Russians as the New Minority

Russians as the New Minority

Ethnicity and Nationalism in the Soviet Successor States

Jeff Chinn

Robert Kaiser

The University of Missouri–Columbia

WestviewPress

A Division of HarperCollinsPublishers

Copyright © 1996 by Westview Press, Inc., A Division of HarperCollins Publishers, Inc.

Published in 1996 in the United States of America by Westview Press, Inc., 5500 Central Avenue,
Boulder, Colorado 80301-2877, and in the United Kingdom by Westview Press, 12 Hid's Copse
Road, Cumnor Hill, Oxford OX2 9JJ

Library of Congress Cataloging-in-Publication Data
Chinn, Jeff.
        Russians as the new minority: ethnicity and nationalism in the Soviet successor states / Jeff
      Chinn, Robert Kaiser.
           p.   cm.
      Includes bibliographical references and index.
      ISBN 0-8133-2249-9 (alk. paper). — ISBN 0-8133-2248-0 (pbk. : alk. paper)
      1. Russians—Former Soviet republics. 2. Nationalism—Former Soviet republics. 3. Former Soviet
      republics—Ethnic relations. I. Kaiser, Robert John. II. Title.
DK35.5.C48 1996
947—dc20   96-6849
                                                                                                      CIP

The paper used in this publication meets the requirements of the America n National Standard for
Permanence of Paper for Printed Library Materials Z39.48-1984.

10   9   8   7   6   5   4   3   2   1

Contents

Part III   Conclusions

Illustrations

Tables

Country Data

Maps

Preface

The decision to focus on Russians outside the Russian Federation in this study of interethnic conflict and conflict management was made for several reasons. First, the disintegration of the USSR caused the 25 million Russians living outside Russia to become overnight the largest ethnic minority in Europe. Second, Russians are found in significant numbers in all of the Newly Independent States (NIS), making a comparative study of interethnic conflict and conflict management throughout the former USSR possible. Third, and perhaps most importantly, Russians were the dominant group in the USSR, and they exercised this dominance not only in Russia but in all of the former union republics. The titular nationalism that arose during the 1980s was frequently and pointedly anti-Russian as well as anti-Soviet; the success of the independence movements thus resulted in a dramatic status change between Russians outside Russia and members of the titular groups. This status shift makes the interaction between Russians and titular nations of particular interest as the latter have become dominant in the newly emerging states.

Our principal objective in writing this book was to re-examine several theories of nationalism in light of the unfolding titular-Russian relationships in the non-Russian successor states. Most studies assessing nationalism in the NIS have adopted decolonization as their overarching theoretical framework. This approach has some utility, but its limitations often outweigh its explanatory power. First, treating the USSR as an empire like any other is problematic, and not only because of its "internal" nature. The state was created in part as an anti-imperial act, and several of the USSR's nationality policies worked at cross purposes with Russian hegemony. Second, the imperial analogy became less accurate over time. Particularly during the post-Stalin period, Russian dominance outside Russia was increasingly challenged by titular elites; in most republics a two-tiered system of ethnic stratification developed with Russians losing their dominant place to upwardly mobile members of the titular groups. Third, the imperial analogy and decolonization are much more accurate depictions of titular-Russian relations in some regions than in others. In Central Asia and Azerbaijan, this approach has much greater merit than in the Baltics, Georgia, and Armenia, yet decolonization is typically treated as if it were equally applicable in all of the NIS. Finally, decolonization approaches tend to oversimplify the titular-Russian relationship. Analysts using this approach see this relationship as unidimensional, with the titular nations as victims of the hegemonic Russians. Local Russians are portrayed as having little legitimate place in the non-Russian republics; the solution to the unfolding conflict is thus the removal of the alien Russians from these non-Russian homelands.

While not rejecting decolonization approaches in their entirety, we have attempted to examine the unfolding titular-Russian relations in the NIS using theoretical frameworks that allow for greater complexity. This book attempts to assess these interethnic relationships from a less russophobic viewpoint while at the same time avoiding the opposite russocentric approach. We were particularly interested in applying the concept of interactive nationalism—a refinement of reactive ethnicity—as both an explanatory and predictive model for inter-ethnic behavior.

The structure of the book reflects two basic positions that we took from the outset. First, we treat nationalism in the NIS as an interactive process. We emphasize that nationalism began long before the 1980s, yet is not a "primordial" sentiment. Part One traces the history of Russian-titular relations during the late Tsarist and Soviet periods, the critical era during which national identity and nationalism developed in this region. Second, we treat the interaction between the titular groups and the Russians as a variable which is not the same in all republics of the former USSR. Part Two thus provides an in-depth assessment of the titular-Russian relationship in the fourteen non-Russian states.

Although both authors were involved in the research, writing, and editing of all the materials incorporated in the book, Professor Chinn initiated the project and was the principal author of Chapters 1, 5, 6, and 7, and Professor Kaiser was the principal author of Chapters 2, 3, 4, 8, 9, 10, and 11.

Jeff Chinn
Robert Kaiser

Acknowledgments

This study benefited from financial support and scholarly input from a variety of sources. The authors gratefully acknowledge the assistance they received from the Missouri University Research Board for research, travel, and released time for this project. Professor Kaiser also received a Social Science Research Council postdoctoral grant, which was instrumental in supporting the research and writing for his contribution to this book. Professor Chinn also received travel support from International Research and Exchanges Board (IREX) to support his research.

In addition to this financial support, the authors wish to express their deep appreciation to the numerous scholars working on related research who provided invaluable input during the research and writing of the book. The authors would especially like to thank Ian Bremmer (Hoover Institution), Ralph Clem (Florida International University), William Crowther (University of North Carolina-Charlotte), John Heyl (University of Missouri), Charles King (Oxford University), Robin Remington (University of Missouri), Michael Sacks (Trinity College), Nikolai Petrov and Vladimir Kolosov (Institute of Geography, Russian Academy of Sciences), Mikhael Guboglo (Institute of Ethnology and Anthropology, Russian Academy of Sciences), Zhanna Zayonchkovskaya and Galina Vitkovskaya (Institute for Economic Forecasting, Russian Academy of Sciences), Professors Alexandr Susokolov and Revaz Gachechiladze (Institute of Geography, Georgian Academy of Sciences), Professor Juozas Lakis (Vilnius Pedagogical University), Professors Edgars Osins, Einars Semanis, and Peteris Zvidrins (University of Latvia), Aksel Kirch and Marika Kirch (Estonian Academy of Sciences), and Professor Nurbek Omuraliev (Center of Social Research, National Academy of Sciences of Kyrgyzstan). The authors also thank *Post-Soviet Geography*, Professor Chauncy Harris, and the Geographic Resource Center, Department of Geography (University of Missouri–Columbia), for their assistance in providing the maps for this work. Finally, the authors acknowledge the students who participated in a graduate seminar on Russians as a new minority during the Fall 1993 semester and who provided valuable insights and feedback at an early stage in the research.

J.C.
R.K.

Part I

The Theoretical and Historical Background

Chapter 1

Introduction

In the newly independent non-Russian states of the former Soviet Union, Russians and their changing status have become the latest and potentially most explosive "national problem." According to the 1989 Soviet census, there are nearly 25 million Russians resident outside Russia; thus, they are the largest minority in Europe today. Russians are a politically significant minority in nearly all of the newly independent states except Armenia. These Russians have become actors in domestic politics of the non-Russian successor states as well as a crucial factor in the emerging foreign relations between the non-Russian states and the Russian Federation.

Not only is the Russian minority large and widespread, it is also essentially new. Until recent years, the Russians living in non-Russian union republics saw themselves and were treated by Moscow as the dominant group throughout the Soviet Union.[1] Indeed, these Russians tended to view all of the USSR as their homeland, and thus did not think of themselves as minorities living in an alien environment. Today, these formerly self-assured and dominant Russians have become vulnerable minorities beyond Moscow's control and protection. The status of Russians in the non-Russian states is increasingly being challenged as titular nationalists reorient their states toward serving the interests of the titular nation rather than the interests of Moscow. The rapidly changing status of Russians in the non-Russian lands and the consequences of these dramatic changes provide the central themes of this book.

During Soviet times, Moscow's policies laid the foundation for the situation that both Russian and indigenous leaderships now face. Linguistic and educational policies, industrial development, and Communist Party organizations favored Russians and Russian-speakers throughout the USSR. Being Russian was rarely disadvantageous in the non-Russian republics.

The russocentric policies were offset to varying degrees by efforts aimed at achieving inter-national equalization. These programs, targeting members of the titular nations for preferential treatment in their home republics (indigenization or *korenizatsiya*), together with the organization of the USSR as a federation of national states, encouraged members of each titular group to develop an exclusionary attitude toward its republic (*e.g.*, Uzbeks in Uzbekistan). These policies and the territorial nationalism that they engendered worked at cross-purposes with policies aimed at merging the entire population into one Soviet people.

During the post-Stalin era, nationality policies "from above" that supported development of territorial nationalism were supplemented by pressure for *korenizatsiya* from below. Growing numbers of titular elites used their positions to promote members of their own groups over nonmembers, pressing for greater titular representation in prestigious sectors of political, economic, and sociocultural organizations. During the postwar period, a two-tiered system of ethnic stratification developed, with Russians continuing to occupy a dominant position in society as a whole, but with each titular group also attaining a privileged standing in its home republic.[2]

In the late 1980s, members of the titular nations became increasingly nationalistic, as they asserted their rights as **indigenes** to exclusive control of their homelands. This national "reawakening," although beginning in the ethnocultural sphere, quickly spread to the socioeconomic and political arenas. This rise in exclusionary nationalism represented a centrifugal threat not only to the unitary political and economic power structures in Moscow but also to the dominant status of Russians living in the non-Russian periphery.

The coming to power of titular nationalists in their newly independent states has eroded the once-dominant position of the Russians living there. In most of these states titular elites have begun the process of deconstructing the old two-tiered system of ethnic stratification in which dominance had to be shared with Russians in order to build a stratification system in which the titular nation stands alone as the hegemonic group.

Russians living in non-Russian areas have thus experienced a dramatic decline in status. Few disagree that the status of the Russians has changed markedly, but the interpretation of this change depends upon the observer's position. Some Russians claim to have become an oppressed minority. Many indigenes agree that Russians have lost status but argue that they have merely lost their dominant position and are now equal to others. Still others argue that Russians as "colonial oppressors" have no legal basis for continuing to reside in the successor states and should be forced out.

With the dramatic change in Russians' status has come rising inter-national and inter-state tension and the potential for conflict. Managing this rising tension and conflict is important both for the parties themselves and for the surrounding states. To understand the changing inter-national relations and to gauge the potential for successful conflict management, this book will examine three questions about the nature of Russian-titular interaction in the newly independent states:

1. How are the newly independent non-Russian states that came into being as vehicles for titular national self-determination dealing with their Russian minorities? Answers to this question can range from the acceptance of Russians

The hyphenated forms "inter-national" and "a-national" are used throughout this book to emphasize our focus on "nation," defined as a community with both backward-looking and forward-looking characteristics. This usage distinguishes the term "inter-national," meaning between or among nations, from the commonly used "international," meaning between states, as applied to foreign policy. We will use the term "inter-state" for such relationships to avoid any confusion. (See "What Is a Nation," in Chapter 2.)

as a co-equal or dominant group in the state (i.e., the status quo ante) to the rejection of a Russian presence in the state and the use of force to remove the minority, up to and including expulsion, ethnocide, and genocide. Of course, between these two extremes lies a wide range of options available to titular elites.

2. How are the Russians in the newly independent states coming to terms with their changed status? Russian reactions range from acceptance and adaptation to their new position as a subordinate minority to rejection and opposition, which may take the form of emigration, political opposition, and/or irredentism or separatism.

3. To what extent do initial choices made by the new states in including or excluding the Russian minorities have an impact on the type of political regimes created and the prospects for the development of democratic institutions?

How Newly Independent States Deal with Russian Minorities

After decades of tension between the titular nations and the Soviet center, independent states representing the dreams of the titular nationalists have become a reality. These new states are political-geographic expressions of a nationalistic ideal. Titular nationalists in the successor states feel entitled to their own state, whose borders ideally are congruent with those of the nations' ancestral homelands.[3] They almost always claim exclusive rights in their homeland and view territorial control as a necessity for their nation's survival.

This view would not be a cause for conflict if the new "nation-states" fulfilled a second nationalistic ideal—ethnic homogeneity of the population. However, nearly all of these post-Soviet states contain multi-national populations. The titular populations' claims to special rights and privileges in their homelands thus come into conflict with the rights and privileges of non-titular groups that inhabit the same territory. This situation impinges particularly on the Russians, who until recently enjoyed special status throughout the USSR as the dominant nation in the Soviet state.

In some republics, the population growth as a consequence of immigration was greater than the natural increase. Especially in the smaller former Soviet republics, the influx of Russians and other Slavs was seen as an assault on their cultures, resulting not only from the migration itself but also from conscious decisions made in Moscow to overwhelm the indigenous cultures and russify the population.

The motives of Moscow's central planners are less relevant than the perceptions that their decisions created. Evidence exists in educational and cultural policy, especially during certain periods, that sovietization through *russification* was an important goal; whether the economic and industrial policies that drove migration were coordinated parts of sovietization/russification policies is less important than the perception created in the non-Russian republics that this was the case. Demographic russification—particularly in the Baltic republics—became a catalyst for rising titular nationalism that was both anti-Soviet and anti-Russian.

The titular nationalists who now control the political institutions of the post-Soviet states are pursuing *territorial nationalism* or *national territoriality*—the restructuring of ethnocultural, socioeconomic, and political relationships to ensure their nation's predominance in the territory perceived to be its historical homeland. In some cases, formal nationalism is evident in the new constitutions, citizenship laws, language laws, and voting rights. In others, a more informal, mass-based anti-Russian and anti-outsider nativism has emerged, even though titular political elites are not promoting formal nationalism.

Since Soviet disintegration, most titular nationalists have been implementing policies to guarantee political and economic as well as cultural dominance. This strategy is not unique to the newly emerging states in Eastern Europe and the former Soviet Union. Titular dominance can be found even in some states that meet the definitional standard of a democracy, because they extend both political and civil rights to their whole population. Nonetheless, one nation maintains institutionalized control. An *ethnic democracy*, according to Smooha and Hanf, provides

> a structured superior status to a particular segment of the population and [regards] the non-dominant groups as having a relatively lesser claim to the state and also as being not fully loyal. . . . Since the state is considered to be the expression of the national aspirations of the dominant group, the nation takes precedence over the state or civil society.[4]

Smooha and Hanf contend that ethnic democracy is a likely outcome in the divided societies of Eastern Europe because "nationalism in Eastern Europe tends to be integral and exclusionary as opposed to Western nationalism, which tends to be open, inclusive and coterminous with citizenship." They thus predict that Eastern European states will follow the model of ethnic democracy where the titular nation uses the state to satisfy its political agenda.[5]

Robert Hayden has identified a similarly exclusionary *constitutional nationalism* in the former Yugoslav republics, which he defines as:

a constitutional and legal structure that privileges the members of one ethnically defined nation over other residents in a particular state. . . . It is a departure, however, from currently accepted democratic constitutional norms which view the individual citizen as the basic subject of constitutions. Instead, constitutional nationalism envisions a state in which sovereignty resides with a particular nation *(narod)*, the members of which are the only ones who can decide fundamental questions of state form and identity.[6]

The developing institutions and laws of the newly independent non-Russian states are expressions of the nationalism of the populations that considered themselves to be disenfranchised and persecuted under Soviet rule. Their versions of "constitutional nationalism," as in the case of the Yugoslav republics, single out members of the titular nation for special treatment, thereby alienating the nontitular populations, including the formerly dominant Russians. The problem with constitutional nationalism in multinational states is that the excluded minorities will be "at best indifferent and at worst hostile to the state."[7]

Constitutional nationalism in the newly independent states varies in the degree to which the titular nation is afforded a privileged place and the nontitular population is excluded from the new sociocultural, economic, and political life that is being created. Nevertheless, to a greater or lesser degree, policies are designed to enhance the status of the titular nation. At best, the nontitular groups under such circumstances have legal protections; both constitutional and symbolic provisions (holidays, anthems, flags) emphasize the dominant status of the titular nations, in whose name the state is proclaimed.

In spite of the often common policy approaches to asserting titular hegemony, the titular nations' views of the Russians living among them are often more varied. Relations among different nations depend on many factors, including history, culture, religion, and economic development. Just as the different titular nations do not view Russians similarly, all members of a single nation do not have the same perceptions of Russians. Thus, a statement that Estonians or Ukrainians have a particular view of the Russians who live in their homeland, while containing a certain degree of validity, would not be a view held by every Estonian or Ukrainian.

Despite this qualification, some generalizations can be made about the ways in which Russians are viewed. The most important distinction applies to Russians who went to non-Russian lands (for example, Kazakhstan or Ukraine) as settlers before the twentieth century. This population is often viewed as native to the area. Similarly, the Baltic peoples categorize Russians as "historic" settlers if they immigrated before the Soviet incorporation of Lithuania, Latvia, and Estonia in 1940. These immigrants lived in the independent interwar states, typically learned the Baltic languages, and otherwise adapted to local life. They and their descendants are thus accorded greater consideration, both in law and in attitudes of the indigenous peoples, than those Russians who migrated during Soviet times.

Even though migration to the non-Russian periphery was significant before the 1917 revolution and during the first decades of Soviet power, the majority of

Russians now living in the non-Russian successor states are post–World War II migrants and their descendants. Postwar reconstruction and economic expansion resulted in massive migratory waves, with most migrants seeking greater economic opportunity for themselves and their families. In addition, Communist Party, military, and security personnel were sent to the non-Russian republics to assure reliability and smooth functioning of political, administrative, and security infrastructures. Economic migrants entering during the Soviet era receive mixed reactions; in some places (Central Asia, for example) they are welcomed on the governmental level because of their skills, though they often are treated with hostility in the stores, on public transportation, and on the streets. Even in the Baltics and Moldova, the economic migrants are not blamed personally for the policies that caused their migration, and titular nationalists typically distinguish between economic migrants and the military, security, and Party personnel who were part of the perceived Russian "occupation."

Many Central Asians see Russians as colonial rulers sent to conquer and exploit indigenous societies. In the Baltics, the term "occupier" is often applied to the Russians, referring to the illegal incorporation of the independent Baltic states into the Soviet Union in 1940, the fifty-year rule by Moscow, and the difficult negotiations over Russian troop removal after independence. Those titular nationalists viewing Russians as colonizers or occupiers have little sympathy for the plight of individual Russians remaining in the newly independent states. How one views this nationalistic perspective depends on one's starting point. In terms of western liberal-democratic theory, exclusion from the political process by national identity, language, citizenship, or voting laws is hardly democratic; yet from the perspective of national liberation or decolonization nationalism, the fact that colonial settlers or retired military officers are losers is less troublesome.[8] The notion of "internal colonialism," implying a non-Russian periphery dominated economically, politically, and culturally by a Russian core, is found in some form in all the successor states and will be discussed in Chapter 2.

The different timing and processes by which the non-Russian successor states came under Russian and Soviet control influence the reactions of the titular nations in these newly independent states to both Russia and Russians today. The titular nationalists' views of the Russians form the basis for development of constitutional and legal approaches to the question of Russians as a minority. Voting rights, citizenship, and language legislation are the most conspicuous issues. Some successor states (Ukraine, Moldova, Lithuania, and initially Kazakhstan) have granted Russians immediate citizenship and considerable cultural autonomy; others (Estonia and Latvia) have made attainment of citizenship relatively difficult and insisted on proficiency in the language of the new state. Some (Estonia and Latvia) have also encouraged Russian emigration in order to reduce the Russian proportion of the population; others (Kyrgyzstan) have sought to convince the Russians to stay. The extremes of the accommodation-exclusion spectrum (maintenance of Russians in their pre-independence status; elimination through the use of physical force, including expulsion and genocide) are not found in the newly independent states. Nonetheless, the fourteen non-Russian successor states vary substantially in the degree to which Russians have been included or excluded from the political, economic, and sociocultural life that is emerging. Chapters 3 and 4 explore the history of the Russian core's imposition of control on the non-Russian periphery. The history of the relationship between titular nations, local Russians, and the Russian/Soviet center is also treated in each of the regional chapters in Part Two.

How Are the Russians Responding?

The 1991 Soviet dissolution dramatically accelerated the pace of cultural, socioeconomic, and political indigenization as well as the decline in the status of Russians outside Russia. The two-tiered ethnic stratification system that developed during the postwar period came under attack by titular nationalists intent on unseating the minority Russians from their position of privilege. Suddenly, the formerly dominant minority found itself a political, economic, and cultural minority. Accepting equal or even subordinate status has been a shock for the Russians. As one scholar observed:

> The changes . . . perceived as a national revival by representatives of the indigenous nation . . . are perceived as a social catastrophe by people belonging to the "imperial" nation. The perception of the status change as social catastrophe is primarily connected with the sudden transition from their position as privileged majority within the Empire to the status of a national minority within a new and incomprehensible state formation.[9]

Our second question, both theoretically and practically, involves Russians' comprehension of and reaction to their new situation. In many ways, this question turns the previous one on its head, as the focus shifts to the formerly dominant and self-assured Russian population in order to gauge its reaction to the "incomprehensible state formation" it is experiencing. Many issues—citizenship, language, and voting rights—remain the same as the analysis moves from the perspective of the titular nations to that of the Russian minorities. So, too, does our cautionary note: Although their circumstances are similar enough to allow generalization and comparison, all Russians are not identical. Careful consideration must be given to differences as well as similarities in the Russian populations, their origins, geographical dispersion, and demographic characteristics as well as political organizations, leadership, and aspirations. Nonetheless, to the degree that there is a lack of differentiation among policies developed by the nationalizing regimes toward the Russians, their responses to policies that threaten their former dominance also tend to be undifferentiated.

Russian minorities are not distributed evenly in the non-Russian republics. Almost half of the Russians living outside Russia live in Ukraine, although they constitute larger proportions of several other republics. Some states, such as

Kazakhstan, have a roughly equal balance between Russian and titular populations. In most of Central Asia and Transcaucasia, the Russian population is small, concentrated in the capital cities, and rapidly decreasing as a result of emigration. Yet in others states, such as Latvia, Estonia, Moldova, Belarus, Ukraine, and Kyrgyzstan, the Russian population constitutes a sizeable minority. In general, areas with high Russian concentrations (northern Kazakhstan, Crimea and "left-bank" Ukraine, Transdniestrian cities in Moldova, northeastern Estonia, and urban areas of Latvia) have been characterized by interethnic tension and conflict; those areas that border Russia have the potential to become inter-state as well as inter-national problems.

For Russians within today's new states, coping with titular nationalism is nothing new; the Soviet government had long been concerned about republic-level nationalism. However, Russians never imagined that the Soviet Union, with its Russian domination, would disintegrate. A considerable cognitive shift is required of the formerly dominant population to accommodate this abrupt change. Part of the Russians' difficulty in adapting results from their vague notion of group identity at the time of Soviet disintegration. One survey found that an almost equal number of Russians viewed themselves as Soviets as viewed themselves as Russians.[10] A majority of Russians surveyed in Tashkent, Chisinau, and Moscow also identified the entire USSR as their homeland.[11] Almost all Russians living outside the Russian republic before Soviet disintegration viewed themselves as the dominant group of the Soviet Union rather than as a minority living in a foreign land.

An example from Latvia illustrates this interpretation. Russian migrants coming to Latvia thought they were moving "to the Soviet west rather than to a once-independent country."[12]

> Many Russian-speakers now feel offended and deeply upset about the change of their status that an independent Latvia has brought: they are discovering that being Russians or "Russian-speakers" with lifelong loyalty to the USSR, as well as a strict preference for the Russian language and concomitant disregard for the Latvian language, are no longer assets in securing advancement. What is more, Russia has not indicated that it would welcome their return.[13]

During most of the Soviet period, failure to distinguish between Russia and the rest of the USSR would have caused few internal conflicts. With Soviet disintegration, Russians now must confront their own culture and homeland in a new way. How do Russians view the place in which they live, and what do they now see as "home?" Because the Russians did not conceive of themselves as a minority before the Soviet breakup, even though they were a numerical minority in the republic in which they lived, they did not develop the group cohesion or cultural identity typical of immigrants. This lack of cohesion now hinders their ability to act effectively as a cultural or political force in the newly independent states. It also means that Russians in the non-Russian states will be more likely to look toward Russia for assistance in solving their new national problems than to attempt to reach new working relations within the political and cultural context in which they find themselves.

> One of the reasons for the prevailing "imperial consciousness" is that the status and position of the Russian population in the national republics is rather vague. In order to be able to play a constructive role, they have to become aware of their own community . . . with its specific interests and values, its way of life, its moral norms. . . . Only then can we speak about a specific Russian community in Estonia (in the Baltic Republics in general), or in Moldavia, Central Asia, and others. Only then, political self-determination, compromises with other movements and constructive cooperation are possible.[14]

In this sense, Russians cannot be treated as "just another minority" in the newly independent states. They are not the same as Poles in Lithuania or Ukrainians in Kazakhstan, and this difference goes beyond the enormous size of the Russian minority. First of all, Russians were the dominant nation of a huge and powerful multinational state. While they migrated in large numbers throughout the former Soviet Union, they never conceived of themselves as a minority in a foreign environment. They never felt the need to acculturate to the indigenous way of life; on the contrary, the non-Russians accommodated them. Furthermore, the Russians cannot be treated as "just another minority" today because of the importance and power of the Russian state. They look to Russia not only as their external homeland but also as their protector, and Russia has accepted this role as one of its foreign policy goals.

Both of these factors reduced the need for Russians to coalesce as minorities in the non-Russian environments. This, too, distinguished them from other minority groups living in the non-Russian republics or from Russians who have emigrated beyond the borders of the former Soviet Union. Thus, Armenians, Georgians, or Uzbeks living outside their homelands were forced to look to each other for cultural and other support in ways that the Russians never had to. These groups had to build their own minority communities, as did Russian emigrants in places like New York. Essentially, the other groups had to recognize that their cultures were subordinate to the predominant culture in the place that they lived. They had to acculturate either to the titular group or, as typically was the case in the former Soviet Union, to the dominant Russian culture. In either case, they and their conationals were forced, unlike the Russians, to form a minority community of interest or to accept the loss of their culture.

The role of the Russian-based educational system was key to both of these phenomena. Russians never acknowledged the status of the titular nation in the non-Russian republics. Third-level nationalities had to acknowledge the subordination of their own culture to both the titular and the Russian one. If their culture was to survive at all, it required the building of a minority community. In today's post-Soviet environment, the absence of such a community among the Russian population is an important factor in our analysis.

Although the leadership of the Russian Federation has articulated a position of support and protection for Russians in the so-called "near abroad," it has not welcomed the return of these Russians to Russia. Russian Federation laws grant citizenship to Russians living in other republics but are not intended to encourage return migration. Rather, they have been enacted to encourage other states to recognize dual citizenship. The economic situation in Russia is troublesome for the existing population, and the return of Russians from the other republics further complicates an already difficult situation. "At the present time Russia is neither materially nor psychologically prepared to take in even greater numbers of potentially re-emigrating Russians, to say nothing of members of other peoples."[15] Nonetheless, over 2 million Russians, especially from violence-prone Central Asia and Transcaucasia, have migrated to Russia in recent years. Victor Perevedentsev, a well-known Russian demographer, predicts that "the majority of the Russian (or, if you will, Russian-language or 'European') population will inevitably leave [Central Asia] even if ideal interethnic relations should prevail in that region."[16]

Analyses of Russians in their new situation must differentiate as well as generalize. Each individual or family migrated at a particular time and usually for a personal reason. Generalizations about economic motives or lack of adaptation may apply to most Russians but not to all. Such distinctions are now particularly important to make, especially as indigenous political forces are determining the rules for participation of Russian minorities in the new political order. Russian adaptation to the titular society is a key variable in the process. Knowledge of the local language, interaction with the indigenous nationality, and intermarriage are important indicators in measuring Russian acculturation.

Each new regime is creating constitutional arrangements specifying citizenship procedures, voting laws, and property rights. Some have granted rights to all people living in their territories, while others have been more exclusionary. One apparent motive of the successor regimes is to break up the Russian minority politically—to emphasize cross-cutting cleavages within the group. A key factor in differentiating among Russians is their willingness to accommodate the new ethnopolitical reality; those who have indigenous contacts (spouses, friends) are expected to behave differently politically from those who do not speak the local language and who interact exclusively with other Russians. One must also explore the Russians' willingness to participate politically in the new order by adopting citizenship in the state, by voting, and by forming and participating in political parties and interest groups. Nonetheless, in spite of such distinctions, the usual nationalist treatment of Russians as a single category often engenders a common Russian response.

Some Russians have actively rejected the new political, cultural, and economic realities of the successor states and have migrated to Russia. Some of this emigration parallels Russian troop withdrawal as support functions tied to the military have become unnecessary. Others, typically recent migrants to non-Russian areas, return to family, friends, and familiar surroundings. Many of these emigrants would have likely returned to Russia even if the Soviet Union still existed; however, under today's circumstances, they will not be replaced by other

Russian immigrants. A third group of emigrants is made up of refugees from the conflicts taking place in Central Asia and Transcaucasia. But the more important group for our analysis is made up of Russians who remain in the successor states and oppose the new political and social order. In some cases this opposition takes the form of separatism or irredentism, as is the case in Transdniestria and Crimea, and to a lesser extent in eastern Ukraine, northern Kazakhstan, and northeastern Estonia. In more typical cases resistance is political or economic, with political opposition groups forming to resist the indigenization of politics and culture, and economic interests organizing to oppose reforms.

The Russian situation differs by location, as do Russian attitudes toward indigenous populations. Thus our question—How will Russians in the newly independent states come to terms with their changed status and re-orient themselves to new political, cultural, and economic realities?—will not lead to a uniform answer. The regional chapters in Part Two explore the similarities and differences in Russian minority responses in the newly independent states.

Initial Choices and Long-Term Consequences

The process of creating successor states is still young. Particularly during this developmental stage, the evolving relationship between members of the titular nations and the Russian minorities is having an important impact on both the states' developing political institutions and the nature of political discussion. The policies initially chosen by ruling titular leaderships toward Russian minorities will have important long-term repercussions by defining the nature of international relations. Furthermore, we contend that policies of accommodation rather than confrontation or exclusion are more likely to enhance development of liberal democratic institutions.

The participation (or lack thereof) of minority Russians in developing political institutions in the newly independent states may be the defining element in the states' attempts to build democratic regimes. These new states will either incorporate all of their peoples in their efforts to build successful political and economic entities or they will be forced to contend with politically powerful minorities that can undermine their independence and complicate their already delicate relationships with Moscow. Finding the formula to channel demands of Russian minorities into legitimate political activities that will support rather than undermine the new states will be a continuing test for the successor states. The concerns of Russian minorities cannot be legislated or wished away; the search for means to channel their interests into democratic political processes will have enormous implications for the outcome of state-building in a multinational environment.

These concerns highlight two issues at the core of understanding nationalizing regimes: the conflicting nature of "rights" and the means to regulate international conflict in multinational societies. Neither question can be settled by this discussion; nonetheless, the interplay between the indigenous majorities' pursuit of hegemony and the Russian minorities' efforts to retain their earlier status provides fascinating comparative case studies.

The existence of an ethnic stratification system during the Soviet period and the changes to it after Soviet dissolution have resulted in repeated references to "rights." Under the old regime, titular nations claimed that their right to self-determination was being abridged. Concomitantly, third-level nationalities, less influential than either the Russians or the titular nations, claimed that they had fewer rights in their own homelands. With the establishment of nationalizing regimes after independence, the Russians believe that their rights are now in jeopardy. Third-level nationalities have generally sought greater territorial and cultural autonomy; while some have been accommodated, others have lost ground and are pursuing a separatist (e.g., Abkhazia) or irredentist (e.g., Nagorno-Karabakh, South Ossetia) agenda of their own. A discussion of the nature of rights (illustrated by the citizenship debates in Estonia and Latvia) will help unravel this situation, at least for analytical purposes. This approach will allow us to differentiate among the various arguments being advanced; however, the conflicting and emotional bases upon which arguments are built will quickly make clear why neither logic nor clarity can unite the parties.

How might the new regimes encompass the aspirations of all of their people? With significant minority populations in most of these new states—and minority Russian populations in all of them—will they incorporate or exclude the nontitular groups as they strive to institutionalize their independence? This question is fundamental to the future political development of the successor states.

The Russian minorities, both because of their size and their connection to a powerful Russian Federation, occupy a unique position. Their participation, or lack thereof, in the developing political institutions of the successor states may prove to be the defining element in the efforts of these entities to build independent political systems. The new states must find ways to manage the seemingly inherent conflicts among their multinational populations—or face an escalation of inter-national conflict that can threaten their independence and complicate the already delicate relationships between them and the Russian Federation. By using the Russian populations as its focus, this book examines the approaches being taken by the dominant indigenous populations toward the non-titular groups to determine how a national minority might be incorporated successfully in emerging political and social structures of the new states. Which of the various representational and territorial means being used to contain national conflict in multinational states might result in its diminution?

The former Soviet Union provides fertile ground for such study: Although the republics each had experience with Russian rule and Russian migration prior to Soviet times, each experienced the major Russian migration to its territory as a part of postwar Soviet economic development. Policies applied by Moscow toward the individual union republics, while not identical, were more similar than different in regard to language, education, politics, and economics. With independence, each of the new multinational states must confront similar political issues—new constitutions, citizenship, voting rights, and language policies. The range of policies being adopted in response to related circumstances thus provides a useful framework for comparative analysis, as do the commonalities of the reaction of the minorities to the successor states' nationalizing agendas.

The remainder of Part One (Chapters 2–4) provides a theoretical and historical examination of the Russians in the non-Russian republics. Chapter 2 examines the literature on nationalism and territoriality that guides our discussion of titular assertiveness and the resulting Russian reaction, focusing especially on nationalism's interactive nature. Chapter 3 reviews the historical movement of Russians from the core to the periphery during the Russian Empire as well as the reactions of the indigenous people to this foreign domination. Chapter 4 then examines ethnic stratification and the Soviet approaches to both nationalism and territoriality. Part Two (Chapters 5–10) presents a series of comparative case studies examining the titular nation/Russian interaction in each of the newly independent states, emphasizing the period of Soviet unraveling (1988–1992) and the early years of independence (1992–present).

These chapters compare the situations of the Russian populations in the context of the successor states' efforts to build both stable and legitimate political systems. They examine the legal foundations of the new states and the degree of accommodation or exclusion faced by the Russian minorities in public policies. The study also examines shifts in public opinion, including attitudes among indigenes toward Russians, and Russian views about their status in the nationalist context of successor-state politics. The interactive nature of nationalism plays an important role in guiding this investigation. So do the groups that claim to speak for Russian minorities, including those found in the Russian Federation.

Part Three draws on the evidence presented in the comparative case studies to determine which theoretical literatures enhance our understanding of the minority Russians in the Soviet successor states as examples of the interaction of majority and minority nations living in the same state. We also explore the implications of titular groups' policies of accommodation or exclusion on the development of political institutions. Finally, what lessons might we draw for the management of inter-national conflict from the differing approaches taken by the newly independent states?

Notes

1. A distinction must be made between minority and majority demographic status, and subordinate and dominant political/economic/cultural status. A demographic minority may be economically, politically and culturally dominant.

2. Robert Kaiser, "Nationalism: The Challenge to Soviet Federalism," in Michael Bradshaw, ed., *The Soviet Union: A New Regional Geography?* (London: Belhaven Press, 1991), pp. 39–65; Robert Kaiser, *The Geography of Nationalism in Russia and the USSR* (Princeton, NJ: Princeton University Press, 1994).

3. Colin Williams, "The Question of National Congruence," in R. J. Johnston and P. J. Taylor, eds., *A World in Crisis? Geographical Perspectives*, 2nd ed. (Oxford: Basil Blackwell, 1989), pp. 229–265. This topic is treated more fully in Chapter 2.

4. Sammy Smooha and Theodor Hanf, "The Diverse Modes of Conflict-Regulation in Deeply Divided Societies," in Anthony D. Smith, ed., *Ethnicity and Nationalism* (Leiden: E. J. Brill, 1992), p. 32.

5. Ibid., p. 33. This comment needs to be qualified, because the "Western" Basque, Catalan, Flemish, Walloonian, Corsican, Scottish, Irish, Ulster, and even Welsh nationalisms also tend to be both integral and exclusionary.

6. Robert M. Hayden, "Constitutional Nationalism in the Formerly Yugoslav Republics," *Slavic Review*, Vol. 51, No. 4 (Winter 1992):655–656.

7. Ibid., p. 669.

8. Martha Brill Olcott, "The Decolonization of the USSR," lecture at the Kennan Institute for Advanced Russian Studies, February 10, 1992, reported in *Meeting Report*, Vol. 9, No. 10.

9. Aleksei A. Semyonov, "The Russian and 'Russian-Speaking' Populations of the National Republics in the Period of the Crisis of Empire," in Helen Krag and Natalia Yukhneva, eds., *The Leningrad Minority Rights Conference* (Copenhagen: The Minority Rights Group Denmark, 1991), p. 116.

10. Roman Solchanyk, "Ukraine, the (Former) Center, Russia, and 'Russia,'" *Studies in Comparative Communism*, No. 25 (1992):34.

11. Leokadia Drobizheva, "Etnicheskoye samosoznaniye Russkikh v sovremennykh usloviyakh: Ideologiya i praktika," *Sovetskaya etnografiya*, No. 1 (1991):5.

12. Dzintra Bungs, "The Latvian-Russian Treaty or the Vicissitudes of Interstate Relations, RFE/RL *Research Report* (February 28, 1992):32.

13. Ibid.

14. Semyonov, "Russian and 'Russian-Speaking' Populations," p. 117.

15. A. Vishnevskiy and Zh. Zayonchkovskaya, *Migratsiya iz SSSR: Chetvertaya volna* (Moskva: Tsentr demografii i ekologii cheloveka, 1991).

16. John B. Dunlop, "Will the Russians Return from the Near Abroad?" *Post-Soviet Geography*, Vol. 35, No. 4 (April 1994):204, citing V.I. Perevedentsev, "Migratsiya naseleniya v SNG: opyt prognoza," *POLIS*, 2, 1993.

Chapter 2

Nations, Nationalism, Inter-National Conflict, and Conflict Management

This chapter develops a theoretical framework for the study of the titular/Russian interrelationships that follows. First, we discuss various meanings of *nation* and *nationalism* employed by other analysts and then define these critical terms as they will be used throughout this work. Second, through the development of a typology of interactive nationalism, we discuss the possible range of answers to the three questions posed in Chapter 1 and develop a set of working hypotheses to test with our regional case studies.

What Is a Nation?

The term nation has been applied to a variety of ethnocultural and political groups, ranging from localized clans and tribal communities to states and even inter-state collectivities.[1] The many uses of the term nation have lent confusion to the study of nationalism, itself a term frequently employed in a variety of contexts (see below).

The meaning of nation and national identity has been the subject of intense discussion among western sociologists and political scientists as well as among Soviet ethnographers and nationalist elites themselves. These debates tend toward over-dichotomization: nations are treated as either primordial or modern communities; as ethnocultural ascriptive identities or as political interest groups; as objectifiable communities whose members share certain tangible characteristics (language, religion, rites, and rituals) or as subjective communities whose members share only a more intangible sense of belonging and sense of destiny (i.e., a national self-consciousness). These dichotomies are frequently clustered. Those who view nations as primordial communities also tend to see them as ethnocultural ascriptive identities whose members are bound by a set of tangible characteristics that have existed essentially unchanged from time immemorial, with a subjective sense of belonging based on common ancestry. Those who view nations as modern communities tend to define them as political interest groups whose tangible characteristics, important for their instrumental utility, were created in the recent past, and whose common genealogical and geographic roots are also myths created in order to bind the national community more closely together.

The Marxist-Leninist view of nations lies within this modernist camp. Nations are seen as creations of the capitalist epoch—as bourgeois instruments to control the proletariat through the creation of false consciousness. Nations would disappear with world communism and be replaced by proletarian international-ism.[2] Within the USSR itself, unequal and antagonistic capitalist nations of tsarist Russia were said to have been transformed into equal socialist nations that had developed brotherly inter-national relations because class antagonisms had been eliminated. Over time, according to Communist Party officials and Soviet ethnographers, national identities were being supplanted by an inter-national or a-national Soviet identity (i.e., the so-called new Soviet people).[3] This Marxist interpretation did not imply that individuals would soon forget their ethnocul-tural origins, but rather that nations as forward-looking political interest groups seeking to control their own destinies would cease to exist.

The conceptual dichotomization in the treatment of nations misses as much as it captures. Primordialist definitions miss the way in which nationalism waxes and wanes over time and ignore the changes in ethnonational identity wrought by the revolutionary sociocultural, economic, and political developments of the nine-teenth and twentieth centuries. Modernist definitions ignore the critical impor-tance that a shared belief in a common ancestry set in the primordial past has on contemporary attitudes of national members. Renan's definition of the nation "as a daily plebiscite"[4] captures the instrumental/circumstantial dimension of national identity but overlooks members' perceptions that they are part of a nat-ural, primordial, and permanent ascriptive community. Once national conscious-ness is attained, members of nations are unlikely to subject this belief to a "daily plebiscite," and they are not likely to cast their national identity aside in favor of membership in another nation or in an a-national interest group.

Definitions integrating elements of primordialism and modernism, such as Smith's perennialism or Scott's oppositional model, are more satisfactory in cap-turing both the ascriptive and instrumental character of nations.[5] In this volume, we define nation as a backward-looking community whose members share a pri-mordial sense of common genealogical and geographic origin, and also as a for-ward-looking, modern political interest group whose members share a desire to control their common destiny.[6]

The nation's tangible characteristics are important both as symbols of the group's historical ethnocultural connectedness and also as present-day instru-ments in the nationalist struggle for control over the nation's destiny. In both cases, language and homeland are the most important characteristics. However, the loss of these tangible attributes does not necessarily mean the end of the nation. Indeed, the opposite is frequently the case. Policies attempting to force assimilation to a common statewide identity often backfire. Loss of linguistic or territorial autonomy often results in the rise of antistate nationalism among national minorities, thus being counterproductive to the goal of assimilation.[7] This was certainly the case with the state-promoted russification programs of the late nineteenth century and again during the Soviet period.

A Sense of Common Origins

The nation is essentially a subjective community whose members share a backward-looking sense of common genealogical and geographic origins and a forward-looking sense of common destiny. Nationalists frequently depict their nations as ancient, even primordial, ethnocultural communities whose members have descended from common ancestors. Such common genealogical origins are for the most part mythical, since most nations are amalgamations of ethnocultural communities. Nevertheless, the myth of common ancestry is important in that it lends the nation an organic and natural appearance and provides members with a sense of being part of an extended family.

Nationalists also typically claim primordial connectedness to an ancestral land in which the nation originated. In national origin myths, the nation is not only said to have been born in a certain place but frequently is said to derive directly from the soil of the homeland. For example, in 1971 the Kyrgyz poet Kozhomberdiyev exorted the Kyrgyz to "remember, even before your mother's milk/You drank the milk of the homeland."[8] In this way, a sense of spatial identity with the homeland—a feeling that members of the nation belong only there and nowhere else—is nearly as potent as the sense of common ancestry. This spatial identity has frequently developed into a sense of exclusivity among members of the indigenous nation. Members feel not only that they belong in the homeland, but that no one else belongs there.[9] This sense of exclusiveness is often triggered by immigration of ethnonational outsiders or by conquest and control of the national homeland by some outside group.[10]

The perception of primordial genealogical and geographic connectedness is one aspect of a nation's subjective sense of belonging. Smith contends that the nation's history—its mythical origins as well as more recent historical events—sets the trajectory for the nation's future.[11] For this reason, one cannot understand nations purely in modern terms, since what nations are and where they are going have been largely predetermined by where they have been and how members perceive the past.

A Sense of Common Destiny

The forward-looking sense of common destiny distinguishes nations from ethnic groups, which remain essentially backward-looking communities of belonging.[12] Nations thus may be viewed as future-oriented, politicized, and territorialized ethnic groups whose members seek to gain control over their destinies. This future orientation converts ethnic groups from primordial communities of belonging into political interest groups, whose members mobilize to achieve self-determination.

The Making of Nations in Russia and the USSR

This "nationalization" of ethnic groups is essentially a phenomenon of the past 150 years, and thus nations as forward-looking politicized and territorialized communities are essentially modern.[13] Hroch depicts nationalization as a three-stage process: (1) beginning with the ethnicization of elites through a process of "enlightened patriotism" during the late enlightenment era in Europe, (2) continuing with the nationalization of elites during the romantic age (a period of "patriotic agitation"), and (3) ending with the nationalization of the masses, which began during the middle of the nineteenth century.[14] Nations as mass-based communities of interest and belonging can be identified in late nineteenth and early twentieth century Europe. However, this final stage in the nationalization process does not have an end point but must be repeated with each successive generation.

Before the nineteenth century, the term nation referred primarily to a state's political and socioeconomic elite and carried little if any ethnic meaning. Peasants were not considered part of the nation and often were not even considered part of the same species by the elites. For example, Pogodin stated in 1826 that "the Russian people is marvelous, but marvelous so far only in potentiality. In actuality, it is low, horrid, and beastly . . . [Russian peasants] will not become human beings until they are forced into it."[15] Peasants, for their part, typically felt little kinship with the urban and rural elites who ruled them. Prior to the end of the nineteenth century, their communities of belonging and interest rarely extended beyond the village or locality, and all outsiders, regardless of ethnocultural identity, were treated with a good deal of suspicion.[16]

Ethnicization of elites occurred during the late enlightenment era, as intellectuals took an active interest in their own roots and especially in the origins of the indigenous languages and cultures. National identity did not exist during this stage, since the elites attached little political significance to their search for roots.[17] At most, they developed an emotional attachment to their ethnic group and a spatial identity with their ancestral homeland. However, little connection existed between elites and the peasant masses, and elites from different ethnic backgrounds felt more related to one another than to peasants who shared their own roots.

With romanticism, the nation was redefined away from the elite and toward the ethnic group and began to be conceived as a community of belonging linked both to the peasants and to the soil of the ancestral homeland. Agrarian life was idealized by the romantic nationalist intelligentsia, though hardly by peasants themselves. During this stage, intellectuals sought to bond with the peasants in order to awaken their national spirit. However, the peasants remained highly suspicious of outsiders, regardless of their ethnic identity.

As non-Russians in the Russian Empire became more literate, more educated, and more urbanized, they increased their contact with ethnic others who held dominant positions in the cities of their homelands (e.g., Germans in Latvia and Estonia; Russians, Jews, and Poles in Lithuania, Belarus, and Ukraine; Russians and Armenians in Georgia and Azerbaijan; and later Russians in Central Asia and Kazakhstan). For many of these non-Russians, national consciousness developed as a positive psychological bond between romantic nationalized elites and "their" people and also as an oppositional movement against the dominant others.[18]

Nationalization of the masses began during the late nineteenth century and has continued throughout the twentieth. As the rural indigenous peasants became more literate, educated, and urbanized, they began to imagine themselves to be part of more expansive ethnonational communities.[19] Nationalization proceeded unevenly in the Russian Empire, occurring earliest in the northern and western regions of European Russia and later in the south and east. It occurred relatively early in the Baltic and Polish regions, but much later in Belarus, Central Asia, Transcaucasia, and among the indigenous groups of Siberia and the Russian Far East. Throughout most of the Russian Empire, nations as mass-based communities of interest and belonging did not exist prior to 1917, with nationalization of the masses beginning in earnest only during the interwar period.

The nationalization process continued throughout the seventy-year existence of the USSR.[20] Far from the period of dormancy or de-nationalization often depicted by nationalists themselves (i.e., by primordialists), the Soviet era was an age of mass-based nationalization that completely altered interethnic and interpersonal relations in the state. However, not every ethnic group became nationally conscious in the USSR. Nationalization of the masses has not occurred among the numerically small peoples of northern Siberia or among groups such as the Karelians, whose members have interacted with Russians for hundreds of years since long before the national idea diffused to the region. The same might be said of the Belarusians. In Central Asia, subnational ethnic communities continue to be potent sources of popular loyalty that often compete with loyalty to the nations themselves, indicating that mass-based nationalization into Tajik, Kyrgyz, Kazakh, Turkmen, and Uzbek nations has been limited. In this region of the former Soviet Union, the subnational ethnic groups themselves appear to be undergoing a process of nationalization, which if successful may create new nations. The nationalization of ethnic groups—previously treated as subnational communities destined for assimilation into large nations—is also occurring in the North Caucasus region of Russia, particularly in Dagestan.

Similarly, Soviet attempts to coercively erase nations clearly failed, providing additional evidence of the counter-productive nature of forced assimilation. The most obvious examples are the nations and ethnic groups deported from their home republics during and immediately after World War II for supposed collaboration with the Nazis (i.e., Chechens, Ingush, Balkars, Kalmyks, Karachay, Crimean Tatars, Meskhetian Turks, and Volga Germans). Rather than causing the elimination of these groups, the forcible nature of their removal from their homelands and their later cruel treatment heightened their sense of national consciousness.

The Crimean Tatars are a striking example. They were deported from Crimea and their nation was officially eliminated from the 1940s to the 1980s, but they retained and increased their sense of national identity. Since the later 1980s, hundreds of thousands of Tatars have returned to Crimea, attempted to reclaim their ancestral homes, and created a great deal of inter-national tension with Russians and Ukrainians who had migrated to the region.

The mass nationalization process that occurred during the Soviet period made the "national problem" faced by Gorbachev even more intractable than that faced by Lenin and Stalin. The USSR's disintegration along national-territorial

lines thus should be seen as the latest stage in a much longer process of nationalization, which acted as a centrifugal force against which the centripetal processes
of sovietization and russification could not compete. The Soviet successor states,
which themselves have no unifying supranational ideology and identity to unite
their multinational populations, face similar disintegrative pressures.

What Is Nationalism?

Just as "nation" has been used alternatively as a synonym for ethnic group and
state, "nationalism" has frequently been defined as the ideology of the state (i.e.,
patriotism) or as ethnocentrism.[21] Following our definition of nation, we treat
nationalism as the ideology and political action program of the nation. The core
tenets of this ideology were perhaps most succinctly expressed by Breuilly: "a)
There exists a nation with an explicit and peculiar character; b) The interests and
values of this nation take priority over all other interests and values; c) The nation
must be as independent as possible. This usually requires at least the attainment
of political sovereignty."[22]

The first of these three tenets states that the nation exists and is unique, and
corresponds with the nationalist depiction of the nation as a primordial group
that has remained essentially unchanged from "time immemorial." As we noted
above, this primordial and natural appearance of nations is critical in that it
strengthens the ties that bind members to the nation.

The depiction of nations as primordial, natural extended families also provides the foundation for the second tenet (i.e., that loyalty to the nation overrides
loyalty to any other human collectivity). This issue of primary loyalty was seen by
Emerson as the quintessential ingredient distinguishing nations from other communities of interest and/or belonging: "The nation is today the largest community
which, when the chips are down, effectively commands men's loyalty, overriding
the claims both of the lesser communities within it and those which cut across it
or potentially enfold it within a still greater society, reaching ultimately to
mankind as a whole."[23] This is not to suggest that loyalty to other communities is
unimportant in the age of nationalism but that the nation wins out in competition
for people's loyalty "when the chips are down." Loyalty to the nation has clearly
overridden the two main competitors of the twentieth century–loyalty to one's
class and to one's state (i.e., patriotism), except where there is congruence
between nation and state. This is the subject of the third tenet.

Just as nation and nationalism have been used as synonyms for state and
patriotism, "nation-state" has been used to define all polities in the world system
regardless of the national composition of their populations. Using the definition
of nation above, relatively few nation-states exist in the world today. Instead, most
states are both multinational and multihomeland in composition. Thus, the ideology of nationalism is a centrifugal force that represents a threat to the majority of
states, since it makes the nation, not the state, the object of primary loyalty.

Nationalists desire their nations to be as independent as possible. This tenet
of nationalism is directly related to the forward-looking aspect of national identity—

the nation has a destiny to fulfill, and members of the nation must be in control of that destiny. This future-oriented sense of shared destiny converts the nation from a community of belonging into a politicized and territorialized interest group, and converts nationalism from an ideology to a political action program. For nationalists, an ethnically pure nation-state in which the government is operated exclusively by and for members of the nation stands as the political-geographic ideal.

The central issue of nationalism as a political action program is political control over geographic space. Here, the national membership's sense of spatial identity with the ancestral homeland is transformed into a sense of exclusiveness toward the homeland as the place where only members of the nation truly belong and as the only place in which the national destiny can be fulfilled. Nationalism thus becomes the essential equivalent of national territoriality, defined as a political strategy through which nationalists seek to control the destiny of the nation by gaining sovereignty over the ancestral homeland.[24] For Gellner, this political action program is the essence of nationalism: "Nationalism is primarily a political principle, which holds that the political and the national unit should be congruent. . . . [It] is a theory of political legitimacy, which requires that ethnic boundaries should not cut across political ones."[25]

Nationalism as a political action program (i.e., national territoriality) makes multinational, multihomeland states, particularly those with highly centralized political structures, anachronistic. Such national territoriality was a central factor in the disintegration of the Soviet Union, Yugoslavia, and Czechoslovakia and has represented a centrifugal force leading to devolution of political power in Belgium, Canada, Spain, and, to a more limited extent, Great Britain and France. National territoriality has also resulted in violent separatist movements in many of the third world states that emerged following decolonization, primarily because the colonial borders, which were drawn "with cavalier disregard for ethnic homelands," were left intact.[26]

Although numerous analyses of societal trends in the post–World War II period proclaimed an end to the age of nationalism, it now appears that nationalism, far from a waning influence, has experienced a strong resurgence, particularly since the 1970s. This ascendancy of nationalism has occurred not only in the multinational, multihomeland states recently created through the process of formal decolonization but also in the developed European core itself. Several conceptual frameworks have been developed in an effort to explain this resurgence; those most relevant for our purposes in this study are presented below.

Why Nationalism?

Modernization Theory

Nationalism became the world's dominant political action program during the twentieth century and shows few signs of abating at the turn of the twenty-first. Yet for much of the 1900s, most western social scientists perceived nationalism to have reached its zenith in the nineteenth century and to be in decline.

According to the liberal democratic/capitalist thesis known as developmentalism or modernization theory, socioeconomic development and globalization processes would eliminate the need for ethnic and national communities, and a global culture would supplant national consciousness with a sense of belonging to humankind as a whole. Nationalism was thus perceived as a primordial sentiment that modernization would overcome. This approach foresaw one world citizenry and world government that would replace the divisive if not anarchic system of nations and states.[27]

Marxism paralleled modernization theory in its treatment of nationalism as anachronistic. True, Marxism did treat nations and nationalism as the products of a particular historical epoch—early capitalism—rather than as primordial communities and sentiments. Nevertheless, Marx clearly believed that socioeconomic development during capitalism would result in the demise of nations and nationalism, as the working class proletariat from all nations joined together to create a classless and nationless world. This future world did look different than that depicted by modernization theorists; in Marx's future communist world vision there would be no need for government, and there would not be the economic stratification that a future capitalist world would require. However, in their treatment of the future of nations and nationalism, both modernization theory and Marxism were in agreement.

With the advantage of hindsight, we can also say that both were fundamentally wrong in their predictions of the demise of nationalism. Modernization theorists were essentially wrong in viewing nations and nationalism as primordial attachments and sentiments that would disappear with development. As noted above, nations are not only backward-looking communities of belonging but also forward-looking and politicized communities of interest. Nationalism thus is not only a primordial sentiment but also a future-oriented political action program. Marx was also incorrect in seeing nations as solely modern communities of interest fabricated by the bourgeoisie to create a false consciousness among the proletariat.

Numerous attempts have been made to explain why nations and nationalism continue to exhibit a vitality unexpected by both modernization theorists and Marxists. Several of these explanations have resulted in prescriptions for solving the "national problem" faced by multinational, multihomeland states.

Internal Colonialism and Uneven Development
One explanation for the continued existence of nations and nationalism under conditions of modernization is referred to as internal colonialism, a title popularized by Michael Hechter with his study of ethnonational identity and solidarity in Great Britain among the Irish, Scots, and Welsh.[28] This thesis argues that a colonial relationship develops between the dominant core group and subordinate peripheral groups in multinational, multihomeland states established by the conquest of one group over others. The continued existence of solidarity among the subordinate peripheral groups is explained by this exploitative colonial relationship. Economic inequality, expressed by a "cultural division of labor," is said to be the cause of the continued strength of nations and nationalism. According to this

model, the least economically developed groups and homelands in multinational, multihomeland states should thus be the most nationalistic. The solution to the national problem, following the logic of internal colonialism, is inter-national and inter-regional equalization.

Lenin added internal colonialism to Marx's treatment of nations and nationalism. According to Lenin, the essence of the national problem in Russia was the development of a core-periphery colonial relationship between the Russians and Russia on the one hand, and the non-Russians and their homelands on the other. Tsarist Russia was described as a "prison of peoples," and "Great Russian chauvinism" was treated as the state's greatest national problem. Lenin's solution to this national problem was rapid socioeconomic development coupled with inter-national and inter-regional equalization. This equalization was not only to be economic; federalization would provide for the political and juridical equality among nations, and *korenizatsiya* (indigenization) policies would provide for sociocultural equalization.[29] Ironically, non-Russian nationalists who rose in opposition to the USSR during the late 1980s and early 1990s also used the rhetoric of internal colonialism in charging that their nations and homelands were exploited by Moscow and that the USSR remained a prison of nations in which all non-Russians were exploited for the benefit of Russians. The disintegration of the USSR has thus been seen as a form of decolonization nationalism.[30]

Since the mid–1970s, internal colonialism has been subjected to a variety of criticisms.[31] It is true that inter-national and interhomeland inequality have been catalysts for rising inter-national tension in multinational, multihomeland states, particularly when that inequality is perceived by subordinate groups as resulting from policies promulgated by a political center dominated by a core nation. According to Donald Horowitz who studied ethnic conflict in the third world, less developed groups in less developed regions are most prone to separatism, a finding consistent with the predictions of the internal colonialism thesis.[32] However, in several multinational, multihomeland states, the most developed "peripheral" nations are the most nationalistic; such has certainly been the case in the USSR and Yugoslavia, two socialist states whose approaches to solving the "national problem" were formulated according to the precepts of internal colonialism. The Baltic nations, with the highest standards of living in the USSR, were most secessionist, while the Central Asians, with the lowest standards of living among those nations with union republic status, were least in favor of independence. In Yugoslavia, the most developed nations—the Slovenes and Croats— were most secessionist. This "most developed, most nationalistic" relationship is also found in Spain among the Basques and Catalans.

In addition to problems with the least developed, most nationalistic formula, equalization does not appear to solve the national problems in multinational, multihomeland states. According to socioeconomic indicators, the nations in the USSR experienced substantial equalization; similar equalization can also be found in post–World War II Czechoslovakia and Yugoslavia.[33] However, this equalization did not dampen nationalism; on the contrary, inter-national equalization has often coincided with heightened national consciousness and rising inter-national tensions.

This pattern is particularly true in multinational, multihomeland states where less developed indigenes have become more geographically and socially mobilized. As interhomeland migration, urbanization, educational attainment, and upward occupational mobility increase, indigenes compete more intensely with nonindigenes for control over the resources of the homeland, including high status positions. This competition often results in increasing inter-national tensions and conflict; indigenes typically believe that the homeland's resources rightfully belong to them and that their very status as indigenes entitles them to preferential treatment.[34] Thus, while growing inequality has been a catalyst for rising nationalism, equalization and even equality have not solved the national problem in multinational, multihomeland states.

Internal colonialism has more explanatory power if it includes the cultural and political inequality that often accompany economic inequality. Even with economic equalization, political and cultural domination of the state by a core nation have been catalysts for peripheral nationalism. In this regard, perception is perhaps more important than reality: equalization may be occurring according to objective measures (e.g., urbanization, educational attainment, occupation structure), but the subordinate nations' feelings of inequality and exploitation frequently continue to exist. This finding is echoed in Connor's conclusion "that when analyzing sociopolitical situations, what ultimately matters is not *what is* but *what people believe is.*"[35]

Relative Deprivation and Reactive Nationalism

The importance of group perceptions in explaining the continued efficacy of nationalism is the focus of a third set of theories, typically organized under the heading relative deprivation and reactive nationalism. Relative deprivation theory explains national identity and nationalism as reactions to perceived injustices that individuals feel regarding their relations and status compared to ethnic others. According to this approach, what matters is changes in inter-national status over time rather than the nation's status per se.

Relative deprivation theory contends that rising nationalism results from a growing gap between an individual or a group's expectations and its capacity to achieve them.[36] If group expectations remain low, an internal colonial relationship alone will not result in peripheral nationalism, unless group capacity to achieve even these limited expectations diminishes. Likewise, if both expectations and capacity rise at about the same rate, then nationalism should not increase. However, when expectations rise faster than a nation's capacity to achieve them, aspirational deprivation occurs; such change frequently has been cited as a cause of rising inter-national tensions and conflict.

Relative deprivation theory suggests that neither internal colonialism, international inequality, nor subordinate standing per se activates national territoriality in an ethnically stratified society. Rather, changes in one nation's status vis-á-vis other nations' status—or changes in group expectations regarding the nation's "proper place"—tend to activate nationalism.[37]

Relative deprivation theory is useful in explaining both the rise in violent antiforeigner "nativism" in relatively underdeveloped Central Asia and the separatist nationalism in the more developed Baltic republics. Two decades of rapidly rising educational attainment among young Central Asians led to rapidly increasing expectations. Economic stagnation during the 1970s, followed by the economic collapse of the 1980s, resulted in a growing gap between socioeconomic expectations and capabilities. Prior to this period, Russians were dominant in the cities of Central Asia, and Central Asians remained overwhelmingly rural. A condition of internal colonialism existed but did not generate an antiforeigner nativism among the indigenous Central Asians. However, with the rise in educational attainment and increasing socioeconomic expectations, upwardly mobile Central Asians found their paths blocked by Russians and other nonindigenes already occupying elite positions throughout urban, industrial Central Asia. This combination of rising expectations and limited opportunities for upward mobility resulted in violent antiforeigner "nativism," comparable to the underlying conditions that resulted in rising "nativism" among India's "sons of the soil."[38] International tensions and conflict increased only when internal colonialism began to break down through a process of inter-national equalization.

In the Baltic republics, a sense of relative deprivation also existed, even though these nations and homelands had the highest standards of living in the USSR. Clearly, the Baltic republics were not an underdeveloped periphery in Russia, yet the Baltic nations felt deprived. Here, indigenous nationalists compared their economic standing not with the rest of the USSR but with western Europe and especially with Finland, which like the Baltic republics, gained its independence from Russia following World War I but retained it after World War II. The Baltic nations believed that they would have had even higher standards of living if they had retained their independence. They attributed their lower living standards to exploitation by Moscow; the only way to close the gap between expectations and capabilities was to gain independence from the USSR.

Russians living in the newly independent republics outside Russia likewise perceive themselves to be deprived of their former cultural, political, and economic status. As the dominant nation during Soviet times, Russians had high expectations that were generally matched by capabilities. Since independence, Russian expectations have remained relatively high but their capabilities have been declining—in some places precipitously. The titular nations in the newly independent states are restructuring ethnic stratification systems to favor members of their own nations, improving titular group achievement capabilities relative to their past status and relative to other national communities currently living in these states. The rate at which titular nationalists improve their nations' capabilities and undermine those of the Russians will vary depending on the severity of the relative deprivation perceived by members of the titular nations. At the same time, the faster the pace of ethnic restratification, the greater the Russian sense of relative deprivation and therefore the greater the inter-national tensions and the potential for conflict is likely to become.

The two socioeconomic extremes in the USSR (i.e., Central Asia and the Baltics) highlight the utility of relative deprivation theory in explaining nationalism among not only less developed groups in less developed regions but also the more developed groups in more developed regions. This model thus has greater explanatory power than internal colonialism or other decolonization models. It also can be extended beyond the socioeconomic realm to take into account relative deprivation in the cultural and political spheres. Of course, relative deprivation theory is not without its problems, the most difficult of which is the subjective nature of the explanatory variables. Perceptions of relative deprivation are not readily quantifiable. Indeed, some measures may indicate an improvement in group status that would imply a decline in inter-national tensions, yet perceptions of relative deprivation may persist or even grow.

Relative deprivation theory is a useful device with which to explore the nature of the new titular nation/Russian relationships and speculate about the future course of inter-national relations in these newly independent states. Unlike modernization and internal colonialism/decolonization theories, relative deprivation theory does not offer simple solutions to inter-national tensions and conflicts. By locating the cause of the conflicts in the growing disparity between expectations and capabilities, it also identifies the problem that inter-national conflict management must address.

Interactive Nationalism

Interactive nationalism is the final model reviewed in this section and may be seen as an augmentation of relative deprivation theory in our analysis of the unfolding titular/Russian relationship in the newly independent states. According to Shantha Hennayake, who recently studied inter-national conflict in Sri Lanka, nationalism on the part of the "majority" nation is "the major causal factor in the emergence of minority ethnic nationalism."[39] When majority nationalism becomes both "overt" and "exclusionary" (i.e., when the majority nation openly seeks to establish its hegemony in the state), a reactive nationalism is stimulated among "minorities" in the state. The overt, exclusionary nationalism of the majority or titular nation in turn arises as a reaction to perceived threats to the nation's existence or perceived opportunities for national aggrandizement. Hennayake argues that overt majority ethnonationalism is stimulated:

1. when the present majority nation has been subordinated previously under colonialism and/or imperialism—for example, the Sinhalese in Sri Lanka;
2. where the majority ethnonationalism, especially its popular element, has been suppressed—as was the case in prerevolution Iran;
3. when the majority nation is threatened by external forces—for example, pre-Bangladesh East Pakistan—or by internal forces—for example,

growing Hindu nationalism in India in the face of growing Islamic fundamentalism;

4. When the economic resources of a multiethnic nation-state are limited—for example, the situation of the Malays in Malaysia;

5. to solicit support for the adventurist politics of a state—as in Nazi Germany;

6. to regain lost pride—as in postwar France;

7. when the survival of the majority nation is threatened—as in Israel today.[40]

All of these conditions identified by Hennayake are present in the rise of overt exclusionary nationalism among the titular nations in the Soviet successor states. The first two are generally expressed by non-Russians throughout the territory of the former USSR as the reasons they needed to become independent and also why the titular nations must attain dominance or hegemony in "their" newly independent states.

The third condition has been voiced by nationalists in several of the newly independent states. Russia is seen as an external threat by titular nationalists in the Baltics, Moldova, Ukraine, Georgia, and Kazakhstan. Azerbaijan is seen as an external threat in Armenia and vice versa, and Uzbekistan is increasingly viewed as an external threat in the non-Uzbek states of Central Asia. Russians are seen as an internal threat in Moldova, Estonia, Latvia, Ukraine, and in Kazakhstan. This view interacts with the perceived external threat that Russia is thought to pose, thus heightening inter-national tensions between members of the titular nations and the Russians living outside Russia. The same interactive effect is visible in Azerbaijan regarding the Armenians living in the state (particularly those in Nagorno-Karabakh), and in Kyrgyzstan and Tajikistan regarding the Uzbeks living in these two states. In Georgia, a more complicated "Russia as external threat, Russians, Abkhazians and Ossetians as internal threat" links minority nationalism with perceived Russian adventurism or imperialism. In Russia, however, the federal structure of the state itself, in providing non-Russians with a measure of territorial autonomy, is viewed as an internal threat by Russian nationalists, while the West in general is increasingly identified as an external threat in a formulation comparable to nineteenth-century slavophilism.

Condition number four, limited economic resources in the state, refers not only to concerns about the economic viability of the state but also to the uneven distribution of economic resources within the state. In Malaysia, the example cited by Hennayake, Malays are the dominant nation politically and the majority numerically, but Chinese are economically dominant. This situation existed in several of the former union republics, where Russians occupied a dominant economic place in the more developed urban/industrial sectors and where members of the titular nations remained more rural and agricultural. Russian economic dominance is strongest in Kazakhstan and Central Asia. Overall resources are particularly limited in several Central Asian republics. The same situation exists in Moldova, where the urban/industrial region on the left bank of the Dniester River is dominated by Russians and Ukrainians; and to some extent in Ukraine, where the industrial heartland of the east has traditionally been dominated by Russians and russified Ukrainians. Within most of the autonomous units, the titular nation of the union republic in which the autonomous territory is located is dominant economically and politically, and has attempted to retain this dominance since the breakup of the USSR (e.g., Georgians re Abkhazia and South Ossetia).

Condition number five, "to solicit support for the adventurist politics of a state," does not truly exist in any of the newly independent states with the possible exception of Armenia and its attempts to merge with Nagorno-Karabakh. An element of adventurism is also apparent in the policies and pronouncements of the Russian government in regard to the "near abroad," even though Russia has signed treaties recognizing the territorial integrity of its neighbors. More worrisome is the rise of Russian nationalists such as Zhirinovsky, whose political agenda clearly includes the territorial aggrandizement of Russia. His popularity in the elections of December 12, 1993, has had the effect of pushing the Yeltsin government in the direction of greater involvement in the so-called near abroad, which in turn raises the level of titular nationalism in response to the growth of this perceived external threat.

Condition number six, "to regain lost pride," is also an element fueling a more overt and exclusionary Russian nationalism in Russia as well as a willingness to become involved in the "near abroad." The loss of empire and with it superpower status have wounded the pride of even the liberal democratic, pro-Western Russians while enraging the more anti-Western chauvinistic/imperialistic Russian nationalists. Lost pride also serves as a mobilizing factor among Russians living outside Russia, who have frequently lost more than the Russians living in Russia.

Condition number seven—threats to the survival of the majority nation—has been combined with conditions one through three in most of the newly independent states. The non-Russian nations' survival was said to be threatened by the denationalizing russification policies of the USSR. This condition was perhaps nowhere more apparent than in Ukraine where one of the main goals of the Ukrainian Popular Front Organization's (*RUKH*) original program was "to wage a relentless struggle against the policy of denationalization and demand the creation of all conditions for the unfettered development and self-preservation of the Ukrainian people on the territory which has been theirs from time immemorial."[41] Although acculturation toward the Russian nation was the threat that served as a catalyst in the activation of national territoriality in republics such as Ukraine, demographic russification through immigration was the principal threat perceived in others, particularly in Estonia and Latvia.[42]

As noted in Chapter 1, titular nationalism in the USSR became both overt and exclusionary during the late 1980s, although its extent and nature varied by republic. Since independence, political elites representing the interests of the titular nations have at minimum sought to secure those nations' positions as "first among equals." Some titular nationalists have attempted to go even further and establish their nations' hegemony within true "nation-states," excluding minorities from participation in the political, cultural, and economic lifes.

This overt, exclusionary titular nationalism, according to Hennayake, is the major cause of minority nationalism:

> As the exclusionary tendency of majority ethnonationalism increases, and the majority nation increasingly defines the state in its own right, the consent that minority ethnic groups extend to the state is equally withdrawn. This withdrawal usually leads to a simultaneous increase in the politicization of the minority ethnic group. Minority ethnic groups, which are threatened and challenged by the increasing exclusionary practices of majority ethnonationalist politics through the state, are not simply *reacting* to it, but rather are *devising* ways and means to counter it too.[43]

Interactive nationalism, by presenting a theoretical basis for both majority and minority interaction, goes beyond other reactive nationalism models and provides a more satisfactory explanation for the unfolding relationships between titular nations and Russians in the successor states. Yet this particular interactive relationship between titular nations and local Russians contains a further complicating factor—the role of Russia itself. A triangular interactive process, including titular nationalism, local Russian "counter-hegemonic" nationalism, and Russia's state support for local Russians, provides a more comprehensive conceptualization of the interaction than the two-dimensional action/reaction approach.[44]

The interactive process, beginning with majority or titular nationalism, operates on several geographic scales in the former USSR. At the all-union scale, Russian domination of the non-Russian homelands was a clear case of majority nationalism in the USSR. From this perspective, the independence movements can be considered counter-hegemonic minority nationalism. At the scale of union republics, rising titular nationalism, even before independence, had the effect of stimulating minority (Russian and other) nationalism, which has increased since the disintegration of the USSR. At the scale of autonomous territories within union republics, several of the titular groups have become more overtly exclusionary vis-à-vis nontitular members living there, in turn providing a catalyst for rising nontitular nationalism in the autonomous territories.

All of these interactive nationalisms interact with the processes unfolding at the other geographic scales. For example, Georgian separatist nationalism stimulated separatism among Abkhazians and Ossetians who feared rising Georgian chauvinism; and Abkhazian and Ossetian exclusionary nationalism in Abkhazia and South Ossetia stimulated a Georgian nationalist reaction, not only in Tbilisi but also among Georgians living in the two autonomous territories. This instability within Georgia was then used by Russian nationalists seeking to reestablish their hegemony in the near abroad.

Dominant nation behavior toward subordinate nations occupies a continuum along which policies may shift: from accommodation and full inclusion to rejection and exclusion, up to and including the extremist policies of forced expulsion, ethnic cleansing, and genocide. Not all minority or subordinate-group nationalism is extremist. The minority response depends both on the nature of majority or dominant-group nationalism (the degree of minority exclusion) and also on the historical relations between the two groups (whether a previous period of exclusionary nationalism by the dominant group coincided with a campaign of violence and repression against the subordinate group).[45]

Subordinate-nation responses also lie along a continuum, ranging from acceptance and adaptation to rejection and opposition, up to and including violent rebellion and/or secession. The reaction by members of the subordinate group is determined by their perception of the new relationship with both the dominant nation and the state. What may appear to members of the dominant nation, and indeed even to outside observers, as relatively accommodative and inclusive policies may be perceived to be much more exclusionary by members of the subordinate nations. Subordinate groups tend to be particularly sensitive to changes that strengthen the position of the dominant nation if there has been a history of inter-national conflict between the two.

Subordinate nations are likely to meet dominant-nation policies of accommodation and inclusion with acceptance and adaptation, and consequently little conflict escalation is expected. The more exclusionary the policies of the dominant nation—as perceived by members of the subordinate nations—the more likely that members of the subordinate nations will reject and oppose the new state and their new status in it, thus causing conflict escalation.[46]

Subordinate-nation rejection/opposition may be manifested in a variety of ways, including:

Emigration.   Voluntary emigration, or "voting with one's feet" in response to the new situation, may be perceived as forced emigration by those leaving a place in which they no longer feel welcome. Emigration becomes forced expulsion as dominant group nationalism becomes more exclusionary. Refugees in turn tend to heighten inter-state tensions if their nation is dominant in a nearby state (e.g., Armenia and Azerbaijan, Russians returning to Russia).

Formation of Political Opposition Parties.   The subordinate nation may choose to remain in the state and to operate within the political system by seeking to establish or enhance its political voice. This approach can range from the nation's accepting the new political and economic realities while seeking limited cultural and/or territorial autonomy for its members, to rejecting the new reality of dominant-nation hegemony and forming political organizations seeking outright independence in a region proclaimed as the subordinate nation's homeland (secession and/or irredentism). Dominant nations rarely allow separatist parties to operate within the political system, thus forcing the separatist minority underground and making terrorism/guerrilla warfare more likely. In addition, if the dominant nation refuses moderate political demands for cultural and/or territorial autonomy, subordinate political opposition often becomes more extreme.

Independence.   The subordinate nation seeks a state of its own that it can dominate, typically on the territory that it considers to be its homeland, or seeks accession to a neighboring state in which the subordinate nation is already dominant (irredentism). Examples of the former include most of the republics of the USSR, Yugoslavia, and Czechoslovakia. Moldova is an example of the latter, where some nationalists saw reunification of Moldova with Romania as their ultimate objective. As an alternative, the subordinate nation may seek to become the dominant or hegemonic group in the state by overthrowing the established order.

The reaction on the part of the dominant nation in turn depends on the extremism of the subordinate nation's response. Through the use of an interactive approach, one can easily see how inter-national conflict escalation occurs, and how once begun, conflicts of this nature are difficult to defuse.

Conclusion

The interactive nationalism model contends that inter-national tensions and conflicts are less the result of ancient, tribal hatreds than the consequence of an interactive process initiated by the majority, titular or dominant nation seeking hegemony in the state. This approach, in contrast to a more primordialist view, implies that inter-national conflicts are amenable to management, because the majority nation can adopt policies to include members of all nations as full and equal participants in the socio-cultural, economic, and political life of the state. According to this theory, accommodation and inclusion should dampen counter-hegemonic reaction on the part of national minorities.

Thus far most dominant nations have failed to accommodate the interests of the subordinate nations or even to recognize the legitimacy of subordinate national interests. This lack of accommodation by the dominant nation leaves subordinate nations with few choices: acceptance of the new status quo (i.e., hegemony of the dominant nation in the state), emigration (perceived as forced emigration or refugee migration), or political resistance/secession/irredentism.

We now turn to the history of Russia's imperial expansion (Chapter 3) and then of the Soviet Union (Chapter 4) to provide the context for today's titular nation/Russian relations. The purpose of these chapters is to analyze the nature and extent of Russian domination of the non-Russian nations prior to the breakup of the USSR. We also look at the nationalization processes occurring among the indigenous ethnic groups in the Russian Empire and the Soviet Union. This discussion will set the stage for Part Two of the book, in which we examine the interactive inter-national relationships between titular nations and Russians in each of the successor states. The interactive nationalism model is central to our analysis. We augment this approach, however, by drawing concepts from relative deprivation theory and by incorporating a triangular relationship between the titular nationality, the Russian minority and the presence of a potentially interventionist Russian state. Together, these tools help explain the dynamic relationships between the titular nations and the Russian minorities in the Soviet successor states.

Notes

1. Walker Connor, "A Nation Is a Nation, Is an Ethnic Group, Is a State Is a . . . ," *Ethnic and Racial Studies,* Vol. 1 (October 1978): 377–400.

2. Karl Marx, "The German Ideology," Part I, and "Manifesto of the Communist Party," in Robert Tucker, ed., *The Marx-Engels Reader,* 2nd ed. (New York: Norton, 1978), pp. 146–200, 469–500; Walker Connor, *The National Question in Marxist-Leninist Theory and Strategy* (Princeton, NJ: Princeton University Press, 1984), pp. 5–20.

3. See Joseph Rothschild, "Nationalism and Democratization in East Central Europe: Lessons from the Past," *Nationalities Papers,* Vol. 22, No.1 (Spring 1994), p. 27, for a discussion of the terms state and nation.

4. Ernest Renan, *Qu'est-ce qu' une Nation?* (Paris, 1882).

5. Anthony Smith, *The Ethnic Origins of Nations* (Oxford: Basil Blackwell, 1986), pp. 7–15; George Scott, Jr., "A Resynthesis of the Primordial and Circumstantial Approaches to Ethnic Group Solidarity: Towards an Explanatory Model," *Ethnic and Racial Studies,* No. 13 (April 1990): 147–171.

6. See Robert Kaiser, *The Geography of Nationalism in Russia and the USSR* (Princeton, NJ: Princeton University Press, 1994), for an elaboration of this definition. This view of the nation as both backward-looking and forward-looking is similar to the definition offered by Rupert Emerson, *From Empire to Nation : The Rise to Self Assertion of Asian and African Peoples* (Boston: Beacon, 1960), p. 95: "The nation is a community of people who feel that they belong together in the double sense that they share deeply significant elements of a common heritage and that they have a common destiny for the future."

7. Walker Connor, "Nation-building or Nation-destroying?" *World Politics,* No. 24 (April 1972): 338–342.

8. As quoted in Edward Allworth, "Regeneration in Central Asia," in Edward Allworth, ed., *The National Question in Soviet Central Asia* (New York: Praeger, 1973), p. 16.

9. Edward Soja, *The Political Organization of Space* (Washington: Association of American Geographers (AAG), 1971): 34. The terms "sense of spatial identity" and "sense of exclusiveness" are identified as the first two ingredients of human group territoriality. We return to the connection between nationalism and territoriality below.

10. Soja, *Political Organization*; Walker Connor, "The Impact of Homelands upon Diasporas," in G. Sheffer, ed., *Modern Diasporas in International Politics* (London: Croom Helm, 1986), pp. 16–46; Tamotsu Shibutani and Kian Kwan, *Ethnic Stratification: A Comparative Approach* (London: Macmillan, 1965), p. 445.

11. Smith, *Ethnic Origins.*

12. According to Connor, a nation is "a self-differentiating ethnic group" ("Nation-Building or Nation-Destroying?" p. 337), or "a self-aware ethnic group" ("A Nation Is a Nation . . . ," p. 388). This definition implies that when ethnic groups begin to interact with ethnic others and realize that they can distinguish themselves from these ethnic others, a nation is born. The definition also implies that the 3,000 or so ethnic subdivisions in the world today should all be considered nations because ethnic interaction has become commonplace globally. However, although appropriate to consider these 3,000 ethnic groups proto-nations, a more refined differentiation between nation and ethnic group is needed.

13. As examples of this more modernist, instrumentalist depiction of nations, see Smith, *Ethnic Origins*; Kaiser, *Geography of Nationalism*; Eric Hobsbawm, *Nations and Nationalism Since 1780* (Cambridge: Cambridge University Press, 1990); Ernest Gellner, *Nations and Nationalism* (Ithaca, NY: Cornell University Press, 1983); Benedict Anderson, *Imagined Communities* (London: Verso, 1983); Eugen Weber, *Peasants into Frenchmen* (Stanford, CA: Stanford University Press, 1976); Walker Connor, "When Is A Nation?" *Ethnic and Racial Studies* 13 (January 1990): 92–103; Miroslav Hroch, *The Social Preconditions for National Revival in Europe* (Cambridge: Cambridge University Press,

1985); Edward Tiryakian and Ronald Rogowski, eds., *New Nationalisms of the Developed West* (Boston: Allen & Unwin, 1985).

14. Hroch, *Social Preconditions*, p. 23.

15. As quoted in Nicholas Riasanovsky, *Nicholas I and Official Nationality in Russia, 1825–1855* (Berkeley: University of California Press, 1969), p. 99.

16. Kaiser, *Geography of Nationalism*, pp. 44–47.

17. For some groups, early research into ethnocultural and linguistic history was conducted by nationalists from neighboring nations, who sought to prove that these ethnic groups and their homelands were historically part of their nations. For example, Polish and Russian nationalist historians sought evidence that Belarusians and Belarus were an integral part of the Polish or Russian nation. This interest in Belarusian roots served as the early ethnicization phase in the region. See Nicholas Vakar, *Belorussia: The Making of a Nation* (Cambridge: Harvard University Press, 1956), pp. 73–82.

18. Kaiser, *Geography of Nationalism*, pp. 39–40.

19. Anderson, *Imagined Communities*; Kaiser, *Geography of Nationalism*; Weber, *Peasants into Frenchmen*.

20. Nationalization, as well as acculturation and assimilation processes in the Soviet Union are discussed at length in Chapter 4.

21. Connor, "A Nation Is a Nation."

22. John Breuilly, *Nationalism and the State* (Manchester: Manchester University Press, 1982), p. 3. A more detailed elaboration of these tenets is found in Juval Portugali, "Nationalism, Social Theory and the Israeli/Palestinian Case," in R. J. Johnston et al., eds., *Nationalism, Self-Determination and Political Geography* (London: Croom Helm, 1988), p. 155.

23. Rupert Emerson, *From Empire to Nation: The Rise to Self Assertion of Asian and African Peoples* (Boston: Beacon, 1960), 95–96.

24. Kaiser, *Geography of Nationalism*. For a discussion of human territoriality as a political strategy, see Robert Sack, *Human Territoriality: Its Theory and History* (Cambridge: Cambridge University Press, 1986); and Soja, *Political Organization*.

25. Ernest Gellner, *Nations and Nationalism* (Ithaca: Cornell University Press, 1983), p. 1. For a similar definition of nationalism, along with detailed case studies, see Colin Williams, "The Question of National Congruence," in R. J. Johnston and P. J. Taylor, eds., *A World in Crisis? Geographical Perspectives*, 2nd ed. (Oxford: Basil Blackwell, 1989), pp. 229–265. Smith, in *Ethnic Origins*, also defines nations as both politicized and territorialized ethnic groups.

26. Connor, "Impact of Homelands," p. 20. Connor makes the point that this is true of state borders generally and not just those delimited by the colonial powers.

27. Karl Deutsch, *Nationalism and Social Communication*, 2nd ed. (Cambridge: MIT Press, 1966); and Connor's critique of Deutsch in "Nation-Building?"

28. Michael Hechter, *Internal Colonialism: The Celtic Fringe in British National Development, 1536–1966* (Berkeley: University of California Press, 1975).

29. See Walker Connor, *Marxist-Leninist Theory*; Robert Kaiser, "Nationalism: The Challenge to Soviet Federalism," in Michael Bradshaw, ed., *The Soviet Union: A New Regional Geography?* (London: Belhaven Press, 1991), pp. 39–66; Kaiser, *Geography of Nationalism*, pp. 96–102.

30. For example, see Alexander Motyl, "From Imperial Decay to Imperial Collapse: The Fall of the Soviet Empire in Comparative Perspective," in Richard Rudolph and David Good, eds., *Nationalism and Empire: The Habsburg Empire and the Soviet Union* (New York: St. Martin's Press, 1992), pp. 15–43. The problems with treating the Soviet Union as an empire like any other are discussed extensively in Chapter 4.

31. Francois Nielsen, "Toward a Theory of Ethnic Solidarity in Modern Societies," *American Sociological Review* 50 (1985): 133–149; Walker Connor, "Eco- or ethno-nationalism?" *Ethnic and Racial Studies* 13 (January 1984): 342–359. See also Michael

Hechter, "Internal Colonialism Revisited," in Tiryakian and Rogowski, eds., *New Nationalisms*), pp. 17–26.

32. Donald Horowitz, *Ethnic Groups in Conflict* (Berkeley: University of California Press, 1985).

33. Robert Kaiser, "National Territoriality in Multinational, Multi-Homeland States: A Comparative Study of the Soviet Union, Yugoslavia and Czechoslovakia" (PhD dis., Columbia University, 1988).

34. Kaiser, *Geography of Nationalism*. This finding supports the competition theory of ethnic solidarity as elaborated by Nielsen, "Towards a Theory of Ethnic Solidarity," pp. 133–149.

35. Connor, "A Nation Is a Nation . . . ," p. 380 (emphasis in original).

36. Ted Gurr, *Why Men Rebel* (Princeton, NJ: Princeton University Press, 1970).

37. Peter Alexis Gourevich, "The Reemergence of 'Peripheral Nationalisms': Some Comparative Speculations on the Spatial Distribution of Political Leadership and Economic Growth," *Comparative Studies in Society and History*, Vol. 21, No. 3 (July 1979): 303–322. Gourevitch argues that peripheral nationalism is more likely in cases where the peripheral region is an ethnic homeland that improves its economic position vis-à-vis the core, which may happen as the result of either decline in the core or relatively greater economic development in the periphery. This thesis argues that peripheral nationalism "reemerges" when internal colonialism begins to break down. This idea can be seen as bridging the gap between internal colonialism and the competition thesis, which is briefly discussed below.

38. Myron Weiner, *Sons of the Soil: Migration and Ethnic Conflict in India* (Princeton, NJ: Princeton University Press, 1978), pp. 274–294. Weiner defines nativism as "intense opposition to minorities because of their foreign origin."

39. Shantha Hennayake, "Interactive Ethnonationalism: An Alternative Explanation of Minority Ethnonationalism," *Political Geography*, Vol.11, No. 6 (November 1992): 526.

40. Hennayake, "Interactive Ethnonationalism," p. 529.

41. *RUKH Program and Charter* (Ellicott City, MD: Smoloskyp Publishers, 1989), p. 12.

42. See, for example, Tonu Parming, "Population Processes and the Nationality Issue in the Soviet Baltic," *Soviet Studies* Vol. 32, No. 3 (July 1980): 398–414; and Juris Dreifelds, "Immigration and Ethnicity in Latvia," *Journal of Soviet Nationalities* Vol. 1, No. 4 (Winter 1990–1991): 43–81.

43. Hennayake, "Interactive Ethnonationalism," p. 530.

44. For a discussion of this tripartite relationship see Rogers Brubaker, "National Minorities, Nationalizing States, and External National Homelands in the New Europe." *Daedalus* Vol. 24, No. 2 (Spring 1995):107–132. This triangular conceptualization also adds clarity to other evolving inter-national relationships, such as the situation of Hungarians in Romania and Slovakia and that of Serbs in the territories of the former Yugoslavia.

45. Hennayake, "Interactive Ethnonationalism." See also Raphael Zariski, "Ethnic Extremism Among Ethnoterritorial Minorities in Western Europe," *Comparative Politics* 21 (1989): 253–272.

46. See Albert O. Hirschman, *Exit, Voice, and Loyalty* (Cambridge: Harvard University Press, 1970).

Chapter 3

Core and Periphery in the Russian Empire

To comprehend the interactions between the titular nations and the minority Russians today, one must first understand the history of relations between Russians and non-Russians as each side perceives it. Certain historical events—the timing of incorporation of non-Russian lands and peoples into the Russian Empire and the USSR, the nature of this incorporation, and intergroup relations afterward—are critically important in giving shape to contemporary international perceptions.

The timing of the Russian conquest of the non-Russian territories in relation to the development of a national consciousness among the indigenous groups is critical. The later incorporation occurred in the nationalization process, the more likely it was to activate a minority nationalism that was pointedly anti-Russian. It is also important to know whether Russian conquest occurred prior to, during, or after the group in question had experienced political independence and/or dominance over others. If the group and its homeland were independent polities when conquered, or were themselves the seats of imperial power, conquest was more likely to serve as a catalyst for indigenous nationalism.

The nature of the conquest and incorporation of non-Russians also plays an important role. First, how did the incorporation take place? What was the extent of hostility involved in Russian expansion and conquest, and did it result in high casualties or devastation to the homeland? Second, was the conquest direct (between Russians and indigenes protecting their homeland), or indirect (between invading Russia and another empire, with the land acquired as the spoils of this war)? Third, was the conquest accompanied by large-scale in-migration of Russians? As noted in Chapter 2, an in-migration of foreigners, especially members of the hegemonic group, often activates an exclusionary indigenous nationalism. Finally, were the group and its homeland wholly or partially incorporated into the empire? Inter-state borders dissecting a group and its homeland provide a potential external base of support for independence, particularly if conationals dominate the neighboring state.

The interaction of Russians and the indigenous group after the incorporation of its territory is another crucial factor. To what degree was cultural and territorial autonomy afforded the group and did that autonomy meet expectations? Nationally self-conscious groups have higher expectations than ethnic groups. As nationalization proceeds, cultural and territorial autonomy must increase in order to satisfy the demands of indigenes.

Some interactions between Russians and the indigenous groups involved coercion. To what extent was force used by the core against indigenous groups in the periphery to "solve the national problem?" Examples cover a continuum from mandatory learning of the Russian language and forced acculturation to expulsion from the homeland and finally genocide.

Similarly, to what extent did Russians themselves dominate the non-Russian periphery? An ethnic stratification system that denied indigenes dominance in their homeland, especially if those indigenes had already become nationally conscious, would likely serve as a catalyst for anti-Russian nationalism. Russian in-migration could also produce this effect. But the reverse is also true: indigenes who have gained greater autonomy and dominance in their own homelands frequently push for greater independence. Finally, to what degree did the Russian core itself dominate the non-Russian periphery?

This chapter traces the development of titular-Russian relationships as perceived both by members of titular nations and by Russians. The theoretical framework for this analysis, outlined in Chapter 2, emphasizes the interactive nature of titular-Russian relationships, while also drawing on theories of colonialism, ethnic stratification, and decolonization nationalism.

The Creation of the Russian Empire

Russia's expansion through conquest of contiguous non-Russian lands and peoples—and the establishment of colonial relations between the Russian core and the non-Russian periphery—was an imperial project that occupied the last 350 years of the Empire's existence.[1] During this period of expansion through conquest the Empire exhibited great variability in the degree of autonomy granted its subjects, with greater de jure autonomy granted to the provinces of the northwest (Finland, Congress Poland, the Baltics) and greater de facto autonomy available to subjects in Siberia and the Far East because of their remoteness from the core.

The extent of regional opposition to rule by Moscow also varied greatly. Opposition tended to be much higher in northern Caucasia at the time of its incorporation and in northern Caucasia and northern Kazakhstan during the massive influx of Russians that followed the conquest and incorporation. Opposition to tsarist rule increased more rapidly over time in the northwestern provinces of Russia. This trend was undoubtedly related to the nationalization of non-Russians in the Baltic **guberniyas** (administrative districts), Congress Poland, and Finland, coinciding with the sociocultural and economic development of the indigenous ethnic communities in this region of Russia.[2] As the nationalization process developed during the nineteenth century, opposition to

Russia's absolute control increased throughout the non-Russian periphery and within the Russian core itself. This nationalization process was one of the critical factors leading to the disintegration of the Russian Empire, though mass-based nations as communities of belonging and interest were only beginning to emerge in much of the non-Russian periphery by World War I.

A Brief Chronology of Russia's Expansion

Russia became a multiethnic empire during the reign of Ivan IV (1533–1584), the first "tsar of all the Russias." Even before the conquest of the Kazan' Khanate in 1552, Muscovy had expanded to incorporate several surrounding non-Russian ethnic groups and their homelands—including Karelians to the north; Nentsy, Zyrians (Komi), and Komi-Permyaks to the northeast; Ukrainians in eastern Ukraine from Chernigov to the northern margins of the Crimean Khanate—and had begun to encroach upon the lands of the Chuvashes, Votyaks (Udmurts), Cheremises (Mari), and Mordvins in the middle Volgas. With the exception of the Chuvash, these groups, with their long history of Russian interaction preceding the beginnings of a national consciousness by centuries, have experienced the greatest degree of linguistic russification, interethnic marriage with local Russians, and intergenerational ethnic re-identification toward the Russian nation.[3]

After the fall of the Kazan' Tatars in 1552,[4] the Astrakhan' Khanate in 1554, and the Khanate of Sibir in 1581, a broad arc of land was acquired by the rapidly expanding Russian Empire. Still hemmed in to the west by the Kingdoms of Poland and Sweden, the Russian Empire began its push to the east. By the end of the century, Russia had enveloped the lands of the Kazan' Tatars, the Khanty and Mansi, and the remaining lands and peoples of the middle and lower Volga basin. It had also conquered the western margins of Bashkiria and extended political and military control to much of the Ob River basin in Siberia and nearly to the Ural River in what is now northwestern Kazakhstan.

After the short-lived "Time of the Troubles" between 1598 and 1618, when Poland and Sweden expanded at Russia's expense in the West, the expansion of the Russian Empire continued. By 1689, Russia had laid claim to all of Siberia and the Far East north of the Amur River basin, and dozens of small nomadic peoples and their lands were incorporated into the Empire. This "incorporation" was frequently more apparent than real; aside from dealings with Russian trappers, traders and explorers, the impact on the day-to-day lives of the indigenous peoples in the East was minimal. This situation was particularly true in the Far East, due to the time and the hardships involved in crossing Siberia.[5] The remoteness of this region lessened only with the opening of the Trans-Siberian Railroad, which barely preceded the collapse of the Russian Empire. Nonetheless, due to the sparse settlement patterns of the nomadic indigenes, Russians had become a demographic majority in Siberia and the Far East by the 1678 population registration (Table 3.1). In the West, Russia also made major gains by incorporating much of the territory controlled by the

Table 3.1

Distribution of Russians in the Russian Empire, 1678–1917

(Absolute number in thousands and percent of total population)

Region	1678 000s	1678 %	1719 000s	1719 %	1782 000s	1782 %	1795 000s	1795 %	1834 000s	1834 %	1858 000s	1858 %	1897 000s	1897 %	1916–17 000s	1916–17 %
Euro Russia	7966	71.1[a]	10801	56.6	17372	59.7	19188	52.2	26659	52.8	32107	53.4	48876	51.9	64485	52.8
C. Ind.	3880	97.0	4535	97.7	5795	96.5	6106	96.2	7428	96.0	8204	95.4	10573	97.1	13855	97.8
C. Agr.	1700	93.4	2805	90.6	4726	87.9	5241	87.4	7420	87.6	8560	86.8	11216	87.3	14382	86.8
North	644	92.0	515	92.0	689	90.9	739	91.3	900	90.8	1105	90.1	1521	90.1	2006	89.8
Lake	900	90.0	1051	89.4	1830	92.0	1916	92.1	2399	88.7	2683	88.4	4406	88.7	5628	90.9
Mid-Volga	462	51.3	935	59.7	1343	64.8	1414	63.2	1974	62.6	2425	62.8	3091	59.8	3918	59.7
Lower Volga	—[b]	—	100	33.0	576	62.4	899	66.7	1883	68.2	2463	67.5	4032	65.4	5553	65.5
North Urals	270	90.0	561	90.8	1412	84.5	1626	84.0	2572	84.8	3553	85.1	5052	83.9	6101	83.2
South Urals	—	—	19	10.5	183	40.9	253	40.2	553	43.4	967	47.5	1966	51.8	3007	54.3
Belorussia and Lithuania	83	4.0	165	4.5	433	9.4	493	9.5	607	9.9	645	9.9	1961	16.9	3510	23.6
Baltics	—	—	3	0.3	13	1.2	13	1.1	49	3.2	63	3.6	114	4.8	180	6.3
Left-Bank Ukr.	—	—	40	2.2	178	5.4	175	5.2	209	4.9	301	6.1	1010	13.3	1249	12.8
Right-Bank Ukr.	—	—	—	—	...[c]	...	4	0.1	15	0.3	33	0.6	413	4.3	426	3.4
Novorossiya	27	6.7	72	15.6	193	22.2	308	19.1	614	18.1	1063	21.6	3213	29.8	4496	30.7
Congress Poland	—	—	—	—	—	—	—	—	5	0.1	6	0.1	298	3.2	167	1.3

41

Finland	—	—	...	...	—	—	1	...	31	2.2	36	2.1	10	0.4	7	0.3
North Caucasia	—	—	4	0.7	17	2.5	111	6.9	279	13.2	373	16.9	1608	42.5	2744	46.9
Transcaucasia	—	—	—	—	—	—	—	—	4	0.2	32	1.0	261	4.7	474	6.3
Central Asia and Kazakhstan	—	—	—	—	—	—	—	—	—	—	50	1.0	588	7.6	1548	14.3
Siberia and the Far East	154	51.8	323	66.9	693	67.6	819	68.9	1702	73.8	2259	74.1	4432	76.9	7425	77.6
TOTAL	8120	70.6[a]	11128	55.3	18082	58.7	20118	50.9	28644	45.3	34821	42.9	55765	43.5	76676	44.6

Notes: The data provided in Table 3.1 for the period 1678–1858 and for 1917 are estimates constructed by Bruk and Kabuzan, and must be treated with caution. No question on ethnic identity was asked in the population registrations prior to 1897, and in the 1897 census only a question on ethnolinguistic group was asked.

[a] The percentages for total population are for the territory of the Russian Empire at the time of the population registration. The figures provided in Bruk and Kabuzan are for the territory comparable to the geographic extent of the Russian Empire in 1897, and so are not the same as those given above.

[b] — indicates a region that was not part of the empire at the time, and/or for which data were not available.

[c] ... indicates that the number of Russians in this region was less than 1,000 or less than 0.1% of the total population.

The guberniyas for the gross regions of the empire in Table 3.1 are as follows:

European Russia: the 50 guberniyas of the empire, plus Congress Poland and Finland.

C. Ind. = Central Industrial: Kaluga, Kostroma, Moscow, Nizhniy Novgorod, Tver', Vladimir, Yaroslavl'.

C. Agr. = Central Agricultural: Kursk, Orel, Ryazan', Tambov, Tula, Voronezh.

North: Arkhangel'sk, Vologda.

(continues)

42

Table 3.1 (continued)

Lake: Novgorod, Olonets, Pskov, St. Petersburg, Smolensk.

Mid-Volga = Middle Volga: Kazan', Penza, Simbirsk.

Lower Volga: Astrakhan', Samara, Saratov.

North Urals: Perm', Vyatka.

South Urals: Orenburg, Ufa.

Belorussia and Lithuania: Grodno, Kovno, Minsk, Mogilev, Vil'na, Vitebsk.

Baltics: Estland, Kurland, Lifland.

Left-Bank Ukraine: Chernigov, Khar'kov, Poltava.

Right-Bank Ukraine: Kiev, Podol'sk, Volynia.

Novorossiya: Don, Yekaterinoslav, Kherson, Tavrida.

Bessarabia guberniya missing from table in Bruk and Kabuzan.

Congress Poland: Kalish, Kel'tsy, Lomzha, Lyublin, Petrokov, Plotsk, Radom, Sedlets, Suvalki, Warsaw.

Finland: Abo-Bjorneborg, Kuopio, Nyland, St. Michel, Tavastehus, Uleaborg, Vasa, Vyborg.

North Caucasia: Chernomorya, Kuban, Stavropol, Tersk.

Transcaucasia: Baku, Batumi, Dagestan, Elisavetpol', Karsk, Kutaissi, Sukhumi, Tiflis, Yerevan, Zakatalsk.

Kazakhstan and Central Asia: Akmolinsk, Fergana, Samarkand, Semipalatinsk, Semirechiye, Syr'-Darya, Uralsk, Zakaspisk.

Siberia and the Far East: Amur, Irkutsk, Kamchatka, Primorya, Sakhalin, Tobolsk, Tomsk, Yakutiya, Yenisey, Zabaykal.

Source: S. Bruk and V. Kabuzan, "Dinamika chislennosti i rasseleniya russkogo etnosa (1678–1917)," *Sovetskaya etnografiya* 1982 (4), 17.

Zaporozhiye Cossacks (i.e., Left-Bank Ukraine and Kiev), first as a protectorate and later as a possession. However, as in the case of the eastward expansion, Russian control of this western province was limited throughout the remainder of the seventeenth century.[6]

During the reign of Peter I (1689–1725), Russia acquired Estonia, Livonia, and Ingria as a result of its success in the 1700–1721 war with the Kingdom of Sweden. This victory brought Finns, Estonians, and Latvians into the Empire, as well as Baltic Germans who had established dominance over the Baltic coastal region. The Russian Empire under Peter I also made temporary gains in Ukraine in the lower Dnieper and Don River basins at the expense of the Ottoman Empire and the Crimean Tatars, and around the littoral of the Caspian Sea at the expense of Persia. The conquest of Kamchatka and the exploration of the Kuril Islands also began during this period.

From 1725 to 1762, Russia expanded southward into the lands of the Kazakh hordes, and explored the Aleutian Islands. In the West, the Russian Empire gained lands in southeastern Finland and on the right bank of the Dnieper River south of Kiev; the latter acquisition placed Russia on the Sea of Azov and gave it access to the Black Sea. However, Russia also lost the lands around the Caspian littoral to Persia during this period.

The rule of Catherine II (1762–1796) was marked by the partitions of Poland (1772, 1793, and 1795), resulting in major territorial acquisitions for Russia in present-day Poland, Latvia, Lithuania, Belarus, Ukraine, and Moldova east of the Dniester River.[7] The Crimean Tatar Khanate was also conquered, representing a major loss to the Ottoman Empire in the region. The Ottoman Empire also lost the lands around Odessa. These acquisitions brought large numbers of Poles, Jews, Belarusians ("White Russians"), Lithuanians, Ukrainians (Malorussy or "Little Russians"),[8] and Crimean Tatars into the Russian Empire. During this period Russia also advanced into northern Caucasia and northern Kazakhstan, though control over these areas was not firmly established until the nineteenth century.

During the nineteenth century, the Russian Empire expanded to its greatest geographic extent, acquiring Finland, Bessarabia, Transcaucasia (including Armenia, Azerbaijan and Georgia), Kazakhstan and Turkestan, and the Amur Basin in the Far East. Finland retained a great deal of autonomy after its incorporation. The Amur acquisition also remained relatively autonomous by virtue of its remote location, at least until the completion of the Trans-Siberian Railroad. In the Caucasus, particularly among the mountainous peoples in the north, there was fierce opposition to Russian rule. Although Georgia joined Russia as protection against the Ottoman and Persian Empires it neither anticipated nor welcomed complete incorporation and subjugation. Armenia, Azerbaijan and Dagestan were won from Persia during the 1820s. Bessarabia, like Armenia, was a relatively undeveloped region without its own indigenous nationalized intelligentsia. In Kazakhstan and Central Asia a nationalized elite had also not developed by the time of conquest and incorporation. Among the more nomadic Kazakhs, Kyrgyz, and Turkmen, no nationalization of elites had occurred, and the internal fragmentation among these groups was used to good advantage by Russia as it extended its control over the region. Among the more sedentary Uzbeks and Tajiks, Islamic elites opposed the nationalization process, which they feared would serve as a centrifugal force within the Muslim world. Consequently, little nationalization had taken place by the end of the nineteenth century; while localized opposition to the infidels to the north existed, it was no match for the advancing Russian military.[9]

Core and Periphery

The distinction between core and periphery in the Russian Empire can be defined in a number of ways. Most generally, the Russian Empire was divided into a core of the fifty European guberniyas, including Russia west of the Urals and north of the Caucasus as well as the Baltics, Lithuania and Belorussia, Ukraine and Bessarabia. The periphery was made up of a ring of colonial holdings including Finland, Congress Poland, North Caucasia and Transcaucasia, Kazakhstan and Central Asia, and Siberia and the Far East. These peripheral areas were treated as an external empire; the indigenous populations held diminished status and the territories were more autonomous (de jure in Finland and Poland, de facto in Siberia and the Far East). With the exception of Congress Poland and the Caucasus region, serfdom was not generally practiced in these peripheral areas as it was in the core guberniyas.

This gross regionalization into core and periphery can be further differentiated. In the periphery, relatively developed and autonomous Finland and Poland were distinguished from the underdeveloped Asiatic colonies populated by nomadic or seminomadic peoples. In addition, during the nineteenth century with the rise of Slavophile nationalism, Russian nationalists viewed Siberia and the Far East as a utopia which would save Russia and the Russians from the degradation of European influence. Perceptually, Slavophilism attempted to move the Russian core away from St. Petersburg—an alien European capital looking westward—and toward Siberia.[10] However, Siberia remained on the periphery of the Russian and Soviet Empires even though Russians became the demographic majority there by 1678 and Russian migration to Siberia increased dramatically after 1881.

European Russia can be dissected into three regions: an inner core consisting of the Russian historical heartland where the administrative, industrial, and agricultural centers were located and where ethnic Russians were concentrated (the Central Industrial, Central Agricultural, North, Lake and North Urals regions); an outer core of Russian frontier expansion and incorporation (the Middle and Lower Volga, South Urals, Belorussia, Left-Bank Ukraine, and Novorossiya regions); and a peripheral ring of non-Russian lands (including the Baltic guberniyas, Lithuania, Right-Bank Ukraine and Bessarabia).

In this context, colonial frontiers refer to regions of core-group resettlement after conquest and incorporation, and colonial peripheries refer to regions of conquest for purposes other than core-group resettlement (i.e., economic exploitation, geopolitical security).[11] The periphery itself can be divided along similar parameters into an inner periphery of Russian frontier expansion (North Caucasia, northern Kazakhstan, Siberia, and the Far East) and an outer colonial periphery without substantial demographic russification (Congress Poland, Finland, Transcaucasia, and Central Asia).

This division of the Russian Empire leaves us with two inner peripheries. The first, though within the European core, was outside Russian demographic dominance. Russian hegemony in this region was never firmly established; in the Baltics, Lithuania, and Right-Bank Ukraine, Germans and Poles were locally dominant, while in Bessarabia first Turkic and then Jewish elites dominated the local economic and political scene. In this way, the "inner" peripheral ring within the core looks more like the outer periphery. The second inner periphery was a zone of Russian frontier expansion and substantial immigration, particularly during the period 1881–1914. Though officially treated as an external colonial zone populated by aliens or *inorodtsy*, this second inner periphery was comparable to the outer core of European Russia, which also served as a frontier zone of Russian resettlement. Reorganizing the Russian Empire with these revisions in mind, we come up with the following colonial structure (Map 3.1):

1. Inner Core: Central Industrial, Central Agricultural, Lake, and North regions.
2. Outer Core: North and South Urals and Middle and Lower Volga.
3. Inner Frontier: Belorussia and Lithuania, Left-Bank Ukraine, and Novorossiya.
4. Outer Frontier: North Caucasia, North Kazakhstan, Siberia, and the Far East.
5. Inner Periphery: Baltics, Right-Bank Ukraine, Bessarabia, Congress Poland, and Finland.[12]
6. Outer Periphery: Transcaucasia, South Kazakhstan, and Central Asia.

The expansion of the empire from its northeastern European core was accompanied by the out-migration of Russians from the inner core, and their redistribution first to the outer core, primarily during the eighteenth century, and then to the inner and outer frontiers, most dramatically after the lifting of travel restrictions in 1881 and *mir* obligations in 1906 (Table 3.2; 3.3).

The inner core, which in 1678 contained 87.8 percent of all Russians in the empire, held only 46.8 percent of all Russians by 1917.[13] The proportion of Russians in the outer core more than doubled from 9.0 percent in 1678 to 20.9 percent in 1795. The relative shift of Russians toward the outer core then slowed; by 1917 this region contained 24.2 percent of all Russians in the Empire. The proportion of Russians in the inner frontier increased at a faster rate, rising from 1.3 percent in 1678 to 4.8 percent in 1795 and to 12.1 percent of all Russians in 1917.

The relative shift toward the outer frontier was even more dramatic, increasing from 1.9 percent in 1678 to 4.7 percent in 1795 and to 15.3 percent in 1917. By 1917, the outer core contained fewer Russians than did the frontier (inner and outer frontiers combined), and these three zones contained more than the number

46

Map 3.1 Russian Empire: Core, Frontier and Periphery

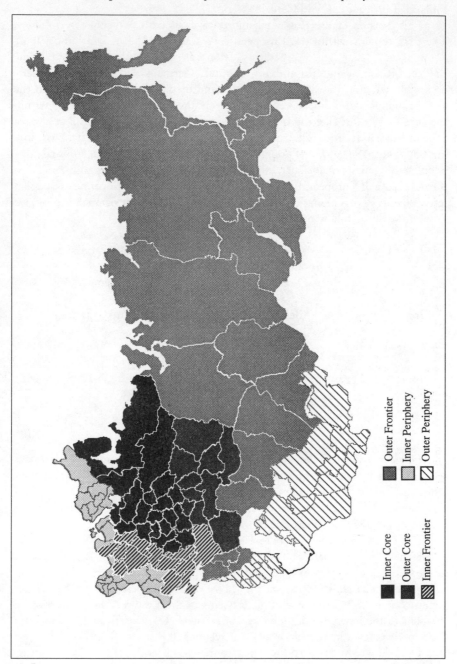

Table 3.2
Distribution of Russians in the Russian Empire, 1678–1917
(Percent of Russians by Gross Region*)

Region	1678	1719	1782	1795	1815	1834	1850	1858	1897	1916–17
Euro Russia	98.1	97.1	96.1	95.3	93.6	93.1	92.6	92.2	87.6	84.1
C. Ind.	47.8	40.8	32.0	30.3	27.7	25.9	24.6	23.6	19.0	18.1
C. Agr.	20.9	25.2	26.2	26.1	26.3	25.9	24.4	24.6	20.1	18.8
North	8.0	4.6	3.9	3.6	3.3	3.2	3.2	3.2	2.7	2.6
Lake	11.1	9.4	10.1	9.5	9.6	8.4	7.9	7.7	7.9	7.3
Mid-Volga	5.7	8.4	7.4	7.0	6.8	6.9	7.0	7.0	5.5	5.1
Lower Volga	—	0.9	3.2	4.5	5.1	6.7	6.6	7.1	7.2	7.2
North Urals	3.3	5.0	7.8	8.1	8.5	9.0	10.1	10.2	9.2	8.0
South Urals	—	0.2	0.9	1.3	1.5	1.9	3.1	2.8	3.5	3.9
Belorussia and Lithuania	1.0	1.5	2.4	2.4	2.2	2.1	2.0	1.8	3.5	4.6
Baltics	—	...	0.1	0.1	0.1	0.1	0.1	0.1	0.2	0.2
Left-Bank Ukr.	—	0.4	0.9	0.9	0.8	0.8	0.7	0.9	1.8	1.6
Right-Bank Ukr.	—	—	...	...	...	...	0.1	0.1	0.7	0.6
Novorossiya	0.3	0.7	1.2	1.5	1.7	2.1	2.5	3.0	5.8	5.9
Cong. Poland	—	—	—	—	—	...	0.2	...	0.5	0.2
Finland	—	...	...	...	...	0.1	0.1	0.1	...	...

(continues)

Table 3.2 (continued)

Region	1678	1719	1782	1795	1815	1834	1850	1858	1897	1916–17
North Caucasia	—	...	0.1	0.6	0.7	0.9	1.0	1.1	2.9	3.6
Transcaucasia	—	—	—	—	...	...	...	0.1	0.5	0.6
Central Asia and Kazakhstan	—	—	—	—	—	—	0.1	0.1	1.1	2.0
Siberia and the Far East	1.9	2.9	3.8	4.1	5.7	6.0	6.3	6.5	7.9	9.7
TOTAL	100.0	100.0	100.0	100.0	100.0	100.0	100.0	100.0	100.0	100.0

Notes: The data provided in Table 3.2 for the period 1678–1858 and for 1917 are estimates constructed by Bruk and Kabuzan, and must be treated with caution. No question on ethnic identity was asked in the population registrations prior to 1897, and in the 1897 census only a question on ethnolinguistic group was asked. Gross regions are defined as in Table 3.1

[a] The percentages for total population are for the territory of the Russian Empire at the time of the population registration. The figures provided in Bruk and Kabuzan are for the territory comparable to the geographic extent of the Russian Empire in 1897, and so are not the same as those given above.

[b] — indicates a region that was not part of the empire at the time, and/or for which data were not available.

[c] . . . indicates that the number of Russians in this region was less than 1,000 or less than 0.1% of the total population.

The guberniyas for the gross regions of the empire in Table 3.2 are as follows:

European Russia: the 50 guberniyas of the empire, plus Congress Poland and Finland.

C. Ind. = Central Industrial: Kaluga, Kostroma, Moscow, Nizhniy Novgorod, Tver', Vladimir, Yaroslavl'.

C. Agr. = Central Agricultural: Kursk, Orel, Ryazan', Tambov, Tula, Voronezh.

North: Arkhangel'sk, Vologda.

Lake: Novgorod, Olonets, Pskov, St. Petersburg, Smolensk.

Mid-Volga = Middle Volga: Kazan', Penza, Simbirsk.

Lower Volga: Astrakhan', Samara, Saratov.

North Urals: Perm', Vyatka.

South Urals: Orenburg, Ufa.

Belorussia and Lithuania: Grodno, Kovno, Minsk, Mogilev, Vil'na, Vitebsk.

Baltics: Estland, Kurland, Lifland.

Left-Bank Ukraine: Chernigov, Khar'kov, Poltava.

Right-Bank Ukraine: Kiev, Podol'sk, Volynia.

Novorossiya: Don, Yekaterinoslav, Kherson, Tavrida.

Bessarabia guberniya missing from table in Bruk and Kabuzan.

Congress Poland: Kalish, Kel'tsy, Lomzha, Lyublin, Petrokov, Plotsk, Radom, Sedlets, Suvalki, Warsaw.

Finland: Abo-Bjorneborg, Kuopio, Nyland, St. Michel, Tavastehus, Uleaborg, Vasa, Vyborg.

North Caucasia: Chernomorya, Kuban, Stavropol, Tersk.

Transcaucasia: Baku, Batumi, Dagestan, Elisavetpol', Karsk, Kutaissi, Sukhumi, Tiflis, Yerevan, Zakatalsk.

Kazakhstan and Central Asia: Akmolinsk, Fergana, Samarkand, Semipalatinsk, Semirechiye, Syr'-Darya, Uralsk, Zakaspisk.

Siberia and the Far East: Amur, Irkutsk, Kamchatka, Primorya, Sakhalin, Tobolsk, Tomsk, Yakutiya, Yenisey, Zabaykal.

Source: S. Bruk and V. Kabuzan, "Dinamika chislennosti i rasseleniya russkogo etnosa (1678–1917)," *Sovetskaya etnografiya*, 1982 (4), 18.

Table 3.3

Proportional Redistribution of Russians Among Zones of the Empire, 1678–1917
(Percent of all Russians, and percentage point change)

Imperial Zone	1678	1719	1782	1795	1815	1834	1850	1858	1897	1917	percent point change		
											1678–1795	1795–1917	1678–1917
Core	96.8	94.5	91.5	90.4	88.8	87.9	86.9	86.2	75.1	71.0	−6.4	−19.4	−25.8
Inner	87.7	80.0	72.2	69.5	66.9	63.4	60.1	59.1	49.7	46.8	−18.3	−22.7	−41.0
Outer	9.0	14.5	19.3	20.9	21.9	24.5	26.8	27.1	25.4	24.2	11.9	3.3	15.2
Frontier	3.2	5.5	8.4	9.5	11.1	11.9	12.6	13.4	23.0	27.4	6.3	17.9	24.2
Inner	1.3	2.6	4.5	4.8	4.7	5.0	5.2	5.7	11.1	12.1	3.5	7.3	10.8
Outer	1.9	2.9	3.9	4.7	6.4	6.9	7.4	7.7	11.9	15.3	2.8	10.6	13.4
Colonial Periphery	0.0	0.0	0.1	0.1	0.1	0.2	0.5	0.4	1.9	1.6	0.1	1.5	1.6
Inner	0.0	0.0	0.1	0.1	0.1	0.1	0.2	0.2	0.9	0.8	0.1	0.7	0.8
Outer	0.0	0.0	0.0	0.0	0.0	0.1	0.3	0.2	1.0	0.8	0.0	0.8	0.8

Source: Table 3.2.

living in the inner core, and more than half of all Russians in the Empire. In contrast, the inner and outer colonial peripheries never became zones of large scale Russian in-migration, although these regions did experience rapid increases in the number of Russian residents during the last four decades of the Russian Empire.

As Russia expanded and Russians dispersed from their inner core, the empire became less Russian. Demographically, Russians declined from 71 percent of the empire's total population in 1678 to 43.5 percent in 1897 (Table 3.1). Culturally, during the late eighteenth and nineteenth centuries, Russian identity began to shift from loyalty to the tsar and Orthodoxy to the ethnocultural community of Russians. This shift coincided with the nationalization of the dominant group and, near the end of the nineteenth century, an attempt to russify the non-Russians. The non-Russians, particularly in the northern and western regions of the state, experienced their own nationalization activated by and directed against the domination of "outsiders" (i.e., a counter-hegemonial process). These interactive nationalization processes were enhanced by greater geographic and social mobilization accompanying modernization. The rise of Russian and non-Russian national consciousness, and the interactive nationalism and inter-national conflicts that developed from it, helped undermine an already decaying empire which finally collapsed with World War I.

The Nationalization Process in the Russian Empire[14]

As noted in Chapter 2, nationalization is a relatively recent process, beginning in the late eighteenth century with the ethnicization of elites, which Hroch defined as "the period of scholarly interest . . . marked by a passionate concern on the part of a group of individuals, usually intellectuals, for the study of the language, the culture, the history of the . . . nationality." This ethnicization of elites was normally followed by the nationalization of elites, which Hroch referred to as a "period of patriotic agitation." Nationalized intellectuals were no longer satisfied merely to study their ethnic roots; they became proselytizers of the new national religion among the masses with whom they shared an ethnocultural bond. If they were successful, a third stage followed, which Hroch described as "the rise of a mass national movement." At this time, national consciousness becomes mass-based, and nationalism becomes an ideology and a political action program embraced by the entire community.[15]

The Ethnicization of Elites
Ethnicization of Russian elites began during the late eighteenth century and focused on the history of the Russian people or eastern Slavs, their folklore, the development of their language, and their geographic roots. An emotional attachment to homeland was evident in the works of Alexandre Radishchev and Nicholas Karamzin, for whom love of fatherland was seen as the principal reason behind their interest in the ethnocultural community.[16] At this time, nation was defined as the enlightened citizens of the state,[17] and was more a class distinction than an ethnocultural one.

Later, during the first half of the nineteenth century, the state's definition of nation, under the rubric of "Official Nationality" (beginning with Nicholas I,

1825–1855), equated Russianness with loyalty to the tsar and the Orthodox faith rather than ethnicity and geography.[18] In both cases, Russian peasants were considered to be subhumans in need of evolution and civilization or as children or "toys to be manipulated at will,"[19] not a part of the nation. An 1826 quote from Pogodin, a proponent of Official Nationality, captures this view: "The Russian people is marvelous, but marvelous so far only in potentiality. In actuality it is low, horrid, and beastly . . . [Russian peasants] will not become human beings until they are forced into it."[20] Furthermore, at this time Russian elites viewed the fatherland as the entire state (*otechestvo*), rather than the more narrowly defined ancestral homeland (*rodina*). Nevertheless, this period initiated the intellectual interest in ethnocultural identity, ethnic and geographic origin and development of the Russian language (which began to overtake Latin and French as the language of choice among the Russian elite during the early nineteenth century).[21]

Among non-Russians in the empire, the ethnicization of elites varied in timing and intensity. For groups in the empire's northwest (Estonians, Latvians, Lithuanians, Poles, and Finns), as well as for Ukrainians, Georgians, and Armenians, evidence of a "period of scholarly interest" in the ethnocultural and geographic origins of "their people" can be found by the 1820s. An ethnicization of elites also appeared relatively early among the Kazan' Tatars, and somewhat later among the Crimean Tatars, Azeris and, Kazakhs. The onset of nationalization was impeded in Central Asia because of the influence of conservative Islam, under which the elites tended to reject ethnic particularism in favor of an overarching Islamic identity. For these groups, as well as for Belarusians, ethnicization of elites barely predated World War I and the disintegration of the Russian Empire.[22]

The very existence of an indigenous "period of scholarly interest" among several of the ethnic communities in Siberia and the Far East is questionable and certainly did not begin prior to the twentieth century. For many of these groups, both ethnicization and nationalization of elites resulted more from the *korenizatsiya* policies of the 1920s and 1930s than from indigenous processes.[23] In addition, for several groups the "period of scholarly interest" in their ethnic and geographic origins began not among indigenous intellectuals, but among non-indigenes. In Estonia, early research into the origins and development of the Estonian language and culture was conducted by local German intellectuals.[24] Similarly, Polish and Russian intellectuals were the first to take an active interest in the ethnocultural origins of Belarusians. However, these Poles and Russians were driven less by intellectual curiosity than by geopolitical concerns; they attempted to establish that the local Slavs who lived in Belarus were actually Poles or Russians, in order to strengthen their respective claims to the region.[25]

The Nationalization of Elites

After 1825, a number of nationalistic strands developed among the Russian intelligentsia, the best known of which was Slavophilism.[26] The Slavophile movement developed during the 1830s in opposition to enlightenment and Westernism. The contrast between romantic Slavophiles and enlightened Russian Westernizers was particularly stark in regard to their ideas of the nation. Westernizers such as Belinsky saw Peter the Great as the molder of the Russian nation because of his European orientation. "Before Peter the Great Russia was merely a people (*narod*); she became a nation (*natsiya*) thanks to the changes initiated by the reformer."[27] The Westernist view saw the nation as a community of enlightened individuals which the peasants could not join until they became sufficiently educated or 'civilized'.

The Slavophiles, in contrast, held that the Westernized Russian elite had alienated itself from the nation, which the Slavophiles considered to be a primordial organism of intimately connected and internally unified village communes. For Slavophiles, the Russian nation was not made by Peter the Great, but was threatened by his reforms and by Westernism generally.[28] According to the Slavophiles, for the Russian nation to be whole once again the intelligentsia must reject the West and return to "a cultivation of the native . . . elements in the social life and culture of ancient Russia."[29]

The nationalization of Russian elites influenced the official policies of the Russian Empire. During the latter half of the nineteenth century, "Official Nationality" gave way to a view of a core community based less on loyalty to tsar and Orthodoxy than on ethnocultural attributes, particularly language. The population of the empire was divided into Russians, consisting of Great Russians, "Little Russians" (Ukrainians), and "White Russians" (Belarusians), who were treated as branches of the same core nation, and *inorodtsy* (aliens), which defined the less European, more feudal and/or nomadic peoples of the South and East, but in a general sense referred to all non-Russians. Those non-Russians with homelands in the European core or "mother country" of the empire were subjected to policies of russification, since the ideal of "Russia, one and indivisible" also meant that the core would become a homogeneous nation-state. The *inorodtsy* in the colonial periphery, and particularly in the zone south and east of the Urals, were seen as unassimilable. Russification of this population was considered unnecessary, since this region was viewed either as a frontier for Russian resettlement to become russified through migration, or as an external colony to be exploited by the European core.

The nationalization of non-Russian elites occurred primarily in response to the subordinate position in which indigenous intellectuals found themselves (i.e., it was an interactive counter-hegemonic process). Most of the indigenous elites were second-class citizens in what they were beginning to identify as their ancestral homelands. Socially mobilized Estonians and Latvians migrating to local cities found Germans in a dominant position; Lithuanians found themselves subordinate to Poles; Georgians and Azeris to Armenians economically and Russians politically; Ukrainians and Belarusians to Jews economically, and Poles and Russians politically and culturally; later Central Asians and dozens of ethnic communities within the Russian republic found themselves subordinate to the increasingly dominant Russians. Prior to the 1850s, the few indigenes who became educated and urbanized assimilated to the locally dominant group. For example, in his study of Latvians in Riga, Henriksson found that before the middle of the nineteenth century "upwardly mobile Latvians had Germanized as a matter of course. Hence there had been no Latvian upper or middle class; to be Latvian was to be lower class."[30] A similar assimilation of upwardly mobile indigenes occurred among Estonians, Lithuanians, Belarusians, Ukrainians, and among dozens of non-Russian groups whose homelands were located within the core region of the empire.

The inferior status of indigenes and the acculturation pressures that accompanied upward mobility became increasingly intolerable for indigenes as increasing numbers of them became more educated, urbanized and upwardly mobile. A reactive nationalism, brought on by a growing perception of relative deprivation among the non-Russian indigenous elites who were relegated to subordinate status in their own homelands, became apparent during the last decades of the Russian Empire's existence. These nationalized elites began to feel a sense of exclusiveness toward their homeland, and expressed increasing resentment against "foreigners" who held dominant positions in them. Under these conditions, russification policies of the tsarist government, coming at a time of rising national consciousness throughout European Russia, proved counter-productive to the goal of assimilation and served as a potent catalyst for anti-Russian and anticolonial nationalism during the last five decades of the empire's existence.

Rather than acculturate to the dominant group as previous generations had done, nationalized indigenous elites began working to secure dominance for themselves and their "nations" in the cities of their homelands. One important development during this time was the beginning of a process of standardization and vernacularization of the indigenous languages. The standardization of an indigenous language using the spoken vernacular was meant both to replace the dominant alien language toward which upwardly mobile indigenes had acculturated in the past, and also to place the peasants and their language at the center of the nation.[31] As socioeconomic development penetrated deeper into the non-Russian countryside, an increasing number of upwardly mobile peasants became nationally conscious and served as transmitters of the national idea to the masses.[32]

The Nationalization of the Masses

Nationalization of the masses is often depicted as a one-way process with elites or the state mobilizing an otherwise inert underclass to serve the purposes of the elite. Enlightened Westernizers and the tsarist regime tended to view the relationship between civilized elites and the "dark masses" in this way, and this view is typical of the modernization thesis generally. In contrast, the Slavophiles and other romantic nationalists saw the peasant *narod* as the real core of the nation. From this perspective it was not the masses who needed civilizing but the elites who needed reawakening.

Both of these views of the peasantry were undoubtedly mistaken. The masses were not inert, and during the nineteenth century impetus for change often came from below.[33] Yet the peasant's life was by no means ideal, holding more appeal for the romantic nationalists than for the peasants themselves. Rather than a unidirectional process, this stage of nationalization is better explained as an interactive, interclass process of adaptation.

For most "nations" in the Russian Empire, nationalization of the masses was only beginning by the time of World War I and the disintegration of the state. Throughout the nineteenth century, the rural population remained highly suspicious of intellectual outsiders and highly localized in its orientation. The peasantry began to respond to broader national concerns only after emancipation, when migration and social mobilization began to break down this localism. The critical elements in the mass nationalization process as they developed between 1861 and 1914 are briefly described below.[34]

The Emancipation of Serfs.   The abolition of serfdom was a necessary precondition for the nationalization of the peasantry. It was certainly viewed as such by Russian nationalists, who increasingly saw serfdom as a stumbling block in the pathway of Russia's national "rebirth."[35] A strong desire for emancipation also existed among the peasantry; however, under ordinary circumstances this desire was not overtly expressed, taking the form of "everyday resistance" rather than outright rebellion.[36] Indeed, the Great Reforms of February 19, 1861, were enacted because of a fear that the serfs were becoming sufficiently politically mobilized to emancipate themselves, representing a potential revolutionary challenge to the empire. In the words of Alexander II, "It is better to abolish serfdom from above than to await the day when it will begin to abolish itself from below."[37]

The 1861 emancipation dealt mostly with Russian peasants in the inner core of the empire, but included those peasants still under serfdom in the outer core, as well as in Ukraine, Belarus, Lithuania, and Georgia.[38] In Siberia, the Far East, Kazakhstan, Central Asia, Bessarabia, and most of Transcaucasia serfdom was not practiced and the reforms thus had only indirect significance (e.g., the increasing number of Russian peasants migrating to the region after emancipation). In the Baltic guberniyas and in Congress Poland, emancipation had come earlier in the century (1807 in Congress Poland, 1816 in Estland, 1817 in Kurland, and 1819 in Lifland). This earlier emancipation, coupled with greater socioeconomic development in these northwestern guberniyas, helps to explain the relatively early nationalization of the peasantry in this region.

The reforms of 1861 did little more than abolish the formal control that landowners exercised over the peasantry. Peasants continued to be tied to the land and both migration and social mobility remained severely constricted. The reforms were intended to avert revolutionary change by formally freeing the serfs while restricting and channeling their migratory and social movement in ways that benefited the empire. The emancipation achieved this aim in the short term. However, some have argued that the revolutions of 1905 and 1917 were the result of rising relative deprivation among the peasantry brought on by an expectation (the promise of complete emancipation) that went unfulfilled.[39]

Migration and Social Mobilization.   Before 1861, the population of Russia was overwhelmingly rural and little migration occurred. Even after formal emancipation, the peasantry was kept immobilized through financial obligations to the commune. Nevertheless, both rural-rural and rural-urban migration increased during the last five decades of the Russian Empire, especially after legal restrictions on movement were lifted in 1881 and redemption payments were canceled in 1906. The migration to Siberia, the Far East and to northern Kazakhstan (the Asiatic Steppe) was particularly intense: "Between 1896 and 1916, the eastward migration of Russians reached tremendous proportions; during this period over 5,000,000 settlers moved into Asiatic Russia. More than 1,500,000 of this number . . . entered Kazakhstan."[40]

Rural to rural migration in search of better or more extensive agricultural lands had a limited effect on the nationalization of the peasantry in tsarist Russia, unless the destination was ethnically different and the in-migrants were numerous. For example, the massive rural in-migration of Russians to northern Kazakhstan and their appropriation of grazing lands from the nomadic Kazakhs resulted in the rise of a pointedly anti-Russian and anti-tsarist national consciousness among the Kazakhs.[41] This "reactive nationalism" was also apparent in other densely settled non-Russian regions that experienced massive rural in-migration of Russians late in the nineteenth century (North Caucasia, Novorossiya and particularly Crimea, and southern Siberia).

Rural to urban migration had a much greater impact on mass-based nationalization, since it usually represented not only geographic relocation but also social mobilization. The initial increase in rural to urban migration after 1861 was temporary seasonal labor migration (*otkhod*) to the cities in order to supplement rural earnings to cover the costs of redemption payments. This new form of nomadism increased dramatically after 1870, but had a limited impact on the nationalization process. Normally, only adult males participated in *otkhod*, so family life continued to be centered in the village. *Otkhodniki* from the same village also tended to migrate together and to live and work in the same place within the city. Such group migration reduced the impact not only of the urban way of life and urban ideas (including nationalism) on the temporary migrants, but also reduced their exposure to and interaction with members of other ethnic groups.[42]

Still, between 1861 and 1914, an increasing number of temporary labor migrants found ways to settle permanently in the cities. The volume of migration was also increasing, resulting in the urbanization of Russia's population. The cities primarily attracted peasants from nearby villages, but the capitals drew peasants from a greater distance.[43] At the same time, the younger, more literate and educated urban migrants were increasingly exposed to nationalization processes, particularly in the capital cities. These nationally conscious peasants then served as transmitters of the national idea and nationalism to the countryside.

Within Russia's core, rural to urban migration drew primarily from the surrounding Russian countryside, diffusing the new Russian national idea to villages throughout the core. Non-Russian rural migrants to Russian cities, and particularly to St. Petersburg, also underwent a process of russification,

although this process normally occurred only after the second or third generation born in the cities.[44] Young non-Russian urban elites migrating to St.
Petersburg for a university education were influenced more by the nationalistic
intellectual currents in the capital, which accelerated the pace of their nationalization as Georgians, Lithuanians, Ukrainians, and so on, rather than their
russification. They in turn served as conduits for nationalization on their
return home.

In the non-Russian periphery, rural indigenes migrating to nearby cities frequently found nonindigenous elites in a dominant economic, cultural and political position. As noted above, prior to 1861, the few indigenes who migrated to
cities typically acculturated to the dominant nonindigenous group. However, after
1861 the number of indigenous peasants migrating to the cities increased dramatically, together with rising industrialization, literacy, and education. This demographic indigenization of cities occurred simultaneously with the diffusion of the
national idea. Rather than continued assimilation, the upwardly mobile indigenes
experienced a growing sense of relative deprivation as rapidly rising expectations
went unfulfilled, partly due to the economic, political, and cultural hegemony of
nonindigenes in the cities. Thus, economic development and the urbanization of
indigenes coincided not with further acculturation and assimilation, but rather
with the nationalization of the urban indigenous masses. Henriksson found the
following pattern in his study of nineteenth century Riga that serves as an example of this reorientation from assimilation to nationalization:

> In the past upwardly mobile Latvians had Germanized as a matter of course.
> Hence there had been no Latvian upper or middle classes; to be Latvian was to
> be lower class. The growth of Latvian national consciousness, the sheer size of
> the Riga Latvian community and the increased opportunities for upward mobil-
> ity created by industrialization, however, all worked against Germanization.
> Fewer and fewer Latvians were assimilated into the German community after
> the 1860s, and by the 1880s Riga had a small but growing Latvian bourgeoisie.[45]

The demographic indigenization of cities was occurring most rapidly in the
Baltic guberniyas, where Tallinn and Riga became cities with an Estonian and
Latvian majority during this period.[46] A similar demographic indigenization was
taking place in the cities of Georgia and Azerbaijan, though Russians were also
migrating to the region's major cities, and Armenians remained a major demographic component. Armenian cities were also becoming more indigenous
through a process of rural-urban migration.

In Ukraine, Belarus, Lithuania, and Bessarabia, cities remained demographically dominated by nonindigenes. Jews and Poles, having held dominant positions
in the past, continued to be present in large numbers; during the last decades of
the Russian Empire, Russians also migrated to the cities of these provinces in
increasing numbers. By 1897 Russians had become more numerous than indigenes in the cities of these four regions. In Central Asia, the urban population
was primarily indigenous, mainly consisting of Uzbeks and Tajiks. However,
almost no rural-urban migration took place among Central Asians; the Central

Asian urban population was either born in the cities or came from outside the region. In the cities of Siberia, northern Kazakhstan, Novorossiya, and North Caucasia, urban growth occurred primarily because of Russian in-migration from the core region of the empire, and not as a result of the urbanization of indigenes. [Table 3.4]

The demographic indigenization of cities throughout the non-Russian periphery made the urban ethnic stratification system that favored nonindigenes increasingly intolerable, particularly where indigenous elites had already become nationalized and begun to agitate against the hegemonic position of outsiders. Indigenous upward mobility and the creation of an indigenous middle class were more advanced in the northwestern periphery of the empire (Congress Poland, Finland, and the Baltic guberniyas). The rising competition between indigenes and "foreigners" (Germans and increasingly Russians), particularly in the Baltic guberniyas, served as a catalyst for rising counter-hegemonic nationalism by the turn of the twentieth century. Interethnic relations were further exacerbated when the tsarist government attempted to restrict the use of indigenous languages and to replace them with Russian. In the Baltic, nationalism was successfully used to mobilize the masses during the 1905 revolution, and again during World War I and the civil war that followed. This region gained its independence from Russia and retained it throughout the interwar years.

In Ukraine, Belarus, and Bessarabia, urbanization, educational attainment and upward mobility among the indigenes were almost nonexistent. A mass-based nationalization did not occur among Ukrainians, Belarusians, or Bessarabians (i.e., Romanians/Moldavians) prior to the disintegration of the Russian Empire, although a nationalization of elites had taken place in Ukraine and to a more limited extent in Belarus by World War I.[47]

In Georgia, upwardly mobile Georgians found Armenians economically dominant and Russians politically dominant in Tiflis. This ethnic stratification produced a rising sense of relative deprivation which triggered a national consciousness among Georgians, who were entering the capital in increasing numbers between 1861 and 1917.[48] A similar situation developed in Azerbaijan; upwardly mobile Azeris were confronted by economically dominant Armenians and politically dominant Russians in Baku. Growing anti-Armenian sentiments culminated in the Armenian-Azerbaijani War of 1905, which further nationalized the Azeri masses. Nevertheless, a mass-based Azeri nation was only beginning to coalesce prior to the disintegration of the Russian Empire.[49] In Armenia, nationalization was limited not because of ethnic stratification within the urban industrial centers but because of limited economic development in Yerevan which remained "a sleepy oriental town of 30,000 in 1914."[50] Socially mobilized Armenians more frequently were found outside Armenia; this geographic isolation of mobilized Armenians from the Armenian homeland undoubtedly slowed the pace of economic development and nationalization processes in Armenia.

In Kazakhstan, reacting to the massive influx of Russian settlers and the repressive policies of the tsarist government, "the Kazakhs increasingly thought

59

Table 3.4
Ethnolinguistic Composition of the Total and Urban Population, 1897 (Percent)

Region	Total Population			Urban Population		
	% Ind.[a]	% of Ind.[b]	% Russian[c]	% Ind.[d]	% of Ind.[e]	% Russian[f]
European Russia	81.5	77.7	81.5	90.6	13.7	90.6
Siberia	11.1	99.5	76.8	1.3	1.1	83.5
Ukraine	68.2	79.2	17.2	28.1	5.4	38.5
Bessarabia	47.6	82.1	8.0	14.2	4.5	24.4
Belarus		72.5			2.6	
and Lithuania	62.7	71.4	5.6	12.9	1.5	17.8
Latvia		74.5			19.6	
and Estonia	82.0	88.3	4.8	51.9	12.3	12.5
Congress Poland	71.8	85.2	2.8	48.8	15.6	8.0
North Caucasia	16.7	82.5	42.2	1.8	1.3	64.9
Dagestan	87.9	73.5	2.3	27.2	2.4	21.4
Georgia	55.7	98.8	5.0	33.1	8.9	19.1
Azerbaijan[g]	59.8	67.5	5.1	51.0	13.0	16.8
Armenia	53.2	37.6	1.6	58.5	12.2	8.4
Northern Kazakhstan	77.2	46.6	17.5	14.8	1.6	68.9
Central Asia	94.7	93.8	3.0	79.6	11.6	11.4

Notes: Indigenous language groups for Siberia = North Siberian Tribes, Yakuts, Buryats; for North Caucasia = Ossetians, Karachays, Kumyks, Nogays, Kabardins, Cherkess, Chechens, and Ingush; for Dagestan = Lezgin language groups, Kumyks, and Nogays; for northern Kazakhstan = Kirgiz (Kazakhs); for Central Asia = Turkmen, Kirgiz, Kara-Kirgiz, Kara-Kalpaks, Kipchaks, Sarts, Uzbeks, Taranchi, Turks, Tajiks, and Kazhgars. Regions: Georgia = Kars, Tiflis, and Kutaissi guberniyas; Armenia = Yerevan guberniya; Azerbaijan = Baku and Elisavetpol' guberniyas; North Caucasia = Kuban, Stavropol', Tersk, and Chernomorya guberniyas; European Russia = 50 European guberniyas, including Baltic, Ukraine (i.e., Novorossiya, Left Bank and Right Bank Regions), Belarus and Lithuania, and Bessarabia. Gross regions as in Table 3.1. [a]% Ind. = the indigenous language group's percent of the total population (e.g., Armenian language speakers as a percent of the total population of Armenia). [b]% of Ind. = the percent of the indigenous language group resident in its home region (separate figures given for Belarusians, Lithuanians, Latvians and Estonians). [c]% Russian = the percent of Russian language speakers in the total population of the region (language of 'Great Russians' only). [d]% Ind. = the indigenous language group's percent of the urban population. [e]% of Ind. = the percent of the indigenous language group living in cities in the home region. [f]% Russian = the percent of Russian language speakers in the urban population of the region. [g]Azeris in 1897 = Tatars. Figure for column 2 = the percent of all "Tatar" speakers living in Caucasia and resident in Azerbaijan.

Source: Nicholas Troynitsky, ed., *Obshchiy svod' po imperii rezul'tatov' razrabotki dannykh pervoy vseobshchey perepisi naseleniya*, Vol. 2 (St. Petersburg: Tsentral'nyy statisticheskiy komitet', 1905).

and acted as a homogeneous community" by the end of the tsarist era.[51] However, this coalescence was not enhanced by the social mobilization of the Kazakhs at that time, and stopped short of full-fledged nationalization. In Turkestan, geographic and social mobilization of the indigenous masses had not yet begun, rural in-migration of Russians was much more limited than in northern Kazakhstan, and nationalization of indigenous elites was hampered by conservative Islam; thus, the preconditions for the nationalization of the masses did not yet exist.[52]

Nationalism and the Disintegration of the Russian Empire

By end of the Russian Empire, nationalization of the masses had proceeded farthest in the northwestern corner of the inner periphery and had begun to diffuse from urban to rural sectors of the inner core and the European parts of Russia. In addition, a reactive nationalism was becoming apparent in regions of massive Russian rural-rural migration to the non-Russian periphery. However, nations as mass-based communities of interest and belonging were only beginning to supplant localism in most of tsarist Russia.

Nationalist opposition to the Russian Empire was limited for the most part to urbanized, indigenous elites who had undergone a process of nationalization during the last decades of the nineteenth century. These nationalists were attempting to awaken the indigenous masses through the creation of standardized languages around spoken rural vernaculars, the introduction of nationalized curricula taught in indigenous languages in rural schools, the publication of nationalistic literature in these languages, and the creation of political movements for greater cultural and territorial autonomy for indigenes in their homelands, which were the geographic creations of these nationalized elites.

Tsarist attempts to counteract non-Russian nationalization and promote an alternative nationalization process through russification policies proved counterproductive; such policies served not as instruments for the denationalization of non-Russians and their renationalization as Russians, but as catalysts for non-Russian nationalism which was both anti-Russian and anti-tsarist in orientation. This result was particularly true in the northwestern inner periphery of the empire, where indigenous nationalization had proceeded furthest. Here, nationalism became more secessionist than elsewhere.

Bessarabia also separated from Russia, but more as a result of Romanian irredentism than the rise of separatist nationalism in Bessarabia. In Ukraine, Belarus, and Transcaucasia, nationalistic political organizations pressed the center for greater autonomy, but were not independence-minded prior to the disintegration of the empire.[53] This situation was also true of the Kazan' and Crimean Tatars. As noted above, a nationalized elite had not yet formed in Central Asia, though localized anti-Russian sentiments and elite Islamic opposition to tsarist rule did exist. Anticolonial opposition to the core and to Russians was on the rise throughout the non-Russian periphery, even though nationalism as a mass-based political movement was only a limited part of the opposition.

In Russia, Russian national consciousness rose along with the migration and social mobilization of the peasants after emancipation. This nationalization occurred most rapidly in the inner core of the empire. Mobilization and nationalization also tended to undermine the autocratic power of the tsar, since the upwardly mobile, nationally conscious peasantry fought for greater freedoms than those provided by the 1861 emancipation. This pressure for change from below was alternatively repressed and accommodated during the period from 1861–1914. As noted above, the lifting of restrictions on migration to Siberia, the Far East, and northern Kazakhstan in 1881 eliminated many of the geographic restrictions (which had worked to the benefit of rural elites in tsarist Russia) on the Russian peasantry.

The cancellation of redemption payments after the 1905 revolution further eroded the old lines of authority. Finally, nationalization of the Russian peasantry shifted the emphasis of one's identity away from loyalty to the tsar and Orthodoxy and toward one's ethnocultural identity, which was itself becoming a politicized and territorialized community of interest. As nation and homeland—rather than tsar and religion—became the focus of Russians' loyalty, the authority of the tsar was curtailed.

Industrialization and urbanization accelerated this process. The political legitimacy of the Russian Empire not only faced a growing challenge in the non-Russian periphery but was also decaying from within the inner core of the empire itself. World War I hastened the disintegrative processes, and brought to an abrupt end an empire that was fated for elimination in any event.[54]

Notes

1. For the best overview of this history of expansion, see Allen Chew, *An Atlas of Russian History: Eleven Centuries of Changing Borders*, rev. ed. (New Haven and London: Yale University Press, 1970).

2. Robert Kaiser, *The Geography of Nationalism in Russia and the USSR* (Princeton, NJ: Princeton University Press, 1994), Chapter 2.

3. Robert Kaiser, *National Territoriality in Multinational, MultiHomeland States: A Comparative Study of the Soviet Union, Yugoslavia and Czechoslovakia* (Ph.D. diss., Columbia University, 1988); Kaiser, *Geography of Nationalism*; Barbara Anderson and Brian Silver, "Estimating Russification of Ethnic Identity Among Non-Russians in the USSR" (paper presented at the annual meeting of the Population Association of America, March 1981, rev. January 1983).

4. Tatar dominance over Muscovy provided the group with a history that almost guaranteed that this group would develop into a nation at the forefront of any independence movements that developed within Russia.

5. Walter Kolarz, *The Peoples of the Soviet Far East* (Hamden, CT: Archon Books, 1969), p. 12.

6. Chew, *Atlas*, p. 44.

7. This left-bank region—not a part of the Bessarabia guberniya that was acquired later—is today the site of the separatist Transdniestrian Republic.

8. Until the collapse of the Russian Empire, "White Russians," "Little Russians," and "Great Russians" were considered branches of the Russian "tribe" (*plemiya*). Statistics prior to 1926 rarely differentiated between the three branches, with the implication that the three branches would become (if they were not already) indistinguishable elements of the Russian nation. Russian nationalists from Solzhenitsyn to Zhirinovsky continue to view Ukrainians and Belarusians as branches of the Russian nation and their homelands as part of "Mother Russia."

9. Kaiser, *Geography of Nationalism*, pp. 41–43.

10. Ladis Kristof, "The Geopolitical Image of the Fatherland: The Case of Russia," *The Western Political Science Quarterly* (1967):941–954; Mark Bassin, "Russia Between Europe and Asia: The Ideological Construction of Geographical Space," *Slavic Review* 50 (Spring 1991):1–17.

11. For a detailed discussion of the difference between frontier and colonial expansion, and its application to Russia's conquest and control of Kazakhstan and Turkestan, see Ralph Clem, "The Frontier and Colonialism in Russian and Soviet Central Asia," in Robert Lewis, ed., *Geographic Perspectives on Soviet Central Asia* (London: Routledge, 1992), p. 19–36.

12. Congress Poland and Finland, though not part of the 50 guberniyas of European Russia, are included as part of the inner colonial periphery because they were relatively developed European colonies that were more fully integrated into the empire's economy.

13. Russians did not, however, experience an absolute decline in numbers in the inner core. See Table 3.1.

14. This section draws extensively on Kaiser, *Geography of Nationalism*, Chapter 2.

15. Miroslav Hroch, *The Social Preconditions of National Revival in Europe* (Cambridge, MA: Cambridge University Press, 1985), pp. 22–23. Hroch's study focused on the rise of national consciousness and nationalism among small and oppressed nations across Europe. However, a similar three-stage process of nationalization also provides an appropriate framework for Russian as well as non-Russian nationalization in the Russian Empire.

16. Kaiser, *The Geography of Nationalism*, p. 35; Alexandre Radishchev, "A Discourse on What It Means To Be a Son of the Fatherland [1789]," in W. Leatherbarrow and D. Offord, eds., *A Documentary History of Russian Thought from Enlightenment to Marxism* (Ann Arbor, MI: Ardis, 1987), pp. 18–24; Nicholas Karamzin, "On the love of the fatherland and national pride [1802]," in Marc Raeff, ed., *Russian Intellectual History; an Anthology* (New York: Harcourt, Brace & World, 1966), pp. 107–112; and N. Karamzin, "A memoir on ancient and modern Russia [1811]," in Leatherbarrow and Offord, eds., *Documentary History* pp. 32–41. For a discussion of Karamzin, see Richard Pipes, *Karamzin's Memoir on Ancient and Modern Russia* (New York: Atheneum, 1974).

17. Radishchev, for example, "had a wholly rationalist and nominalist view of the nation as a 'collection of citizens' rather than a supra-individual whole endowed with a 'collective soul'." Andrzej Walicki, *A History of Russian Thought from Enlightenment to Marxism* (Stanford, CA: Stanford University Press, 1979), p. 40.

18. Nicholas Riasanovsky, *Nicholas I and Official Nationality in Russia, 1825–1855* (Berkeley: University of California Press, 1969); Jeffrey Brooks, *When Russia Learned to Read* (Princeton: Princeton University Press, 1985), p. 214.

19. Ben Eklof, *Russian Peasant Schools: Officialdom, Village Culture, and Popular Pedagogy, 1861–1914* (Berkeley: University of California Press, 1986), p. 1.

20. As cited in Riasanovsky, *Nicholas I,* p. 99.

21. Kaiser, *Geography of Nationalism*, p. 35.

22. Kaiser, *Geography of Nationalism*, 36; Richard Pipes, *The Formation of the Soviet Union: Communism and Nationalism, 1917–1923*, rev. ed. (New York: Atheneum, 1968), p. 10; Hroch, *Social Preconditions*, pp. 76–86; Toivo Raun, *Estonia and the Estonians*, 2nd ed. (Stanford, CA: Hoover Institution Press, 1991), p. 56; Ronald Suny, *The Making of the*

Georgian Nation (Bloomington, IN: University of Indiana Press, 1989), pp.123–125; William Hanaway, Jr., "Farsi, the Vatan, and the Millat in Bukhara," in Edward Allworth, ed., *The Nationality Question in Soviet Central Asia* (New York: Praeger, 1973), pp. 143–150; Hans Braker, "The Muslim Revival in Russia," in Erwin Oberlander et al., eds., *Russia Enters the Twentieth Century 1894–1917* (New York: Schocken Books, 1971), pp. 182–198; Nicholas Vakar, *Belorussia: The Making of a Nation* (Cambridge, MA: Harvard University Press, 1956), pp. 73–82.

23. These policies are discussed in Chapter 4.

24. Raun, *Estonia and the Estonians*, p. 56.

25. Vakar, *Belorussia: The Making of a Nation*, pp. 73–82.

26. For a detailed discussion of this movement, see Andrzej Walicki, *The Slavophile Controversy* (Notre Dame, IN: University of Notre Dame Press, 1975).

27. As quoted in Walicki, *The Slavophile Controversy* , p. 401.

28. Nicholas Riasanovsky, *A Parting of Ways: Government and the Educated Public in Russia 1801–1855* (Oxford: Clarendon Press, 1976), p. 189.

29. Andrzej Walicki, *History of Russian Thought* (Stanford, CA: Stanford University Press, 1979), p. 92.

30. Anders Henriksson, "Riga: Growth, Conflict, and the Limitations of Good Government, 1850–1914," in Michael Hamm, ed., *The City in Late Imperial Russia* (Bloomington, IN: Indiana University Press, 1986), p. 180.

31. Kaiser, *Geography of Nationalism*, pp. 40–43.

32. Ibid., pp. 39–43.

33. Ben Eklof, "Peasants and schools," in B. Eklof and S. Frank, eds., *The World of the Russian Peasant: Post-Emancipation Culture and Society* (Boston: Unwin Hyman, 1990), pp. 115–132.

34. For a more detailed discussion of the nationalization of the masses in the Russian Empire, see Kaiser, *Geography of Nationalism*, pp. 47–83.

35. Riasanovsky, *Parting of Ways*, p. 262.

36. Rodney Bohac, "Everyday Forms of Resistance: Serf Opposition to Gentry Exactions, 1800–1861," in E. Kingston-Mann and T. Mixter, eds., *Peasant Economy, Culture, and Politics of European Russia, 1800–1921* (Princeton, NJ: Princeton University Press, 1991), pp. 236–260. See also Martin Gilbert, *Atlas of Russian History*, 2nd ed. (New York: Oxford University Press, 1993), p. 57.

37. Quoted in Terence Emmons, "The Peasant and the Emancipation," in Wayne Vucinich, ed., *The Peasant in Nineteenth-Century Russia* (Stanford, CA: Stanford University Press, 1968), pp. 47–71.

38. Gilbert, *Atlas of Russian History*, p. 58; Geroid Robinson, *Rural Russia Under the Old Regime* (London: Longmans, Green, 1932), pp. 85–86.

39. Boris Mironov, "The Russian peasant commune after the reforms of the 1860s," in Eklof and Frank, eds., *World of the Russian Peasant*, p. 33.

40. George Demko, *The Russian Colonization of Kazakhstan 1896–1916* (Bloomington, IN: Indiana University Press, 1969), p. 78. See also Frank Lorimer, *The Population of the Soviet Union: History and Prospects* (Geneva: League of Nations, 1946), pp. 24–28. Lorimer defines the Asiatic Steppe as Akmolinsk, Semipalatinsk, Turgay and Uralsk Oblasts.

41. Martha Olcott, *The Kazakhs* (Stanford, CA: Hoover Institution Press, 1987), pp. 101–112.

42. Kaiser, *Geography of Nationalism*, pp. 60–61.

43. A. Rashin, *Naseleniye Rossii za 100 let* (1811–1913), (Moskva: Gosstatizdat, 1956), pp. 142–143.

44. Nataliya Yukhneva, *Etnicheskiy sostav i etnosotsial'naya struktura naseleniya Peterburga* (Leningrad: Nauka, 1984), pp. 191–193. Yukhneva notes that the russification of Ukrainians and Belarusians in St. Petersburg is difficult to assess accurately.

Ethnonational identity in the Russian Empire was most frequently equated with language, and "Russian" was used as the label for Ukrainian and Belarusian, as well as for the language of the "Great Russians." Likewise, "Russian" was used as an overarching ethnic category encompassing Great Russians, White Russians and Little Russians.

45. Henriksson, "Riga: Growth, Conflict," pp. 180–181.

46. Raun, *Estonia and the Estonians*, p. 91; Yukhneva, *Etnicheskiy sostav*, p. 191.

47. Hans Rogger, *Russia in the Age of Modernization and Revolution 1881–1917* (London: Longman, 1983), pp. 184–185; Violet Conolly, "The 'Nationalities Question' in the Last Phase of Tsardom," in E. Oberlander et al., eds., *Russia Enters the Twentieth Century 1894–1917* (New York: Schocken Books, 1971), pp. 152–181; Bohdan Krawchenko, *Social Change and National Consciousness in Twentieth Century Ukraine* (New York: St. Martin's Press, 1985), p. 28; Vakar, *Belorussia: The Making of a Nation*, p. 85.

48. Ronald Suny, *The Making of the Georgian Nation*, pp. 139–140.

49. Tadeusz Swietochowski, "National Consciousness and Political Orientations in Azerbaijan, 1905–1920," in Ronald Suny, ed., *Transcaucasia: Nationalism and Social Change* (Ann Arbor, MI: University of Michigan Slavic Publications, 1983), pp. 209–232.

50. Richard Hovannisian, "Caucasian Armenia between imperial and Soviet rule," in Suny, ed., *Transcaucasia*, p. 260.

51. Olcott, *The Kazakhs*, p. 112.

52. Rogger, *Russia in the Age of Modernization, and Revolution 1881–1917*, p. 197; Braker, "The Muslim Revival in Russia."

53. Pipes, *Formation of the Soviet Union*, pp. 11–21.

54. Alexander Motyl, "From Imperial Decay to Imperial Collapse: The Fall of the Soviet Empire in Comparative Perspective," in R. Rudolph and D. Good, eds., *Nationalism and Empire: The Habsburg Empire and the Soviet Union* (New York: St. Martin's, 1992), pp. 15–44.

Chapter 4

The "National Problem"
in the USSR

A consensus has developed in the West and in the NIS that the former Soviet Union was in many ways a continuation of the Russian Empire. The nationalism which triumphed over the USSR and sovietization is treated as a form of "decolonization nationalism." Non-Russians view Russians as the hegemonic nation against which their counter-hegemonic nationalism is directed. Russian nationalists, however, view themselves as fellow victims rather than as beneficiaries of this "last empire;" they describe the Communist party elites as the favored or hegemonic group, and all nations (including the Russian nation) as equally subordinate.

While depicting the USSR as a colonial empire has some analytical utility, studies that treat the USSR as an imperial power like all others are misleading. So too are those that view Russians as the hegemonic group and all non-Russians as equally oppressed colonial subjects. In theory, the 1917 Bolshevik Revolution and the creation of the USSR were intended to be anticolonial acts.

First, the goal of the Soviet Union was to overcome global imperialism, viewed by Lenin as the last stage of capitalism. The Soviet Union was to serve both as an alternative model and as a catalyst for the destruction of worldwide imperialism. Second, Lenin's writings on the national question displayed a decidedly counter-hegemonic orientation consistent with this anti-imperial mission. The new state was to favor non-Russians over Russians until inter-national equality had been achieved. Third, the socialist political elites in the core were to be inter-nationalist or a-nationalist. In principle, the state was not to favor one ethnonational community over others.

These founding principles were subverted over time by political elites both at the center and in the periphery; nonetheless, the inter-national political agenda did influence core/periphery and Russian/non-Russian relations in the USSR. Thus, "welfare colonialism"[1] or "imperial socialism" is a more useful description of the USSR than are more traditional views of colonialism and imperialism occurring within the capitalist world system.

In addition to the distinctive nature of the ruling Marxist-Leninist ideology in the "Soviet Empire," the USSR was distinguished by a federal structure, with republics organized along national-territorial lines (Map 4.1). This congruence between national and territorial boundaries increased the probability that the ethnic groups indigenous to the state would become politicized and territorialized nations, and that these nations would ultimately develop political agendas whose goal—placing the fate of the nations in the hands of their national memberships—would be realized territorially. This territorial nationalism was enhanced by Soviet nationality policies which provided preferential treatment for members of the nation living in their homelands (*korenizatsiya*), but not for those who lived beyond the home republic's borders.

This chapter highlights the development of nations and nationalism during the Soviet period, focusing particularly on the relationship between Russians and non-Russians and the disintegrative processes which occurred under Gorbachev. The specific geopolitical changes taking place since the mid–1980s in the individual republics are examined in Part Two of the book.

Lenin and Great Russian Chauvinism

Lenin was a "strategic Marxist," who used Marx's theories to provide the foundation for his own political action program.[2] His writings and policy pronouncements on the national problem reflected his assessment of this issue's political importance for bringing about revolutionary change in Russia. Lenin's support for equality of Russians and non-Russians was not based on the belief in inherent rights of peoples to an independent ethnocultural, socioeconomic, and political existence, but rather on the conclusion that equality among peoples and an end to national oppression of other peoples by Russians was the only route to the ultimate communist objective of assimilation—the supplanting of a national self-consciousness with an inter-national or a-national identity.[3]

Like Marx, Lenin was a proponent of the modernization thesis. This approach contended that nations and national identity were products of the capitalist epoch which would give way voluntarily to an inter-national proletarian identity in late capitalism:

> Is there anything real left in the concept of assimilation, after all violence and all inequality have been eliminated?
>
> Yes, there undoubtedly is. What is left is capitalism's world-historical tendency to break down national barriers, obliterate national distinctions, and to *assimilate* nations—a tendency which manifests itself more and more powerfully with every passing decade, and is one of the greatest driving forces transforming capitalism into socialism. . . . No one unobsessed by nationalist prejudices can fail to perceive that this process of assimilation of nations by capitalism means the greatest historical progress, the breakdown of hidebound national conservatism in the various backwoods, especially in backward countries like Russia.[4]

Lenin cited turn-of-the-century New York City—viewed as a melting pot into which peoples of different national background entered and out of which

Map 4.1 Federal Divisions of the Union
of Soviet Socialist Republics, 1989

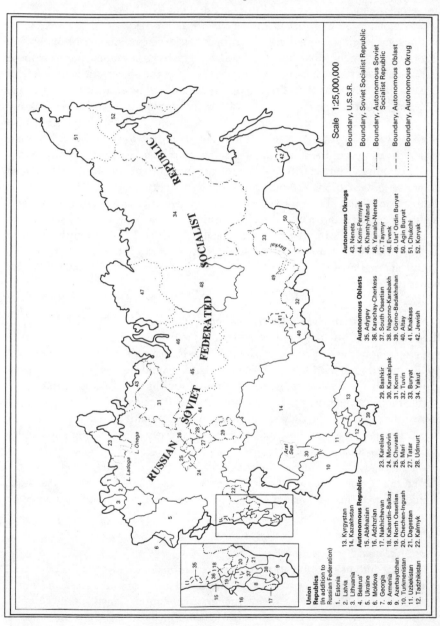

Scale 1:25,000,000

Boundary, U.S.S.R.

Boundary, Soviet Socialist Republic

Boundary, Autonomous Soviet Socialist Republic

Boundary, Autonomous Oblast

Boundary, Autonomous Okrug

Autonomous Okrugs
43. Nenets
44. Komi-Permyak
45. Khanty-Mansi
46. Yamalo-Nenets
47. Taymyr
48. Evenk
49. Ust' Ordin Buryat
50. Agin Buryat
51. Chukchi
52. Koryak

Autonomous Oblasts
35. Adygey
36. Karachay-Cherkess
37. South Ossetian
38. Nagorno-Karabakh
39. Gorno-Badakhshan
40. Altay
41. Khakass
42. Jewish

29. Bashkir
30. Karakalpak
31. Komi
32. Tuvin
33. Buryat
34. Yakut

23. Karelian
24. Mordvin
25. Chuvash
27. Mari
28. Udmurt

Union Republics
(In addition to Russian Federation)

1. Estonia
2. Latvia
3. Lithuania
4. Belarus'
5. Ukraine
6. Moldova
7. Georgia
8. Armenia
9. Azerbaydzhan
10. Turkmenistan
11. Uzbekistan
12. Tadzhikistan
13. Kyrgyzstan
14. Kazakhstan

Autonomous Republics
15. Abkhazian
16. Adzhrian
17. Nakhichevan
18. Kabardin-Balkar
19. North Ossetian
20. Chechen-Ingush
21. Dagestan
22. Kalmyk

Source: R. Kaiser, *The Geography of Nationalism,* p. 155

Americans emerged—as evidence that socioeconomic development was the key to solving the national problem.[5] Inter-national Soviet citizens would similarly be forged in the industrial cities of Russia and the USSR.

Although Lenin believed in the historical inevitability of the demise of nations and their assimilation into an inter-national community, he spoke and wrote of a stumbling block on the road to a global communist future without nations and states. National consciousness among the masses in Russia was at least in part driven by the existence of a system of ethnic stratification in which Russians were the hegemonic "oppressor nation" exploiting all other nations and homelands in the empire.[6] So long as this condition of internal colonialism persisted, the working masses would tend to side with their own bourgeois nationalists in opposition to their international community of interest—the proletariat.

Beginning from the Marxian precept that "no nation can be free if it oppresses other nations,"[7] Lenin developed a dialectical approach to the national problem in Russia. The proletariat of the oppressor nation (i.e., Russians) must fight for equality and national self-determination (i.e., the right to secede and form independent nation-states) of national minorities. Concomitantly, the proletariat of the non-Russian nations had a duty to work for the assimilation of all ethnic and national communities into one inter-national or a-national collective identity.

The Right of Nations to Self-Determination

Lenin's advocacy of the right of nations to self-determination was devised to overcome non-Russian concerns about Great-Russian chauvinism.[8] One aspect of Russian domination over non-Russian lands would be eliminated if nations could decide for themselves whether to join a multinational socialist state or to form their own independent nation-states. However, Lenin distinguished between support for the right of national self-determination, which was the duty of all Russian Marxists, and support for actual secessionist movements, which must be individually assessed to determine their progressive or regressive nature. Like Marx, Lenin generally preferred large centralized states to small states. Given the option of seceding or voluntarily joining a larger multinational state, Lenin believed that national minorities would act in their economic self-interests and join or remain part of larger international states.

Inter-National Equalization

Lenin's second major principle regarding the national question was inter-national equality. To Lenin, the key to solving the national problem in the Russian Empire was overcoming Russian hegemony through inter-national equalization. Coupled with modernization and political socialization to inculcate a socialist orientation, equalization would overcome the Russian Empire's interethnic antagonisms, and reorient the masses away from bourgeois nationalism and toward proletarian inter-nationalism.[9]

This inter-national equalization was needed in the sociocultural, economic, and political spheres, and was to serve as the focal point of Soviet nationality policies. The federal structure of the state was intended to provide non-Russian nations politico-juridical equality with Russians. *Korenizatsiya*, giving titular members preferential treatment in their home republics, was designed to provide socio-cultural and economic equalization of nations in the state. Each of these policies had both intended and unintended consequences, but the overwhelming effect of federalization and *korenizatsiya* was to accelerate the nationalization of ethnic indigenes. In this way, the nationality policies made the national problem more intractable over time.[10]

Territorial Autonomy and Federalism

The third major principle of Lenin's approach to the national problem was **territorial autonomy** for nations whose members opted to remain in the multinational socialist state. Not only was territorial autonomy seen as a means of overcoming the colonial relationship between core and periphery, it was also viewed as a way to make large multinational states such as Russia more economically efficient. The autonomous territories were to be as nationally homogeneous as possible:

> A uniform national population is undoubtedly one of the most reliable factors making for free, broad and really modern commercial intercourse. It is beyond doubt that not a single Marxist, and not even a single firm democrat, will stand up for the Austrian crown lands and the Russian guberniyas and uyezds, or challenge the necessity of replacing these obsolete divisions by others that will conform as far as possible with the national composition of the population. Lastly, it is beyond doubt that in order to eliminate all national oppression it is very important to create autonomous areas, however small, with entirely homogeneous populations, towards which members of the respective nationalities scattered all over the country, or even the world, could gravitate, and with which they could enter into relations and free associations of every kind.[11]

Lenin counterposed national-territorial autonomy to national-cultural autonomy, which was being promoted by Austrian Marxists as a means of preserving the multinational Austro-Hungarian state in a post-imperial setting. National-cultural (or extraterritorial) autonomy advocated the creation of national unions to which individuals would belong regardless of their place of residence. These unions would provide their national members with social services, including education, as well as political representation.

Lenin saw national-cultural autonomy as anti-Marxist, because it made nations rather than classes the basic building blocks of society. Lenin found nationalist control of educational curricula and nationally-based political parties particularly offensive.[12] Lenin's multinational state would consist of nationally homogeneous autonomous territories where indigenes could study in their own language and be represented politically by members of their own nation; however, instruments of political socialization (education, government, media) would be controlled by a-national communists at the center.

The autonomy envisaged by Lenin was thus limited. In his early writings he strongly preferred economically and politically centralized states over federated or confederated states:

> But while, and insofar as, different nations constitute a single state, Marxists will never, under any circumstances, advocate either the federal principle or decentralization. The great centralized state is a tremendous historical step forward from medieval disunity to the future socialist unity of the whole world, and only *via* such a state . . . can there be any road to socialism.[13]

Lenin's opposition to federalism changed with Russia's changing circumstances. Declarations of independence in several border regions during World War I required a rethinking of support for national self-determination. Because the nations in the periphery had not actually voted for secession in referendums, the Bolsheviks could claim that these independence movements were merely exercises in bourgeois nationalism. In this way, the Bolsheviks could justify the use of the Red Army to reintegrate the lost lands. The border regions themselves viewed a federal structure as more acceptable than mere autonomy in a centralized Russian state. Thus federalism could satisfy some of the border nations' territorial demands, while at the same time providing the center with a means to gather lost lands back into the USSR.

Lenin became increasingly concerned about the Great-Russian chauvinism emerging at the center of his own party. Territorial autonomy might be sufficient to ensure inter-national equality in a socialist state with an inter-nationalist or a-nationalist center. However, until the political core became truly a-national, non-Russians in an autonomous state structure would be unable to overcome Russian hegemony. Federalization thus became the structural instrument for politico-juridical equalization between the Russian and non-Russian nations, and served as the most acceptable compromise between national self-determination (now a counter-revolutionary act) and national-territorial autonomy (now insufficient to equalize inter-national relations). However, the hierarchically structured Communist party placed severe constraints on the federal nature of center-republic relations. The USSR had become a federation in form, but in essence remained a unitary state which provided only limited territorial autonomy for non-Russians in their republics.[14]

Stalin and the National Question

While Lenin constructed the theoretical framework for solving the national question, Stalin enacted policies that gave this theoretical framework concrete form. Stalin was poorly suited for implementing this national policy agenda, both because he was not committed to equalization and federalization as necessary preconditions for solving the national problem, and because he, though born a Georgian, became a Great Russian chauvinist over time.

In an early work, "Marxism and the National Question (1913)," Stalin listed the right of nations to self-determination, regional autonomy for "such crystallised units as Poland, Lithuania, the Ukraine, the Caucasus," inter-national equality, and inter-national unity in a single party as essential elements to solving Russia's national problem.[15] These elements were seemingly consistent with Lenin's thinking; however, on closer examination significant differences can be seen.

First, in the section "The national problem in Russia," Great-Russian chauvinism was not mentioned once, though it was central to Lenin's thinking. The "right of nations to self-determination" was mentioned, but Stalin did not discuss this right as a critical instrument to solve the national problem in Russia. "Regional autonomy," as envisaged by Stalin, would not be based on nationally homogeneous units, but rather would consist of multinational economic regions designed to facilitate inter-national integration rather than national segregation. Stalin discussed "national equality" in the context of providing minorities in autonomous regions with their own schools and the use of their own languages, but this would not necessarily result in the inter-national equalization between Russians and non-Russians in the USSR as a whole. Stalin's divergence from the essence of Lenin's thinking regarding the national question led Lenin to publish his "Critical Remarks on the National Question" later that year.

During the 1920s, Stalin's writings on the national question consistently identified three national problems. Great-Russian chauvinism was the first, and was treated as the most serious of the three during the early 1920s. The second, counterposed to Great-Russian chauvinism, was "local" or non-Russian nationalism. The third was identified as inter-national and inter-regional inequality that had been inherited from the Russian Empire and continued to persist after the socialist revolution, even though politico-juridicial equality had been achieved through the federalization of the state.

In 1921 Stalin depicted Great-Russian chauvinism, favoring Russians over non-Russians, as a problem of Russia's imperial legacy. Local Russian peasants who had settled in the border regions were described as kulaks who oppressed non-Russians, took their best lands, and served as a fifth column for tsarist expansionism.[16] The struggle against Great-Russian chauvinism was thus tied to the "dekulakization" drive of the early 1920s, through which the center consolidated power in the countryside. By 1923, Stalin blamed the rise of Great-Russian chauvinism on the New Economic Policy (NEP), and thus linked the solution of the national problem to the end of the economic program, which he had opposed from the outset.[17] However, the center under Stalin became even more Russocentric with the end of NEP and the initiation of the collectivization and rapid industrialization programs.

During the early 1920s, Stalin depicted local nationalism as a defensive reaction to Great-Russian chauvinism. The national problem could be solved only by waging a "determined war on Great-Russian chauvinism."[18] However, even in the early 1920s, Stalin noted that "defensive nationalism" could become "aggressive nationalism" or "local chauvinism" on the part of the dominant local nation and directed against its own national minorities. As examples Stalin cited Georgian chauvinism toward Abkhazians, Ossetians, and Armenians, Azeri chauvinism toward Armenians, and Uzbek chauvinism toward Turkmen in Bukhara.[19] Stalin believed that defensive local nationalism would disappear once Great-Russian chauvinism was eliminated, but that a more active effort would be needed to rid the country of local chauvinism.

Stalin viewed the third national problem—national and regional inequality— as the cause of the two other national problems. Inter-national and inter-regional equalization were thus defined as keys to solving all national problems inherited from the Russian Empire. According to Stalin, the USSR had eliminated politico-juridical inequality among nations by passing laws declaring the equality of nations, and by constructing the USSR as a "confederation of sovereign republics" which retained the right of secession. However, actual cultural and economic inequality would take longer to overcome. Therefore, one of the most pressing tasks during the 1920s was to equalize levels of sociocultural and economic development between the Russian center and the non-Russian periphery through *korenizatsiya,* or indigenization:

> The task of the Party is to help the toiling masses of the non-Great-Russian peoples to catch up with Central Russia, which is ahead of them, and to help them a) to develop and consolidate their own Soviet state system in forms consistent with the national character of these peoples; b) to organize their own courts, administrative bodies, economic organs and government organs functioning in the native language and recruited from among local people acquainted with the customs and psychology of the local population, and c) to develop a press, schools, theatres, clubs and cultural and educational institutions generally, functioning in the native language.[20]

In addition to this indigenization in the republics, Stalin also argued that the national communities must have representation in the central administration and legislature, in order to ensure that the non-Russians would come to view the USSR as their own state. Stalin also wrote of the need to relocate industries to the underdeveloped border regions in order to dismantle the exploitative imperial economic geography of the past and to bring about inter-regional economic equalization.[21]

By 1930, a shift in the treatment of local nationalism and Great-Russian chauvinism can be seen in Stalin's speeches and writings. Great-Russian chauvinism, still identified as the principal danger facing the USSR, was redefined as a reaction against the inter-national equalization policies—as an anti-federalist, anti-*korenizatsiya* and pro-assimilationist orientation among Russian political elites—particularly those in the non-Russian republics. Local nationalism was no longer defined as a defensive reaction to Great-Russian chauvinism, but rather as a proactive attempt by non-Russians to use equalization policies to isolate and separate their nations from the inter-national proletariat, and from the inter-nationalist center of the USSR.[22] Inter-national equalization policies, portrayed as the solution to the national problem in the early 1920s, were recast as the main national problem by the early 1930s. Nationality policies designed to promote inter-nationalism through equalization were instead promoting nationalization of the masses and a sense of exclusiveness among titular nations toward their proper status in their home republics.[23]

During the 1930s, Stalin reversed positions on which of these two deviations posed the greatest danger to the USSR. In 1934, Stalin held that the greatest threat was posed by "the deviation against which one has ceased to fight and has thus enabled to grow into a danger to the state." As an example, Ukrainian nationalism was cited as the major danger in Ukraine, with the implication that "local nationalism" had overtaken Great-Russian chauvinism as the USSR's most significant national problem.[24]

Throughout the remainder of the 1930s, indigenous political elites in the republics were purged for local nationalism, culminating in the Great Purges of 1937–1938. At the same time, the center continued to develop native-language schools, and to recruit socially mobilized indigenes for elite economic and political positions in their home republics. Mass-based *korenizatsiya* continued even though indigenous elites—themselves frequently products of earlier indigenization efforts—were being purged.

The Great-Russian-chauvinist phase of Stalin's national policy began in 1938 and continued until his death in 1953. The Russian language became a mandatory subject in all schools. Russians were depicted as the "teachers, civilizers, cultural leaders, and protectors of the non-Russian nationalities." After World War II the center sought to eliminate "the non-Russian nationalism that had been intensified by the militant patriotism of the war period."[25] The deportation of entire national communities from their homelands for supposed collaboration with Nazi Germany illustrates the fervor of this crusade against local nationalism.

The Status of Russians and Non-Russians in Post-Stalin USSR

The post-Stalin period approached the national question somewhat differently. The most consistent message between the 1950s and the 1980s was that inter-national equalization had occurred, and therefore the national problem had been solved. Soviet political elites and ethnographers contended that a "new Soviet people" was becoming a primary identity for most of the people in the USSR. While sovietization did not mean that individuals were losing their ethnocultural identities, it did imply that these ethnic groups were no longer forward-looking politicized and territorialized communities (*i.e.*, nations). This also meant that nationalism as an ideology and a political action program had been supplanted by inter-nationalism. As discussed below, this belief in the success of sovietization was one of the major errors regarding the national question in the post-Stalin USSR in general, and in the Gorbachev era in particular.

After Stalin's death, Russians continued to be treated as elder brothers, though without the excessive pro-Russian stance of the late Stalin era. Brezhnev was perhaps the most chauvinistic of the post-Stalin leaders in this regard, but his praise of the Russian nation emphasized their socialist-revolutionary rather than their national character:

> All the nations and nationalities of our country, above all the Great Russian people, played a role in the formation, strengthening and development of this mighty union of equal peoples that have taken the path of socialism. The revolutionary energy, selflessness, diligence and profound internationalism of the Great Russian people have rightfully won them the sincere respect of all the peoples of our socialist homeland.[26]

Both Andropov and Gorbachev were also russocentric if not Russophiles.[27]

Russians and the Russian language were dominant by the end of World War II and they maintained their hegemonic position until the state itself disintegrated in 1991. On this basis alone, one might argue that the Russian Empire had been restored in the USSR. However, this stance oversimplifies inter-national and center-periphery relations in the postwar USSR. Elevating Russians and the Russian language to the status of "first among equals" was not intended to realign the USSR around Russian nationalism, but rather to facilitate the drawing together of nations into one Soviet people. Nevertheless, the dominance of Russians and the Russian language—regardless of the rationale used to justify it—did confer superior status on one group over all others in the state as a whole.

The dominance of Russians in the USSR occurred concomitantly with an indigenization of each of the state's union republics. During this period, mass-based nationalization of the titular groups continued apace as socially mobilized indigenes increasingly attempted to use their indigenous status as an advantage against Russians and other outsiders in competition for high-status jobs, higher standards of living and greater access to the resources of the homeland. By the end of the Soviet period, a two-tiered system of ethnic stratification had emerged, with Russians as the hegemonic nation in the country as a whole, but with titular nations dominant in their own home republics. Indigenization, not sovietization or russification, was the primary trend in the union republics in the post-Stalin period, and it paved the way for the disintegration of the state during the late 1980s.[28]

The National Problem Solved

Post-Stalin Soviet leaders proclaimed that inter-national inequality and the Russian-dominated ethnic stratification system had been eliminated and that the national problem in the USSR had been solved. Khrushchev's 1961 Communist

Party program linked equality with the coming of communism and the decreasing significance of the Soviet federation:

> The borders between the union republics within the USSR are increasingly los-ing their former significance, since all nations are equal, their life is organized on a single socialist foundation, the material and spiritual needs of each people are satisfied to the same extent, and they are all united into one family by common vital interests and are advancing together toward a single goal—communism.[29]

Commemorating the fiftieth anniversary of the formation of the USSR, Brezhnev likewise proclaimed that the national problem had been solved as a result of the Soviet Union's achieving inter-national and interrepublican socioeco-nomic equalization.[30] After this 1972 speech, interrepublican equalization disap-peared as a major criterion in economic planning.[31]

In the same speech, Brezhnev added that while the major national problem inherited from the past had been resolved, new national problems continued to arise even at the stage of developed socialism.[32] This formulation—that equal-ization had solved **the national problem**, but that new national problems con-tinued to arise as members of different nations interacted in their daily lives—became the new standard which appeared in speeches by Andropov and Gorbachev.[33]

During the 1960s and 1970s, the creation of one united Soviet people became the focal point of research on the national question. According to the national dialectic, nations had blossomed (*rastsvet*) as a result of the twin poli-cies of *korenizatsiya* and federalization. By the 1980s, the nationalization that was the product of this *rastsvet* was said to be essentially complete.[34] Nations were also said to be drawing together (*sblizheniye*) into one Soviet people, even while they retained their sense of national identity. At some point in the future, the nations of the USSR and in principle all nations of the world would merge (*sliyaniye*) into one inter-national or a-national community. Although few Soviet leaders or ethnographers spoke of the complete assimilation of all peo-ples, most agreed that a Soviet people had come into being and that friendship among peoples and Soviet patriotism had supplanted narrower nationalistic interests.

Gorbachev was a firm believer in the sovietization myth. The underlying assumption of *perestroika* itself was that a loyal Soviet people existed. Once freed from bureaucratic constraints by *glasnost'* and *demokratizatsiya*, this Soviet people would use its newly found freedoms to pull the USSR from its stagnation, rein-vigorate the Soviet economy, and accelerate the USSR's historical progress toward communism.[35] Even as late as 1989, at the Communist Party plenum held to dis-cuss national problems facing the USSR, Gorbachev asserted:

> We have grown up in a social atmosphere literally permeated with international-ism. Friendship of the peoples was not some kind of abstract slogan for us, but

an everyday reality. Can we really forget that? Can we renounce the internationalist legacy of the revolution?[36]

Unfortunately for Gorbachev, his reforms did not mobilize a sovietized people to revitalize the Soviet economy and society. Rather, they enabled nationalists in the republics to pursue political action programs oriented toward the creation of greater independence for the titular nations in their homelands. Throughout the non-Russian periphery, but particularly in the western union republics, organizations founded in support of *perestroika* such as *RUKH* and *Sajudis* almost immediately redefined their missions away from restructuring the Soviet socialist economy and toward national rebirth.

Clearly, Gorbachev, the other postwar leaders, and Soviet ethnographers erred dramatically in their assessments of the national problem which remained in the USSR. In the following section, we briefly consider the reasons for their overly optimistic outlook regarding an end to inter-national antagonisms and the emergence of a new Soviet people.[37]

Sovietization, Russification, or Indigenization?

Soviet political elites and ethnographers cited several societal trends as evidence that sovietization was occurring. Rapid socioeconomic development, including the rapid rise in education, urbanization, and industrialization which both Marx and Lenin linked directly to assimilation, was viewed as facilitating sovietization. Data showing inter-national and interrepublican socioeconomic equalization were cited as evidence that an inter-nationalist drawing together into one Soviet people was occurring. Interhomeland migration was also viewed as a demographic process facilitating integration. Finally, ethnocultural statistics indicating linguistic assimilation toward Russian, rising international marriage rates, and the so-called natural assimilation of the children from such marriages were all seen as evidence that nations were drawing together into one Soviet people.[38]

Socioeconomic Development and Equalization

Socioeconomic development occurred in the USSR, with certain time periods (*e.g.*, the 1930s) characterized by extremely high rates. Rapid industrialization, urbanization, and collectivization broke down the localism that dominated the countryside. However, this localism was replaced not by an inter-national orientation, but rather by a national consciousness. Members of the indigenous communities migrated to their homeland's cities in search of work and often found nonindigenes blocking upward mobility. The nationalization of indigenous groups was also facilitated by Soviet nationality policies which had structured the state as a federation of national republics typically named after one indigenous group, and which had targeted that group for preferential treatment in access to education and to high status economic and political employment.

During the post-Stalin era, center-initiated *korenizatsiya* policies were increasingly supplemented by *korenizatsiya* from below. Indigenes who attained positions of authority increasingly used their power to hire "their own," thus facil-

itating indigenous upward mobility while at the same time enhancing the importance of national identity. Socioeconomic development, coupled with nationality
policies favoring indigenes in their own homelands and supplemented by efforts
to accelerate indigenization in the republics, facilitated rising national consciousness, nationalism, and inter-national antagonisms, not sovietization.

Inter-national equalization also occurred throughout the post-Stalin period, at
least by socioeconomic and political measures (i.e., educational attainment, urbanization, occupational mobility, political representation). However, inter-national
equalization in the USSR occurred as a result of each titular nation gaining greater
privileges (i.e., becoming more dominant) in its respective home republic. When
viewed from the perspective of union republics rather than the USSR as a whole,
the USSR was experiencing a shift from Russian hegemony to a two-tiered system
of ethnic stratification with Russians and titular nations competing for dominance,
and with all other minorities in the republics increasingly left behind.

By 1989 titular nations at the union-republic level were over-represented in
elite positions in education (students in higher education), the economy (enterprise directors), and the political system (deputies in the Congress of Peoples
Deputies, the Republican Supreme Soviets and the local soviets) (Table 4.1). In
higher education, only Russians, Ukrainians, and Belarusians were relatively
under-represented in their homelands. In high-status economic employment,
only Russians, Moldovans, and Uzbeks were relatively under-represented in their
homelands. For political representation, the more local the geographic scale, the
higher the degree of titular over-representation. Nine of the fifteen nations were
over-represented in the Congress of Peoples Deputies, ten of the twelve nations
for which data are available were over-represented in the Supreme Soviets of
their home republics, and all nine nations for which data are available were
over-represented in the local soviets of their homelands.

The most counter-intuitive aspect of these data is that Russians were the only
nation relatively under-represented across the board; this is certainly not what one
would expect to find if the USSR was truly operating as a new Russian empire. Even
within the Russian Federation, several of the indigenous minorities with
autonomous territories were over-represented in these high-status activities, resulting
in a relative under-representation of Russians in their homeland. However, Russians
were relatively over-represented outside their home republic, indicating that their
status as dominant state-nation was preserved to the end of the Soviet era. Titular
over-representation thus occurred most frequently at the expense of non-Russians.

Inter-national equalization and titular over-representation were occurring
throughout the post-Stalin era; however, interrepublican equalization was not
achieved. Investment decisions made after 1972 resulted in growing inequality
across republics.[39] Most notably, Central Asian economic development lagged
behind, while its population and educational attainment were rapidly increasing.[40] Not surprisingly, these factors have resulted in a growing sense of relative
deprivation among Central Asians, who have become increasingly incapable of
meeting their rapidly rising expectations. This growing gap between expectations

Table 4.1
Indigenous Proportions of Total Population,
Students Entering Higher Education, Directors of
Economic Enterprises, and Political Representatives, 1989 (Percent)

Nation	% of Total Population	% of Students	% of Directors	% of Political Representatives in: CPD[a]	RSS[b]	LS[c]
Russian	82	80	77	71	78	—
Ukrainian	73	67	79	69	75	86
Belarusian	78	71	78	70	74	86
Moldovan	64	71	50	72	69	77
Uzbek	71	71	68	70	78	79
Kazakh	40	54	40	40	54	54
Kyrgyz	52	65	55	59	64	69
Tajik	62	63	66	67	75	69
Turkmen	72	78	72	76	74	81
Georgian	70	89	89	73	—	—
Azeri	83	91	94	76	—	—
Armenian	93	99	99	88	—	—
Lithuanian	80	88	92	85	87	—
Latvian	52	54	63	78	70	83
Estonian	62	78	82	81	77	—

Notes: [a]Congress of Peoples Deputies. [b]Republican Supreme Soviets. [c]Local Soviets.

Source: Robert Kaiser, *The Geography of Nationalism in Russia and the USSR* (Princeton: Princeton University Press, 1994), pp. 233, 241, 349.

and capabilities has served as a catalyst for sporadic, spontaneous acts of violence against nonindigenes. This situation is unlikely to improve significantly in the years ahead.

Until its demise the USSR remained a highly centralized state, though economic and political decision-making were devolving to titular elites in the union republics. This centralized power structure was at odds with the USSR's federal structure, and increasingly at odds with the desired center-republic relations perceived by titular political elites in the republics. The discontent resulting from this incongruity grew as the number of highly qualified indigenes occupying decision-making positions in the republics increased. Gorbachev's reforms provided republican elites with the opportunity to express their discontent, first through calls for greater cultural and economic independence from Moscow, and later through demands for greater political independence.

The Soviet experience indicates that neither socioeconomic development nor equalization necessarily solve national problems in multinational, multihomeland states. In the Soviet case, modernization and equalization resulted in the nationalization of indigenes, not in their denationalization or sovietization. Rather than abandoning national identity as they became more educated, urbanized, and socially mobilized, indigenes used their indigenous status as a means to gain a competitive edge over "outsiders." Contrary to predictions that modernization and equalization would facilitate the drawing together of nations into one Soviet people, they heightened national consciousness, inter-national tensions and the potential for conflict.

Interhomeland Migration

After the revolutionary upheavals of the 1920s and 1930s, interhomeland migration, with the exception of the Russians, was quite limited. The low incidence of interhomeland migration is particularly evident in the post-Stalin era when most migration was voluntary. Even as their members became more educated, urbanized, and upwardly mobile, most nations remained highly concentrated in their home republics. Nonetheless, most republics became more nationally mixed, particularly between 1926 and 1959, as economic development induced Russian out-migration to the non-Russian periphery (Table 4.2).

The growing number of Russians in Central Asia was particularly dramatic, and included both migration to rural areas because of collectivization and the Virgin Lands Program, and also migration to urban areas because of increasing industrialization. Major cities in Central Asia became Russian enclaves by the 1960s. Between 1959 and 1989, Russian in-migration also resulted in a dramatic demographic russification of Latvia and Estonia, two republics forcibly reincorporated into the state after interwar independence. Russian in-migration was also high in Ukraine and Belarus.

Aside from the Baltic and Slavic republics, a demographic indigenization occurred between 1959 and 1989, and was especially intense after 1970. Both increased concentration of titular nations in their respective republics (especially Armenia) and Russian out-migration, beginning in the 1960s, contributed to this process. In Central Asia, demographic indigenization occurred primarily because of high birthrates among Central Asians compared with Russians and other non-Central Asians. This demographic indigenization was enhanced beginning in the 1970s, as Russians and other European groups began to leave Central Asia, with out-migration accelerating during the 1980s.

Interhomeland migration partially inter-nationalized the population. Individuals living outside their homelands adopted the Russian language more frequently and married members of other national communities at higher rates than individuals remaining in their homelands. This inter-nationalization was especially pronounced in subsequent generations: children of inter-national families often adopted a national identity other than that of the parent living outside his

Table 4.2
National Composition of Population by Union Republic, and National Concentration in the Home Republic, 1959–1989
(% and % point change)

| | National Composition of Total Population | | | | | | | | | | % of Titular Nation in Home Republic | | | | |
| | Indigenes | | | % point chg | | Russians | | | % point chg | | | | | % point chg | |
Republic	1926	1959	1989	1926–59	1959–89	1926	1959	1989	1926–59	1959–89	1926	1959	1989	1926–59	1959–89
Russia	78	84	82	6	−2	78	84	82	6	−2	93	86	83	−7	−3
Ukraine	81	77	73	−4	−4	9	17	22	8	5	74	86	85	12	−1
Belarus'	81	81	78	0	−3	8	8	13	0	5	85	83	79	−2	−4
Moldova	—	65	65	—	0	—	10	13	—	3	—	85	83	—	−2
Uzbekistan	74	62	71	−12	9	5	14	8	9	−6	85	84	85	−1	1
Kazakhstan	57	30	40	−27	10	20	43	38	23	−5	94	77	80	−17	3
Kyrgyzstan	67	41	52	−26	11	12	30	22	18	−8	87	86	88	−1	2
Tajikistan	75	53	62	−22	9	1	13	8	12	−5	63	75	75	12	0
Turkmenistan	70	61	72	−9	11	8	17	10	9	−7	83	92	93	9	1
Georgia	67	64	70	−3	6	4	10	6	6	−4	98	97	95	−1	−2
Azerbaijan	62	68	83	6	15	10	14	6	4	−8	84	85	86	1	1
Armenia	84	88	93	4	5	2	3	2	1	−1	47	56	67	9	11

Lithuania	81	79	80	-2	1	2	9	9	7	0	100	93	95	-7	2
Latvia	75	62	52	-13	-10	11	27	34	16	7	96	93	95	-3	2
Estonia	92	75	62	-17	-13	4	20	30	16	10	91	90	94	-1	4

Note: Data are for republics as delimited at the time of the census. [a] 1930s data from the Estonian census of 1934, the Latvian census of 1935, and the Lithuanian census of 1938, and are found in Tonu Parming, "Population Processes and the Nationality Issue in the Soviet Baltic," *Soviet Studies* Vol. 32, No. 3 (July 1980):399. Parming notes that "the 1934 data for Estonia are for the current territorial area of the Estonian SSR; the data for Latvia in 1935 and Lithuania in 1938 are for the territorial areas of the interwar Republics." [b] The total number of indigenes used in calculating these percents is equal to the census figures taken from Parming plus the number of Lithuanians, Latvians and Estonians, respectively, living in the USSR according to the 1937 Soviet census, as published in Yuri Polyakov et al., "Polveka mclchaniya (vsesoyuznaya perepis' Naseleniya 1937 goda)," *Sotsiologicheskiye issledovaniya* No. 7 (1990):58.

Source: Yu. Arutyunyan and Yu. Bromley, *Sotsial'no-kul'turnyy oblik sovetskikh natsiy* (Moskva: Nauka, 1986), pp. 32–37; Robert Kaiser, *The Geography of Nationalism in Russia and the USSR*, p. 174.

or her homeland. However, this inter-nationalization of out-migrants is only apparent among individuals who voluntarily left their homeland; forced deportation of groups (e.g., Chechens, Ingush, Crimean Tatars, Kalmyks, Balkars, Karachays) resulted in rising nationalism.

On the other hand, the in-migration of outsiders is one of the most potent catalysts for rising indigenous nationalism. This feature was especially apparent in the Baltics, where demographic russification since the 1950s became the central feature of resurgent territorial nationalism. Nationalists rallied around perceived threats to the future viability of the Latvian and Estonian nations (see Chapter 5). This anti-outsider nativism was evident in nearly all former Soviet republics. From the evidence of the post-Stalin period, it is clear that increased inter-national interaction resulting from the in-migration of nontitular groups is more likely to result in rising inter-national tensions than in the drawing together of nations into one inter-national community of interest.

Even national members who left the homeland and underwent a process of assimilation toward either the Russians or the titular nations have served as a catalyst for rising nationalism back home. Indigenous nationalists typically use the assimilation of these individuals as examples of the central authorities' efforts to "denationalize" the group. This is particularly true among Ukrainian nationalists, whose membership was reduced dramatically during the interwar years through the assimilation of Ukrainians living outside Ukraine (in addition to casualties of the famine of 1933). The loss of members to assimilation is cited as an example of what can and will happen to the nation as a whole if it is not able to gain control over its destiny by gaining sovereignty in its homeland.[41]

For these reasons, interhomeland migration—particularly Russian out-migration to the non-Russian republics—did not have the desired effect of inter-nationalizing or sovietizing the indigenous populations. The in-migration of often educated and skilled ethnic others heightened a sense of national consciousness among upwardly mobile indigenes, who frequently found themselves at a competitive disadvantage with these skilled nonindigenes. The presence of these nontitular elites provided a potent symbolic target against which titular nationalists attempted to mobilize their nations. Indigenous status itself, as noted above, was increasingly used to gain a competitive edge over such outsiders. The impact of interhomeland migration as a catalyst for rising nationalism in the USSR conforms to the experience of multinational, multihomeland states generally.

Ethnocultural Russification Versus Indigenization

While Soviet political leaders and researchers asserted that a sovietization of the population was occurring, western analysts—frequently non-Russian emigres from Soviet-bloc countries—perceived a process of forcible russification of non-Russians. According to the russification school, the national problem in the

USSR was being solved through the forced acculturation to the Russian language, which would ultimately result in the assimilation of non-Russians to the Russian nation. The USSR would thus become a Russian nation-state.

Soviet analysts used data showing increasing usage of Russian as evidence that sovietization was occurring. Even learning Russian as a second language was hailed as a first step toward assimilation:

> Bilingualism is a necessary (and obligatory) stage in the transition of a single individual or group of individuals from their native language to another language. Therefore, it is necessary to consider bilingualism as an important phase and as a component part of the process of linguistic assimilation.[42]

Beyond linguistic assimilation, inter-national marriage was also used as evidence either of sovietization or russification. Inter-national marriage is critical to the assimilation process, since it represents the inter-nationalization of families and is the one concrete path to voluntary integration of nations over the course of generations. Soviet ethnographers used the term "natural assimilation" to refer to the process experienced by children of inter-national families. Such assimilation, as noted above, meant a loss among national members living outside their respective home republics. While analysts in Moscow treated this process as "natural," western analysts and nationalists whose nations were losing adherents viewed it as a coercive effort by central authorities to russify the population.

Both sovietization and russification provide misleading views of the USSR's acculturation and assimilation trends. Russian bilingualism was spreading because of the mandatory study of Russian in schools and the dominance of Russian as the official language in the Soviet Union. Learning Russian as a second language, however, was not a preliminary stage in the assimilation process, but rather was an accommodation that non-Russians were forced to make in order to get ahead or even to get along in their own homelands.[43] Learning Russian was frequently resented by members of the titular nations; Russian bilingualism thus had the paradoxical effect of raising anti-Russian and anti-Soviet sentiments among upwardly mobile indigenes, who were often forced to compete for the resources of their homelands not only with outsiders but also in an alien language.

Linguistic russification—the adoption of Russian as one's native language—was accurately viewed by Soviet and western analysts as a measure of acculturation and the preliminary stage in the process of assimilation. However, the emphasis that analysts placed on this trend seems to have been unwarranted. Given the increasingly dominant status of Russian in Soviet society, it is surprising how little linguistic russification actually occurred. Between 1959 and 1989, the number of non-Russians who were linguistically russified increased from 10.2 million to 18.7 million (from 10.8 percent to 13.3 percent of all non-Russians in the USSR). Most of this linguistic russification occurred before 1979, when 16.3 million—13.1 percent of all non-Russians—considered Russian to be their native language; almost no linguistic russification took place during the 1980s.[44]

The vast majority of members of all nations whose homelands were designated as union republics retained the titular language as their language of first choice throughout the 1959–1989 period (Table 4.3). Only Ukrainians and Belarusians experienced substantial linguistic russification. In these cases, the russification appears to have been part of a concerted effort to "denationalize" these fellow eastern Slavs, who Russian nationalists do not consider as separate nations but merely as ethnic branches of the Russian nation.[45] On the other hand, Armenians and Estonians experienced a linguistic derussification between 1959 and 1989; Azeris linguistically derussified during the 1980s; and Turkmen, Tajiks, and Georgians experienced no additional linguistic russification after 1979.

Linguistic russification was a stronger trend among national communities whose homelands were designated autonomous republics, oblasts, and okrugs in the Russian Federation. Even among these groups, linguistic russification was limited to two clusters of ethnonational communities. First, ethnonational groups with homelands in the northwestern or Volga-Urals region of Russia which were absorbed by the Russian Empire very early and whose members had interacted intensely with Russians for centuries (i.e., Karelians, Komi, Mari, Mordvinians, Udmurts, and Chuvashes) experienced substantial linguistic russification, with the rate of linguistic assimilation as high in the 1980s as in previous decades. Second, numerically small ethnic groups of northern Siberia (whose homelands were designated "autonomous okrugs") also experienced substantial linguistic russification which accelerated as their members became more socially mobilized. For these groups, the "modernization thesis" appears to hold, but this is an exception that proves the rule. They had not experienced the nationalization processes described in Chapter 3, and the indigenous masses had never become nationally self-conscious. For members of these groups (i.e., Khanty, Mansi, Chukchi, Koryaks), russification was thus not a process of denationalization, but rather a process of nationalization.[46]

Linguistic russification occurred primarily among individuals living in cities outside their home republics (Table 4.4). Both the initial rate of linguistic russification in 1959 and the rate between 1959 and 1989 were, on average, much higher outside than inside the homeland. This finding applied to all groups except those at the autonomous okrug level, where linguistic russification in the homeland was as extensive as it was among members living outside. This trend toward russification in the homeland provides further evidence of the lack of national consciousness among these small groups compared with the other nations in the USSR.

For most non-Russians, linguistic russification was as far as assimilation went. Inter-national marriage, an intermediate stage in the process of assimilation, remained a relatively rare occurrence in Soviet society, although it increased with rising urbanization and education rates. As with linguistic russification, intermarriage was particularly low for the members of titular nations living in their home republics, and occurred most often among members who lived in cities outside their homelands.[47]

Table 4.3

Native Language Retention and Linguistic Russification, 1959–1989 by Nation
(Percent of National Community and Percentage Point Change)

Nation	Native Language Retention					Linguistic Russification				
	1959	1970	1979	1989	% point change	1959	1970	1979	1989	% point change
Russian	99.8	99.8	99.8	99.8	0.0	—	—	—	—	—
Estonian	95.2	95.5	95.3	95.5	0.3	4.7	4.4	4.5	4.4	-0.3
Latvian	95.1	95.2	95.0	94.8	-0.3	4.6	4.6	4.8	5.0	0.4
Lithuanian	97.8	97.9	97.9	97.7	-0.1	1.2	1.5	1.7	1.8	0.6
Ukrainian	87.7	85.7	82.8	81.1	-6.6	12.2	14.3	17.1	18.8	6.6
Belarusian	84.2	80.6	74.2	70.9	-13.3	15.3	19.0	25.4	28.5	13.2
Moldovan	95.2	95.0	93.2	91.6	-3.6	3.6	4.2	6.0	7.4	3.8
Kazakh	98.4	98.0	97.5	97.0	-1.4	1.2	1.6	2.0	2.2	1.0
Uzbek	98.4	98.6	98.5	98.3	-0.1	0.5	0.5	0.6	0.7	0.2
Kyrgyz	98.7	98.8	97.9	97.8	-0.9	0.3	0.5	0.5	0.6	0.3
Tajik	98.1	98.5	97.8	97.7	-0.4	0.5	0.6	0.8	0.8	0.3
Turkmen	98.9	98.9	98.7	98.5	-0.4	0.6	0.8	1.0	1.0	0.4
Georgian	98.6	98.4	98.3	98.2	-0.4	1.3	1.4	1.7	1.7	0.4
Azeri	97.6	98.2	97.8	97.7	0.1	1.2	1.3	1.8	1.7	0.5
Armenian	89.9	91.4	90.7	91.7	1.8	8.3	7.6	8.4	7.6	-0.7
Averages[a]										
Union Republic	95.6	95.4	94.4	93.9	-1.7	4.0	4.4	5.5	5.9	1.9
Auton Republic	91.6	90.4	88.3	86.1	-5.5	5.7	7.5	9.6	12.1	6.4
Auton. Oblast	91.6	91.5	90.4	88.5	-3.1	7.3	7.9	8.9	10.6	3.3
Auton. Okrug	80.3	74.4	69.5	60.0	-20.3	14.8	20.5	25.2	33.5	18.7

Notes: [a] The averages are for ethnonational communities whose homelands were categorized in one of the four federal units in the USSR (Union Republic, Autonomous Republic, Autonomous Oblast, Autonomous Okrug). The percents here and above are for the ethnonational communities taken as a whole, and not the total population of the federal unit. Averages treat each ethnonational community as one observation. For a list of ethnonational communities included below the union republic level, refer to the source.

Source: Robert Kaiser, *The Geography of Nationalism in Russia and the USSR*, pp. 266–268.

Table 4.4
Linguistic Russification in the USSR, 1959–1989
(Percent claiming Russian as the first language, and percentage point change)

Nation	Homeland Urban			Homeland Rural			Outside Urban			Outside Rural		
	1959	1989	% pt Chg	1959	1989	% pt Chg	1959	1989	% pt Chg	1959	1989	% pt Chg
Ukrainian	15	19	4	1	2	1	54	57	3	42	50	8
Belarusian	22	30	8	1	3	2	61	64	3	46	52	6
Moldovan	9	11	2	1	1	0	36	36	0	8	11	3
Uzbek	1	1	0	0	0	0	3	5	2	0	1	1
Kazakh	2	3	1	0	1	1	7	9	2	2	4	2
Kyrgyz	1	1	0	0	0	0	7	7	0	0	1	1
Tajik	2	2	0	0	0	0	3	4	1	0	1	1
Turkmen	2	2	0	0	0	0	12	13	1	1	1	0
Georgian	1	0	-1	0	0	0	31	33	2	12	17	5
Azeri	2	1	-1	0	0	0	11	16	5	1	3	2
Armenian[a]	1	0	-1	0	0	0	27	30	3	5	9	4
Lithuanian	0	0	0	0	0	0	21	38	17	9	23	14
Latvian	2	3	1	1	1	0	54	56	2	31	43	12
Estonian	1	2	1	0	0	0	55	61	6	29	42	13
Groups whose homelands are:[b]												
ASSRs	9	13	4	0	1	1	23	30	7	8	15	7
A. Oblasts	14	9	-5	3	3	0	34	33	-1	14	21	7
A. Okrugs	29	49	20	12	26	14	40	53	13	18	32	14

Notes: [a]Armenians outside the homeland exclude those in Nagorno-Karabakh Autonomous Oblast. The figures for Armenians in Nagorno-Karabakh are: Urban: 1959=7%, 1989=3%; Rural: 1959=1%, 1989=0%. [b]Averages are unweighted, with each national community treated as one observation.

Source: Robert Kaiser, *The Geography of Nationalism in Russia and the USSR,* pp. 276–281.

As noted above, Soviet ethnographers viewed "natural assimilation" as an intergenerational process occurring primarily among children of inter-national families. However, the national identity chosen by such children again indicates that indigenization was a competitor with russification. When one parent was a member of the titular nation and the other parent was not, children most often opted for a titular national identity. This tendency occurred even when the nontitular parent was Russian, indicating "natural assimilation" involving the titular nation was toward indigenization rather than russification. Individuals living outside their homeland tended to intermarry with much greater frequency, and their children most often chose the titular identity (if the other parent was a member of the titular nation) or a Russian national identity (if the other parent was a Russian). This segment of the national community living outside of its homeland was undergoing a process of denationalization. However, this portion of most nations' populations was small, so few nations were assimilating either to a Soviet inter-national or a Russian national identity.[48]

Conclusions

During the Soviet era the status of Russians and the Russian language as "first among equals" was firmly established. Yet the dominant status of Russians was increasingly challenged by titular nations whose members were becoming more urbanized, educated, and upwardly mobile over time. The "modernization" of the non-Russians in their respective homelands coincided not with their sovietization or russification, but with nationalization and subsequently rising nationalism. First through indigenization policies, and later through an indigenization from below, members of titular nations out-competed members of nontitular groups for elite positions within the homeland. Within each union republic, economic and political elites were increasingly converted from spokespersons for the center into lobbyists for their nations.

The theoretical foundations on which Soviet nationality policies rested—that modernization, equalization, and territorial autonomy would solve the national problem—were fundamentally flawed. These factors, by helping to nationalize the indigenous masses in each republic, made the national problem more intractable. Gorbachev's reforms assumed that the national problem had been solved and that a Soviet people existed; what *glasnost'* and *demokratizatsiya* uncovered were mass-based nations mobilized to take control of their futures by gaining sovereignty within their homelands. The extent of such nationalization varied by republic. The Baltic nations were more nationally cohesive and conscious than the nations in Central Asia or the titular groups whose homelands were autonomous territories within the USSR. Nonetheless, once nationalism became an overt political action program in the Baltics, it quickly diffused to other nations and helped nationalize the masses in areas where nations had not become mass-based.

In this way, the newly independent states of the former Soviet Union were created primarily to give geopolitical expression to titular nationalism, which had become anti-Soviet, anti-outsider, and particularly anti-Russian in the decades preceding Soviet disintegration. As noted in Chapter 1, the new national problem facing each of the successor states is how to pay proper homage to exclusionary nationalism—the force that brought these states into being—while at the same time coping with their populations' multinational composition. That dilemma, particularly as it involves the Russians in the non-Russian states, will be the focus of Part Two.

Notes

1. This term has been used to describe the relations between Moscow and Central Asia. See Martin Spechler, "Regional Development in the USSR, 1958–78," in U.S. Congress, Joint Economic Committee, *Soviet Economy in a Time of Change* (Washington, DC: Government Printing Office, 1979), Vol. 1; and Michael Rywkin, *Moscow's Muslim Challenge: Soviet Central Asia* (Armonk, NY: M. E. Sharpe, 1982).

2. Walker Connor, *The National Question in Marxist-Leninist Theory and Strategy* (Princeton, NJ: Princeton University Press, 1984), p. 30.

3. This is most clearly stated in V. Lenin, "Critical Remarks on the National Question," written in 1913. See *National Liberation, Socialism and Imperialism. Selected Writings by V. I. Lenin* (New York: International Publishers, 1968), pp. 12–44.

4. Lenin, "Critical Remarks," in *Selected Writings* pp. 21, 23.

5. Vladimir Lenin, "The National Programme of the RSDLP," in *Selected Writings*, p. 10; and "Against Great-Russian Chauvinism," in Robert Tucker, ed., *The Lenin Anthology* (New York: W. W. Norton, 1975), pp. 659–660.

6. Lenin, "National Programme," p. 10; and "Against Great-Russian Chauvinism," pp. 659–660.

7. Tucker, *Lenin Anthology*, p. 198. Lenin repeatedly cites this phrase as the theoretical justification for his national program.

8. Lenin, "The Right of Nations to Self-Determination," and "On the National Pride of the Great Russians," in *Selected Writings*, pp. 45–109; and "Against Great-Russian Chauvinism," pp. 659–660.

9. Lenin, "Critical Remarks," pp. 32–36.

10. Robert Kaiser, *The Geography of Nationalism in Russia and the USSR* (Princeton, NJ: Princeton University Press, 1994), ch. 3.

11. Lenin, "Critical Remarks," p. 42.

12. Lenin, "Critical Remarks." See also Joseph Stalin, "Marxism and the National Question," in Joseph Stalin, *Marxism and the National and Colonial Questions* (New York: International Publishers, 1934), pp. 3–61. This tract—Stalin's first statement regarding the national question—was written at Lenin's behest as a response to Austrian Marxists. Dissatisfied with Stalin's product, Lenin wrote and published his "Critical Remarks" at the end of 1913 to set the record straight. Note: all subsequent references to Stalin are taken from this edition of his works.

13. Lenin, "Critical Remarks," p. 38. See also Connor, *The National Question in Marxist-Leninist Theory*, pp. 217–222; and Gregory Gleason, *Federalism and Nationalism* (Boulder: Westview Press, 1990), pp. 19–36.

14. Robert Kaiser, "Nationalism: The Challenge to Soviet Federalism," in Michael Bradshaw, ed., *The Soviet Union: A New Regional Geography?* (London: Belhaven, 1991), pp. 39–65. See also Richard Pipes, *The Formation of the Soviet Union*, rev. ed. (New York: Atheneum, 1968), and Connor, *The National Question in Marxist-Leninist Theory*.

15. Stalin, "Marxism and the National Question," pp. 56–61.

16. Stalin, "Theses on the Immediate Tasks of the Party in Connection with the National Problem (1921)," in *Marxism and the National and Colonial Questions*, pp. 93–96.

17. Stalin, "Report on National Factors in Party and State Development," in *Marxism and the National and Colonial Questions*, p. 149.

18. Stalin, "Theses on National Factors in Party and State Development (1923)," in *Marxism and the National and Colonial Questions*, p. 143.

19. Stalin, "Theses on National Factors," p. 143.

20. Stalin, "Theses on the Immediate Tasks," pp. 94–95.

21. Stalin, "Theses on National Factors," p. 155–168.

22. Stalin, "Deviations on the National Question (1930)," in *Marxism and the National and Colonial Questions*, pp. 257–262.

23. Already in 1925 Stalin complained of an effort in Ukraine to use *korenizatsiya* to force Russians to learn the Ukrainian language. Stalin, "Extract From a Letter to Comrade Kaganovich and Other Members of the Central Committee of the Communist Party of the Ukraine," in *Marxism and the National and Colonial Questions*, pp. 229–230.

24. Stalin, "Deviations Toward Nationalism," in *Marxism and the National and Colonial Questions*, pp. 267–268.

25. Lowell Tillett, *The Great Friendship: Soviet Historians on the Non-Russian Nationalities* (Chapel Hill, NC: University of North Carolina Press, 1969), pp. 86–90.

26. Leonid Brezhnev, speech before the Twenty-fourth Party Congress, 1971, as quoted in Connor, *The National Question in Marxist-Leninist Theory*, p. 489.

27. Connor, *The National Question in Marxist-Leninist Theory*, p. 489; Yaroslav Bilinsky, "Nationality Policy in Gorbachev's First Year," *Orbis* Vol. 30, No. 2 (Summer 1986):331–342.

28. Kaiser, *Geography of Nationalism*.

29. "Programma Kommunisticheskoy Partii Sovetskogo Soyuza (1961)," *Kommunist* No. 16 (1961): 84.

30. Walker Connor, *The National Question in Marxist-Leninist Theory*, p. 478.

31. Gertrude Schroeder, "Nationalities and the Soviet Economy," in Lubomyr Hajda and Mark Beissinger, eds., *The Nationalities Factor in Soviet Politics and Society* (Boulder: Westview Press, 1990), p. 43.

32. Connor, *The National Question in Marxist-Leninist Theory*, p. 478.

33. See *Programma Kommunisticheskoy Partii Sovetskogo Soyuza Prinyata XXVII S'ezdom KPSS*, novaya redaktsiya (Moskva: Politizdat, 1986), pp. 43–45.

34. Yulian Bromley, "Etnograficheskoye izucheniye sovremennykh natsional'nykh protsessov v SSSR," *Sovetskaya etnografiya* No. 2 (1983): 9.

35. Mikhael Gorbachev, *O natsional'noy politike v sovremennykh usloviyakh. Doklad i zaklyuchitel'noye slovo no Plenume TsK KPSS 19, 20 Sentyabrya 1989 goda* (Moskva: Politizdat, 1989), p. 13.

36. Mikhael Gorbachev, *O natsional'noy politike*, p. 13.

37. For a more complete examination of this issue, see Kaiser, *Geography of Nationalism*, and Kaiser, "Nationalism: The Challenge to Soviet Federalism." For an earlier work devoted to the "enduring national problem" faced by the USSR, see Connor, *The National Question in Marxist-Leninist Theory*.

38. For this last measure, western analysts frequently argued that the data pointed to russification of the non-Russian population, not sovietization.

39. Schroeder, "Nationalities and the Soviet Economy;" Ronald Liebowitz, "Spatial Inequality under Gorbachev," in Bradshaw, ed., *The Soviet Union*, pp. 15–37.

40. Robert Kaiser, "Social Mobilization in Soviet Central Asia," in Robert Lewis, ed., *Geographic Perspectives on Soviet Central Asia* (London: Routledge, 1992), pp. 251–278.

41. See, *RUKH Program and Charter* (Ellicott City, MD: Smoloskyp Publishers, 1989). On the assimilation of Ukrainians living outside Ukraine during the interwar period, see Robert Lewis et al., *Nationality and Population Change in Russia and the USSR* (New York: Praeger, 1976), pp. 218–220. On excess mortality in Ukraine during the 1930s, see Stephen Wheatcroft, "More Light on the Scale of Repression and Excess Mortality in the Soviet Union in the 1930s," *Soviet Studies*, Vol. 42, No. 3 (1990):355–367.

42. Mikhael Guboglo, "O vliyanii rasseleniya na yazykovyye protsessy," *Sovetskaya etnografiya* No. 5 (1969):17.

43. Ralph Clem, "The Ethnic Dimension, Part II," in Jerry Pankhurst and Michael Sacks, eds., *Contemporary Soviet Society* (New York: Praeger, 1980), p. 40.

44. Tsentral'noye statisticheskoye upravleniye pri Sovete Ministrov SSSR (TsSU SSSR), *Itogi vsesoyuznoy perepisi naseleniya 1959 goda* (Moskva: Gosstatizdat, 1962), Svodnyy tom, p. 184; Gosudarstvennyy komitet SSSR po statistike (Goskomstat SSSR), *Itogi vsesoyuznoy perepisi naseleniya 1979 goda* (Moskva: Goskomstat SSSR, 1989), Vol. 4, Part I, Book 1, p. 5; Statisticheskiy komitet sodruzhestva nezavisimykh gosudarstv (Statkom SNG), *Itogi vsesoyuznoy perepisi naseleniya 1989 goda* (Minneapolis: East View Publications, 1992), Vol. 7, Part I, p. 10.

45. John Dunlop, *The Faces of Contemporary Russian Nationalism* (Princeton, NJ: Princeton University Press, 1983), pp. 154–156.

46. Kaiser, *Geography of Nationalism*, p. 272.

47. Kaiser, *Geography of Nationalism*, pp. 295–317.

48. Kaiser, *Geography of Nationalism*, pp. 317–321.

Part II

The Newly Independent States

Chapter 5

The Baltics

Estonia, Latvia, and Lithuania were incorporated into the Soviet Union in 1940 as the result of the Molotov-Ribbentrop Pact that launched World War II and led to a temporary partition of Europe between Hitler's Germany and Stalin's USSR. The three Baltic countries had been part of the Russian Empire prior to World War I and each gained independence after the war and maintained it during the interwar period. This twenty-year period of independence distinguishes the Baltics from the other post-Soviet states. While Ukraine, Moldova, and the Transcaucasian republics had moments of independence before Soviet incorporation which today feed their nationalist reconstruction of history, they never experienced the nation- and state-building processes that took place in the Baltics from 1920–1940. The Baltic states cultivated the memory of their interwar statehood while under Soviet rule and used Gorbachev's *glasnost'* and *perestroyka* to reestablish independence.

The Baltic states share many historical experiences. Their early development was influenced by external elites: Polish in Lithuania and German in Latvia and Estonia. By the mid-nineteenth century each had developed a nationalized elite which spread the national idea to the masses. With post–World War I independence, each developed comparatively prosperous economic systems. The Molotov-Ribbentrop Pact resulted in each of the state's being brought into the Soviet Union as union republics for what became a half century of Soviet rule (1940–1991).

Their independence movements also share many attributes. The Baltic republics led the anti-Moscow and antiunion struggle of the late 1980s and achieved independence after the 1991 coup, some months ahead of the other republics. Unlike the other newly independent states, they have no formal links with the Commonwealth of Independent States (CIS) today—nor have they considered this possibility. They also share the common challenge of developing stable political and economic systems and untying their economies from Russia.

One important factor distinguishes the Baltic states from the other new states formed after Soviet dissolution. Today's Estonia, Latvia, and Lithuania consider themselves to be the legal successors of the states created in the aftermath

The Baltics: Areas Of Russian Concentration

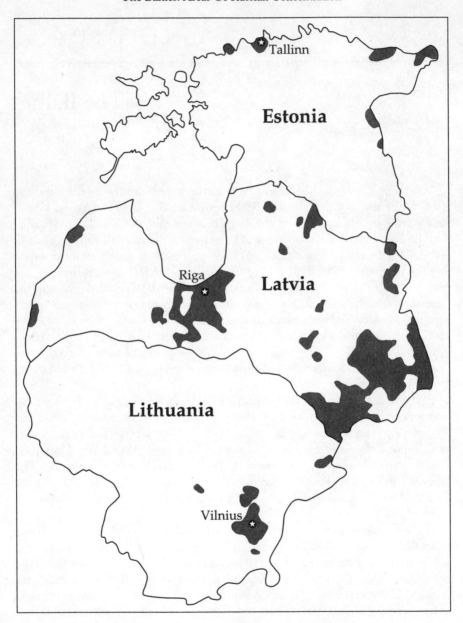

BALTICS

	Lithuania	Latvia	Estonia
Territorial Size (km2)	65,200	64,600	45,200
Population Size (1993)	3,730,000	2,566,000	1,517,000
Percent Titular (1/1/94)	81	54	64
Percent Russian (1/1/94)	9	33	29
Urban Population (1993)	2,541,000	1,776,000	1,068,000
Percent Titular (1989)	76.4	44.0	51.2
Percent Russian (1989)	12.4	40.7	39.0
Size of Capital City (1/1/91)	576,747[a]	910,200	481,500
Percent Titular (1989)	50.5	36.5	47.4
Percent Russian (1989)	20.2	47.3	41.2
Natural Increase (/1000, 1989)	4.8	2.4	3.7
Titular NI (1989)	5.1	1.6	2.7
Russian NI (1989)	3.2	2.7	5.1
Net Migration To (2)/From (1) Russia (1989–93)			
Total	−39,248	−59,130	−42,604
Titular	3,007	1,040	328
Russian	−35,025	−50,086	−36,627
Life Expectancy (1989)	Men: 67.1 Women: 76.4	Men: 65.8 Women: 75.2	Men: 66.2 Women: 74.9
Titular e^0 (1989)	Men: 67.6 Women: 76.8	Men: 66.0 Women: 75.6	Men: 66.1 Women: 75.2
Russian e^0 (1989)	Men: 66.5 Women: 74.7	Men: 65.3 Women: 74.4	Men: 65.9 Women: 74.3
Employment[b] (1993)	84.3	91.0[c]	92.8[d]
Trade (Export/Import Ratio, 1993)			
Intra-NIS Trade[e]	0.85	0.88	1.41
Extra-NIS Trade[f]	1.43	1.36	0.75

Notes: [a] Population total for Vilnius is for 1989. [b]Employment given as a percent of the working-age population. [c]Latvian employment is for 1992. [d]Estonian employment is for 1991. [e]Intra-NIS ratios based on figures provided in the national currencies. [f]Extra-NIS ratios based on figures provided in US dollars.

Sources: Goskomstat SSSR, *Chislennost' naseleniya soyuznykh respublik po gorodskim pose-leniyam i rayonam na 1 yanvarya 1991 g.* (Moskva: 1991); Aksel Kirch, Marika Kirch and Tarmo Tuisk, *The Non-Estonian Population Today and Tomorrow* (Tallinn: Estonian Academy of Sciences, December 1992); Goskomstat Rossiyskoy Federatsii, *Chislennost' i sotsial'no-demograficheskiye kharakteristiki russkogo naseleniya v respublikakh byvshego SSSR* (Moskva: 1994); Statkom SNG, *Itogi vsesoyuznoy perepisi naseleniya 1989 godo* (Minneapolis, MN: East View, 1992), Vol. 7, Part 2; Mikhael Guboglo, "Demography and Language in the Capitals of the Union Republics," *Journal of Soviet Nationalities* Vol. 1, No. 4 (Winter 1990–1991): 14–19; The World Bank, *Statistical Handbook 1994: States of the Former USSR* (Washington, DC: World Bank Studies of Economies in Transformation No. 14, 1994).

of World War I. As such, they are *restored* states, not *new* states.[1] This legal connection to the interwar states provides the starting point for the reestablishment of their constitutions and laws.[2] Yet the 1991 republics differ dramatically from the interwar states: Latvia and Estonia, and Lithuania to a lesser extent, are now multinational polities with large proportions of Russians and other Slavs. Such similarities provide sufficient reason to treat the Baltics together, but should not obscure their differences. Geography, history, and circumstance result in each of the state's confronting similar challenges; but an examination of their policies since independence demonstrates that each is charting an independent political and economic course.

Nationalization in the 1800s, reenforced by a substantial period of independence in modern times, furnishes the background for today's Baltic politics. The demographic and cultural russification that followed the Soviet takeover provides the most troublesome contemporary issue. Baltic political, economic, and administrative officials were replaced by Russians. Thousands of indigenous elites were exiled or killed. The Nazi occupation caused additional casualties and triggered emigration to the West. When the Soviets regained control, the Russian political and economic influx continued. Political reliability became the most significant test for personnel recruitment during the 1940s and early 1950s (the late Stalin period). This early Soviet period was more important for the nature of the positions that Russians occupied than for the number of Russians entering the region.

The economic reconstruction and industrial expansion of the 1960s and 1970s then resulted in mass migrations of Russians and other Slavs. Because of their developed economies and their European character, the Baltic states became desirable destinations for Russians wishing to improve their living conditions. Concomitantly, their western location and perceived political unreliability resulted in their becoming home to thousands of Soviet troops and their dependents, many of whom remained after retirement from the military. Particularly in Latvia and Estonia, demographic russification was also facilitated by the small size of the indigenous nations and by the low indigenous birthrates.

Fifty years of Soviet control thus resulted in dramatic changes in the Baltic populations. The rural areas today remain populated almost exclusively by the titular nations; Russians and other immigrants are clustered in the cities. The capitals and larger urban areas lost their indigenous character, and the Balts feared that continuing nonindigenous immigration would further submerge their national cultures. The Russian migrants had little sense that they were living in a foreign land and little desire to acculturate; rather, Russians expected indigenes to behave as if they were in a Russian environment. Needless to say, this Russian attitude caused resentment on the part of the Balts, who were particularly sensitive because of their small populations and perceived cultural vulnerability. This demographic legacy has been the principal political issue—played out over citizenship and language—in both Estonia and Latvia. The relatively smaller Russian presence in Lithuania has resulted in less controversy.

Estonia

Population

During interwar independence, Estonians comprised just under 90 percent of their republic's population. War losses, border adjustments, and emigration resulted in an even greater concentration of Estonians by 1945, when only 23,000 Russians lived in Estonia.[3] At the time of independence in 1991 the Russian population had grown to 475,000, and the total Slavic population to 551,000 (35 percent of the population). The indigenous population had grown modestly from 831,000 (1945) to 893,000 (1959) to 965,000 (1992).[4] Since then both the Slavic and the total population have declined somewhat as a result of emigration (80,000) and more deaths than births. Estonians today comprise about 64 percent and Russians 29 percent of the population.[5]

Migration to Estonia declined in the late 1980s, in part because of Soviet economic stagnation and in part because of increasingly hostile interactions between Russians and Estonians. This decline in migration was occurring throughout the USSR largely as a result of the economic downturn. Titular peoples in some republics were increasing their proportions of their republics' population because of both a decline in migration and a high indigenous birthrate. Although Estonia experienced a decline in migration, it did not experience much indigenous growth because Estonians typically have had one of the Soviet Union's lowest birthrates.

Some Russian emigration occurred as the military and its support units withdrew from Estonia. In the mid-1980s as many as 125,000 Soviet troops with 25,000 dependents were in Estonia.[6] Troops were not counted in the population figures, but some dependents and civilian support personnel were included. With the final departure of Russian troops on August 31, 1994, some of these individuals have also departed. Nonetheless, the Estonian proportion of the population has only increased slightly. The migration flow has reversed, but Estonia's relatively high standard of living, its economic success compared to other successor states, and the absence of outright conflict work against the development of a large enough outflow of Russians to affect the population balance.

Immigrants are typically more transient than longtime residents; new arrivals often return home or decide to move on to another opportunity.[7] Even during the period with the fastest growth of the Russian population, many Russians immigrated to Estonia, but almost as many Russians left.[8] Today, Russian immigration has been reduced almost to zero, while the outflow of earlier migrants continues relatively normally. Thus, the net direction of the flow has reversed, but mostly from the reduction of immigration rather than from changes in the behavior of Russians already in Estonia. In the absence of economic collapse or inter-national violence, the flow of Russians leaving Estonia will also decline, because the Russians remaining in Estonia will have had more time to establish homes, families, and careers. With each passing year they become less likely to emigrate. Of today's Russian population in Estonia, 78 percent have lived in Estonia 21 or more years, 15 percent from 11–20 years, and only 7 percent for 10 or fewer years.[9] With the reduction in immigration, the proportion of these Russians who know no other home will grow rapidly.

The Question of Citizenship

The demographic russification of Estonia, coupled with the growing majority of Russians who know no home but Estonia, creates a troublesome citizenship question for both Estonians and Russians. Like their Latvian and Lithuanian neighbors, Estonians have constructed their approach to citizenship on the concept of a restored state. They contend that Russians and others who migrated to Estonia as a consequence of an illegal occupation have no inherent political rights. With the legal basis of the state traced to the interwar republic, only citizens of that entity and their descendants can determine the rules by which other individuals might be included in today's body politic. If the fifty-year occupation was illegal, how can the occupiers claim to have political rights in the restored state?

Estonian arguments are emotional as well as legal. The occupation resulted in mass purges, killings, and terror. Many non-Estonians came to administer the country; others came with the military or security forces as occupiers.[10] Why should these oppressors have political rights equal to the oppressed? And why should the West be concerned with the political rights of those who took part in the occupations? Estonian (and Latvian) nationalists point out that western powers did not have the same concern for the political rights of colonists during the decolonization period who were forced out of countries that they occupied (e.g., the French forced from Algeria).

But Russians now living in Estonia can also construct a powerful argument. The majority came as economic migrants to better their own lives, not as military, police, or administrative officials. When they immigrated, Estonia was an integral part of the Soviet Union: the migrants had no comprehension that they were moving to another country. They never envisaged waking up one morning (as they did in August 1991) and finding themselves living "abroad." In addition, most of today's non-Estonians were either born in Estonia or have lived there for decades. How can they not be citizens if they were born or had spent their entire adult lives in Estonia?

The demographic russification that took place during Soviet rule makes this issue crucial. Estonians, with a titular population just under one million, argue that their country's character was changed by the migration of a half million non-Estonians. They contend that a country with over a 90 percent titular population (1945) is fundamentally different from one with only 64 percent titular today, in which the capital itself is almost half Russian (Tallinn has a population of 442,000, of whom 217,300 are Estonian and 180,000 Russian).[11]

Most non-Estonians want to continue living in Estonia, not only because Estonia has a high standard of living, but because they have no other home. Many even supported Estonian independence in the precoup years.[12] This setting frames the citizenship dilemma that has consequences for both Estonians and

Russians; it also helps determine whether the Estonian approach to the Russian minority will lead to containment of ethnic conflict and development of democratic institutions.

The citizenship question was settled, at least legally, in 1993 after two years of difficult debate. The outcome was closer to the Estonian-nationalist than to the Russian position, but the extreme nationalist stance was moderated to bring citizenship within reach of most Soviet-era immigrants. The citizenship debate illustrates Estonia's nature as a nationalizing state, so the positions are described in some detail below. Because the Latvian debate, though more prolonged and difficult, was essentially similar, we will not restate the logic of the arguments in the discussion of the Latvian case that follows.

On March 30, 1990, the Popular Front–led Estonian Supreme Soviet declared that Estonia would begin its transition to independence, following procedures outlined by Gorbachev in response to Lithuania's unexpected declaration of independence.[13] The Popular Front had originated as a reform movement within the Estonian Communist Party when few believed that complete independence could be achieved. At first, Popular Front leaders hoped that *perestroyka* and *glasnost'* would allow decentralization and a less unitary, more confederal Soviet Union. As Popular Fronts in other republics escalated their demands for greater economic and political independence from Moscow, the notion of republican citizenship began to take on new meaning. The Estonian Popular Front at first articulated an inclusive approach to citizenship, often called the "zero option." The zero option would have established naturalization procedures for anyone migrating after March 30, 1990, but would have qualified all for citizenship who were resident in Estonia before that date.[14] The primary goal was to reduce future migration.

The nationalist and anti-Russian Congress of Estonia, which developed from informal Estonian Citizens' Committees formed early in 1989 to register citizens of the interwar republic and their descendants, championed a restrictive citizenship. As the advocate for genuine independence, the Congress argued that since the Soviet annexation had been illegal, the legal continuity of the state was linked to the independent interwar republic. Thus, only the citizens of the interwar republic or their offspring could automatically be considered citizens of Estonia with the right to determine legal and constitutional changes. Those who had migrated after 1940 could not be citizens without naturalization. The Congress stressed that its position was neither discriminatory nor racist; interwar citizens and their descendants continued to be legal citizens regardless of their national identity (including about 100,000 non-Estonians[15]). Nonetheless, almost one-third of the people in Estonia would be disenfranchised through this prescription of legal continuity.[16]

The conflict between the Congress of Estonia and the Popular Front reflected a constitutional dilemma: the Estonian Popular Front, like its counterparts in other republics, developed within the Estonian Supreme Soviet. In the 1990 election, the first in which opposition and reform candidates were allowed to challenge Party-backed candidates, the Popular Front had gained a majority of reformist deputies. Although voting for independence in 1991, the Supreme Soviet nonetheless was considered illegitimate by many Estonians because it was a Soviet institution with no link to the interwar republic. Thus, the Supreme Soviet could not "legitimately" approve either citizenship legislation or a new constitution.

The Congress argued that only interwar citizens and their descendants could vote on the new constitution, which would in turn determine standards for naturalization of noncitizens. The Estonian Popular Front, along with the former communists, advocated a more liberal position on who should vote on the new constitution. While conceding that migrants who came after 1940 could become citizens only through naturalization, the Popular Front contended that the adoption of a new constitution required broad participation to ensure its legitimacy:[17] those intending to become citizens should vote to cement their loyalty. The conservative Congress prevailed. Only citizens of the interwar republic and their descendants were allowed to vote, thus excluding 500,000 of the 600,000 non-Estonians from participation. The constitution was approved by 92 percent of the "historic citizens" on June 28, 1992.[18]

By limiting the electorate to historic citizens, the titular nationalists successfully asserted Estonian hegemony in the nation-state that they were creating. This move ensured that all 101 members of the newly elected *Riigikogu* (Popular Assembly), the successor to the Supreme Soviet, were Estonians.[19] In contrast, 20 percent of Supreme Soviet members had been Russian-speakers. During its initial term, this entirely Estonian parliament has been able to set the direction of Estonia's political development.

With the passage of the constitution and the election of the first post-Soviet parliament, deputies turned to the citizenship law. The Popular Front's first draft had maintained the legal distinction between historic and naturalized citizens: all historic citizens and their descendants were citizens; others (who had permanent residency in Estonia on March 30, 1990, when Estonia declared its intention to seek full independence) could be naturalized if they wished. Immigrants after that date would face a residency requirement, a language test, and a loyalty oath.[20]

The opposition to this draft made clear the depth of the nationalist feeling:

> The main arguments against the initial draft revolved around the very factor that had fueled Estonians' anxiety for years: that the massive postwar immigration would ultimately result in their cultural annihilation . . . aggravated by their own low birth rate. In order to preserve the Estonian culture, language, and way of life, the opponents of the draft law argued, all those who sought naturalization should have lived in Estonia for ten years and must demonstrate knowledge of the language.[21]

After heated debate, the two sides compromised. The newly elected *Riigikogu* passed a law containing a three-year residency and language requirement for naturalization, modeled on the naturalization law of the interwar republic. After passage of the law, the government applied a visa regime to all crossing points with Russia and established a low annual immigration quota.

The three-year residency was modest. The law nonetheless contained provisions that, together with the language requirement, initially limited the number and political power of naturalized citizens. First, the law required would-be citizens to demonstrate two years' residence in Estonia after March 30, 1990. They then must wait an additional year for citizenship to be granted.[22] In addition, as a direct concession to the Congress of Estonia, citizenship was barred for those who served in foreign military or intelligence services, criminals, and the jobless. Naturalized citizens were required to surrender other citizenship. Vello Pettai notes:

> (I)t was now the prerogative of the restored legal authorities ... to legalize [noncitizen] presence as they deemed fit. *Naturalized citizenship* for the Soviet-era immigrants under terms determined by the restored state authorities would be the answer. ... If the naturalization terms were set high, leading to an effective barrier to noncitizen (and hence mostly Russian) participation in political life, then ethnic nationalism would clearly benefit.[23]

The local election law, passed on May 19, 1993, was more inclusive, permitting permanent residents and citizens of other countries (who had lived in Estonia for five years) to vote. Only citizens, however, could hold office. This measure was particularly important for the Russian majority, numbering almost 150,000, in Estonia's northeast. Without this concession, few in Narva, Kohtla-Jarve, and Sillamae would have been eligible to vote for municipal officials.[24] Under a special provision of the law bestowing citizenship for special service to the state, the *Riigikogu* granted citizenship to some Russians, thereby allowing them to run for office during the October 1993 local elections. Arguing also that approximately 30,000 noncitizens had registered with the Congress of Estonia prior to independence, thereby risking their futures and demonstrating their commitment to an independent and non-Soviet Estonia, parliament waived the waiting period and language exam for this group and thus strengthened Estonia's public case that its citizenship policies were nondiscriminatory.[25]

The first post-Soviet municipal elections demonstrated the Russians' political muscle at the local level, as well as the extent to which their exclusion from parliamentary and presidential politics fostered titular hegemony. Almost 20 percent of registered voters were noncitizens. The conservative parliamentary parties did poorly in local elections. In Tallinn, Russian-backed candidates won 31 of 64 seats in the local council; in the northeast, of course, Russian support was required to win any seats. However, moderate Russian candidates tended to be most successful. According to Toivo Raun, the success of these moderate Russians indicates that a portion of the Russian population is willing to work within the Estonian political system.[26]

In contrast, the Estonian-controlled parliament has not been particularly moderate, demonstrated by the controversy over the initial version of an aliens' law passed in 1993.[27] Meant to clarify the status of noncitizens, this law originally required noncitizens to apply for permission to live in Estonia, with reapplication every five years. The proposed procedure rejected any residence permits issued during the Soviet period. Those who failed to apply or those rejected were subject to deportation. Needless to say, retired military or security personnel were ineligible for residence permits. This proposal also had a second purpose: to deal with the estimated 50,000 individuals living in Tallinn who were neither citizens nor holders of the required Soviet residence permit *(propiska)*. These unofficial migrants came to Estonia because of its standard of living and existed outside the official economy. With registration required to obtain work permits and housing, the government would be able to deal more effectively with this population.[28]

Many Russians characterized this attempt to codify the status of noncitizens as "ethnic cleansing." Russians in northeastern cities threatened to secede. One western diplomat called the passage of the law "the greatest crisis of the post-Soviet era in the Baltic states."[29] President Meri, stung by reaction from western democracies, asked the Commission for Security and Cooperation in Europe (CSCE) and the Council of Europe to review the law. Both bodies, as well as close ally Sweden, asked Meri to return the law to the *Riigikogu* for modification.[30] Meri did so, and parliament modified the law to guarantee that noncitizens resident before July 1, 1990, would be granted residency permits. Noncitizens must apply for temporary residence permits by July 1995, and certify that they have a job, housing, and local registration. Military and security personnel are subject to special regulations.[31] While the final law was not as severe as the initial version, it was one more victory for nationalists attempting to restructure the power balance.

Language

As noted in Chapter 4, russification during the Soviet era was most evident in regard to language. Many non-Russians believed that the very existence of their languages were threatened by the dominant position of Russian throughout the USSR.

> Under the guise of internationalization, Russian became the only language for business . . . and for communication among government organs, enterprises, and institutions. . . . (T)he spread of the Russian language came to be considered the equivalent of internationalism, and the propagation of the national language—a manifestation of nationalism. . . . (T)he erosion of national languages reached levels that threatened their existence.[32]

In school or the workplace, Estonians were forced to adapt to the migrants, rather than vice versa. Communication between Estonians and Russians was conducted in Russian. Russians lived together, worked together, and assumed that Estonians would accommodate their mono-lingualism.[33] While most Estonians acquired enough Russian to function in the Soviet society, they, more than most of the titular nations, resisted linguistic russification (Tables 4.3 and 4.4). Thus, language policy has been a primary area of inter-national conflict after the adoption of the state language law in 1989.[34]

Language laws show the attempts of the titular governments to remove Russian from its former hegemonic place and to replace it with the titular languages. The Estonian language requirement for both citizenship and employment is indeed a difficult hurdle. Estonian is a Finno-Ugric language, unrelated to Russian and more difficult for Russians to master than Slavic, Germanic, or Romance languages. Russians thus argue that the language law is discriminatory and intended to exclude them from citizenship.

An operational level of language competence for citizenship has been defined as the ability to use approximately 1500 words for everyday conversation. Examinees must have the ability to understand news and information items, converse about their family, read short texts, fill out a biographical questionnaire, and know some Estonian history and geography.[35] Because of the difficulty of the language, even this level requires an important commitment by those desiring citizenship. According to the 1989 census, only 13.7 percent of the Russians in Estonia were fluent in Estonian.[36] In Tallinn, just 15 percent of the almost 200,000 Russians claimed to speak Estonian.[37] By 1993, 38 percent of Russian respondents to a survey claimed to be able to carry on a conversation in Estonian.[38] Nonetheless, most Russians still have a long way to go to reach the required competence for citizenship, even though it is set at a level less than fluency.

To date, many Russians have spent more energy complaining about this requirement than trying to master Estonian. Yet several Estonians commented during Summer 1993 that younger people now attempt to greet people and ask for items in stores in Estonian rather than Russian. These Estonians had little concern with the Russians' linguistic competence; their attempt to use Estonian, not their ability, is what mattered. By using even imperfect Estonian, the Russians acknowledged that they were living in Estonia and not Russia. To most Estonians, that acknowledgement was the critical factor.[39]

While Estonian was taught in Russian-language schools during the Soviet period, it was not taken seriously by either students or teachers. Circumstances have now changed: beginning in 1995, students attending non-Estonian-language secondary schools must pass an Estonian-language test to graduate. This graduation exam will also satisfy the language requirement for citizenship. In Narva, the curriculum has been extended from ten to eleven years to accommodate additional language instruction.

According to the rector of the Tallinn Technological University, Olav Aarna, newly enrolling Russian students are showing significant improvement in their Estonian ability. Unlike earlier times when Russian students often claimed to be "proud" that they knew not one word of Estonian, they now make an effort not only to use what they know but to learn more. During the 1993–1994 and 1994–1995 academic years, Aarna reports that all courses at the technical university will be available in both languages. Later, many courses will be taught in one language—the language most comfortable for the instructor—so all students must be prepared to study in either language.[40]

Estonian officials argue that the alien and language laws, rather than being anti-Russian, have created the motivation for many Russians to make the decision to acculturate:

> "These laws have created a basis to overcome the great-nation psychology under which the Estonian language was considered too small to bother to learn it," (said Alar Jaanis, head of the remigration section of the Estonian Migration Board). Mr. Jaanus added that among the younger generation of non-Estonians, the effect of the new legislation can already be seen. "There's growing interest in learning the language."[41]

The 1989 state language law (unconnected to the language requirement for citizenship) required that governmental officials and persons serving the public speak Estonian. Graduated requirements were outlined depending on the nature of one's work. Enterprises and offices can request yearlong (and renewable) extensions for key personnel. This law to date has caused little controversy and has not resulted in replacement of non-Estonian personnel.

Ending Russian television broadcasts in Estonia in Spring 1994 has been a more controversial step. The Russian television service, Ostankino, failed to pay Estonian Television for broadcasting its signal. The cancellation of Russian-language television can be viewed as one more step in the nationalizing agenda because it exposes Russian speakers to more Estonian language, and no doubt provides another incentive to learn the language.

By making knowledge of the Estonian language the principal impediment to citizenship for Russians, Estonian nationalists have emphasized the importance of their nation's language as an instrument of Estonian hegemony. In political life, in the workplaces, and in the schools, Russian has lost status—both as the language of inter-national communication and as the foreign language studied by young Estonians. Young Russians living in Estonia, forced to pass a language exam for school graduation as well as for citizenship, seem willing to adapt to their new situation. The older generations, however, are both slower and less willing to accommodate the new stratification system with which they are confronted.

The Military Legacy

The final issue to be examined is linked to the withdrawal of former Soviet (now Russian) troops, dependents, and their civilian support from Estonia. Few have argued that active troops on foreign territory had any political rights. Our analysis of minority Russians thus considers military retirees, their dependents, and others who supported the military.

Soviet forces were stationed in the Baltics under the command of the North West Group of Forces. These troops defended the Soviet Union from the perceived NATO threat and assured Moscow's control of three republics whose loyalty, from the Soviet perspective, was questionable. Over the years of Soviet control, millions of individuals at one time or another served in the Baltic forces. Additional thousands of civilians worked at military factories and port facilities closed to Estonians.

The absolute number of Russians who served in Estonia is important because of the standard of living that they encountered. Housing was better; food and consumer goods were more plentiful; life was more European. Since military retirees were free to locate anywhere in the Union except Moscow and Leningrad (now St. Petersburg), many chose to retire to the Baltics or to other hospitable places (in terms of climate or standard of living) such as Crimea and Moldova.

Today's nationalist regimes distinguish between these migrants and those who came to better their lives and the lives of their families. Thus, in the popular rhetoric, the military retirees fall into the category of "occupiers" and "colonials" who came to impose unwelcome political and economic systems. Rights for those with military or security backgrounds are thus perceived differently from rights for economic migrants.

Rights for military retirees became linked to the withdrawal of remaining troops from Estonia and Latvia. The Russian side sought "social guarantees," including residence permits and pensions, for military retirees and dependents remaining in Estonia.[42] Estonia, supported by most Western powers and international organizations, wanted the issues separated, arguing that the "illegal" occupation was the issue: troops carrying out an illegal occupation had no right to remain. Estonia wanted Russian servicemen who retired since independence (with families estimated at 35,000 people) to leave the country, and those who retired before that time (with families estimated at 44,000) to pledge that they no longer worked for Russia.[43] Estonia contended that these individuals were not harmless pensioners: 6000 were under sixty years of age, 1000 were under fifty, and 360 were younger than 45. In addition, as many as 5000 not eligible for pensions had left the military and remained in Estonia.[44] This issue went beyond citizenship: what social and legal rights did they have in Estonia? Could they own property? Who would pay their pensions?

In order to achieve the final withdrawal on August 31, 1994, Estonia compromised by agreeing to consider permanent residency for the retirees on a case-by-case basis (with the assumption that most would be permitted to remain in Estonia). Russia, of course, was using the troops to bargain for the rights of all Russian noncitizens and show its muscle in Estonian domestic politics.

The issue of thousands of retired military (and particularly their families) is indeed troublesome. The Russian side wanted Estonia to make concessions before Russia agreed to a final troop withdrawal. Since most of the retirees and families would not return to Russia under any scenario, what will be their place in Estonian society? If they are to remain in Estonia, can they (or at least their children) be brought into the body politic to play a constructive role in building the new state? But to nationalists intent on Estonian hegemony, incorporating the

Russian minority—particularly that portion connected to the Soviet and Russian military—is a most undesirable outcome.

Public Opinion

In spite of these divisive issues, relations between the titular and the Russian population in Estonia have improved considerably since the late 1980s. In February 1993, Aksel and Marika Kirch found that 88 percent of Estonians considered inter-national relations to be normal or good, compared to 45 percent five years earlier. Non-Estonians (mainly Russians) agreed, with 89 percent believing that relations between the groups were normal or good, compared to 60 percent in 1988. In April 1992, 30 percent of the Russians said that relations with Estonians were bad. By February 1993, this figure had fallen to 17 percent.[45]

Rose and Maley (1993) found that 49 percent of Estonians describe Estonian/Russian relations to be good (and 1 percent very good), and 31 percent not very good (and 2 percent bad); Russians in Estonia are more favorable, with 71 percent describing relations as good and 3 percent very good, and only 13 percent saying not very good and 1 percent bad. On a related question, only 26 percent of Estonia's Russians agreed and 5 percent strongly agreed that "Noncitizens and minority nationalities are being badly treated here." Of those surveyed, 46 percent disagreed and 12 percent strongly disagreed with that characterization.[46]

Aksel Kirch argues that Russian self-identification is changing: "Russians identify more with the Estonians than they do with the Russians in Russia. They don't want to think and live like Russians in Russia." Kirch contrasts Russians in the northeastern cities with those in Tallinn. Because Russians in the northeast face fewer daily challenges to their position and way of life, they perceive international relations more favorably than do Russians in Tallinn, who must interact daily with increasingly assertive Estonians. Narva Russians, in particular, live in what Kirch calls an "extraterritorial" city, viewing the Narva River as a psychological and geographical border between East and West. They identify with neither Russia nor Estonia but consider themselves "western."[47] Kirch views discontent in the northeast as being fomented by the old local leadership which, since the 1993 constitutional and parliamentary elections, has lost its Soviet-era power and status along with its citizenship. The absence of major protest in Narva over the disenfranchisement of 90 percent of the population for the 1993 elections and the success of Russians in local elections show that Russian anxieties may well lessen with economic and political progress.[48]

The director of the Institute of Philosophy, Sociology and Law, Priit Jarve, agrees with this optimistic analysis:

> Russians are mostly loyal to the new Estonian state. Two years ago they were Moscow-oriented; now they can see with their own eyes that life is better here than in Russia. This is especially true in Narva. Most came to Estonia for economic opportunity. Economic progress is important for their loyalty. Most who

want to return to Russia have already done so. Besides, Russia doesn't want them to come back; what would they do there?[49]

An increasing proportion of non-Estonians have concluded that Estonian citizenship is desirable.[50] A June 1993, poll indicated that 56 percent of non-Estonians (then without citizenship) would prefer to become Estonian citizens.[51] An April 1992 survey suggested that half of non-Estonian respondents desired full Estonian citizenship. These figures were approximately double that found by Kirch in September 1990.[52] Of the others, 28 percent indicated a desire for Russian, Ukrainian, or Belarusian citizenship together with permission to work in Estonia.[53]

Estonian political hegemony has required Russians to reformulate any notion of a binational or consociational state. As Cynthia Kaplan notes, Estonians and Russians live in two societies, differing in language, place of birth, religion, urban versus rural, wealth, and type of work; they interact in only a limited way.[54] According to sociologist Marika Kirch, Russians also begin with a major political difference: they have never experienced "citizenship" in a civil society.[55]

Different interests and agendas are represented within the Russian community. Though some still long for Soviet times, a growing number of Russians identify with independent Estonia and want citizenship. But interest groups or parties representing Russians in Estonia, or in any of the successor states, are a new phenomenon because Russians outside Russia previously did not view themselves as a community with common interests. The withdrawal of Russian troops accents the separation of Estonia from Russia, and makes members of the Russian minority more cognizant of their common interests.

An example of the Russians' new sense of common interest and willingness to become active in Estonia's political life is the coalition formed to contest seats in the March 1995, parliamentary election. Running under the banner, "Our Home is Estonia," this coalition included the Estonian United People's Party, the Russian Party, and the Russian People's Party. Two months before the election the group submitted a list of 81 candidates for the 101 member parliament.[56] In order to win places in the parliament, the coalition must pass the 5 percent threshold outlined in the constitution. The electorate for the second parliament after independence was similar to that of the first. Between the September 1992, election and the March 1995, election, only 45,000 of the noncitizens had been naturalized.[57] However, unlike the first parliament, this election did result in Russian representation. "Our Home is Estonia!" received 5.87 percent of the votes and seated six deputies in the *Riigikogu*.[58] Thus, while the newly naturalized citizens make up a rather small part of the total electorate (which numbers just under 800,000), they no doubt were critical in propelling the Russian coalition beyond the required threshold.

Pro-Moscow groups make up the other extreme of the political spectrum and are conservative even in the context of Russian Federation politics. By early 1994,

42,000 of the 436,500 Russian population in Estonia had taken Russian citizenship, giving Estonia the largest number of Russian Federation citizens of any of the former republics. This high number can be explained by the provision of the aliens law requiring noncitizens to decide which citizenship they desire.[59] Eleven thousand of these Russian Federation citizens voted in the 1993 Russian parliamentary elections, with 48 percent Estonia-wide and 59 percent in Narva supporting ultranationalist Vladimir Zhirinovsky.[60] Similarly, the Union of Russian Citizens in Estonia recently declared its "all-round support for Russia's military invasion of the Chechen Republic" and expressed its concern for the "200,000 ethnic Russians living in Chechnya."[61] Such groups, though small, remain extremely anti-Estonian.

The Estonian Intermovement *(Interdvizhenie)*, a more mainstream Russian political group that provided opposition to the Estonian Popular Front and to the late 1980s Communist Party reform movement, found leadership among factory directors and workers in Estonian enterprises serving the all-union market. The more moderate United Council of Work Collectives (OSTK) has focused on the economic well-being of Estonia's Russians. Kaplan cites data perhaps indicative of lessening Russian political polarization and identification with the Soviet Union:

> 37 percent of the non-Estonians associate themselves above all with Estonia, followed by home town (32%) and finally, the Soviet Union (21 percent) . . . Only a decade ago the non-Estonians determined themselves first of all as citizens of the Soviet Union, followed by home town and the world.[62]

By the 1991 coup and independence, as much as half of the Russian population in Estonia, as in Latvia, Lithuania, and Moldova, indicated (through polls and referenda) that sovereignty was desirable.[63] At this point many perceived Moscow as the enemy because of its economic policies. With independence and the subsequent implementation of policies (citizenship, language, alien law) intended to establish Estonian hegemony, some of this hostility has been redirected toward Tallinn. Nevertheless, few Russians appear to be interested in giving up their Estonian residency and resettling in Russia.

The Estonian leadership, while not yielding its nationalistic agenda, has taken steps to address this loss of Russian support. In July 1993, in an attempt to soften the hostile reaction to the law on aliens both within Estonia's Russian community and from western organizations, President Meri formed a "Roundtable" to open communication with Russian non-citizens and calm the outcry that followed the passage of the aliens' law. The Russian Assembly, the most important Russian organization in Estonia today and the umbrella for moderate and westernizing Russian interests, has been cooperating with this Roundtable. The slavophile Russian *Sobor,* more radical and interested in maintaining ties with the Russian Federation, has thus far not participated. But this dichotomy conveys an overly extreme view; according to Priit Jarve, "Polls show that about a third of

Estonia's Russians are undecided or have no opinion about political questions. Russians as a group are not nearly as politicized as their leaders."[64]

Latvia

Population

Latvia provides the most extreme demographic situation for the titular population in the Baltics and, with the exception of Kazakhstan and Kyrgyzstan, of any former Soviet republic. Migration trends and birthrates in the 1970s and 1980s convinced Latvian demographers that Latvians would be a minority in their own homeland by the turn of the century. Migratory patterns have changed since the move toward independence began, and the Latvian proportion of the population has since increased. Still, at the beginning of 1994, Latvians constituted only 54.2 percent of the population of their republic.[65]

Latvia illustrates one extreme in our comparison of the non-Russian successor states: a regime that aggressively promotes the interests of the titular nation. This position triggers a minority reaction which has potential long-term consequences on Latvia's developing institutions. The government's exclusionary political agenda is most obvious regarding citizenship—the main irritant between Latvians and Russians. A citizenship law was finally passed in summer 1994, but the three-year conflict about the status of postwar migrants in the body politic will have a long-term impact on inter-national relations.

Latvia is the second smallest (after Estonia) of the newly independent states, with 2,657,000 people of the following ethnic groups:[66]

Percent of Population	
Latvian	54.2
Russian	33.1
Ukrainian or Belarusian	7.2
Other	5.5

This population composition is often exaggerated by the titular nation as "half Latvian, half Russian," lumping all non-Latvians as Russian-speakers. The postwar migration to Latvia was no greater than to Estonia; however, Latvia's titular population was only 77 percent in 1935, compared to almost 90 percent in Estonia. Thus, Latvians' enhanced sensitivity to the demographic situation results from fear of minority status in their own country. Of course, Soviet policies accentuated Latvians' belief that their language and culture were being annihilated and have given impetus to the current regime's exclusionary policies.

Latvian approaches to citizenship and language are intended to diminish the status of Russians within Latvia. Such policies have triggered a political reaction that has been exacerbated by Moscow. Russians currently living in Latvia are thus caught in a dilemma not entirely of their own making:

> In the mid-1970s, a pop tune promoted the myth of the Soviet melting pot. "My address is not a house," went the words. "My address is the Soviet Union." . . . Russians sent out to the republics to ensure Moscow's rule found life better there and gladly stayed. Now, abruptly, they have all had a change of address.
>
> Yet in the independent republics, "Russians go home" is the new pop refrain. . . ."When Latvians fought for independence, they wanted our support," says Katya Borshchova, an editor, born in Riga, whose Russian father was an officer of the occupying army. "But now even good Russians aren't acceptable. It's us and them."[67]

During Latvia's struggle for independence, the Soviet military newspaper, *Krasnaya zvezda*, characterized the situation similarly:

> For most newcomers to Latvia, migration is a normal process associated with the chance to improve one's standard of living. For them the Baltic republics are attractive. . . . Many migrants consider that they are simply taking advantage of their rights as Soviet citizens when moving from one part of the USSR to another, and they ignore the fact that they are actually going from one national republic and its culture to another. . . . [68]

These statements emphasize the psychological challenge faced by nonindigenes in Latvia and other republics. When Russians migrated, they felt no need to acculturate. As the dominant nation in the Soviet Union, Russians thought it logical that their culture and language would be the common denominator. Most migrated for the improved standard of living created by the postwar industrial expansion; they did not see themselves colonizing or occupying another land.

Even officers and troops of the North West Group of Military Forces understood their primary adversary to be the West. While providing assurance of Moscow's dominance in the Baltics, they perceived their mission as defense of the USSR. Upon discharge or retirement, many chose to stay in the Baltics for the high standard of living. By settling in cities with substantial Russian populations, they also maintained their Russian way of life.

Some raised children in Latvia, while others brought dependents from elsewhere. Today, the absolute majority of Russians and other nonindigenes—considering that peak years of migration were the 1960s and 1970s—were born in Latvia. The editor cited above is typical; her father came to Latvia with the army, but she was born in Latvia. Since migrants were usually young, moving after school or military service but before careers were well underway, even those not born in the republic have spent most of their adult lives in Latvia.[69] With independence, the Russians and other migrants are in a very uncomfortable situation—Latvia is the only home they know, yet independent Latvia is being governed by and for members of the Latvian nation.

The dilemma of the migrants and their descendants does not lessen Latvians' outrage when they consider Latvia's Soviet experience. Thousands of Latvians were killed or exiled during Soviet consolidation before and after World War II; thousands more were lost to the war and wartime emigration. These experiences depressed the traditionally low Latvian birthrate, further reducing the titular population. Yet the primary cause of today's inter-national hostility was the postwar dilution of the Latvian population by massive migration of Russians and other Slavs to fill jobs in newly built enterprises.

Latvians began to question Soviet industrialization policy in the 1950s. Even Latvian communists had misgivings about the super-industrialization that was triggering huge migrations of non-Latvians. But when these concerns were expressed to Nikita Khrushchev in 1959, he charged republican political leaders with nationalism and removed them. As a result, Moscow kept close watch on Latvia to prevent further development of a locally oriented indigenous leadership.[70]

After this early challenge to Moscow failed, industrialization proceeded rapidly. Between 1959 and 1989, the Russian population in Latvia grew by 350,000, while the Latvian population increased by only 90,000. Most of the migrants settled in Latvia's cities; Russians constituted a majority in Riga and in Latvia's next seven largest cities.[71] Facing this daily reality exacerbated Latvians' fears that they were being forced to relinquish their national identity to accommodate the migrants.

In addition to economic immigrants, Latvians were concerned with two special groups: military pensioners and prisoners. Riga, headquarters for the North West Group of Military Forces, had an especially large officer corps stationed nearby. As individuals retired or were discharged from the military, many decided to remain in Latvia. Some 50,000 World War II veterans and 60,000—100,000 retired Soviet officers reside in Latvia today. Of course, this number is increased substantially by their families.[72]

Prisoners raise a second concern for Latvians. Just as non-Russian soldiers usually performed their military service outside their home republics, prisoners were often incarcerated far from their homes. Upon completion of their terms, they could settle anywhere except Moscow and Leningrad (St. Petersburg). Because the Latvian economy was strong, many found jobs and thus received residence permits. According to Latvia's best known demographer, Peteris Zvidrins, soldiers and prisoners together contributed 7,000–8,000 annually to the growth of Latvia's nontitular population throughout the 1980s.[73]

Latvians were vocal about the threat to their nation from Russian migration. Zvidrins and demographer Parsla Egilite publicized the situation through carefully researched scholarly articles on migratory patterns and low Latvian birthrates. The latter provided a safer subject on which to publish, but was nonetheless quite effective in acquainting Latvians with the "demographic threat to the Latvian nation." Egilite notes even today that "chances for the survival of the Latvian nation are slim, even if migration stops and the ecological situation is rectified."[74] Egilite points out, however, that Russian fertility in Latvia, contrary to the common belief, is even lower than Latvian fertility, and has been so throughout the postwar period.[75] This fact can be explained by the concentration of Russians in Latvia's cities, where fertility rates are lower than in rural areas.

With the support of the former communist government, Latvians quickly took advantage of *glasnost'* and passed Resolution No. 46, "On Measures to Halt the Unjustified Mechanical Growth of the Population of the Latvian SSR." This legislation was intended to reduce further migration by halting industrial projects requiring labor beyond that available locally.[76] Immigration did decline after 1989, but the decline cannot be directly attributed to Resolution No. 46. The political and social situation was changing, and the titular nations were becoming increasingly hostile both to the center and to local Russians. Unlike the Caucasus and Central Asia, few violent interpersonal incidents occurred in the Baltics. Nonetheless, indigenous people were becoming assertive on the streets and in the workplaces; perhaps for the first time, Russians were forced to recognize that they no longer lived in Russia.

The first demonstrable result of this changing popular mood was the decline in Russian migration to Latvia. The economic slowdown had been evident throughout the 1980s and migration from Russia to Latvia had already decreased. With the political challenges to Moscow in the late 1980s and the freedom to discuss national problems openly, migration to Latvia sharply declined. This decline can be attributed more to the potential migrants' recognition that they would be unwelcome than to the migration legislation itself.

By 1990 more non-Latvians were emigrating than immigrating. This reversal parallels the Estonian case. The most recent migrants were the first to leave, and the change in the net flow resulted more from the reduction of immigration than from changes in the behavior of those already living in Latvia. Absent international violence, the passage of time will slow emigration as well. New migrants who do not adapt or who miss family or friends leave quickly; the longer they live in Latvia the more likely they will remain permanently. Since most migrants came to Latvia for improved economic prospects, they are likely to tolerate some social and political difficulties both because of Latvia's economic promise and also because of the dismal economic situation now found in Russia.

Citizenship

The citizenship debate took place against this backdrop. Latvians feared for their future as a nation; their precipitous demographic drop from over three-fourths in the 1930s to just over half of the population in 1989 provided the substance for this fear. The migration that resulted in Russian majorities in all of Latvia's urban centers, coupled with a low indigenous birthrate and consequently an aging population, further exaggerated the demographic trends.[77] One way to reverse decades of demographic dilution—at least in a political sense—was to exclude immigrants from the new polity by reserving citizenship for those with roots in Latvia prior to 1940, when 77 percent of the citizens were Latvian and only 8 percent Russian.[78] In championing such titular prerogatives, nationalist political forces triggered an internal Russian response and provided an excuse for external Russian involvement.

Latvian citizenship is not as simple as the "half-Latvian, half-non-Latvian" popular conception. By December 1994, 2.5 million people were registered in Latvia, with 1,776,000 (71 percent) classified as citizens. Of all citizens, 78.8 percent are Latvian and 16.2 percent are Russian. Of the million non-Latvians, 364,036 (36 percent) are citizens. The remaining noncitizens number approximately 734,000, most of whom are Russian.[79] This group remains at the center of the citizenship controversy.

The Latvian Supreme Council introduced a citizenship bill immediately after independence in October 1991. The initial proposal would have restored citizenship to interwar citizens and their descendants on request, and established a naturalization procedure for individuals who met the following conditions: (1) sixteen-year residency, (2) knowledge of Latvian, (3) relinquishment of other citizenship, (4) knowledge of Constitution, and (5) oath of allegiance. This proposal also outlined conditions excluding an individual from citizenship, including membership in the Soviet military or security forces (and retirees) who settled in Latvia after June 17, 1940, service as a Communist Party or Komsomol official in Latvia after that date, criminal behavior, or the absence of a source of income.[80]

Latvia's initial approach to citizenship thus paralleled Estonia's. The most inclusive "zero option" approach, favored by Russians and others who migrated to Latvia after 1940, would have granted citizenship to all legally resident when Latvia declared its independence (August 23, 1991). The most restrictive approach, advocated by the Latvian Citizens' Committee, would have limited citizenship to citizens of the interwar republic and their descendants.

In spite of their differences, the two sides agreed on a fundamental point: only citizens—the 1,776,000 individuals who could trace their lineage directly or through parents or grandparents to the interwar republic—could determine the naturalization process for others. This stance undercut the Supreme Council, since this legislative body had no legal tie to the interwar republic, and therefore could not "legitimately" decide fundamental constitutional questions of the newly independent state. Most Latvians favored the restrictive view, while non-Latvians, supported by Russia, many western democracies, and the CSCE, have promoted more inclusive policies.

The Citizens' Committee, claiming to represent the interests of interwar citizens, wanted to reserve more power for Latvians by restricting citizenship for Soviet-era migrants. While not changing Latvia's demographic composition, this approach significantly changed the national composition of voters. The feeling that Soviet incorporation of Latvia was illegal and those who carried out or benefited from that deed must not be included in the body politic was based on the genuine belief that "criminals" should not benefit from the crime.

The Popular Front, as reformers from within the system and advocates for Latvia's minorities, adopted the inclusive position. This position, recognizing the consequences of a divided society and relations with the mighty neighbor to the east, had both Latvian and Russian advocates. Former Foreign Minister and now opposition leader Janis Jurkans (forced from office in November 1992, because he advocated a five-year residency requirement based on the 1919 Latvian Constitution) noted the linkage between an inclusive citizenship policy and foreign relations with Russia:

> We cannot permit the appearance of a huge number of residents without citizenship in Latvia. . . . many people came to Latvia from Russia without realizing that they had come to a state that was once an independent country. Our duty is to understand the fate of these people, who, like we, are victims of the (Soviet) system.[81]

The length of residency had symbolic importance for Latvians far exceeding any real consequence. According to demographer Zvidrins, even the sixteen-year requirement would have initially reduced the potentially eligible pool of voting-age non-Latvians by no more than a quarter.[82] With each passing year, more of the later migrants would meet even that residency requirement.

Entering 1994 with no citizenship legislation and recognizing that residency provisions alone would not accomplish its exclusionary agenda, the parliament adopted in June a plan for naturalization that would have divided the non-Latvian population by imposing a language requirement for all and a quota for some. This proposal would have allowed those born in Latvia to be naturalized between 1996 and 2000. Only after 2000 could migrants be naturalized, and then only according to a quota set at 0.1 percent of the previous year's citizenry (thus allowing approximately 2000 naturalizations per year).[83] The quota evoked great controversy. As envisaged, it would preserve Latvia as a "single-nation" state by assuring that Latvians comprise the overwhelming majority of eligible voters.[84] While controversial with western democracies and international organizations, this quota was a central feature of the exclusionary political action program of the nationalists.

Western and Russian protests led to a presidential veto and subsequently a modification of the law as originally passed by the parliament. Several western organizations were active mediators in the dispute in Latvia as they had been in Estonia. Both the Council of Europe and the CSCE High Commissioner on National Minorities, Max van der Stoel (formerly the Dutch Foreign Minister), criticized the notion of a "single-nation" state because it compromised the rights of non-Latvians. Both organizations specifically criticized the quota, arguing that it made naturalization either remote or unpredictable. While accepting that citizenship could be phased in over time, the organizations urged a formula that provided certainty in the form of dates and requirements for those wishing to become citizens.[85]

The citizenship law finally adopted on July 22, 1994, eliminates the quota, but phases in eligibility for naturalization. The first group eligible to be naturalized (beginning February 1995) includes those married to citizens as well as ethnic Estonians and ethnic Lithuanians.[86] Those born in Latvia can then be naturalized before 2000; immigrants to Latvia can become naturalized only after 2000.[87] While less stringent than the original proposal, the law as adopted is the most exclusive to be found in any of the successor states. It effectively results in titular control of the political process for the first decade of Latvia's renewed independence, leaving those who cannot trace citizenship to the interwar republic with a limited stake in the success of the newly independent state.

Latvians, however, seem prepared to accept international criticism and a partially disenfranchised population in order to accomplish their political goals. From a nationalist perspective, this hegemonic political action program is vital for the survival of the Latvian nation; Latvian nationalists thus are unlikely to be dissuaded from pursuing their exclusionary political agenda.

Language

During the Soviet era, Russian migration outside Russia did not imply cultural adaptation. Russians lived and worked together, sent their children to Russian schools, consumed Russian entertainment and media, and assumed that communication with others would be in Russian. Language data support this perspective: only 22 percent of non-Latvians knew Latvian in 1989,[88] and only 15.4 percent of Russians in Riga could speak Latvian.[89] By late 1993, however, 63 percent of Russian respondents to a survey claimed to be able to carry on a conversation in Latvian.[90] Likewise, the Latvian Language Commission in summer 1993 indicated that "some 67 percent of those for whom a knowledge of Latvian was necessary for their job or profession passed Latvian language examinations at their required level."[91] Thus, a meaningful change had taken place since the 1989 census, even though the data cited are not perfectly comparable.

Nonetheless, language requirements have the potential to exclude more non-Latvians from citizenship than do long residency requirements. And unlike residency, language is an active rather than passive requirement. Migrants desiring citizenship must make an effort to learn and use the titular language. Language requirements thus foster cultural accommodation and imply some commitment to the community in which migrants live.

Estonia required an approximately 1500-word proficiency for citizenship, with a separate employment requirement depending on the nature of the job. Moldova granted citizenship to all without a language test, but initially imposed a language requirement demanding that those with supervisory or public-contact jobs be more proficient in the language than others. Latvia likewise has linked language to naturalization and employment. Directors and supervisors are required to be quite proficient in the language, individuals serving the public need intermediate ability, and others need only to understand everyday conversations.

By pressuring Russians to learn Latvian, Latvians are reversing years of russification in which the titular language was discouraged at work or school. Latvians also repressed their own language in everyday conversations, though 97 percent still regarded Latvian as their native language.[92] Juris Dreifelds cites a 1989 Riga study in which "only 17 percent of Latvians used Latvian in opening conversations with strangers, but 96 percent of Russians and 85 percent of other groups used Russian." Countrywide, only 36 percent of Latvians opened conversations with strangers in Latvian, and 90 percent of Russians opened conversations in Russian.[93]

During Soviet rule, Russian-language schools taught Latvian as a foreign language, but in Latvia as elsewhere, most students did not take the titular language requirement seriously. Thus, Russians graduated with only minimal knowledge of Latvian and felt no need to improve it. Latvians enrolled in the Latvian-language schools took the study of Russian more seriously, knowing that they would have to use it for further education and in most jobs. This situation began to change in the late 1980s and the change has accelerated since independence. The number of pupils in Russian schools has declined by 23,000 in recent years as a result of the withdrawal of Soviet troops, the sharp drop in the non-Latvian birthrate, and the inclination of mixed families after independence to send their children to Latvian schools. In 1994–1995, 59 percent of all pupils in Latvia were studying in Latvian schools; in Riga only 37 percent studied in Latvian, while 85 percent in the Latvia's nonurban districts studied in the indigenous language.[94]

Russian children attending Russian-language schools now consider Latvian to be a serious subject and realize that they must show competence to graduate. At the same time, greater fluency in Latvian is required at the postsecondary level, and Russians are forced to improve their competence if they want to pursue educational opportunities. Latvians also are becoming more assertive: they more often use their own language and expect those with whom they interact to understand and respond in Latvian.

Russians are not expected to give up their own language and culture; in fact, schools in Russian, Ukrainian, Belarusian, and other languages receive governmental support. Latvians, like the Estonians, merely want Russians to display respect for the indigenous culture and to make a commitment to the new state. Neither a pledge of loyalty to the new constitution nor the relinquishment of other citizenship for naturalization demands the same commitment to Latvia as does the use of the titular language.

Troop Withdrawal

Latvia, like Estonia, spent much of 1993 and early 1994 negotiating the withdrawal of Russian troops. Latvian and Russian negotiators reached an agreement in March 1994, specifying withdrawal of all troops by August 31, 1994, except those at the Skrunda radar station. This base will be leased to Russia for four years, followed by eighteen months during which Russian specialists will be present for its dismantling. The Latvian delegation agreed that military pensioners "with legal residence in Latvia prior to January 28, 1992 (when Russia took over responsibility for the former Soviet army), will be allowed to stay in Latvia on the same conditions as other Soviet-era immigrants." This provision includes about 30,000 pensioners, with about 2,000 more recent retirees forced to leave.[95] This agreement drew opposition from Latvian conservatives as well as from Estonia, both for the Skrunda lease and for allowing military retirees to gain permanent residency. As Latvian president Guntis Ulmanis stated, "The question of the military pensioners is a very serious compromise for Latvia."[96]

Russia used its troop presence in both Latvia and Estonia as a bargaining chip to gain concessions for Russians living in the two countries. Both Latvia and Estonia made concessions on military retirees and on citizenship that they were initially not inclined to make. Much of the pressure for concessions came from the western democracies and organizations such as the CSCE and the Council of Europe; both countries compromised in order to maintain support from the west on Russian troop withdrawal. The troops were finally withdrawn from both states on August 31, 1994.

Lithuania

Lithuania differs in important ways from its Baltic neighbors. First, Lithuania had an early experience with independence, controlling its own and surrounding territories periodically before the sixteenth century. As a result of this history and its close ties to the West through Poland and Catholicism, its own nationalization process took place relatively early, with the elites and then the masses assuming a national identity in the first half of the nineteenth century. Though part of the Russian Empire from 1795 to 1917, Lithuania resisted russification and Orthodoxy. Like Estonia and Latvia, Lithuania gained its autonomy in 1920 and experienced twenty years of interwar independence; this experience, carried in personal memories and collective myths of the Lithuanian nation, served as the greatest single impetus for renewed independence.

Population
The second area of greatest difference from Estonia and Latvia is population. Lithuania has a somewhat larger population (3,739,000 in 1994), with Lithuanians now making up 81.1 percent of the total. Russians constituted 9.4 percent (344,455) in 1989, but this proportion has fallen to 8.5 percent (318,000), almost identical to the 8.6 percent reported in the 1970 census. Poles, with about 7 percent of the population, are the other significant minority.[97]

Since the 1989 census, emigration has exceeded immigration by 57,000. The net emigration of Russians was 7376 in 1991 and 21,118 in 1992; a somewhat smaller outflow was expected in 1993, with emigration declining as a result of lower immigration in the immediately preceding years. Most of the emigrants cite family ties, not discrimination, as their motive for leaving.[98] Alfred Senn credits Lithuania's inclusive approach to citizenship for encouraging some of the Russian outflow: "Russians took citizenship, received investment coupons which they used to buy their apartments, sold the apartments, and moved to Russia where they could find housing for less cost and have a small nestegg left over."[99]

Most Russians in Lithuania are longtime residents. According to a survey by Richard Rose and William Maley in late 1993, 81 percent of Lithuania's Russians have lived in Lithuania for 21 or more years. An additional 10 percent have been resident for 11–20 years, with only 8 percent of all the Russians having lived in Lithuania for 10 or fewer years.[100] A similar question posed two years earlier by the Lithuanian Department of Nationalities showed that 46 percent of Lithuania's Russians were born in the republic, and 41 percent had lived in the republic for 10 or more years.[101] Lithuanian Russians were evenly divided in response to the question, "If you had to do so, could you find a place to live somewhere in Russia?"[102]

Just as the sense of being overwhelmed by migrants has defined the political and social environment in Estonia and Latvia, the more moderate proportion of nonindigenes in Lithuania has resulted in a more relaxed attitude on the part of Lithuanians toward Russians. This attitude, however, did not result in a more accommodative posture toward Moscow in the 1980s; Lithuania was the first and most strident of the republics in demanding both economic and political independence. While characterizing Moscow as the enemy, Lithuanians were not hostile to Russians living among them. In contrast to the segregation of Tallinn and Riga, Russians live among Lithuanians in Vilnius and most other cities; the lack of residential segregation, especially in Vilnius, has also resulted in a more common view of some of the state's challenges.[103] In contrast to Latvia and Estonia, Vilnius is only 20 percent Russian, Kaunas is 8 percent Russian and Klaipeda is 28 percent Russian; Snieckus, home to workers at the Ignalina nuclear plant, is the exception to this population pattern, with 64 percent Russian and only 8 percent Lithuanian (1989).[104]

The earliest Russian migration can be traced to the sixteenth century, with a second wave taking place during the interwar period as many intellectuals left the USSR for the West. In the late 1980s descendants of both groups identified politically with the aspirations of the indigenous population for an independent Lithuanian state.[105] Postwar migration, however, was of most concern to Lithuanians, just as to their northern neighbors. Russians migrated to Lithuania for the same reasons as to Estonia and Latvia: the standard of living was high relative to Russia, jobs were plentiful, and the lifestyle was western. Factories were built without regard to local resources or availability of labor; the last migration took place to staff huge technological enterprises, such as the nuclear plant near Snieckus and the oil refinery in Mazeikiai. These latest Russian migrants have not yet decided their role in the new state:

> To date, these people have psychological problems concerning their identity. Although they consider themselves "Soviet" people, they recently began their search for their national roots. Each of these waves of immigrants has a different attitude and point of view toward Lithuania's independence.[106]

Although migration played an increasingly large role in Lithuania's population growth (12 percent of the increase resulted from migration from 1959–1970, 24 percent from 1970–1979, and 32 percent from 1979–1989),[107] it did not lead to a demographic russification of the population as in Estonia and Latvia because of Lithuania's relatively larger population size. In this respect Lithuania is more like Ukraine, Belarus, and Moldova. The availability of a larger rural labor pool that could be utilized in support of industrial development also limited migration and mitigated its impact. In addition, Lithuanians had a higher birthrate and a larger natural rate of population increase than their Baltic neighbors.

Lithuania was the first republic to demand an end to political, military, and economic ties with Moscow. The Lithuanian Popular Front, *Sajudis,* quickly evolved from a reform-Communist movement to a full-fledged national-liberation movement. Lithuanians wanted to be politically free of Moscow, but did not have the same perception of being overwhelmed demographically and culturally in their own homeland. Russians wielded disproportionate influence within the Lithuanian economic and political systems. However, Lithuanians perceived the situation to be political rather than interpersonal, and directed their hostility toward Moscow rather than toward individual Russians. As one western diplomat noted, the good inter-national relations are surprising in light of Lithuanian history: over 300,000 Lithuanians were deported by Stalin and 30,000 were killed in a guerrilla war that lasted into the 1950s. Most of the surviving elite fled to the West. Nonetheless, Lithuanians view the Russians among them as fellow victims of the Soviet system. Communists, not ordinary Russians, were to blame.[108]

The status of the Polish minority has historically been more difficult for the Lithuanians, and today discrimination claims are heard more often from Poles than Russians. Stalin's invasion in 1940 resulted in Vilnius' being attached to Lithuania rather than Poland, a sensitive issue for Poles even today. Unlike Riga with its Russian majority and Tallinn with a divided population, Vilnius now is over 50 percent Lithuanian, in contrast to less than 5 percent before World War II, when Vilnius was 40 percent Polish and 40 percent Jewish. The Lithuanian leadership has thus far shown little interest in acquiescing to the Polish minority's requests for political or territorial concessions.

Citizenship

The sense that center-periphery political relations were more important for the nation's future than the domestic demographic and sociocultural conditions led Lithuania to pursue a different path from Latvia and Estonia. No group like the Congress of Estonia or the Latvian Citizens' Council developed as an advocate for interwar citizens because Lithuanians did not feel the same threat to their existence as a nation. One result has been a more inclusive approach to citizenship. This strategy has reduced inter-national tension domestically and ameliorated Moscow's concern for Russians in Lithuania.

One reason for Lithuania's inclusive approach was a lesser cultural threat; a second was timing. Lithuania was the first republic to declare the inapplicability of Soviet laws on its territory and the first to challenge the drafting of its men into the Soviet military. During these steps toward independence in 1988 and 1989, few envisaged Soviet disintegration and the success of the secession movement. In asserting independence and pursuing sovereignty, Lithuanians sought support from all domestic groups, including the Russian minority. They also tried to avoid provoking Moscow into military intervention. Preventing a confrontation with the Russian minority and asserting that Russians living in Lithuania themselves wanted independence were two of their strategies.

The Lithuanian Supreme Council adopted a citizenship law on November 3, 1989. This resolution, approved twenty months before the first coup attempt, paralleled the steps in Estonia and Latvia by restoring citizenship to interwar citizens and their descendants. However, unlike its neighbors' approaches, Lithuania's law granted citizenship to all who were born in the republic, or whose parents or grandparents were born in Lithuania. Those not included in the above categories but living in Lithuania in November 1989, could become naturalized citizens. Naturalization required a formal request within two years of the law's passage, a loyalty oath, and the relinquishing of other citizenship. This two-year period was subsequently extended with the intention of including all eligible persons who desired citizenship.

By 1994, 95 percent of the Russians in Lithuania had acquired Lithuanian citizenship through birth or naturalization. They thus have equal access to the political system with Lithuanians. One analyst noted that the distinction is between the citizens and noncitizens, not Lithuanians and Russians. Citizens participate normally and are quiet; protests come primarily from the small percentage of noncitizens.[109] Military retirees and CPSU or Komsomol officials were treated for citizenship purposes as were other individuals, though security service personnel were excluded. Migrants after 1989 were subject to typical conditions for naturalization: a ten-year residency, a knowledge of the language, and a source of income.[110]

One consequence of this approach to citizenship troubles some Lithuanians. Many non-Lithuanians chose citizenship because they believed that they would fare better economically as Lithuanian citizens. Thus, citizenship for many became an economic question, not one of political loyalty. But Russian motives should not be surprising:

> Russians are alienated from the general cultural and political process, which means that the fruits of independence already enjoyed by Lithuanians (the return of cultural values, the feeling of pride for being a member of the world community, etc.) are irrelevant to Russians, who are more sensitive to economic difficulties. . . . [111]

Language

During the Soviet era, linguistic russification was promoted in Lithuania as elsewhere. Russian was taught in schools beginning in kindergarten. Many subjects in Lithuanian-language high schools and university programs were taught only in Russian, assuring that students in certain fields were fluent in the Russian language. In addition, all doctoral dissertations after 1975 were written only in Russian.[112] The majority of Lithuanians sent their children to Lithuanian-language schools; however, some parents chose to enroll children in Russian-language schools, thinking that a Russian education would improve their children's life chances.

Lithuania's new language legislation was passed a year before (November 19, 1988) citizenship legislation. Lithuanian became the state language; public officials were initially given two years to learn the language, but this period was extended until 1992 and again until 1995 to accommodate non-Lithuanians. One official doubted that anyone would lose a job as a result of language, but thought that inability to communicate in Lithuanian could block advancement. Those more highly educated have learned Lithuanian and are not threatened by the new requirements.[113] Russians generally have more education than Lithuanians (37 percent of Russians have higher or secondary-specialized education, compared to 29 percent of Lithuanians).[114] The 1989 census reported that 37.5 percent of Russians in Lithuania spoke the titular language, the highest figure for any of the former Soviet republics. Four percent of Russians considered Lithuanian to be their native language. According to the Rose and Maley survey in late 1993, 70 percent of Russians in Lithuania report that they can carry on a conversation in Lithuanian, compared to 63 percent of the Latvian Russians who can converse in Latvian, and 38 percent of Estonian Russians who can speak Estonian. The same survey indicates that only 33 percent of Lithuania's Russians think that they "should not be made to learn a Baltic language." Corresponding figures are 34 percent in Latvia and 37 percent in Estonia.[115]

The 1988 language law made knowledge of Lithuanian a requirement for officials, not for the entire population, and was not tied to citizenship for those living in Lithuania prior to 1989. The language law accommodated minority languages, allowing their parallel use for official purposes in areas where minorities were concentrated. In 1995, however, the language law was strengthened, making Lithuanian the official language for all institutions, enterprises, and organizations, and requiring officials to have command of the language. The Polish faction in the parliament opposed these changes, but its attempt to legalize bilingualism in certain locations was defeated.[116] In a parallel move to tighten language regulations, the parliament enacted legislation to require Lithuanian companies to choose names that will follow the grammatical rules of the Lithuanian language and to use Lithuanian terminology in advertising.[117]

In spite of strengthening the state language laws, the government supports minority-language schools and other educational activities, preparation of teachers for minority-language schools and cultural organizations, minority-language media, and religious organizations. (In 1992, Lithuania had 188 Russian-language schools at the primary, nine-year, and secondary level, and 123 Polish-language schools.[118]) While this policy is particularly important to Poles and Russians, it is also applied to much smaller groups. Non-Lithuanian schools have increased instruction in Lithuanian, but finding qualified language teachers and suitable texts remains a problem in Lithuania as elsewhere. Entrance requirements for Lithuanian universities may be taken in Lithuanian, Polish, or Russian.[119]

Lithuania's policy toward its Russian minority is often contrasted with the policies of Estonia and Latvia. One must be careful, however, not to ignore the similarities and overstate the differences. All three states support education and culture in minority languages; all three require (or will require) facility in the indigenous language for public employment; and all three have based citizenship on legal continuity to the interwar republic. The important difference is Lithuania's exempting non-Lithuanians born or living in the republic before 1989 from residency and language requirements for citizenship. Although requiring migrants to be naturalized, this approach is much more inclusive. By early 1994, nearly 95 percent of adults in Lithuania had chosen Lithuanian citizenship.[120] In addition, noncitizens have all the civil rights of citizens, with the exception of "electing or being elected to the representative bodies of state power . . . (or participating) in referenda."[121]

Most Russians supported the Lithuanian Democratic Labor Party (former communist leader Algirdas Brazauskas) in the 1992 Parliamentary elections. Because most were citizens, Russians were able to make their preferences known through normal voting processes, and their participation was high. Groups appealing primarily to Russians have had little success; in general, Russians have found the Lithuanian political process to be open to them, and have not felt the need to engage in counter-hegemonic politics.

Relations with Russia

The variable treatment of Russians in the Baltic states has resulted in differentiated Russian Federation policies toward them. Soviet policy was most severe toward Lithuania–the first republic to demand separation from the union. Yet the Russian Federation now points to Lithuania as a positive example because naturalization requirements have been waived for most Russians. The Russian Federation used Lithuania's inclusive policy as justification for the withdrawal of its military forces by August 31, 1993. Withdrawal of forces from Latvia and Estonia was periodically halted because Russia claimed that both states were violating the rights of their Russian minorities. Again in contrast to its rhetoric on Estonia and Latvia, Russia considers that "normal conditions exist for Russians" in Lithuania.[122]

The situation, as usual, is more complex. Latvia provided the headquarters for the North West Group of Military Forces, thus housing the largest number of retired officers, and historically had the largest troop concentration. Estonia also had a disproportionately large number of military retirees. Lithuania had smaller and less important bases because of the large deployment of troops in Kaliningrad, the Russian oblast located west of Lithuania. Kaliningrad remains Russian territory, with access requiring transit through Lithuania. Lithuania also provides electricity and transports fuel for the base. Thus, troops in Lithuania were not as important to the Russians as troops in the other Baltic republics, and Russia continues to require services from Lithuania to support Kaliningrad.

Early in the independence movement, *Sajudis* sought Russian-minority support; intellectuals from all groups were invited to participate in the restructuring movement. According to parliamentarian Nikolai Medvedov, this approach was consistent with Lithuania's tradition as a regional power earlier in its history: as a multiethnic state with 40 percent Lithuanians and 60 percent Slavs, citizenship was available for all. Neither group was confrontational. *Sajudis* then lost support when it turned to the right, blaming communists for every problem.[123] The Brazauskas government continues Lithuania's more tolerant tradition. Even when dealing with sensitive issues like military and KGB retirees, "let them grow old in peace" is the unofficial policy. Accommodation and inclusion, not confrontation and exclusion, best describe the path Lithuania has chosen to follow toward a civic rather than a national state.

Conclusions

Since independence, the Estonian and Latvian governments have been controlled by those with nationalistic political action programs. Important steps have been taken—the development of new constitutions and legislation on citizenship, voting rights, and language—to assure titular control of the political process for the immediate future. Estonia, however, moved quickly to establish the rules by which Russians could enter the body politic. The relative clarity and reasonableness of these rules, together with general optimism about the economy, have been important factors in reducing inter-national tension. Language remains the primary obstacle to Estonian citizenship, but the decision to learn Estonian and thus be eligible for citizenship is in the would-be citizens' hands. Perhaps the Estonian case will test whether clearly defined rules of political participation, even if accompanied by titular nationalism, can lead to political and social integration. Of course, as in most situations, the question is confounded by other variables. In Estonia, the relative strength of the economy may be an equally important factor in persuading Russians to accept a somewhat disadvantageous political position in order to improve their standard of living.

Latvian nationalists, feeling more threatened by demographic and cultural russification, struggled longer with the citizenship issue and ultimately adopted a more exclusionary position. In Latvia, two factors work against inter-national cooperation: the exclusionary policy outcome of the citizenship debate and the divisive discussions that finally led to its enactment in Summer 1994. In late 1993, Russians in both Latvia and Estonia responded similarly to a survey question on whether noncitizens and minority nationalities were being badly treated (29 percent in Latvia and 31 percent in Estonia agreed with this characterization).[124] One can only speculate that the earlier resolution of the issue in Estonia, with a relatively more inclusive outcome, and the postsurvey resolution in Latvia, with a more exclusionary outcome, would now result in different responses.

The Lithuanian case provides a contrast. The initial policy on citizenship emphasized inclusion, and a civic rather than a national state has remained the goal. Unlike their neighbors, however, the Lithuanians never were as culturally and demographically threatened, and thus have not used independence to assert a cultural hegemony that had previously been threatened.

Notes

1. Rogers Brubaker, "Citizenship Struggles in Soviet Successor States," *International Migration Review*, Vol. 26, No. 2 (Summer 1992): 278–279; United Nations High Commissioner for Refugees, Regional Bureau for Europe, "Nationality Laws in Former USSR Republics," July 1993, p. 28.

2. Vello Pettai, "Contemporary International Influences on Post-Soviet Nationalism: The Cases of Estonia and Latvia," Paper presented to the 25th National Convention of the American Association for the Advancement of Slavic Studies (AAASS), Honolulu, November 1993.

3. Raivo Vetik, "Ethnic Conflict and Accommodation in Post-Communist Estonia," *Journal of Peace Research*, Vol. 30, No. 3 (1993): 273.

4. Aksel Kirch, "Russians as a Minority in Contemporary Baltic States," *Bulletin of Peace Proposals*, Vol. 23, No. 2 (1992): 205–206. See also Riina Kionka, "Migration to and From Estonia," Radio Liberty, *Report on the USSR*, September 14, 1990, pp. 20–21; and Baltic News Service (BNS), December 22, 1994.

5. *Eesti Ringvaade*, Internet Edition, Vol. 4, No. 22 (May 30–June 5, 1994). Alar Jaanes, head of the Re-migration Bureau of the Estonian Citizenship and Migration Board, reports that emigration has been steady at 12,000–14,000 per year, with the same expected for 1994. The Estonian government provides 1000–2500 Estonian kroons ($77–$192) to assist emigrants. The Estonian government has been exploring ways to increase direct payments for those Russians who leave Estonia. See also BNS, December 22, 1994.

6. Riina Kionka, "A New Level of *Glasnost* in Estonia," RFE/RL *Report on the USSR*, January 5, 1990, pp. 22–23.

7. Jeff Chinn, "Ethnic Cleavages in the Baltic States," in Gary D. Wekkin, Donald E. Whistler, Michael A. Kelley, and Michael A. Maggiotto, eds., *Building Democracy in One-Party Systems* (New York: Praeger, 1993), p. 194.

8. Rein Taagepera, "Estonia's Road to Independence," *Problems of Communism*, November–December 1989, p. 14, estimates "that since 1945, 7.5 million people have come to Estonia but 7 million have left again."

9. Richard Rose and William Maley, "Nationalities in the Baltic States: A Survey Study," No. 222 (Glasgow: Centre for the Study of Public Policy, 1994): 53.

10. See Romuald J. Misiunas and Rein Taagepera, *The Baltic States: Years of Dependence, 1940–1980* (Berkeley: University of California Press, 1983).

11. BNS, December 22, 1994.

12. Aksel Kirch, Marika Kirch, and Tarmo Tuisk, "The Non-Estonian Population Today and Tomorrow: A Sociological Overview (Preprint)," (Tallinn: Estonian Academy of Sciences, December 1992).

13. Rein Taagepera, *Estonia: Return to Independence* (Boulder, Westview Press, 1993), p. 176.

14. For an expanded discussion of the early stages of this debate, see Riina Kionka, "Who Should Become a Citizen of Estonia?" RFE/RL *Report on the USSR*, September 27, 1991, pp. 23–26.

15. Raivo Vetik, "Ethnic Conflict and Accommodation," p. 277.

16. Riina Kionka, "Who Should Become a Citizen of Estonia?," RFE/RL *Report on the USSR*, September 27, 1991, 23–26

17. Vetik, "Ethnic Conflict and Accommodation," p. 278.

18. *The Baltic Independent* (Tallinn), July 3–9, 1993, 1.

19. The first Russian deputy, Sergei Zonov, joined the parliament on March 22, 1994, replacing an Estonian deputy who was appointed to head a governmental office. Zonov expressed interest in helping to integrate the Russian speakers into the Estonian society. RFE/RL *Daily Report*, No. 57, (March 23, 1994).

20. Kionka, "Who Should become a Citizen of Estonia?" pp. 23–26.

21. Ibid., p. 24.

22. This law was modified in January 1995. New immigrants are now required to wait five years before applying for citizenship, and then an additional year for processing. This change, effective April 1, 1995, does not affect Soviet-era migrants who are already permanent residents of Estonia, who still must meet the two-plus-one requirement. OMRI, No. 24, II, (February 2, 1995); Estonian Ministry of Foreign Affairs, *Estonia Today*, January 24, 1995.

23. Pettai, "Contemporary International Influences," pp. 19–20.

24. "Preliminary figures show that 170,685 noncitizens have registered to vote, including 83,297 in Tallinn, 25,750 in Narva, 16,657 in Kohtla-Jarve, and 8,725 in Sillamae. Since there are 699,356 adult citizens in Estonia, this means that noncitizens will constitute 19.6% of potential voters (Tallinn 33.4%, Narva 79%, Kohtla-Jarve 54.5%, and Sillamae 94%)," Ann Sheehy, "The Estonian Law on Aliens," RFE/RL *Research Report*, September 24, 1993, p. 11, citing *Estoniya*, September 1, 1993. Noncitizens participated in the local elections in a higher proportion than citizens.

25. UN High Commissioner for Refugees, "Nationality Laws in Former USSR Republics," July 1993, p. 27.

26. Toivo U. Raun, "Post Soviet Estonia, 1991–1993," *Journal of Baltic Studies*, No. 1 (1994). See *The Baltic Independent*, October 22–28, 1993.

27. See Commission for Security and Cooperation in Europe (CSCE), *Human Rights and Democratization in Estonia*, Washington, D.C. September 1993, pp. 14–17.

28. Aksel Kirch, personal interview, Tallinn, June 1993. Kalev Katus estimates this number at 45,000, "Eesti demoarengu hetkeseis," *Postimees*, January 2, 1992, p. 2.

29. Personal interview, June 1993.

30. Letter from Max van der Stoel, CSCE High Commissioner on National Minorities, to President Lennart Meri, Tallinn, July 1, 1993.

31. Chancy D. Harris, "Ethnic Tensions in the Successor Republics in 1993 and Early 1994," *Post-Soviet Geography*, Vol 35, No. 4 (April 1994), 189.

32. Albert S. Pigolkin and Marina S. Studenikina, "Republican Language Laws in the USSR: A Comparative Analysis." *Journal of Soviet Nationalities*, Vol. 2, No. 1 (1991): 38–39.

33. Kionka, "Migration to and from Estonia," p. 23; Rein Taagepera, "Ethnic Relations in Estonia, 1991," *Journal of Baltic Studies*, Vol. 23, No. 2 (Summer 1992): 121–125.

34. See M. Rannyt, *O zakone o yazike*, (Tallinn: Znanie, 1989).

35. "Estonia Alters Language Needs," *The Baltic Independent* (Tallinn), April 23–29, 1993, p. 3.

36. CSCE, *Human Rights and Democratization in Estonia*, p. 12.

37. Mikhail Guboglo, "Demography and the Language in the Capitals of the Union Republics," *Journal of Soviet Nationalities*, Vol. I, No. 4 (1990–1991): 40.

38. Rose and Maley, "Nationalities in the Baltic States," p. 52.

39. Imbi Reet-Kasik, teacher, personal interview, Tallinn, June 1993.

40. Olav Aarna, rector, Tallinn Technological University, personal interview, Tallinn, June 1993.

41. Lisa Trei, "From Russia with Love," *Baltic Independent*, June 17–23, 1994, p. 7.

42. *Eesti Ringvaade* (Internet Edition), Vol. 4, February 21–27, 1994.

43. RFE/RL *Daily Report*, No. 24, February 24, 1994.

44. Estonian Ministry of Foreign Affairs, Backgrounder (Internet), March 1, 1994.

45. Kirch, personal interview, June 1993.

46. Rose and Maley, "Nationalities in the Baltic States," p. 56.

47. The Ida-Virumaa region in Estonia's northeast is home to 148,000 Russians, with 68,300 living in the city of Narva. BNS, December 22, 1994.

48. Aksel and Marika Kirch, personal interviews, Tallinn, June 1993; see also Aksel Kirch, Marika Kirch, and Tarmo Tuisk, "Russians in the Baltic States: To Be or Not To Be," *Journal of Baltic Studies*, Vol. 24 (1993): 178.

49. Priit Jarve, director of the Institute of Philosophy, Sociology and Law, personal interview, Tallinn, June 1993.

50. By February 1994, some 11,000 people had been naturalized as Estonian citizens. According to the Russian Embassy in Tallinn, 42,300 people living in Estonia had registered as Russian citizens. RFE/RL *Daily Report*, No. 22, February 2, 1994.

51. ITAR-TASS (Internet), July 8, 1993.

52. Kirch, "Russians as a Minority," p. 208. This 1990 survey also found that 49% responded that they must think about the citizenship question, and 25% responded negatively.

53. Vello A. Pettai, "Estonia: Old Maps and New Roads," *Journal of Democracy*, Vol. 4, No. 1 (January 1993): 123.

54. Cynthia Kaplan, "Estonia," Paper presented to the National Convention of the American Association for the Advancement of Slavic Studies, Phoenix, November 1992. See also Cynthia Kaplan, "Estonia: A Plural Society on the Road to Independence," in *Nations and Politics in the Soviet Successor States*, Ian Bremmer and Ray Taras, eds., (Cambridge: Cambridge University Press, 1993).

55. Marika Kirch, personal interview, June 1993.

56. Baltic News Service, January 19, 1995.

57. BNS, December 7, 1994.

58. BNS, March 9, 1995.

59. *The Baltic Independent*, June 17–23, 1994, 7.

60. Rostislav Khotin, "Zhirinovsky Wins Votes, Little Backing in Estonia," Reuters, December 16, 1993; *Eesti Ringvaade* (Internet Edition), December 9–12, 1993.

61. BNS, December 27, 1994.

62. Kaplan, "Estonia: A Plural Society," p. 215, citing Andrus Saar, "Inter-ethnic Relations in Estonia," *The Monthly Survey of Estonian and Soviet Politics*, November–December 1990, 12–15.

63. The March 3, 1991, vote on independence did not provide a direct indication of the vote by ethnic identification. Rein Taagepera has calculated that perhaps a quarter of the non-Estonians voted in favor of independence. "Ethnic Relations in Estonia, 1991," *Journal of Baltic Studies*, Vol. 23, No. 2 (Summer 1992): 126. As a result of Moscow's pressure on Estonia between the spring vote and the August coup, Russian opinion was shifting in favor of independence (Aksel Kirch, personal interview, June 1993).

64. Jarve, personal interview, June 1993.

65. State Statistics Committee, reported by Ministry of Foreign Affairs, *Dienas Bizness* (Internet), June 6, 1994.

66. Ibid.

67. Barry Newman, "Colonial Refugees: Soviet Union's Demise Strands Many Russians in Hostile Republics," *The Wall Street Journal*, February 4, 1992, 1.

68. Dzintra Bungs, "Migration to and from Latvia," Radio Liberty, *Report on the USSR*, September 14, 1990, p. 29, citing *Krasnaya zvezda*, February 15, 1989.

69. Rose and Maley, "Nationalities in the Baltic States," pp. 52–53, report that 86% of Russians in Latvia have lived there 21 or more years, 9% for 11–20 years, and only 5%

for 10 or fewer years. Only 24% of the Latvian Russians were born in Russia, while 52% were born in Latvia.

70. Einars Semanis, Chair of Political Science Department at University of Latvia, now an officer in the Foreign Ministry, personal interview, Riga, May 19, 1992.

71. Statistics Committee, *The Ethnic Situation in Latvia Today*, (Riga: Institute of Philosophy and Sociology, 1992), p. 4.

72. "The role of the former Soviet Occupation Army in influencing the demographic and social structural changes in Latvia is unclear. It is estimated that there are some 160,000 persons in Latvia who are associated with the Occupation Army (including wives and children)." Latvian Statistics Committee and the Department of Citizenship and Immigration, May 3, 1993; see also Dzintra Bungs, "Soviet Troops in Latvia," RFE/RL *Research Report*, August 28, 1992, p. 20.

73. Peteris Zvidrins, demographer, personal interviews, Riga May 17 and 19, 1992.

74. Dzintra Bungs, "Are the Latvians Dying Out?" Radio Liberty, *Report on the USSR*, April 19, 1991, p. 16.

75. Parsla Egilite, demographer, personal interview, Riga, May 19, 1992.

76. Bungs, "Migration to and from Latvia," p. 29.

77. This situation might be contrasted with Kyrgystan or Kazakhstan, where the indigenous proportion of the population is similar to that in Latvia. In these cases, however, the high indigenous birthrate is resulting in the population balance changing in favor of the indigenous nation. Thus, the Russian nation, not the titular nation, fears for its future.

78. V. P. Karnups, Director of the Latvian Department of Citizenship and Migration, unpublished paper, July 5, 1993.

79. *The Baltic Independent*, February 25–March 3, 1994, 8; *Diena*, January 26, 1994; BNS, December 28, 1994.

80. Dzintra Bungs, "Latvia Adopts Guidelines for Citizenship," Radio Liberty, *Report on the USSR*, November 1, 1991, p. 18.

81. RFE/RL *Research Report*, August 21, 1992, p. 77.

82. Zvidrins, personal interviews, May 1992 and June 1993.

83. Tim Morris, "Citizenship law navigates second reading," *The Baltic Independent*, June 17–23, 1994, p. 4; RFE/RL *Daily Report*, No. 109, June 10, 1994.

84. Edward Lucas, "Keeping the Status Quota," *The Baltic Independent*, February 25–March 3, 1994, 8.

85. *The Baltic Independent*, February 25–March 3, 1994, 8.

86. RFE/RL *Daily Report*, No. 139, July 25, 1994; BNS, February 1, 1995.

87. Steven Erlanger, "Latvia Amends Harsh Citizenship Law That Angered Russia," *New York Times*, July 24, 1994; BNS, February 1, 1995.

88. Pigolkin and Studenikina, "Republican Language Laws," pp. 59–60.

89. Mikhail Guboglo, "Demography and Language," p. 40.

90. Rose and Maley, "Nationalities in the Baltic States," p. 52.

91. Karnups, unpublished paper, July 5, 1993.

92. Statistics Committee, *Ethnic Situation*, p. 10.

93. Juris Dreifelds, "Immigration and Ethnicity in Latvia, *Journal of Soviet Nationalities*, Vol. I, No. 4 (1990–1991): 55, 64–65.

94. BNS, February 17, 1995.

95. Tim Morris and Edward Lucas, "Opposition Demands Poll on Troops Deal," *The Baltic Independent*, March 25–31, 1994, 4.

96. Tim Morris and Vello Pettai, "Government Defends Troop Deal," *The Baltic Independent*, April 1–7, 1994, 4.

97. BNS, February 22, 1994.

98. Severinas Vaitiekus, Department of Nationalities, personal interview, Vilnius, June 1993.

99. Alfred Erich Senn, "Lithuania's First Two Years of Independence," *Journal of Baltic Studies*, Vol. 25, No. 1 (Spring 1994): 85.

100. Rose and Maley, "Nationalities in the Baltic States," p. 53.

101. Department of Nationalities of the Government of the Republic of Lithuania, "Ya i moya zhizn' v Litvye," unpublished survey.

102. Rose and Maley, "Nationalities in the Baltic States," p. 58.

103. Juozas Lakis, Director, Research Group on National Minorities, Vilnius Pedagogical University, personal interview, Vilnius, June 1993.

104. Department of Nationalities of the Government of the Republic of Lithuania, *National Minorities in Lithuania*, Vilnius, 1992, p. 14.

105. Halina Kobeckaite, Director General of the Lithuanian Department of Nationalities, personal interview, June 1992.

106. Department of Nationalities, *National Minorities in Lithuania*, p. 3.

107. Saulius Girnius, "Migration to and from Lithuania," Radio Liberty, *Report on the USSR*, September 14, 1990, p. 25.

108. Personal interview, Vilnius, June 1993.

109. Lakis, personal interview, June 1993.

110. Saulius Girnius, "The Lithuanian Citizenship Law," Radio Liberty, *Report on the USSR*, September 27, 1991, p. 21.

111. Vladis Gaidys, "Russians in Lithuania," *The New Russian Diaspora* (Armonk, NY: M. E. Sharpe, 1994), p. 101.

112. Stanley Vardys, "Lithuanians," in Graham Smith, ed., *The Nationalities Question in the Soviet Union* (London: Longman, 1990), p. 73.

113. Lakis, personal interview, June 1993.

114. Department of Nationalities, *National Minorities in Lithuania*, p. 23.

115. Rose and Maley, "Nationalities in the Baltic States," pp. 52 and 56.

116. BNS, February 1, 1995; Open Media Research Institute (OMRI), No. 23, II, February 1, 1995.

117. BNS, December 7, 1994 and January 11, 1995.

118. Halina Kobeckaite, "National Minorities in the Republic of Lithuania," Unpublished report of the Lithuanian Department of Nationalities, 1992.

119. Ibid.

120. *Baltic News Service*, February 22, 1994.

121. *"Law on the Legal Status of Foreigners in the Republic of Lithuania,"* No. 1–1750, September 4, 1991, *Parliamentary Record*, No. 5, 1992.

122. ITAR-TASS (Internet), March 7, 1994.

123. Nikolai Medvedov, parliamentarian, personal interview, Kaunas, November 1992.

124. Rose and Maley, "Nationalities in the Baltic States," p. 56. However, Latvians were less strong in their disagreement about "bad treatment," and also had more answering "don't know."

Chapter 6

Belarus and Ukraine

Belarusians and Ukrainians, like Russians, are eastern Slavs who share historical, cultural, and linguistic traditions. Because of the location of their homelands, both peoples have frequently interacted with Europe, and Russians have often thought of these areas as "the West." Most importantly, Russians have internalized the view that the three Slavic groups are *edinokrovnye*, of one blood, and that Ukraine and Belarus are integral parts of Mother Russia, thus making today's Belarusian and Ukrainian independence particularly difficult for Russians to accept.

This Russian view is not reciprocated equally by Belarusians and Ukrainians, many of whom resent cultural and political domination by their "big brothers." Belarus, with a 1.3 million Russian minority (13.2 percent), has a weak tradition of nationalism, a history of cultural domination by both Poland and Russia, and a government interested in cooperating as much as possible with Russia. Ukraine, with an 11 million Russian minority (21.9 percent), presents a more complex situation with a nationalist tradition in the western regions, a largely russified indigenous population in the East and South, and a government determined to maintain independence. After several years of independence, both Belarus and Ukraine, dependent on Russia for resources and especially energy, are facing economic collapse; in comparison to their situations, Russia's ailing economy is a success, and reunification with Russia for economic motives is attractive to some.

The sections that follow on Belarus and Ukraine diverge because of the differing nature of the interaction between the titular nation and the Russians. Belarus is characterized by the absence of indigenous nationalism; because Belarusians have not been forcing an exclusionary nationalistic agenda, the Russian minority is less threatened than elsewhere. In contrast, the regime in Kiev has pursued a more nationalistic political action program vis-à-vis Moscow. Anti-Moscow actions have often been perceived within Ukraine as anti-Russian, thus contributing to the interactive process between Ukrainians and local Russians. Ukrainianization, strongly favored by nationalists in the historically pro-Ukrainian/anti-Russian western regions and opposed by Russians and russified Ukrainians alike in the East and South, adds a regional dimension that leads

Belarus and Ukraine: Areas of Russian Concentration

to a consideration of both irredentism and federalism. Belarus' relative lack of both a nationalistic agenda and of Russian mobilization, together with Ukraine's anti-Moscow nationalism and the concomitant domestic Russian (and russified Ukrainian) reaction, provides further evidence of the explanatory power of the concept of interactive nationalism.

Belarus

Belarus differs from its Baltic and Ukrainian neighbors in its level of national self-consciousness and in its relationship to Russia. While Belarus' national movement in the late 1980s and independence after the 1991 coup paralleled patterns in neighboring republics, they differed in depth and popular acceptance. Belarus has thus far displayed timidity in pursuing an exclusionary nationalistic agenda.

BELARUS AND UKRAINE

	Belarus	Ukraine
Territorial Size (km^2)	207,600	603,700
Population Size (1/1/94)	10,367,300	52,114,400
Percent Titular (1989)	77.9	72.7
Percent Russian (1989)	13.2	22.1
Urban Population (1993)	6,988,000	35,297,000[a]
Percent Titular (1989)	73.3	65.8
Percent Russian (1989)	17.5	29.0
Size of Capital City (1/1/91)	1,633,600	2,635,000
Percent Titular (1989)	72.1	72.4
Percent Russian (1989)	20.0	20.9
Natural Increase (/1000, 1993)	−1.1	3.5
Titular NI (1989)	4.4	1.7
Russian NI (1989)	8.0	2.7
Net Migration To (2)/From (1) Russia (1989–1993)		
Total	18,595	160,846
Titular	9,267	130,553
Russian	6,158[b]	14,251[b]
Life Expectancy (1989)	Men: 67.1 Women: 76.3	Men: 66.4 Women: 75.0
Titular e^0 (1989)	Men: 66.6 Women: 76.2	Men: 66.5 Women: 75.1
Russian e^0 (1989)	Men: 68.5 Women: 76.7	Men: 66.3 Women: 75.3
Employment[c] (1993)	83.5	83.1[d]
Trade (Export/Import Ratio, 1993)		
Intra-NIS Trade[e]	0.75	0.66
Extra-NIS Trade[f]	0.95	1.70[g]

Notes: [a]Ukraine's urban population total is for 1992. [b]A net outmigration of Russians to Russia was recorded for 1993 from Ukraine and for 1990 and 1993 from Belarus'. [c]Employment given as a percent of the working-age population. [d]Ukraine's employment percent is for 1992. [e]Intra-NIS ratios calculated from trade measured in the national currencies.[f]Extra-NIS ratios calculated from trade measured in US dollars. [g]Ukraine's extra-NIS trade ratio is for 1992

Sources: Goskomstat SSSR, *Chislennost' naseleniya soyuznykh respublik po gorodskim poseleniyam i rayonam na 1 yanvarya 1991 goda* (Moskva: 1991); Goskomstat Rossiyskoy Federatsii, *Chislennost' i sotsial'no-demograficheskiye kharakteristiki russkogo naseleniya v respublikakh byvshego SSSR* (Moskva: 1994); Statisticheskiy komitet SNG, *Statisticheskiy byulleten'* No. 20 (June 1994): 35–36; Statkom SNG, *Itogi vsesoyuznoy perepisi naseleniya 1989 goda* (Minneapolis, MN: East View, 1992), Vol. 7, Part 2; Mikhael Guboglo, "Demography and Language in the Capitals of the Union Republics," *Journal of Soviet Nationalities* Vol. 1, No. 4 (Winter 1990–1991): 9–13; The World Bank, *Statistical Handbook 1994: States of the Former USSR* (Washington, DC: World Bank Studies of Economies in Transformation No. 14, 1994).

Belarusian leaders oppose Belarusian nationalism, seeking accommodation to Russians at home and to the external Russian state. While perhaps 10 percent of the parliament and 15 percent of the population support the nationalistic agenda of the Belarusian Popular Front, they have been overwhelmed by an apathetic populace and conservative supporters of the old regime. Those in power do not see themselves representing the interests of the titular nation; and, unlike Russians in most of the other republics, the 13 percent minority has neither lost power nor faced challenges to its status.

Today's limited nationalism is consistent with Belarusian history. Unlike many former Soviet republics, Belarus has broken only tentatively with its Soviet past. In spite of its European location, this new state, traditionally dependent on Moscow, had little experience with independence. Ukraine, Moldova, and the Baltics were striking out independently prior to the coup; Belarus, led by conservative bosses loyal to Moscow, resisted nationalist agendas. This absence of aggressive separatist nationalism is both an advantage and disadvantage: Belarus has experienced little of the inter-national tension present in other republics. Yet a unique national consciousness, a sense of nationhood, and a drive for meaningful independence are absent even today. As a journalist recently wrote in response to Belarus' consideration of economic and military union with Russia:

> A huge segment of the Belarusian population does not appreciate its national identity or . . . independence. . . . people are willing to support any alliance as long as it can make the slightest improvement in their own lives. The influential corps of directors, especially those from the military-industrial complex, and many members of the executive branch of government are ready and willing to support the new alliance [with Russia] completely. . . . the republic population has displayed a strong tendency to remember the years before perestroyka with . . . nostalgia. The people had no independence or freedom then, but they did have sausage and a sense of security.[1]

Belarusians have long been identified as a distinct ethnic group. But a sense of nationhood, linking real or imagined past glories to future goals, has not materialized. Other successor states may ultimately fail to maintain independence because of economic or military weakness; however, their titular nations have internalized self-images as nations that deserve independence. The Belarusian people and state still lack the self-image necessary to create a unified, independent polity.

Belarus has strong ethnic and linguistic ties to Russia. For centuries Russians and Belarusians perceived each other as close kin. That all three Slavic peoples (Russians, Belarusians, and Ukrainians) developed from common ancestors color Russians' attitudes toward Belarusians. Ostankino reported as recently as January 12, 1994, after a summit between Russian President Yeltsin and then Belarusian Supreme Soviet Chairman Shushkevich, that "talks were necessary in order to remove barriers restricting cooperation *in what is essentially a single people.*"[2]

Similarly, a 1993 poll indicated "32 percent of ethnic Belarusians considered the history of Russia and Belarus to be the same; 37.6 percent . . . had no knowledge of Belarusian culture; and 55 percent said that 'nationalism' had no positive potential."[3]

After a year of Belarusian independence, Parliamentary Chairman Shushkevich acknowledged Belarus' limited notion of nationhood:

> The history of Belarus is more or less like this: one part said all happiness comes from Poland, the other part said all happiness comes from Russia. There was nothing Belarusian here. We want good relations with Poland and good relations with Russia, but we have our own remarkable traditions and cultural monuments. . . . What we need to do is not so much to develop but to resurrect our nation.[4]

A Belarusian Nation?

Before the twentieth century, Belarusians identified themselves by locality rather than language or culture. In 1897, 98 percent lived in rural areas or very small towns. As town size increased, Belarusian presence declined.[5] Because of their rural existence and limited education, Belarusians failed to participate in early modernization efforts; the upper strata of society—urban and ethnically Russian, Polish, or Jewish—pushed for modernization. Both literacy and an urban critical mass were necessary for an intelligentsia to develop and articulate the goals of national mobilization. Belarusians had neither.[6]

Being caught between stronger Polish and Russian states resulted in numerous wars and border adjustments. Yet rather than developing their own nationalism, urban Belarusians assimilated to the dominant external power. Guthier notes that at the turn of the century both the Russians and the Poles were better equipped to pursue modernization. "Belorussians faced . . . serious obstacles, including poverty; high illiteracy; weak representation in the cities, middle class, and professions; and the absence of a primate city to concentrate the limited intellectual and material resources of the Belorussian people."[7]

Political identification began tentatively, and then only in the twentieth century. According to Nicholas Vakar:

> The ten-year period of 1906 to 1917, known as the Adradzen'ne (Revival) period, can be correctly described as the formative years of Belorussian political nationalism. . . . The new generation saw its task . . . (as) organizing the national memory; of fostering the process of national self-determination according to the requirements of modern political science; of defining the national goal in terms of general culture and practical policies; and of educating a personnel capable of assuming the national leadership.
>
> Everything was tried to awaken and enliven the national consciousness of the people. . . . Myths were deliberately created to foster the dynamics of national revival, and to hasten the attainment of the political goal.
>
> Belorussia had everything . . . required for statehood: a territory, a people, a language. It only needed self-government to become a full-fledged nation. But it was not easy to . . . make it the wish of the masses, woefully ignorant and indolent.[8]

During World War I and the Russian Revolution, the small Belarusian elite made an effort to gain sovereignty but could not enlist mass support. The rural majority had not yet internalized a national consciousness. The overthrow of the tsar in 1917 was viewed by activists as a first step in creating a Belarusian state. But even Belarusian nationalists did not envisage a Belarus independent of Russia. They formed a National Committee to represent Belarusian interests in Petrograd, hoping to develop a federal arrangement with Russia. However, they soon discovered that Petrograd was interested in military matters, not Belarusian political aspirations.[9] For several months nationalists and communists jockeyed for position in Minsk. On March 25, 1918, the Rada declared Belarus independent, leading to:

> the ten month period of symbolic independence (that) has left an indelible
> impression. . . . A fact, historically accidental and trivial, has grown into a heroic
> legend. The date of March 25, 1918, is celebrated by nationalists as the birthday
> of the Belorussian state and it has now become a symbol about which all doubts
> are shouted down as sacrilege.[10]

But Belarus was far from independent, nor was it controlled by Belarusian nationalists who sought independence as their ultimate goal. Zaprudnik notes that "97.4 percent of the urban population consisted of non-Belarusians . . . dominated by Russian, Polish, and Jewish parties with their own goals not necessarily coinciding with—and in some cases antagonistic to—the Belarusian revival."[11]

When the Germans, who occupied Minsk in February 1918, left in December, the Russian army arrived. Most Belarusian Rada members left Minsk before the Soviet occupation. On January 1, 1919, the Belorussian SSR was formed with the appearance of an independent state. However, Moscow's control became evident when it ordered the union of Belarus and Lithuania in a state called Litbel.[12]

The Treaty of Riga (1921) divided interwar Belarus between Poland and the Soviet Union. Western areas of Russia containing ethnic Belarusians were attached to the BSSR. Lenin's indigenization policies resulted in "fostering the Belarusian language in all spheres, including the higher echelons of the government and the Communist Party."[13] Belarusian became widely used in education and administration in the 1920s.

In Polish-controlled western Belarus, Poles and Belarusians eliminated all traces of Russian culture, banning Russian from schools and using the Latin alphabet, instead of the Cyrillic, for Belarusian transcription.[14] By the mid-1920s, polonization resulted in the closing of Belarusian schools and cultural organizations; much of the small Belarusian intelligentsia from the Polish territory emigrated to the West.

According to Guthier, "The failures of the national movement to establish a popular base in 1917–18 suggests that in terms of mobilization and consciousness the Belorussian people had not substantially improved upon their condition of

1897." Preconditions for the nationalization of the masses—urbanization, literacy, nonagricultural employment—remained absent. Nonetheless, joining territories populated by Belarusians to create the Belarusian SSR, even though subordinate to Moscow, together with belarusification policies in the republic, encouraged people to identify as Belarusians and thus take a step toward national consciousness.[15]

The early Leninist policy of indigenization fostered Belarusian cultural institutions and higher education. The Belarusian Academy of Sciences and the first Belarusian university were founded in Minsk. Legislation stipulated that both Belarusian and Russian be taught in schools and used in public administration. In reality, Russian was largely banned.[16] However, by the end of the 1920s, Stalin reversed positions and began a russification of governmental personnel, replacing Belarusian nationalists in administrative positions with individuals from other parts of the USSR.

Belarusian identification remained weak. Just as educated Belarusians earlier became polonized, after the 1920s they became russified. Unlike the situation in other union republics, russification in Belarus met little indigenous resistance. The 1926 census reported that three-fourths of Belarusians who became literate had learned Russian, not Belarusian; in the cities this figure was 89 percent. More educated Belarusians were thus entering the mobilized environment through the vehicle of the Russian language, thus increasing the likelihood of assimilation to the Russian culture. In contrast, only 7 percent of the Russians learned the Belarusian language.[17]

Yet belarusification in the early 1920s in the Polish-dominated West and throughout the decade in the Soviet-controlled East for the first time created the notion of homeland and nation among many Belarusians. Wider education and urbanization enabled Belarusians to distinguish between themselves and their Russian, Polish, and Ukrainian cousins. Nevertheless, when confronted with full-scale polonization and russification, Belarusians were not sufficiently self-conscious to resist the onslaught.

> In the course of the twenty years of separation of the two Belorussias, the degree of unity achieved before partition was lost. A new generation had grown up in two cultures, developing independently in Vilna [at that time part of Poland] and in Minsk. With Polonization on one hand and Russification on the other, the two centers came to differ widely in their language, literary standards, and education generally, drawing further apart every year.[18]

Stalin's purges also decimated Belarusian culture by targeting the intelligentsia. Hundreds of thousands were killed or exiled. Purges were but one dimension of the "communist genocide":

> In 1933 a language reform was decreed, bringing Belarusian orthography and vocabulary closer to Russian at the expense of the natural character of the

Belarusian language. . . . The Belarusian language was banned from high official places and from higher education. Speaking Belarusian in formal gatherings became a sign of "bourgeois nationalism."[19]

During the 1939 Soviet-German division of Poland, the USSR seized western Belarus, thus uniting the lands inhabited by Belarusians under a single political regime. After the German invasion, all Belarusian territories remained together under German wartime rule, and were then reincorporated into the USSR as a single entity after the war.

The postwar period witnessed extraordinary industrial development and rapid urbanization, together with mass Belarusian migration to other parts of the USSR. Russian migrants replaced the Belarusian administrative class, then filled thousands of jobs in expanded industries. Russians and other nonindigenes replaced Belarusians in party and governmental positions. By Stalin's death, Russians occupied most leadership positions.[20]

Postwar development also resulted in a huge migration of rural Belarusians to urban areas. By 1959 Belarusians had become the numerical majority in the republic's cities, and Belarusian speakers for the first time outnumbered speakers of other languages in Belarusian cities. "The tendency of mobilized Belorussians to adopt the Russian language was reversed. . . . Both the Belorussian nationality and language were gaining numerical preponderance in the most socially and politically active sectors of the population."[21]

Even with this demographic belarusification of cities, the Russian urban culture retained its powerful attraction. Between 1959 and 1970 the proportion of Belarusians claiming Russian as their native language increased from 7 percent to 10 percent, and in Minsk from 25 percent to 35 percent.[22] Of all the titular nationalities, Belarusians have the lowest level of native-language loyalty and the greatest knowledge of Russian. The many Belarusians who migrated outside their native republic typically used Russian as their medium of interaction and also exhibited a high intermarriage rate with Russians. Both of these tendencies enhanced the prospects for Belarusian assimilation.[23]

Still, the locally recruited Belarusian political leadership had opportunities to raise symbolic national issues. The republic's first secretary, P.M. Masherau, regularly emphasized the contributions of Belarusian partisans to the Soviet war effort and used the Belarusian language on state occasions.[24] The World War II partisans filled leadership positions until Masherau's 1980 death. Nevertheless, in spite of Belarus' indigenous leadership, Belarus was dominated politically, culturally, and linguistically by Russia and Russians.

The leaders of the Belorussian Communist Party adhered to positions of national nihilism, which has long-standing roots. Thus, standing on the steps of Belorussian University, Nikita Khrushchev proclaimed that Belorussia would be the first to embark on communism inasmuch as the Belarusians would learn to speak Russian before the other peoples. This behest of Khrushchev's was fervently executed by the Belorussian communists. . . . Byelarus stands out among the former Union republics in that its people have . . . virtually lost their national singularities.[25]

Not surprisingly, Belarus took no leadership role during the Gorbachev years. Nationalists claimed that Belarus had the territory, people, language, and culture to take a place among the nations of central Europe. But this view never caught on with the masses or leadership. Unlike the Baltic nations, few Belarusians seemed to believe that independence was worth either economic or political sacrifice.

The twin issues of reforming the economy and developing a new relationship with the center did not resonate in Belarus as in the other republics. With a comparatively high standard of living, Belarusians were content, exhibiting little hostility toward Russia or Russians' status in Belarus. In spite of the huge postwar migration, Russians still made up a relatively small proportion (13 percent) of the population. Unlike other titular groups, Belarusians did not coalesce around language as the symbolic issue of their political, economic, or cultural subordination. This popular sentiment, coupled with conservative leadership, resulted in limited support for Gorbachev and his political and economic reforms. Not all Belarusians were content with the status quo, just as not all Lithuanians were anxious to go to the barricades. But comparatively, Belarusians exhibited less nationalism, consequently provoking less Russian reaction, than other nations.

Nationalism, to the extent that it developed in Belarus in the late 1980s, was triggered by three issues: the decline in the use of Belarusian, the discovery of mass graves from Soviet purges in 1937–1941, and the fallout from the Chernobyl accident. Each symbolized a threat to the Belarusian nation, thus galvanizing that portion of the population ready to express its national identity.

Language
In the late 1980s language was a common concern in most republics and provided a relatively safe way to challenge Moscow. Language arose as an issue in Belarus in 1986 when several intellectuals requested in a letter to Gorbachev that Belarusian be used in education and government. The appeal to support Belarusian culture and language echoed a sentiment being expressed more forcefully in the Baltics and Moldova; neither Gorbachev nor the Belarusian Communist leadership responded.

> The Russian language pervaded Belarusian culture from education to publications. Popular Front leader Paznyak noted that by ". . . the mid-1970s, in Belorussia's 95 cities and in 'almost all' of the republic's 117 towns, not a single school or kindergarten remained with Belorussian as the language of instruction."[26]

At present, approximately three-fourths of all children in Belarus attend schools where the primary language is Russian,[27] and as many as half of the population consider Russian to be their native language.[28]

Even with independence, this situation has not changed radically. In 1992 over one million copies of Russian-language daily papers were published, compared to 80,000 copies of the single Belarusian daily. The gap is larger for weeklies; in addition, two million copies of Moscow publications are read in Belarus.[29] Former Supreme Council Chairman Shushkevich expressed concern that out of every 100 newspapers, the government subsidized 92 in Russian and only eight in Belarusian.[30] A publication's choice of language has political significance. Russian-language publications tend to be more conservative because, from the nationalist point-of-view, "use of the Belarusian language has always been both a means of national survival and a national goal; not only has Belarusian been the language of dissent, but its very use has constituted an act of dissent."[31]

Belarusian became the state language in 1990, but the pro-Russian Kebich government made little effort to implement the new law. Kebich speaks mostly Russian. Like left-bank Ukraine (discussed below), Belarus lacks the sense of assertive nationalism found in many of the other republics that was first and most strongly asserted through language.

The Graves of the Kurapaty Forest

The second issue, the discovery of mass graves from the Stalinist purges in the Kurapaty forest near Minsk, stunned the population and propelled archeologist and historian Zyanon Paznyak onto the political stage. Paznyak's revelations in the Writers' Union journal[32] led to the first spontaneous mass demonstrations demanding governmental action. "Martyrology of Belarus," founded to document these historic events and commemorate the victims, provided leadership for the initial protests. The Belarusian Popular Front (BPF, founded in Vilnius in June 1989, because Belarusian authorities prevented the organization from meeting within the BSSR) evolved from these protests.[33] Paznyak was selected as its first chairman:

> The BPF is a mass socio-political movement. Its goal is to create a society and to renew the identity of the Belorussian nation based on principles of democracy and humanism, to secure conditions for a free and full-fledged development of culture both of the majority of inhabitants and of Belorussia's national minorities.[34]

While hoping to represent an awakening Belarusian nation, the BPF noted that no groups voiced the minority Russians' interests. Aware of a potential Russian reaction to "belarusification," the Popular Front invited Russians to join: "All the nationalities that comprise the Belorussian state will find a place within it. We are not excluding from it our brothers the Russian people with whom we share our land and fate, who for a long time have innocently suffered together with us."[35] This statement, coming from the most nationalist segment of the Belarusian elite, provides striking evidence of the limited scope of a Belarusian national consciousness. While the most nationalistic force within the Belarusian political spectrum, the Popular Front has pursued a moderate agenda, limited by its lack of mass support and by the concern among its leadership that its own stand could radicalize that taken by the Russian minority.

Chernobyl

Chernobyl provided the impetus for Stanislau Shushkevich, former parliamentary chairperson and head of state, to undertake a political career. Like his rival Paznyak, Shushkevich was an academic who joined the political fray because of his outrage over governmental inaction following the Chernobyl accident. Chernobyl—located just five miles south of the Belarusian border—caused greater contamination in Belarus than in Ukraine because of the prevailing winds. Both Moscow and Minsk greatly underestimated the severity of the accident and thus exposed many to radiation. Belarus reportedly continues to allocate as much as 20 percent of its annual budget to the cleanup and medical care associated with this accident.[36]

Chernobyl, like the discovery of the Karapaty graves, became a symbol of a threat to the Belarusian nation. In addition to being a technical and medical disaster, Chernobyl became a unifying event around which both elites and masses could rally. Thus, Chernobyl, like the storming of the Vilnius television tower and the Tbilisi massacre, has become a powerful political symbol that led to a changed political climate.

The Political Climate

The potential for at least modest political change became evident in Belarus during the 1990 Supreme Soviet elections. Communists lost seats, though they maintained a decisive majority; the Belarusian Popular Front gained 10 percent of parliamentary seats (Shushkevich and Paznyak, both allied with the Popular Front, won their races). This Soviet-era parliament remained in power until 1995, having ignored petitions to advance the date of elections. Former BSSR leaders currently fill most top governmental positions and the Popular Front continues in opposition.

Belarus' conservatism remains evident. In the March 1991, vote on preservation of the union, Belarus followed Moscow in policy and spirit. While other republics declined to participate or modified the questions put to the electorate, Belarusians voted on the referendum determined by Moscow. Eighty-three percent favored the preservation of the union, compared to 76 percent throughout the whole USSR.[37] Belarus' leadership also quickly supported the August 1991 coup. Only after Gorbachev returned to power did Belarus follow the other republics and declare sovereignty.

With the exception of Shushkevich, elected chairman of the Supreme Soviet after the coup, other officials were holdovers from the precoup regime. Belarus, with only limited nationalist ambitions, still favored a new union treaty. Shushkevich merely requested a "fair union."[38] Only after Ukraine's December 1991 vote did Belarus change its position. Shushkevich joined Yeltsin and

Kravchuk in establishing the Commonwealth of Independent States. Yet within the CIS, Belarus still looked to the old "center."

Some nationalists feared that the presence of the CIS capital in Minsk would rob Belarusians of a national core and facilitate further russification. As Popular Front supporters noted:

> The new commonwealth is a compromise between Russia, which wants to take over the role of the Soviet Union together with its property, and Ukraine, which is striving toward independence. Belarus remains an economic and political appendage of Russia. . . . Minsk should not be a bureaucratic creature of the commonwealth, the center of mafia structures, a place to dump worthless rubles and further Russify us. Our country should not be Russia's window on Europe but an independent [and equal] European state.[39]

Referendum/ Parliamentary Elections.   Unlike most other successor states, Belarus delayed the first postcommunist parliamentary or presidential elections. Content with the status quo, parliament waited until Spring 1994 to define the relationship among the government, chief executive, and legislature in a new constitution. This constitution places executive power in the hands of a president and further states that Belarus will remain neutral and nuclear free.

Throughout Winter/Spring 1992, the Popular Front collected over 500,000 signatures calling for a referendum on new elections in an effort to replace deputies who had been elected in 1990 for five-year terms under conditions to assure Communist Party control. Communist Party holdovers still controlled three-fourths of the parliamentary seats and most governmental positions. Parliamentarians, including then-chairman Shushkevich, opposed new elections, claiming that the existing parliament was adequate. The election commission validated the signatures on Popular Front petitions and declared them sufficient. Nonetheless, the parliament voted overwhelmingly against holding a referendum on new elections. Popular Front leader Paznyak called this vote "a holding on to power by unlawful means."[40] The parliament's only response to the petitions was to shorten terms to four years, with the next elections scheduled in March 1994. As the date approached, this "early" election failed to materialize.

Supporters of new elections argued that the existing communist-dominated parliament could not introduce the reforms necessary for Belarusian integration into the western community. The parliament's supporters maintained, however, that Belarus would attract western support and investment precisely because of its political stability. Nonetheless, western attention paid to Belarus has been minimal, a situation likely to continue because of Belarus' dependence upon Moscow and inability to reform.

> The most acute and fundamental problem in the Belarusian parliament and political life overall is the lack of a "center" to ease the way to compromise and accord. Deputies are sharply split into radical and conservative factions. A still weak sense of statehood has left Belarus with a barely formulated national agenda.[41]

Shushkevich, the closest to a centrist political figure, lost parliamentary support. He found himself in constant conflict with the pro-Russian Prime Minister Kebich, but never adopted the more nationalist political action program of the Popular Front. The strongest legislative bloc remains the People's Movement of Belarus (PMB), formed in March 1993, from procommunist organizations (including the Party of Communists of Belarus and the Slavic Assembly) that favor confederation with Russia. It attributes Belarus' current problems to Soviet dissolution, contending that reconstituting the USSR will solve Belarusian problems.[42] This group, noting that two-thirds of Belarusian trade remains with Russia, believes that a renewed linkage is both desirable and natural. According to a spokesperson for the organization, the PMB is

> a left-centrist organization. The key concept for us is justice. This is social guarantees and the right of workers and peasants to determine the forms of economic management for themselves, the freedom of private and collective initiative directed toward the welfare of the fatherland, and the protection of our spiritual heritage from "Americanization" and "mass culture."[43]

Despite its failure to dissolve parliament, the Popular Front remains the most serious Belarusian nationalist force. From its beginning, the BPF opposed ties between Belarus and Russia, opposed participation in the CIS, and championed democratic reforms. While advocating political separation from Moscow and policies protecting Belarusian culture, the BPF has taken moderately accommodative positions on international relations, citizenship, and language. Its founding documents stressed Belarus' multinational composition and the need to foster majority and minority cultures. The BPF supported the provision in the Declaration of Sovereignty stating that "citizens of the Belarusian SSR of all nationalities . . . constitute the Belarusian people"[44] and the July 1993 citizenship law conferring citizenship on all legal residents of Belarus.

A summer 1993 public opinion poll showed the BPF was supported by only one-sixth of the population. Eighteen percent of Belarusians and only 8 percent of Russians supported the BPF.[45] Paznyak earned the confidence of only 16 percent of the population, while 47 percent expressed no confidence in him.[46] Thus, the strongest nationalist party continues to have only limited support.

Belarus' political stalemate came to a head in January 1994 when Parliament held "no confidence" votes on both Shushkevich and Kebich. Shushkevich, the moderate parliamentary chairman out of step with the conservative majority, lost by a 209 to 36 margin. Prime Minister Kebich was retained by a margin of 175 to 101.[47] Popular Front leader Paznyak called the ouster of Shushkevich a "communist *coup de etat*" by conservative hard-liners.[48]

The 1994 Presidential Election.   The Belarusian constitution gave executive power to a president, with the first election for the position to be held in Summer 1994. Prior to this election, the chairman of the parliament had served as chief executive and head of state. In the first round of voting, Prime Minister Vyacheslav Kebich, the architect of the plan for Belarus to join the Russian economic zone, and populist Alyaksandr Lukashenka took the most votes. Lukashenka then defeated Kebich with 80 percent of the vote in the run-off. Both former parliamentary chairman Shushkevich (a centrist) and Popular Front leader Paznyak (a nationalist) failed to make the runoff.

Thus, both of the candidates in the final vote favored closer relations with Russia. Lukashenka, the winner, is a former state farm director who gained notoriety by crusading against governmental corruption. While an advocate of closer relations with Russia in both monetary and political spheres, Lukashenka is a flamboyant politician with a limited public record. Thus, Belarus' future under his leadership is less clear than it might have been had Kebich, Shushkevich, or Paznyak prevailed. Lukashenka's first year in office has not led to the major changes he promised in his campaign, namely a union with Russia or a halt to privatization.

The Military

Belarus had to break free of former Soviet military structures to build an independent state. Like Ukraine, the Belarusian military had a preponderance of Russian officers. By mid-1992 only 30 percent of the officers in Belarus were Belarusian, another 20 percent were Ukrainian, and over 50 percent were Russian. Defense Ministry staff was only 20 percent Belarusian.[49] Ukraine moved quickly to establish its own military, challenging Moscow for military jurisdiction on Ukrainian soil. In contrast, the Belarusian Military District's commander favored maintaining a unified military.[50]

One nationalist goal was achieved when Belarusian became the language of the military in mid–1992. Shushkevich had opposed the Russian demand for bilingualism, calling it "usual laziness and inability to learn Belarusian."[51] By the end of 1993, the military had been reduced to under 100,000.[52] In spite of calls to maintain Russian connections, derussification of the military proceeded. Nonetheless, 40,000 Russian troops remained in Belarus, some because of strategic missile facilities and some because Russia claimed housing shortages.[53]

The military itself has both pro-Russian and nationalist organizations. The Belarusian Association of Servicemen, a nationalist organization advocating defense of Belarusian independence, supports the creation of an independent military to defend Belarusian sovereignty. It, like the Popular Front, strongly backs derussification. The rival Union of Officers of Belarus opposes Belarusian independence. It "assailed the Belarusian popular front and its 'offspring,' the Belarusian Association of Servicemen, for having cooked up the idea of neutrality as an excuse to 'tear Belarus away from Russia' and clear the way for the creation of a Baltic-to-Black Sea cordon sanitaire between Western Europe and Russia."[54]

Neutrality

Belarus' Declaration of State Sovereignty served as fundamental constitutional law prior to the approval of a new constitution in Spring 1994. An important principle of this declaration was neutrality. Because of the presence of Russian troops and Belarus' close ties with Moscow, this neutrality created a dilemma, as noted by Shushkevich:

> To move quickly toward genuine sovereignty . . . and real neutrality, is impossible. . . . We're in close military union with Russia. . . . Neutrality is out of the question in such a union, but each step we take is aimed at loosening the ties. . . . Speeding up these processes [of forming an independent army] would be senseless; we've seen what has happened in other places, and we don't want to injure . . . the dignity of officers.[55]

While acknowledging the connections between Belarus and Russia, Shushkevich opposed Belarusian participation in collective security arrangements with the CIS states, and blocked Belarus' participation in the May 1992, security agreement approved by the CIS Tashkent meeting. Prime Minister Kebich, however, strongly supported the agreement, arguing that military and economic ties between Russia and Belarus would rescue Belarus' ailing economy. Following Kebich's lead, the Supreme Council in April 1993, approved Belarusian membership in the Tashkent pact, ignoring the neutrality provision of Belarus' Declaration of Sovereignty. Polls, however, showed 55 percent of the population supported neutrality.[56] Military, communist, pan-Slavic, and Russian supremacist groups—all opposing derussification—supported Kebich's vision of a common economic and military space with Russia.[57]

The Popular Front opposed the pact, fearing for Belarusian sovereignty. Shushkevich refused to sign the agreement, appealed for a referendum, and threatened resignation. The stalemate continued throughout 1993, with no agreement, no referendum, and no resignation. With Shushkevich's ouster in January 1994, Belarus approved the agreement and reestablished one more link with Russia. From Russia's perspective, the agreement was important; because of the republic's strategic location and forested landscape, the Soviet Union had concentrated much of its military in Belarus. With the Baltics resolutely independent and Ukraine on a nationalistic course, Belarus now has even greater geostrategic significance for Moscow.

Union with Russia

In late 1993 Belarus and Russia strengthened ties in both economic and military spheres. On November 18, the parliament ratified a monetary union with Russia, despite Shushkevich's opposition. But neither economic nor military union have actually been implemented. As Kebich's supporters then argued:

> We have to think about the survival of our people! By forging an economic and military-political alliance with Russia and Kazakhstan . . . we will return to the earlier system of strong integration, we will gain access to raw material and sources of energy at low preferential prices, and Belarus' numerous military plants can expect orders and financing again. . . . what good is independence if the life of the people is growing worse and worse?[58]

The agreement removed Russian tariffs on Belarusian goods sold in Russia, allowing the accumulation of currency to buy Russian raw materials. Even Shushkevich agreed that closer economic connections with Russia and the CIS would strengthen Belarus' economy. The tariff issue has been used by Moscow against many successor states to force them to make either economic or military concessions.

Moscow's reformers opposed this renewed union and its approval contributed to Deputy Prime Minister Gaidar's January 1994 resignation. Russian economists feared that Belarus' lagging reforms would endanger Russian economic progress. Belarusian procommunist groups actively lobbied for union with Russia on economic grounds, at the same time arguing that the Russian language should receive equal status with Belarusian. The Popular Front and other groups representing national minorities in Belarus continue to oppose closer ties with Russia.[59]

The historically late and still incomplete nationalization process thus remains evident in current Belarusian politics. Belarus' lack of a nationalist political action program has meant that the international relations between Belarusians and Russians domestically have lacked the hostility found in many of the other successor states, and inter-state attitudes between Minsk and Moscow have been relatively unchanged. In contrast, we now turn to Ukraine, which has long had a sense of nationhood. This sense of national self-consciousness among much of the Ukrainian population, especially in the West, has characterized both international and interstate relations.

Ukraine

More than eleven million Russians live in Ukraine. These Russians, constituting 21.9 percent of Ukraine's 51.7 million people, comprise the largest Russian population outside Russia itself. Eighty percent of these Russians live on the historically Orthodox, Russian-speaking left bank of the Dnipro River, particularly in the highly industrialized Donbas, Novorossiya, and Crimean areas. This regional cleavage, with the historic russification of left-bank Ukrainians in contrast to the Ukrainian-speaking and Catholic West, is key to understanding inter-national relations in Ukraine today.

Because of size, urban concentration, and economic productivity, Russians have disproportionate influence in independent Ukraine and on inter-state relations. Some Russians want certain Ukrainian oblasts attached to Russia; others prefer citizenship in an independent Ukraine. However, as economic conditions have deteriorated after independence, both Russians and Ukrainians, led by the Communist Party especially in the East and South, have increasingly looked to greater linkage with Russia as a remedy for Ukraine's economic difficulties.

Except for a short period after the Bolshevik Revolution, Ukraine has never been independent. Nevertheless, Ukrainian independence after the August 1991, coup and the December 1991, referendum was hardly unimaginable. Ukrainians, particularly in the West, had internalized a sense of national identity, even though Polish, Russian, and Soviet domination had blocked its political fulfillment. Occupying a large territory with abundant resources and population, Ukrainians had long had an independence movement. In fact, Moscow encouraged development of Ukrainian identity during the early years of Soviet power through indigenization policies. Stalin reversed direction in the 1930s, reducing titular control and promoting russification. First famine and then World War II brought further trauma. Khrushchev's ascension led to renewed ukrainianization, only to be reversed by Brezhnev.

Under Gorbachev, Ukrainians again could express nationalist sentiments. *Glasnost'* enabled such sentiments to blossom, especially in response to the Chernobyl accident; nonetheless, Ukraine lagged behind other republics in pursuing a nationalistic political action program. Not until 1988 did the Ukrainian writers union, targeting language policy, advocate more nationally conscious reform.[60] Nationalist advocacy came primarily from the west around Lviv, a formerly Polish territory with the highest Ukrainian concentration, which became the center for *RUKH*, the Ukrainian movement for *perestroyka*. The March 1990 parliamentary election, in which the noncommunist and *Rukh*-supported opposition won a quarter of Supreme Soviet seats, then opened public discussion of Ukrainian sovereignty.

On July 16, 1990, opposition activities culminated in the Supreme Soviet's almost unanimous declaration of sovereignty (355 in favor, four against, one abstention), which claimed primacy for Ukrainian laws on Ukrainian territory and the right to a republican army.[61] The parliament also addressed "free development of the cultures of all nationalities residing in Ukraine," regulation of "emigration processes," "the functioning of Ukrainian language in all spheres of social life" and defense of Ukrainian citizens outside the republic.[62] Republican citizenship, though still nested within Soviet citizenship, was defined.

Because their languages, cultures, and histories are so closely linked, Russians in both Ukraine and the Russian Federation were shocked by Ukraine's declaration of sovereignty. To Russians, Ukrainians (and Belarusians) were "peoples of one blood *(edinokrovnye)*," linked organically with Russia, differing only by dialect.[63] Russians living in Ukraine did not feel that they were living in a foreign land:

> According to a study done by the Moscow Center for the Study of Public Opinion in 1991, most Russians in Ukraine do not feel themselves strangers there. Ninety percent of the Russians in the Crimea, 89 percent in the eastern region, 86 percent in the central and southern regions, 72 percent in the southwestern region (Bukovina), and 68 percent in Galicia answered in the affirmative when they were asked: "Do you agree with the statement 'I do not feel myself as a stranger in this Republic'?"[64]

Ukrainian sovereignty was thus more traumatic for Russians than Baltic or Caucasian independence. Ukrainian independence separated Russia from its roots and effectively ended the multinational state known first as the Russian Empire and later as the Soviet Union. For Ukrainians, a new relationship with Russia was an important step in developing a new national self-image as well as a foreign-policy goal.

This section examines the Russian minority within a newly independent Ukraine. It analyzes the extent to which Ukraine has been able to accommodate its Russian minority, construct a functioning multinational state, and develop new relations with the Russian Federation. Like the Baltics but unlike Belarus, Ukraine and Ukrainians fit our definition of a *nation* as a backward-looking community of belonging and a forward-looking community of interest. But that notion must be qualified in left-bank areas where russophone Ukrainians identify as strongly with their Russian neighbors as with their Ukrainian ancestors. This common interest has limited Kiev's ability to act as a nationalist regime, and has led to an inclusive policy toward Russians and political conceptions of a civic state.[65] For the most part, the Ukrainian leadership has pursued policies in the name of all Ukrainian citizens rather than in the name of the Ukrainian nation. *RUKH* has been split on this issue, though it has consistently advocated a more nationalistic agenda than either the Kravchuk or Kuchma governments.

Citizenship provides one example of the inclusive approach of the Ukrainian elites. The October 1991, citizenship law granted citizenship to all who were resident in Ukraine when the law passed. No naturalization process and no language requirement were attached to citizenship. This "zero option" method paralleled the Kazakh and Moldovan approaches, but differed from the more exclusionary Estonian and Latvian ones. It differed also from the Lithuanian method, which, though inclusive, required naturalization. Ukrainanian citizenship placed civic identification ahead of national identification and carried rights for individuals, not groups. Citizenship without regard to national identity thus provides an important starting point in distinguishing the Ukrainian from the Baltic strategy.

Inter-National and Inter-State Relations

The presence of so many Russians in an independent Ukraine complicates Russian-Ukrainian inter-state relations. Without anticipating the next two years' developments, Ukraine and Russia signed a treaty on November 19, 1990, specifying the inviolability of existing borders. Nonetheless, when Ukraine declared sovereignty, Russia raised border questions. Moscow's mayor, Gavril Popov "said that negotiations must be held on the territories of the Crimea, Odessa, the Dniester region, and northern Kazakhstan."[66] Similarly, Foreign Minister Kozyrev spoke in support of Russian minorities in the "near abroad," and St. Petersburg's mayor, Anatolii Sobchak, warned of "forced ukrainianization" of the Russian minority and a potential territorial conflict.[67]

Strong assertions of Ukraine's independence vis-à-vis Russia brought Kravchuk and others support from nationalistic Ukrainians, especially in the western areas that came under Soviet control only in 1939. However, an exclusionary nationalist agenda vis-à-vis Russians domestically has been muted from the beginning. Before the coup, Kravchuk contrasted the situation of Russians in Ukraine with that in other republics, reiterating Ukraine's need to respect minority rights: "Russians in Ukraine should not be compared with the Russians in the Baltic republics. Here they are indigenous residents, they have lived on this land for hundreds of years. . . . we will not permit any kind of discrimination against them."[68]

Western areas exhibit strong Ukrainian nationalism, and eastern and southern areas show Russian separatism. Donbas and Crimea have the highest Russian concentrations. Kiev, while thus far choosing the model of a unitary state, has nonetheless made specific concessions to Donbas and especially Crimea. Because of these significant regional differences, Kiev may be forced to consider greater regional autonomy through a federal system. Federal approaches, however, sometimes unwittingly foster secession by institutionalizing regionalism.[69] Because so many of the cleavages in Ukraine are regional, we will examine the two areas with the highest Russian concentrations, Donbas and Crimea, before focusing on the issues of public opinion and language.

Donbas. Including the Donetsk and Luhansk oblasts, Donbas borders Russia; in 1989, 51 percent of the population was Ukrainian and 44 percent Russian. However, Ukrainians in Donbas, frequently more fluent in Russian than in Ukrainian, resist ukrainianization. Donbas language usage illustrates the degree of russification and regional differentiation: only 32 percent consider Ukrainian to be their native language, while 66 percent name Russian. Only 3 percent of Donetsk children and 7 percent in Luhansk study in Ukrainian.[70] Thus, making Ukrainian the state language has fostered resentment among both Russians and Russian-speaking Ukrainians. Local referenda held in Donbas cities during the Spring 1994 parliamentary elections indicated that most favored designating Russian a state language together with Ukrainian. Such a move would most likely provide local Russian-speakers an excuse for not learning or using Ukrainian rather than create the basis for a genuinely bilingual region.

Economic politics dominate heavily industrialized Donbas. While producing 21 percent of Ukraine's industrial output, Donbas faces economic decline. Both Ukrainians and Russians here "believe that the region gets less money from Kiev than it contributes to the state budget."[71] In fact, Kiev's subsidies of Donbas' antiquated industries and mines have slowed economic reform, and Donbas' threats of separatism have kept Kiev from adopting bolder economic strategies. The breaking of ties between enterprises and former all-union economic structures have made the Soviet breakup especially difficult for Donbas, and many Ukrainians as well as Russians wish to rebuild these former connections. In mid-1993, one commentator noted that in Donbas, "the idea of independence is now bankrupt. Russia will hardly be able to remain aloof from supporting the mounting pro-Russian sentiments in eastern Ukraine. . . . The political conflict in Ukraine could confront Russia with a dilemma—to take or not to take the left bank of the (Dnipro) under its economic protection."[72]

The regional and cultural identity that links Donbas' Russians and Ukrainians is more salient than is national identity within the region. Both groups are united by economic circumstances and ties to central economic structures that have been disturbed by Ukrainian independence. Language and culture are not issues between them; Donbas Ukrainians have been russified, not so much by force or policy—but by history and proximity. The cleavage is not between Donbas Russians and Ukrainians, but between a Russian-leaning region and those Ukrainians with a nationalistic agenda, whether represented by governmental institutions in Kiev or by nationalist groups in western Ukraine.

Crimea.   National identity (Russians, Ukrainians, and Tatars), jurisdiction (Russian control, Ukrainian control, or territorial autonomy), and military affairs (the Black Sea fleet) come together in Crimea, Ukraine's only oblast with a Russian majority. Russians comprise approximately 1.6 million of Crimea's 2.4 million people. Ukrainians number 626,000, half of whom name Russian as their native language. Over 280,000 Crimean Tatars constitute another historically and demographically significant group.

Since wresting Crimea from Ottoman control in the 18th century, Russians have considered Crimea to be not only part of their state but part of their homeland. The current dispute dates from 1954 when Nikita Khrushchev transferred jurisdiction of Crimea from Russia to Ukraine in celebration of 300 years of Russian and Ukrainian unity. Nonetheless, this Russian-dominated oblast remained economically and militarily tied to Moscow; Kiev had only limited authority over Crimea under Soviet laws.

Following Soviet dissolution, the Russian Federation parliament and some Crimean Russians have attempted to reclaim Crimea for Russia. Crimea's Ukrainian minority, though russified and concentrated mostly in the peninsula's north, threatened secession from a Russia-controlled Crimea, thus distinguishing themselves from the even more Russian-oriented Ukrainians in Donbas.[73]

Ukraine's sovereignty sent shock waves through Crimea's Russian community. Independence provided the opportunity for Ukrainians to develop a full national identity; Crimea's Russians perceived a status shift from dominance to subordination. But little actually changed for Russians in Crimea: "They have television in Russian, newspapers, schools, theaters—all cultural life in Crimea is lived in Russian."[74] Despite Kravchuk's assurances that Crimeans could manage their own affairs, the Republic Movement of Crimea nonetheless accused "Kiev of discriminating against the predominantly Russian-speaking population by replacing Russian television and radio programs with Ukrainian ones and by sending documents written only in the Ukrainian language."[75] Governmental documents and media (together with education) were indeed the areas where Kiev, in spite of its generally inclusive policies, pursued a nationalizing political action program.[76] The Russian majority's sensitivity to these issues provoked a debate on Crimea's political allegiance.

As Ukraine struggled to consolidate independence, Crimea's Communist Party forced debate on Crimea's future status: Should Crimea be an independent union republic, a part of Ukraine, or a part of Russia? The ultimate goal for most of Crimea's Russians was reunification with Russia. On January 20, 1991, 93.3 percent voted to "reestablish the Crimean Autonomous Soviet Socialist Republic as 'a subject of the USSR and a party to the Union Treaty.'" The Russian majority in Crimea felt that Kiev had made decisions on language and sovereignty without its participation. On February 12, 1991, bowing to local sentiment, the Ukrainian Supreme Soviet designated Crimea a "republic" of Ukraine, reinstating Crimea's pre-1945 autonomous status and conceding local power to the Crimean legislature.[77]

Crimean voting patterns in the December 1, 1991, Ukrainian independence vote lacked unanimity. Although *Krymskaya pravda* noted "that (independence) will, of course, call forth a sharp negative reaction from the absolute majority of inhabitants of Crimea,"[78] opinion was divided. A slight majority (54.2 percent) of Crimean voters supported Ukrainian independence, though the turnout was low and many Russians stayed away from the polls. A January 1992, poll showed that 42 percent favored Crimea's remaining in Ukraine, 15 percent favored returning to Russia, 22 percent favored republic status in the CIS, and 8 percent favored independence.[79]

Later data from Simferopol noted a divergence of Russian and Ukrainian attitudes on Ukrainian independence that was likely present in the December vote as well. Bremmer's October 1992, survey showed that 79 percent of Ukrainians in Simferopol wanted to be citizens of a Ukrainian state, while 27 percent of the Russians held similar views. When asked whether they would like their children to study in Ukrainian schools, 43 percent of the Ukrainians answered positively (the low number showing evidence of russification), but only 9 percent of the Russians agreed. Regarding the Soviet breakup, 42 percent of the Ukrainians and 75 percent of Russians preferred that the USSR still exist. Russians surveyed in Lviv and Kiev were much more positive toward Ukrainian citizenship, less negative on Ukrainian schools, and less desirous of Soviet continuation.[80]

After Soviet dissolution, Crimea and the Black Sea Fleet continued to occupy center stage in the Ukrainian-Russian inter-state conflict. The conservative Russian parliament contributed to the controversy by instructing two of its committees to examine the 1954 Crimean transfer, in spite of the 1990 agreement between Yeltsin and Kravchuk reaffirming existing borders. Naturally, Ukrainian suspicion of Russian motives intensified; Ukrainian counter-statements to Russia were perceived as nationalist by the Russian minority in Ukraine, which then reacted with its own rising minority nationalism. The external Russian state continued to be a player in the domestic interaction between the Ukrainian and Russian populations.

On February 26, 1992, the Crimean Supreme Soviet renamed the peninsula the Republic of Crimea. Although President Kravchuk reiterated Ukrainian respect for Crimean autonomy, he appealed to Crimean lawmakers and residents to reject a local referendum on secession from Ukraine, arguing that separatists were "sowing discord between Crimea and Ukraine" and setting "Russia against

Ukraine by playing the Crimean card." Kravchuk guaranteed Crimeans broad autonomy while demanding protection of Ukrainian and Tatar minority rights in Crimea.[81]

By April 1992, Crimeans had collected over 250,000 signatures for a referendum on Crimean independence. The Ukrainian parliament reacted with a law reiterating that Crimea was Ukrainian. The Crimean parliament scheduled a referendum for August 2 as a step toward Crimea-Russian reunification.[82] Ukraine annulled the Crimean parliamentary moves, and the Crimean parliament backed down. On the same day, the Russian parliament voted to declare the 1954 transfer invalid, inviting Kiev's protests. On June 1, 1992, Ukrainian and Crimean parliamentary heads compromised. A joint Ukrainian-Crimean declaration "defined the peninsula as 'an integral part of Ukraine'" but with special economic status and the right "to enter into social, economic, and cultural relations with other states."[83] According to the Crimea's 1992 constitution, reinstated in 1994, relations between Crimea and Kiev are governed by treaties as though Crimea were an independent state.

This jockeying has now continued for several years, with Crimean authorities pressing for greater autonomy and threatening reunification with Russia, and Kiev's conceding control on local issues but insisting on Crimea's continued Ukrainian status. Kiev has already conceded significant autonomy to avoid Crimean secession. According to Gennadi Siunkov, editor of *Krymskie izvestia*: "The federative tendency is ripening. After the Crimea, the Donbas may separate, and western Ukraine. Ties will remain but (the areas) will dispose of their resources as they see fit, without submitting to the center (Kiev)."[84] Likewise, former Party chief Bagrov argues: "Within Ukraine there is a republic of Crimea. And the republic should have broader rights than any other area within Ukraine."[85]

During the January 1994, election for the Crimean presidency, Bagrov took a relatively moderate stand, advocating Crimea's continuation as an autonomous republic within Ukraine. Yuri Meshkov, his overtly pro-Russian—"in spirit, the Crimean people have been and remain part of the Russian people"[86]—and anti-Tatar opponent, won by championing a referendum on Crimea's status and possible union with Russia. The Ukrainian parliament then responded by granting Ukraine's president authority to overrule those Crimean actions that violate Ukraine's constitution and laws.[87] The salience of these issues to both Moscow and Kiev has been reduced during much of 1994 and early 1995, as most energy has been directed at internal squabbling between Meshkov and the Crimean parliament. Kiev continues to pressure Crimea to make its laws conform to Ukrainian laws; Moscow, at least for the moment, is staying clear of the controversy.

Crimea illustrates both interactive nationalism and Russia's role as an external homeland. The Russian majority in Crimea remains sensitive not only to potential nationalist policies of the Kiev government, but to any action that Kiev might take vis-à-vis Moscow to underscore its independence. At the same time, Crimea opens a discussion of jurisdiction and secession as a result of its arbitrary transfer from Russia to Ukraine in 1954:

According to . . . theoretical and ethical discussions about . . . self-determination, the demands for independence from Ukraine made by Russians living in Crimea have questionable legitimacy, since the Russians are not indigenous (and) have a separate homeland available to them. . . . If . . . population distributions are given greater weight, and if we recognize that Crimea became a part of Ukraine only in 1954, then Russian claims do fall within the legitimacy principle of nationalism which dictates that "ethnic boundaries should not cross political boundaries." In addition, the right to secede generally includes a claim by the secessionist group that it was incorporated against its will. If the Russians can demonstrate through referendum that a majority of the population of Crimea does prefer full independence from Ukraine, then a continued insistence by Kiev to holding on to Crimea could give rise to the argument of involuntary incorporation.[88]

Crimea is important to Moscow for both symbolic and military reasons. However, many areas of the Russian Federation might be compared to Crimea. If Crimeans become independent or change jurisdiction, then what about the status of national groups (Tatars, Chechens) living in defined homelands within the Russian Federation? Do they have the same right to disengage from Russia that Russia would grant to Crimea? For this reason the most clamor on Crimea comes from conservative parliamentarians rather than Yeltsin or his government. But that too might change as Yeltsin is forced to acknowledge the political strength of his conservative opponents. Whatever the outcome, the interactive, triangular process is clear; each step by Kiev to underscore Ukrainian autonomy leads to Russian reaction, both from the Russian population and leadership in Crimea and from Moscow. Because of the presence of the Black Sea Fleet, this interaction is particularly notable in the military sphere.

Military Forces.   One of Ukraine's first acts after Soviet dissolution was to assert control over troops stationed on Ukrainian soil. The original order included the Black Sea Fleet, headquartered in Crimea, again complicating the Crimean relationship for both Russia and Ukraine. Ukraine ordered troops to pledge allegiance to defend Ukrainian independence. But "more than 44 percent of soldiers based in Ukraine were ethnic Russian, 40.3 percent were ethnic Ukrainian. . . . 75 percent of all officers in Ukraine were ethnic Russians. . . . 19 percent of all [Black Sea Fleet] officers were Ukrainian, and . . . among petty officers and seamen roughly 30 percent were Ukrainian."[89]

President Kravchuk, trying to avoid inter-national conflict in the military, attempted to gain the loyalty of Russian as well as Ukrainian officers. He assured all that they were Ukrainian citizens, whatever their national identity. Many were thus willing to swear loyalty to Ukraine, quickly providing Kravchuk with a force nominally responsive to Kiev.

The Black Sea Fleet became the most complicated military issue. Ukraine first claimed the fleet because of its Crimean headquarters. Then Russia and Ukraine agreed to divide it, with negotiations on how to do so continuing without success. The restructuring of the military and the Black Sea Fleet controversy provide symbolic issues for both Ukrainians and Russians: Exclusionary nationalist actions by Ukrainians provoke reactions from the Russian Federation as well as from Ukraine's Russian minority. Likewise, Russian reactions, either by Moscow or by the Russian minority (for example, in Crimea) are seen as a threat to the Ukrainian nation, causing still further nationalist responses.

The military is one area where the Ukrainian leadership has pursued more determined nationalization. Unlike other Russians who have crosscutting loyalties because of ties to families and jobs in Ukraine as well as to a Russian culture or homeland, the Russian officer corps has no such linkage to Ukraine. Its loyalty was to the USSR and, after its demise, to Russia. Thus, the Kravchuk government was quick to restructure the military in spite of potential Russian reaction, realizing that independence, without the availability of force to protect it, would be ephemeral.

Indicators of Russian Opinion in Ukraine

Russians were first confused by the Ukrainian independence movement because of their difficulty in accepting Ukrainians as a distinct nation and Ukraine as a distinct homeland. Public opinion then evolved to the point where perhaps as many as half of Ukraine's Russians favored independence for the Ukrainian state. This support then declined as economic realities replaced earlier hopes. Evidence from polls and votes, culminating in the 1994 parliamentary and presidential elections, underline the growing differences in perspective between the eastern and western areas of the country.

Little evidence can be found of governmental anti-Russian behavior, though the more nationalist wing of RUKH has tended to be anti-Russian as well as anti-Russia. The Ukrainian state has taken steps to secure independence, but independence for all groups living in Ukraine. Many Russians, however, perceived Ukrainian independence itself to be a threat. "Inter-nationalism," a term (from the Soviet or Russian perspective) connoting cooperation among nations, was often used as the banner for Russian mobilization against indigenous assertiveness.

One of the first Russian groups to coalesce was the Donbas Inter-movement. The initial catalyst was language legislation, though this law put little pressure on Russians to learn Ukrainian. In fact, the oblast center, Donetsk, did not have a Ukrainian-language school until 1990. Russian groups opposing Ukrainian nationalism, supporting the union treaty, and favoring ties to Russia and the USSR were also developing in the southern area of Ukraine known as Novorossiya (Odessa, Nikolaev, Kherson, and Dnepropetrovsk oblasts) and in Crimea.[90] Such regionally based sentiment, along with that developing in Transcarpathia (with its Ruthenian/Rusyn population) and in nationalist western Ukraine, has led to talk of federalizaton.

On March 17, 1991, a poll was held on the union's future throughout the USSR. Some republics substituted their own referenda, while others added additional questions. Ukrainian voters, in addition to the all-union question, were asked: "Do you agree that Ukraine should be part of a union of sovereign states on principles of the declaration on state sovereignty of Ukraine?"[91]

An overwhelming 80.2 percent voted "yes," thus qualifying the similarly positive result of the all-union referendum on Union preservation. Though somewhat contradictory, the results likely meant that the majority favored continuation of the Soviet federation, though with greater sovereignty for its constituent parts. In this early vote, Donbas and Crimea strongly supported both Moscow's statement of union and Kiev's statement of sovereignty.

In contrast, Moscow's referendum on union continuation was rejected by over three-fourths of the voters in the western oblasts of Ivano-Frankivsk, Lviv, and Ternopil. Together, the West showed only 15 percent in favor of the union as defined by Moscow, 19.3 percent in favor of staying in the union even on the limited terms defined by the republic, and 89.9 percent for complete independence.[92] These more nationalistic western regions from the beginning of the independence movement have taken a political approach distinct from that of the left bank.

The August 1991, coup was decisive for Ukraine as well as for the other republics. Kravchuk at first took a "wait and see" position, not challenging the Emergency Committee as did Yeltsin and Nazarbaev. After the coup collapsed, Kravchuk banned the Communist Party and worked for greater sovereignty. Postcoup comments from Moscow about border adjustments and nuclear weapons made Kravchuk increasingly wary of Moscow; his reactions to Moscow's statements caused increased concern among Ukraine's Russians about their status in an independent Ukraine.

The most significant postcoup event was the vote on independence and the presidency of December 1991. The referendum asked: "Do you endorse the proclamation of the independence of Ukraine?" Numerous pre-referendum polls showed the population's favoring independence but, like the December vote, divided regionally and nationally. One poll showed 63 percent favoring independence and 17.3 percent against. Another poll found the margin to be 74 percent for and 12 percent against.[93] Western Ukraine had the highest percentage in favor of independence, though even Crimea had a majority supporting independence. By oblast, favorable percentages were Lviv: 86, Ternopil: 92, Odessa: 83, Donetsk: 65, Transcarpathia: 76, Kiev: 88 Chernovitsy: 76, Chernigov: 60, and Crimea: 53.[94]

Between September and October 1991, Russian support for Ukrainian independence grew from 45.9 percent to 58.3 percent.[95] A second October poll showed that among Russians, 55 percent favored independence, 16 percent opposed it, and 29 percent were undecided. In addition, 78 percent of the Russians opposed border changes, while 9 percent thought that parts of Ukraine should belong to Russia.[96]

These polls traced both psychological and political changes. In 1990, "sovereignty" connoted a new concept of union, with constituent republics gaining more autonomy within the Soviet federation. Soon this thinking became outmoded, with greater proportions of the population, particularly in the western oblasts, imagining that Ukraine could become an independent European state. After the 1991 coup, the desire for independence became widespread. Even a majority of Ukraine's Russians viewed an independent Ukraine favorably.

Polling data cannot convey the powerful message given by the electorate on December 1, 1991. This vote, both a referendum on independence and a presidential election, broke historic Ukrainian-Russian ties. In western and central

Ukraine, over 90 percent of those voting supported independence. The vote's overwhelming margin showed Russians as well as Ukrainians supporting independence. Concomitantly, Leonid Kravchuk was elected president with 62 percent in a six-candidate field:

> (T)he vote for independence in the key industrialized but Russified oblasts was: in Donetsk, 83.9 percent; in Dnepropetrovsk, 90.3 percent; in Zaporozhe, 90.6 percent; in Kharkov, 86.3 percent; in Lugansk, 83.8 percent. In the southern Black Sea oblasts, support for independence was also very high: in Odessa, 85.3 percent of the votes were in favor; in Nikolaev, 89.4 percent; and, in Kherson, 90.1 percent. Even in the Crimea . . . 54.1 percent of the participants voted for independence.[97]

These votes underscore the process toward redefinition of the relationship with Moscow that was well underway; the margins indicated that Russians as well as Ukrainians were rethinking assumptions that Ukraine must remain subordinate to Moscow. However, the reality of independence soon intruded on the euphoria of Ukrainian nationalists and the cautious hopes of Ukraine's Russians. Rather than improved living conditions as a result of the break with Russia, the first years of independence have brought severe economic recession.

Ukrainians and Russians alike are reevaluating their 1991 decisions and wondering if linkage with Russia might enhance their deteriorating economic situation. A poll conducted in April 1994, indicated that 34 percent of Ukrainian respondents would prefer to be "united in a single state" with Russia.[98] Some 40 percent were willing to compromise sovereignty to improve living conditions, while only 32 percent were not.[99] Nevertheless, during December 1994, 64 percent surveyed continued to support Ukrainian independence, a figure 8 percent higher than in a December 1993, poll.[100] Of course, such data also suggest that in spite of economic hardship, two-thirds of Ukrainian citizens still prefer independence.

The 1994 presidential election is the latest indicator of the East-West cleavage. In the first round, Kravchuk, defining himself as the guardian of Ukrainian independence and pursuing a Europeanist policy, won up to 90 percent of the vote in some western areas and emerged with a plurality; Leonid Kuchma, an advocate of closer cooperation with Russia, won overwhelmingly in the industrialized east, with over 80 percent in Luhansk and Crimea.[101] In the runoff, Kuchma won with 53 percent of the vote to Kravchuk's 46 percent. This total is not nearly as telling as the voting by oblast. In the west, Kravchuk won with 94–95 percent of the vote in Lviv, Ternopil, and Ivano-Frankivsk. In the east and south, Kuchma recorded victory with 88 percent in Luhansk, 79 percent in Donetsk, 71 percent in Kharkiv, 67 percent in Odessa, and 90 percent in Crimea.[102]

Language

The 1989 language law had four provisions: Ukrainian would become the language of state administration, Ukrainian must be taught in all schools, higher education would eventually shift to Ukrainian, and signs would be in

Ukrainian.[103] In designating Ukrainian as the state language in 1989, legislators anticipated a gradual transition from Russian to Ukrainian and specified no firm implementation timetables. In places where a non-Ukrainian group comprised the majority, another language was permitted for official matters.[104] The law neither forced the learning of Ukrainian nor restricted the use of Russian, a fact particularly salient in Donbas and Crimea. In the years immediately after its passage, the language law had relatively little impact.

Contrary to the initial gradualist approach, Dominique Arel argues that after independence in 1992, three central institutions—the presidential apparatus, the Ministry of Education, and Ukrainian television—forced the language issue by adopting a nationalizing agenda. From the governmental side, documents emanating from Kiev increasingly were written in Ukrainian. Thus, russophone officials often felt that they were at a disadvantage in the workplace. While most Russians had a passive understanding of Ukrainian, many were uncomfortable using Ukrainian for oral communication. Even Leonid Kuchma, as Prime Minister in 1993, spoke Ukrainian in public only from a prepared text.[105]

Russian has threatened Ukrainian since the tsarist-era ban on the use of Ukrainian in government and education. With the exception of the period of indigenization in the 1920s, schools and government increased the use of Russian; individuals, educated in Russian, increasingly spoke Russian at home. During the 1988–1989 school year, only 47.5 percent of school children studied in Ukrainian, though Ukrainians made up almost three-fourths of the population. This choice of Russian was not only the result of governmental policy; just 16.5 percent of the parents of first-grade children in Kiev in 1988 used Ukrainian at home, and only 4.7 percent used Ukrainian at work.[106]

This situation is now being reversed. An increasing proportion of Ukrainian children are studying in Ukrainian compared to the preindependence period. In the survey of first-grade parents cited above, 92 percent hoped to raise the prestige of Ukrainian.[107] By 1992:

> the proportion of children being taught in Ukrainian was still marginally smaller than those receiving instruction in Russian —49.3% and 50% respectively. In the western oblasts of Ukraine between 91.8% and 97.6% of children are taught in Ukrainian, while in the Luhansk, Donetsk, and Crimean Oblasts between 93.3% and 99.96% are taught in Russian. In Kiev 30.9% of children are taught in Ukrainian. In the country as a whole, 83% of children attending village schools are taught in Ukrainian, while 66% of those in cities are taught in Russian.[108]

In 1992 this situation began to change more rapidly. The education ministry instructed "(l)ocal educational organs . . . to bring the proportion of *first graders* 'into optimal concordance with the national composition of the population in each region.' This would mean that in a city such as Kharkiv, where half of the population is Ukrainian, half of the school-age children should eventually be enrolled in Ukrainian schools, up from one percent in 1991."[109] Thus, the linguistic structure of the schools would depend on the national composition of the population in each place, not on the population's language preference. Such an approach would radically restructure the educational system in most left-bank urban areas. Some western Ukrainians wish to pursue such ukrainianization, but Ukraine's large number of Russians and Russophone Ukrainians in the east acts as a brake on such intentions:

> Around 40 percent of all the residents of Ukraine, the overwhelming majority in 11 out of 12 cities with populations of over half a million people . . . consider their native language to be Russian. For very many of them, Russian is their native culture. . . . for these people Russia will never be simply a foreign state.[110]

The extreme nationalists deplore this situation and even oppose parents' rights to choose the language of their children's education. Ukrainian poet, nationalist leader and parliamentarian Dmytro Pavlychko, in a June 1990, interview in Canada, argued against parents' rights to make their children's language choices. He explained nationalist language policy as a conflict between individual and national rights. For such nationalists, Ukrainian independence must result in instruction of Ukrainian children in the indigenous language.

> At present . . . the law permits parents to choose the language of instruction for their offspring. . . . In theory, it seems to uphold individual rights . . . but, in practice . . . the rights of the individual and those of the nation come into direct conflict. . . . if we allow the rejection of the native language in a nation simply because another culture [Russian] is predominant, then this right is profoundly antinational. We need a new law. A Ukrainian mother cannot freely choose the language that her child must learn, because, in selecting the language, she determines the national allegiance. In this way, the law has made our mothers national traitors. They have wanted their children to have good careers . . . and therefore they have sent them to Russian schools. At first they were oblivious to the national aspect of this affair. . . . The right of the native Ukrainian population to be educated in its native language should be enshrined in a law for the defense of the people.[111]

If the Ministry of Education enforces enrollment of first grade pupils corresponding to the national composition of the population in each locality, "ethnic Ukrainians who consider Russian their mother tongue may no longer have the practical choice of sending their children to Russian schools."[112] Similarly, the move to Ukrainian in higher education would have the same consequence. Thus, in spite of the rhetoric of building a civic rather than a national state, at least some of Ukraine's institutions can be accused of undertaking a nationalizing project.

Ukrainian and Russian youth seem much more tolerant on this issue than their parents or politicians. Asked if non-Ukrainians should study and use Ukrainian in place of their native language, only 21 percent of Ukrainian high school students and 10 percent of Russian high school students answered positively. Underlying this opinion is the view of 57 percent of Ukrainian students and 66 percent of Russian students that young people of different nationalities get along better than adults. Only 4 percent of Russians and 24 percent of Ukrainians report that "My national identity is very important to me." This point is underlined by noting that only 18 percent of the Russians in Ukraine report that they interact mainly/only with other Russians, and only 36 percent of the Ukrainians interact mainly/only with other Ukrainians. The survey nonetheless notes one important difference on language: 45 percent of the Ukrainian students speak Russian all the time, and 57 percent speak Ukrainian all the time (since Russian has become "just another foreign language" in Ukrainian-language schools, this situation is likely to change). Only 18 percent of Russian students in Ukraine report speaking Ukrainian all the time, while 81 percent speak Russian all the time. As the authors noted, "There was very little attitudinal support for divisive ethnonationalism among Ukrainian youth of either national origin."[113] This finding parallels what we found elsewhere: Russian young people are adjusting to the new political situation by learning the state languages and interacting more freely with non-Russians; their parents, however, have been slow to change attitudes and behaviors.

Inter-National Accommodation

The inter-national accommodation displayed in the above survey underscores the political leadership's often articulated position that Ukraine is a multinational state whose policies must contribute to positive inter-national relations. In an interview in October 1990, then chairman of the Ukrainian Supreme Soviet Kravchuk cautioned about pushing too hard and too fast for independence, arguing that nationalism advocated by the western region could trigger secessionist feelings in the East:

> I start from the premise that Ukraine is multinational. . . . I would consider it the greatest tragedy if interethnic strife were to break out here as it has in other republics. I will do everything I can to prevent that. Even so, I will do everything I can to ensure that the country becomes sovereign and self governing.[114]

From the beginning of Ukraine's most recent independence movement in the late 1980s, most political leaders took a moderate and inclusive approach to an independent Ukraine. Ukrainian interests thus have been defined in state and strategic rather than national terms. To the outside observer, only a few policies adopted by the Ukrainian government or parliament can be defined as hegemonic. Perception and reality, however, are often not identical: Ukrainian independence threatens the Russian minority's self-perception and standing in Ukrainian society.

Today, with Ukraine suffering economically, the Dnipro's left and right banks perceive different interests. The right-bank population is committed to independence, more integration with Europe and more economic reform. It sees Ukraine's progress inhibited by left-bank mines and factories tied to former Soviet structures. This view clashes with the left-bank's more Russian-oriented economy and russophone culture, especially in Donbas and Crimea, that sees its future more closely tied to Eurasia. These differing perceptions threaten Ukraine as a unitary state.

Differing Courses

While Ukraine and Belarus have close cultural linkages with Russia and with each other, they have taken different political courses since the Soviet breakup. Ukraine under the leadership of former president Kravchuk pursued independence with determination, though not necessarily with concomitant success. Although for the most part eschewing an exclusionary nationalistic agenda domestically, Ukraine adopted an independent foreign policy that is often perceived as being anti-Moscow and has served as a vehicle to mobilize Ukraine's large Russian minority. Russians and russophone Ukrainians living in the Donbas and Novorossiya regions and in Crimea share common goals based on the maintenance of economic ties to Russia and resistance to linguistic ukrainianization. This position is in sharp distinction to more defined national interests exhibited by Ukrainians living in the country's center and West. The interaction of these interests invariably results in a perceived provocation by the other group: Russians see western Ukrainian nationalism as a threat to their status, while nationalists see ties to Russia as a threat to Ukraine's independence and the nation's future. Whether the more Russian-oriented president, Leonid Kuchma, can bridge this division is yet to be seen.

Belarus might be compared to the russified areas of Ukraine, but without the complication of an opposing western nationalism. Only a small minority in Belarus seems interested in pursuing a nationalist agenda. Issues that invite reaction elsewhere have little salience. Citizenship is available to all. Few seem disturbed that Russian is the dominant language, so belarusification is a non-issue. Sovereignty itself has only limited interest; a majority seems ready to choose Russian domination if it brings better economic conditions. Domination, however, is a perceptual term. Without a developed sense of national identity, Belarusians, unlike many Ukrainians, seem less concerned with the reattachment of their nominally independent state to Russia. Russians in Belarus, not having to contend with indigenous nationalism, find that the inter-national situation remains relatively unchanged from Soviet times.

Notes

1. Sergey Plytkevich: "Can Stanislav Shushkevich Recover?" *Narodnaya Gazeta* (Minsk), April 7, 1993, pp. 1,3, cited in *FBIS–USR–93–058*, May 10, 1993.

2. RFE/RL *Daily Report*, No. 8, January 13, 1994 (emphasis added).

3. Ustina Markus, "Belarus," RFE/RL *Research Report*, April 22, 1994, p. 10, citing David Marples, "Belarus: The Illusion of Stability," *Post-Soviet Affairs*, Vol. 9, No. 3 (1993): 265.

4. Kathleen Mihalisko, "Belarusian Leader on First Year of Statehood," RFE/RL *Research Report*, January 15, 1993, pp. 11–12.

5. Steven L. Guthier, "The Belorussians: National Identification and Assimilation, 1897–1970," Part 1, 1897–1930, *Soviet Studies*, Vol 19, No. 1 (January 1977): 43.

6. Thomas Hammond, "Nationalism and National Minorities in Eastern Europe," *Journal of International Affairs*, Vol. 20, No.1 (1966): 9–31.

7. Guthier, "Belorussians: National Identification," Part I, p. 39.

8. Nicolas P. Vakar, *Belorussia: The Making of a Nation* (Cambridge: Harvard University Press, 1956), pp. 91–92. Emphasis in original.

9. Ivan S. Lubachko, *Belorussia Under Soviet Rule, 1917–1957* (Lexington, KY: University Press of Kentucky, 1972), pp. 17–25.

10. Vakar, *Belorussia: The Making of a Nation*, pp. 105–106.

11. Jan Zaprudnik, *Belarus: At a Crossroads in History* (Boulder: Westview Press, 1993), p. 67.

12. Lubachko, *Belorussia Under Soviet Rule*, pp. 29–30.

13. Zaprudnik, *Belarus: At a Crossroads in History*, p. 77.

14. Vakar, *Belorussia: The Making of a Nation*, p. 121.

15. Guthier, "Belorussians: National Identification," Part I, p. 50.

16. Vakar, *Belorussia: The Making of a Nation*, p. 142.

17. Guthier, "Belorussians: National Identification," Part I, pp. 55–56.

18. Vakar, *Belorussia: The Making of a Nation*," p. 155.

19. Jan Zaprudnik, *Belarus: At a Crossroads in History*, p. 88.

20. Lubachko, *Belorussia Under Soviet Rule*, p. 173.

21. Guthier, "Belorussians: National Identification," Part II, *Soviet Studies*, Vol. 29, No. 2. (April 1977), p. 273.

22. Ibid., p. 274.

23. Ralph S. Clem, "Belorussians," in Graham Smith, ed., *The Nationalities Question in the Soviet Union* (London: Longman, 1990), p. 110.

24. Michael Urban and Jan Zaprudnik, "Belarus: A Long Road to Nationhood," in Ian Bremmer and Ray Taras, eds., *Nations and Politics in the Soviet Successor States* (Cambridge: Cambridge University Press, 1993), p. 106.

25. Igor Sinyakevich, "The Referendum as a Method of Struggle for Power: The Internal Political Crisis Intensifies," *Nezavisimaya gazeta* (Moscow), June 5, 1992, cited in *FBIS–USR–92–077*, June 24, 1992.

26. Jan Zaprudnik, "Belorussian Reawakening," *Problems of Communism*, Vol. 38 (July—August 1989): 42, citing Zyanon Paznyak, "Bilingualism and Bureaucratism," *Raduga* (Tallinn), April 1988, p. 37.

27. Chancy D. Harris, "Ethnic Tensions in the Successor Republics in 1993 and Early 1994, *Post-Soviet Geography*, Vol 35, No. 4 (April 1994), p. 187.

28. Marples, "Belarus: The Illusion of Stability," *Post-Soviet Affairs*, Vol. 9, No. 3 (1993): 253–277.

29. Alexander Lukashuk, "Belarus", RFE/RL *Research Report*, October 2, 1992, p. 21.

30. Mihalisko, "Belarussian Leader," RFE/RL *Research Report*, January 15, 1993, p. 12.

31. Lukashuk, "Belarus," p. 21.

32. *Litaratura i Mastatstva*, June 3, 1988.

33. Urban and Zaprudnik, "Belarus: A Long Road," pp. 110–111.

34. Zaprudnik, "Belorussian Reawakening," p. 51.

35. Ibid., p. 51, citing Vasil' Bykaw, *Litaratura i Mastatstva*, July 7, 1989.

36. RFE/RL *News Briefs*, December 6–10, 1993, p. 11.

37. Kathleen Mihalisko, "Belorussia: Setting Sail Without a Compass," RFE/RL *Research Report*, Jan. 3, 1992.

38. N. Derkach, "The House That Shushkevich Is Building," *Za Vilnu Ukrayinu* (Lvov), February 11, 1992, pp. 1–2, cited in *FBIS–USR–92–029*, March 17, 1992, p. 53.

39. Kathleen Mihalisko, "Belarus," RFE/RL *Research Report*, Feb. 14, 1992, p. 9, citing *Chyrvonaya zmena*, December 16–22, 1991.

40. Igor Sinyakevich: "The Supreme Soviet Has Lost Its Legitimacy: So Considers the Parliamentary Opposition," *Nezavisimaya gazeta* (Moscow), November 7, 1993, cited in *FBIS–USR–92–155*, December 4, 1992, p. 128.

41. Kathleen Mihalisko, "Political Crisis in Postcommunist Belarus," RFE/RL *Research Report*, May 29, 1992, pp. 28–29.

42. Ustina Markus, "Belarus a 'Weak Link' in Eastern Europe?" RFE/RL *Research Report*, December 10, 1993, p. 21.

43. Nina Sheldysheva, "We Must Return Not to the Past, But to the Eternal," *Sovetskaya Belorussiya* (Minsk), October 30, 1993, p. 2, cited in *FBIS*–USR–93–152, December 11, 1993, p. 50.

44. Urban and Zaprudnik, "Belarus: A Long Road," p. 115.

45. Kathleen Mihalisko, "Politics and Public Opinion in Belarus," RFE/RL *Research Report*, October 15, 1993, p. 54.

46. Mihalisko, "Politics and Public Opinion," p. 50.

47. RFE/RL *Daily Report*, No. 18, January 27, 1994.

48. RFE/RL *Daily Report*, No. 18, January 27, 1994.

49. Kathleen Mihalisko: "Belarus: Neutrality Gives Way to 'Collective Security,'" RFE/RL *Research Report*, April 23, 1993, p. 28.

50. Ibid., pp. 47–49.

51. Ustina Markus, "Belarus Debates Security Pacts as a Cure for Military Woes," RFE/RL *Research Report*, June 18, 1993, p. 72, citing ITAR-TASS, June 1, 1992.

52. Reuters, December 31, 1992.

53. Ustina Markus, "Belarus a 'Weak Link' in Eastern Europe?" RFE/RL *Research Report*, December 10, 1993, p. 24.

54. Kathleen Mihalisko, "Belarus: Neutrality Gives Way to 'Collective Security,'" RFE/RL *Research Report*, April 23, 1993, p. 28, citing *Narodnaya hazeta* (Minsk), March 3, 1993.

55. Mihalisko, "Belarusian Leader," p. 11.

56. Mihalisko, "Belarus: Neutrality Gives Way,'" p. 24.

57. Ibid., p. 25.

58. Sergey Plytkevich: "Can Stanislav Shushkevich Recover?" *Narodnaya gazeta* (Minsk), April 7, 1993, pp. 1,3, cited in *FBIS*–USR–93–058, May 10, 1993.

59. RFE/RL *News Briefs*, August 30–September 3, 1993, pp. 15–16.

60. Peter J. S. Duncan, "Ukrainians," in Graham Smith, ed., *The Nationalities Question in the Soviet Union*, (London: Longman, 1990), p. 103.

61. Francis X. Clines, "Ukrainians Declare Republic Sovereign Inside Soviet System," *New York Times*, July 17, 1990.

62. Kathleen Mihalisko, "Ukraine's Declaration of Sovereignty," Radio Liberty, *Report on the USSR*, July 27, 1990, p. 18.

63. Peter J. S. Duncan, "Ukrainians," pp. 96, 100.

64. Evgenii Golavakha, Natalia Pnina, and Nikolai Churilov, "Russians in Ukraine," *The New Russian Diaspora* (Armonk, NY: M. E. Sharpe, 1994), p. 65.

65. See, for example, Alexander J. Motyl, *Dilemmas of Independence: Ukraine and the Politics of Post-Totalitarianism* (New York: Council of Foreign Relations, 1993), pp. 79–90.

66. RFE/RL Research Institute, *Report on the USSR*, September 6, 1991, p. 81.

67. Roman Solchanyk, "Ukraine: From Sovereignty to Independence," RFE/RL *Research Report*, January 3, 1992, p. 38.

68. Roman Solchanyk, "Ukraine and Russia: Before and After the Coup," RFE/RL Research Institute, *Report on the USSR*, September 27, 1991, p.15, citing *Pravda*, July 16, 1991.

69. Vicki L. Hesli, William M. Reisinger and Arthur H. Miller, "Public Support for Regional Autonomy in Ukraine: The Potential for Further Disintegration," (paper presented at the 1993 National Convention of the American Association for the Advancement of Slavic Studies, Honolulu, November 1993), p. 5.

70. Andrew Wilson, "The Growing Challenge to Kiev from the Donbas," RFE/RL *Research Report*, August 20, 1993, p. 8.

71. Ibid., pp. 8–9.

72. Leonid Mikhailov, "Leonid Kuchma—A New National Leader," *Sevodnya,* August 31, 1993, p. 3, in *The Current Digest,* Vol. 45, No. 35 (September 29, 1993): 20–21.

73. Fred Hiatt, "Independence Fever Infects Crimea," *Washington Post National Weekly Edition,* June 15–21, 1992.

74. Aleksandr Yemets, "Russia Frequently Acts by the Bulldozer Method: 'Were Russia to Recognize its Role of Elder Brother, We Could Avoid Many Conflicts'," *Segodnya* (Moscow), March 16, 1993, p. 10, *FBIS*–USR–93–043, April 7, 1993.

75. Chrystyna Lapychak, "Ukraine Sees Crimean Move as Russian Ploy," *Christian Science Monitor,* May 26, 1992, p. 5.

76. Dominique Arel, "Language Politics in Independent Ukraine: Towards One or Two State Languages?" *Nationalities Papers,* Vol. 23, No. 3 (September 1995).

77. Kathleen Mihalisko, "The Other Side of Separatism: Crimea Votes for Autonomy," RFE/RL Research Institute, *Report on the USSR,* February 1, 1992, pp. 36–37, citing *Molod' Ukrainy,* September 20, 1990.

78. Ibid., p. 38, citing *Krymskaya pravda,* October 18, 1991.

79. Roman Solchanyk, "Ukrainian-Russian Confrontation over the Crimea," RFE/RL *Research Report,* February 6, 1992, p. 29.

80. Ian Bremmer, "The Politics of Ethnicity: Russians in the New Ukraine," Unpublished paper (Tables 24, 30, 33), 1993.

81. RFE/RL *Research Report,* May 1, 1992, p. 81.

82. *The Economist,* May 9, 1992, 60.

83. RFE/RL *Research Report,* June 12, 1992, p. 57.

84. Hiatt, "Independence Fever."

85. Ibid.

86. RFE/RL *Daily Report,* No. 21, February 1, 1994.

87. RFE/RL *Daily Report,* No. 14, January 24, 1994.

88. Hesli, Reisinger and Miller, "Public Support for Regional Autonomy," p. 4.

89. RFE/RL *Research Report,* January 17, 1992, p. 50.

90. Roman Solchanyk, "'Intermovement' Formed in Donbas," Radio Liberty, *Report on the USSR,* December 21, 1990, p. 10.

91. Ann Sheehy, "Fact Sheet on Questions in the Referendum of March 17 and Later Referendums," RFE/RL Research Institute, *Report on the USSR,* March 22, 1991, p. 5.

92. Roman Solchanyk, "The Referendum in Ukraine: Preliminary Results," RFE/RL Research Institute, *Report on the USSR,* March 29, 1991, p. 6.

93. RFE/RL Research Institute, *Report on the USSR,* October 18, 1991, p. 37.

94. RFE/RL Research Institute, *Report on the USSR,* November 15, 1991, p. 37.

95. Roman Solchanyk, "Centrifugal Movements in Ukraine on the Eve of the Independence Referendum," RFE/RL Research Institute, *Report on the USSR,* November 29, 1991, p. 13.

96. Jaroslaw Martyniuk, "Ukrainian Independence and Territorial Integrity," RFE/RL *Research Report,* March 27, 1992, pp. 66–68.

97. Bogdan Nahaylo, "The Birth of an Independent Ukraine," RFE/RL Research Institute, *Report on the USSR,* December 13, 1991, p. 2.

98. RFE/RL *Daily Report,* No. 108, June 9, 1994. A similar question in Belarus resulted in 41% of respondents' indicating a preference for unification with Russia.

99. Reuters, March 1, 1994.

100. OMRI, No. 20, II, January 27, 1995; OMRI, No. 7, January 10, 1995.

101. Lida Poletz, "Kravchuk Lead Grows, But Run-off Vote Could be Tight," *Christian Science Monitor,* June 29, 1994, p. 3.

102. Information-press Service of the Ukrainian Republican Party (internet), July 16, 1994.

103. "O yazikakh Ukrainskoy SSR," *Pravda Ukrainy,* November 3, 1989.

104. If applied by oblast, only Crimea can take advantage of this provision.

105. Arel, "Language Politics."

106. Bohdan Krawchenko, "Ukraine: The Politics of Independence," in Ian Bremmer and Ray Taras, eds., *Nations and Politics in the Soviet Successor States*, (Cambridge: Cambridge University Press, 1993), pp. 85, 89.

107. Ibid., p. 89.

108. RFE/RL *Research Report*, May 8, 1992, p. 68.

109. Arel, "Language Politics," citing Decree No. 123 of the Ministry of Education, September 1992.

110. Vladimir Malinkovich: "To Part Ways without Saying Farewell: On 'Normalization' of Russian-Ukrainian Relations," *Nezavisimaya gazeta* (Moscow), April 9, 1993, pp. 1,3, cited in *FBIS–USR–93–051*, April 24, 1993, p. 15.

111. David Marples and Chrystia Freeland, "Inside Ukrainian Politics: An Interview with Dmytro Pavlychko," Radio Liberty, *Report on the USSR*, July 13, 1990, pp. 22–23.

112. Arel, "Language Politics."

113. John P. Robinson, Ted Robert Gurr, Erjan Kurbanov, Stephen McHale, and Ivan Slepenkov, "Ethnonationalist and Political Attitudes Among Post-Soviet Youth: The Case of Russia and Ukraine," *PS: Political Science and Politics*, Vol. 26, No. 3 (September 1993): 519–521.

114. Bohdan Nahaylo and Kathleen Mihalisko, "Interview with Ukrainian Supreme Soviet Chairman Leonid Kravchuk," Radio Liberty, *Report on the USSR*, November 23, 1990, p. 15.

Chapter 7

Moldova*

Until the August 1991 coup attempt, Moldova, previously known as Bessarabia and the Moldavian Soviet Socialist Republic, had known independence only briefly,[1] having been part of the Russian Empire, Romania and the Soviet Union during its recent history. Moldova's changing rulers and borders, together with Moscow's industrialization policies, have resulted in today's multinational population.

The interaction between the majority Moldovans and the minority Russians is the defining characteristic of contemporary Moldovan politics. Minorities on the right bank of the Dniester River, including many Russians, have joined the process of creating a new Moldovan state. Transdniestrian Russians, however, continue to pursue territorial independence. The indigenous Moldovan leadership, like that in most of the successor states, must assuage the Russian minority or risk internal inter-national conflict and external conflict with Moscow.

Democratic state-building is difficult when national demands cannot find expression within legitimate political processes. Moldova provides an example of efforts by the political leadership to seek a positive balance between the assertiveness of the titular majority and the rights of minority groups. Initially, the nationalizing agenda of the Moldovans led to minority reaction, threatening both the development of democratic institutions and the existence of the new state. The titular political leaders then moderated their positions and made accommodation of the minorities—Russian, Ukrainian, Gagauz, and others—the central thrust of their policies. While Chisinau has made progress in incorporating right-bank minorities, including the Gagauz, into the state-building process and the multinational government, it has had less success with left-bank Russians.

The territory between the Prut and Dniester rivers known as Bessarabia was a pawn of the Russian and Ottoman Empires. After its 1812 success in its war with the Ottoman Empire, Russia ruled Bessarabia until 1917. With the fall of the Russian Empire, Bessarabia was incorporated into the interwar Romanian state. It came under Soviet influence as the result of the 1939 Molotov-Ribbentrop pact. Following the Nazi invasion in 1941, Moldova was reincorporated into Romania. Only after 1944 did Moldova begin functioning as a Soviet Socialist Republic. The strip of land known as Transdniestria, the "left" bank of

163

Moldova: Areas of Russian Concentration

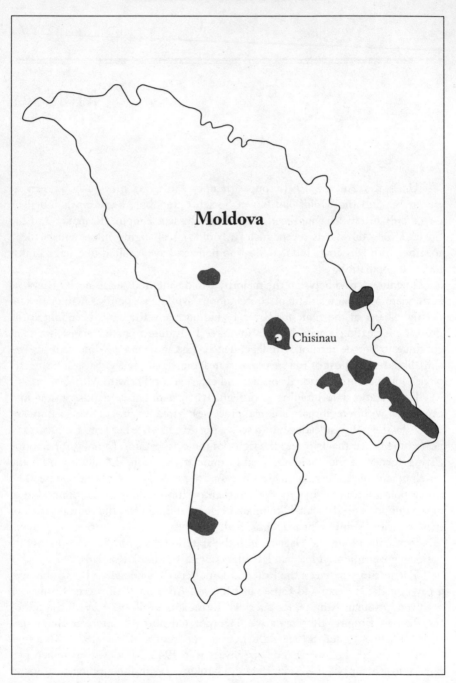

MOLDOVA

Territorial Size (km2)	33,700	
Population Size (1/1/94)	4,352,700	
Percent Titular (1989)	64.5	
Percent Russian (1989)	13.0	
Urban Population (1992)	2,029,000	
Percent Titular (1989)	46.3	
Percent Russian (1989)	23.9	
Size of Capital City (1/1/91)	676,700	
Percent Titular (1989)	49.2	
Percent Russian (1989)	26.4	
Natural Increase (/1000, 1993)	4.4	
Titular NI (1989)	12.0	
Russian NI (1989)	4.5	
Life Expectancy (1989)	Men: 65.5	Women: 72.1
Titular e^0 (1989)	Men: 65.2	Women: 71.1
Russian e^0 (1989)	Men: 66.5	Women: 74.7
Net Migration To (−)/From (+) Russia (1989-1993)		
Total	−19,757	
Titular	7,884	
Russian	−22,351	
Employment[a] (1992)	85.6	
Trade (Export/Import Ratio)		
Intra-NIS Trade[b] (1992)	0.65	
Extra-NIS Trade[c] (1993)	0.83	

Notes: [a]Employment given as a percent of the working-age population. [b]Intra-NIS ratios calculated from trade among the republics of the former USSR and measured in the national currencies. [c]Extra-NIS ratios calculated from trade with countries outside the former USSR and measured in US dollars.

Sources: Goskomstat SSSR, *Chislennost' naseleniya soyuznykh respublik po gorodskim poseleniyam i rayonam na 1 yanvarya 1991* goda. (Moskva: 1991); Goskomstat Rossiyskoy Federatsii, *Chislennost' i sotsial'no–demograficheskiye kharakteristiki russkogo naseleniya v respublikakh byvshego SSSR* (Moskva: 1994); Statisticheskiy komitet SNG, *Statisticheskiy byulleten'* No. 20 (June 1994): 35-36; Statkom SNG, *Itogi vsesoyuznoy perepisi naseleniya 1989 goda.* (Minneapolis, MN: East View, 1992), Vol. 7, Part 2; Mikhael Guboglo, "Demography and Language in the Capitals of the Union Republics," *Journal of Soviet Nationalities* Vol. 1, No. 4 (Winter 1990–1991): 9–13; The World Bank, *Statistical Handbook 1994: States of the Former USSR* (Washington, DC: World Bank Studies of Economics in Transformation No. 14, 1994).

the Dniester River (the eastern bank is designated "left" in relation to the river's flow to the Black Sea), was transferred from Ukraine to Moldova in 1940 and incorporated into the Moldavian Soviet Socialist Republic. In contrast to the remainder of today's Moldova, Transdniestria was never subject to Romanian rule.

Moldova neither restores a previously autonomous state (like the Baltics) nor satisfies a long-suppressed nationalist aspiration (like Ukraine). Many contend that Moldovans, in fact, are Romanians, sharing the same language, faith, and history.[2] The extent to which Moldovans today perceive themselves to be a nation separate from Romanians remains an open question.[3] Both the tsars and the Soviets wanted Bessarabia to distinguish itself from the developing Romanian state to its west.

Tsarist Russia encouraged immigration to Bessarabia by offering land to non-Romanian ethnic groups, including Russians, Ukrainians, Germans, Jews, Bulgarians, and Gagauz. These nineteenth century policies diluted the Romanian population in Bessarabia. Romanians, who comprised 86 percent of the Bessarabian population in 1817, made up 48 percent in 1897 and 56 percent in 1930.[4] Soviet economic policies after World War II resulted in the immigration of thousands of Russians and Ukrainians, again diluting the indigenous population and fostering large Russian-speaking urban enclaves. Moscow encouraged "Moldovan" identification to sever linguistic and cultural ties with Romania, yet attempted to limit a political consciousness that might be turned against the Soviet center.[5]

Moldova today has a population of 4,359,100,[6] with 2.8 million Moldovans constituting the majority (64.5 percent). Ukrainians are the largest minority, numbering 600,000. Moldova is the only successor state in which Ukrainians (13.8 percent) outnumber the Russians (13.0 percent).[7] Of the Ukrainians, 67 percent are native to Moldova and 29 percent to Ukraine.[8] Most urban Ukrainians migrated after World War II to work in developing industrial enterprises; most rural Ukrainians have lived in the same ancestral villages for generations.

Some 52 percent of the 562,000 Russians were born in Moldova and 36 percent were born in Russia.[9] Transdniestria is home to only 27 percent (153,400) of Moldova's Russians, most of whom are postwar migrants. Many Moldovans view the Russian presence as an extension of Soviet—specifically Stalinist—policies, which included mass deportations of Moldovans and an influx of Russians and other Slavic groups.[10]

> The Russian population of the republic grew from 6% of the total in 1940 to 10.2% in 1959 . . . and in 1989 stood at 13% . . . The Russians . . . settled in the urban centers [and] became a colonial elite in Moldova . . . with Russified Ukrainians assuming the role of their junior partners.[11]

The Soviet-era migration not only affected Moldova's demography, but also its occupational and educational balance. As many Moldovan intellectuals fled to Romania at the end of World War II or were purged during the late Stalin era,

Russians and Russian-speakers moved to Moldova's cities, took technical jobs, and filled educational institutions. Consequently, Russian culture dominated urban, technical, and educational life.[12] This situation is now slowly reversing. After substantial immigration during the industrial expansion from 1950–1980, the net inflow of non-Moldovans has ended. While some Russians and other non-Moldovans are emigrating, most perceive Moldova's inter-national relations and living conditions to be comparatively good, making a large-scale outflow unlikely.[13]

Language[14]

Language has been a central issue in the interaction of Moldovans and Russians since the late 1980s. The first Moldovan moves away from Moscow were initiated by the rediscovery of Moldova's Romanian heritage. Similarly, the response of the Russian minority was fueled by the fear of "romanianization."

When the Soviet Union annexed Moldova, not only did Russian became the language of public life, but the Latin alphabet that had been used to write the Romanian language was replaced by Cyrillic. The 1989 language law[15] made Moldovan the state language. Latin letters displaced Cyrillic for its transcription, and place names were written in the state language or in the language of the local majority. This process proceeded smoothly on the right bank. However, language was the trigger for secession in the Transdniestrian and Gagauz areas.

The question of the Latin or Cyrillic alphabet was especially symbolic because Cyrillic was seen as a facet of Soviet cultural imperialism. Affirming that "Moldovan" was different from "Romanian" and best understood using Cyrillic script had been "a litmus test of one's acceptance of the legitimacy of Soviet rule."[16] However, the Romanian Orthodox Church and the princely courts had historically used Old Church Slavonic with its Cyrillic alphabet until the 1840s when the Latin alphabet began replacing Cyrillic.[17] Nonetheless, nationalists reconstructed the past to serve current political needs: they insisted that "Romanian" become the state language, the Latin alphabet be adopted, and that the identity of Romanian and Moldovan be acknowledged.

Indeed, the Soviet claim that Moldovan and Romanian were two languages was false. The different alphabets were intended to make the languages appear to be different and to help foster the theory that the peoples on either side of the Prut were separate (though related) nations. While the Soviets conducted a long and complex campaign to convince Moldovans that they spoke a separate language from Romanians, they were unable to change the reality that the languages were identical. Russian words may have been used for technical or political subjects in Moldova, but their use did not change the language itself. When the barriers to interaction between Moldova and Romania were removed in the late 1980s, all could see that the language written and spoken on either side of the Prut, even though rendered in different alphabets, was the same.

Initially led by the pro-Romanian Popular Front in the late 1980s, Moldovans formed groups in support of restructuring, seizing the opportunity provided by *perestroyka* and *glasnost'* to create a national movement and push the state-language debate into the Supreme Soviet. Gorbachev himself lobbied for maintaining Russian; Mircea Snegur, then Chairman of the Supreme Soviet and currently President, gained notoriety by publicly pressing for Moldovan. Language thus became the vehicle for the titular nation's nationalistic agenda and the focus of inter-national friction. The rediscovery of Moldova's Romanian character precipitated a Russian backlash; Russians feared that designating Moldovan as the state language was the first step toward union with Romania. Reunification was indeed the priority of Moldova's Popular Front.

As momentum built to change from Russian to Moldovan, so did the reaction of the Russian-speaking population. Non-Russians felt especially threatened by the language movement. Gagauzi, Ukrainians, and other minorities feared having to learn both Russian and Moldovan in addition to their native language.[18] On the right bank, the Popular Front's pro-Romanian, pro-unification, and anti-Russian rhetoric severely damaged inter-national relations by causing strong anti-Russian sentiment to emerge during Moldova's budding independence movement.[19]

In passing the state language law of August 1989, the Supreme Council required those interacting with the public and those holding enterprise leadership positions to speak both Russian and Romanian by 1994. As the deadline approached, few Russians had learned Romanian, so the Moldovan majority, itself almost entirely bilingual, remained unable to use its language in everyday activities. Some five years after passage of legislation making Moldovan the state language, language persists as an unresolved issue between Russians and Moldovans. Few Russians have acquired even a rudimentary knowledge of the state language. This situation frustrates Moldovans, especially those political leaders who from early in the independence movement advocated incorporating the Russians and other minorities into the new state. Russian school-age children are making the shift, but most of their parents still expect Moldovans to use Russian for inter-national communication. As one Moldovan educator reported: "When the Soviet Union annexed Moldova, the Russians just pointed a gun at our heads and said to learn Russian. We did. Now after four years, the Russians say they can't learn Romanian."[20]

The 1989 language law, though designating both Moldovan and Russian languages of inter-national communication, provided the catalyst for the Transdniestrian and Gagauz insurrections. Crowther appropriately labels these movements "reactive nationalism":

> Threatened by efforts of the majority ethnic group to destabilize the status quo in its own favor, members of other minorities themselves entered into an independent political movement in order to increase the cost to the state of concessions to the Moldavians ... [appealing] to the national-level political leaders [Moscow] either (1) to defend the status quo, (2) to guarantee that any concessions to the Moldavian majority do not damage the position of minorities in the

republic, or (3) . . . to permit the other minorities to detach themselves from the present political unit and form a political entity of their own.[21]

Since the law's passage, most Russians have not learned Moldovan, but right-bank Russian attitudes have changed. Alexander Belopotapov, the Director of the Russian Cultural Center in Chisinau, now refers to Moldovan as the "state" language and accepts the need for Russians to learn it. Instead of opposing bilingualism, he discussed the inadequate resources (classes, books, teachers) and the short time to learn the language.[22] On the right bank, Russians, Romanians, and Gagauz now acknowledge the identity of Moldovan and Romanian. But recognizing their identity does not close the question: during the February 1994, parliamentary campaign, President Snegur argued that Romanians and Moldovans are distinct peoples with a common language.[23] Snegur had previously avoided "the 'Moldovanism' of the most radical Agrarian Democrats, a view of Moldovan-Romanian separateness which contained uncomfortable echoes of the Soviet policy discredited in 1989."[24] On the other hand, Transdniestria continues to treat Moldovan and Romanian as different languages, arguing that Moldovan is the version of the language with many Slavic words that is written in Cyrillic. Schools teach exclusively in Russian, and no Moldovan-language schools exist in Tiraspol' for its 25,000 Moldovan-speakers.

The status distinction between the languages during Soviet times originated in education; instruction beyond the primary levels in urban Moldova was conducted in Russian. Only 11 percent of the Russians in the capital spoke Moldovan.[25] Just 10 percent of Chisinau kindergartens used Moldovan as the primary language. In the Chisinau technical university, Moldovan was treated as a "foreign" language.[26] Instruction in specialized and higher education was primarily in Russian, necessitating fluent Russian for skilled and administrative jobs.

This situation has changed since 1989. Romanian and many mixed families send their children to often overcrowded Moldovan-language schools. From the 1989–1990 academic year to the 1992–1993 academic year, students studying exclusively in Moldovan increased from 424,000 to 447,000; during the same period, students studying exclusively in Russian fell from 290,000 to 262,000.[27] Most Russian families continue to send their children to Russian-language schools, but both the quality of their Moldovan-language instruction and student seriousness about learning Moldovan have increased. Russians now complain about shortages of Moldovan instructors and materials. The most serious protests involve specialized secondary and higher education, where Chisinau's nationalizing policies have had the greatest negative impact on the Russians.

The proportion of students in Moldovan-language postsecondary institutions increased from 45 percent of the total in 1990–1991 to 58.2 percent in 1992–1993. The proportion going to Russian-language institutions fell from 54.6 percent to 38.8 percent in the same period.[28] Technical education in Russian has been severely reduced, so young people wishing to develop technical skills must study in Moldovan or pursue training outside the republic. Those wishing to pursue Russian-language higher education face limited options and increased competition. Growing numbers of Russian youth reportedly are seeking postsecondary education in Russia, with Chisinau's Russian Cultural Center assisting with enrollment in institutions in Russia.[29]

Many Russian educators have lost jobs because their subjects are now being taught in Moldovan, and some former university teachers from Chisinau have reportedly moved to Transdniestria to work.[30] Other educators and professionals willing to learn Moldovan face a predicament: Despite acquiring conversational ability, they have not gained sufficient sophistication to work in their areas of expertise.[31]

Moldovans' concerns about education include overcrowding and lower instructional quality provided by hastily recruited teachers. Some want to use excess space available in Russian schools to relieve overcrowding in Moldovan facilities, but that step would ignite yet another controversy.

The language law's requirement that supervisors and public service employees be able to respond in the language of their employees or customers originally was to have taken effect in January 1994. Because many Russians were still unable to meet these requirements, Prime Minister Sangheli in February 1993, directed that all governmental functions continue in both Russian and Moldovan. A year later, one of the first acts of the newly elected parliament was to suspend the law requiring language testing of people in supervisory positions.[32] Similarly, laws no longer were to refer to Russian as a foreign language.[33] While moving toward wider use of Moldovan, political leaders are striving to undo the polarization caused by the Popular Front's initial linguistic romanianization agenda of the late 1980s.

While continuing to be accommodative on the language issue, some Moldovans are losing patience. As Presidential Counselor Viktor Grebenshchikov (a Moldovan-speaking Russian) stated:

> Romanians wonder about having to use a foreign language in their own country. Speaking the language of the state of which you are a member is in no way discrimination. Russians here must understand that the Republic of Moldova is no longer the Russian gubernia of Bessarabia, or the Soviet Socialist Republic of Moldavia, but the independent Republic of Moldova.[34]

The Politics of Independence

Following parliamentary elections in Spring 1990, power shifted from the Communists to the Popular Front. Mircea Snegur was elected Chairman of the Moldovan Supreme Soviet, then president, after the Supreme Soviet created the post. Popular Front supporters replaced the government in May 1990, and Mircea Druc became prime minister. By summer 1990, reformers, mostly Moldovans, controlled Moldova's governing structures. Russians, with Ukrainian and Gagauz support, assumed opposition status.

On June 23, 1990, the Supreme Soviet adopted a declaration of sovereignty (stating that Moldovan law superseded Soviet law) and suspended the Soviet military draft. Having sided with the Transdniestrians by refusing to defend the territorial integrity of the republic, Gorbachev lost leverage. Support for a new union treaty dissipated and the pro-unification and anti-Russian Popular Front became the leading political force. For the first time, complete independence from the Soviet Union appeared on the political agenda.

National and ideological cleavages coincided. In December 1990, the Popular Front called a Grand National Assembly (a popular demonstration in the Romanian and Moldovan tradition); 800,000 took to Chisinau's streets to communicate popular sentiment against Moscow's pressure. In February 1991, the Popular Front-dominated Supreme Council rejected holding the all-union referendum on Moldovan territory and endorsed an association of fifteen equal sovereign states with no central power, the so-called "fifteen plus zero" confederation. Left-bank Russian deputies boycotted the Supreme Soviet, thereby weakening the pro-union faction.

The boycott against participation in the union referendum succeeded. Chisinau had by then moderated its position toward non-Moldovans on language and citizenship. The right-bank Russian population was divided, with some seeing advantage in supporting the Moldovan majority, opposing Moscow, and seeking independence. Gagauz and left-bank Russian support for the continuation of the USSR remained high.

Determining the extent to which non-Moldovans favored breaking with Moscow is difficult. In a series of polls conducted by the Moldovan Institute of Sociology, by June 1991, 58 percent of respondents backed separation from the Soviet Union. By the August coup, 79 percent supported independence, thus "support for independence extended beyond the 65 percent share of ethnic Moldovans in the republic's population," perhaps triggering "the decision of the republican leadership to proclaim Moldova's independence from the USSR on August 27, 1991."[35]

The August 1991, coup cemented the divisions between the right- and left-bank positions. Snegur and other leaders immediately stated that the Emergency Committee's decrees had no validity in Moldova. In moves reminiscent of the Baltics, the leadership mobilized popular support to deter Russian troop activities. Moldovans barricaded entrances to Chisinau, and military columns never attempted to push past the unarmed civilians. Right-bank Russians avoided the confrontation. Left-bank Russians and the Gagauz sided with the coup leaders. In the self-proclaimed "Dniester Republic," city and enterprise leaders as well as the Transdniestrian Supreme Soviet cabled support to the Emergency Committee,[36] underscoring the extent to which Chisinau had already lost control of Transdniestria. The left-bank Communist Party maintained control of its property, financial assets, and media. Although the Moldovan leaders initially arrested some left-bank separatists, they were forced by strikes and blockades to release them.

Immediately after the coup, Moldova declared independence. Fifty-two of the 130 non-Moldovan deputies voted for independence, including six of the twelve Gagauz deputies. Snegur tried to convince non-Moldovans that Moldova would reverse the Soviet policy of cultural dominance by "resolving ethnic grievances, establishing a system of guarantees for the observance of human rights, and developing the facilities for the cultural and linguistic expression of the ethnic communities."[37] Rather than replacing russification with romanianization, Chisinau promised to respect local languages and customs. To show his commitment to a civic rather than a nationalizing state, Snegur announced on February 24, 1992, that all residents of Moldova would be offered citizenship. The Moldovan citizenship decree made no exceptions for military personnel, Party and Komsomol officials, or recent migrants, in sharp contrast to Latvian and Estonian policies.[38]

In spite of these steps, ideological and inter-national conflict with Transdniestria increased. Left-bank leaders contended that pro-Moldovan groups opposed the interests of the Russian-speaking (Russian, Ukrainian, and Gagauz) population. While the dispute can be seen as ideological with right-bank reformers' being opposed by left-bank conservatives, it was characterized as inter-national by Transdniestrians and Gagauzi. As hostilities intensified in Spring 1992, Snegur downplayed this inter-national characterization, arguing that these leaders were attempting "to disguise the military-communist nature of the phantom 'Dniester republic' . . . to win support from the national-patriotic forces of Russia" and to violate Moldova's territorial integrity.[39]

Transdniestrian Secession

What began in 1989 as protest developed into revolt in 1990 and secession in 1991. Russian and Ukrainian workers, organized by the right-bank *Edinstvo* and the left-bank Union of Work Collectives, went on strike after passage of the language law, crippling large industries. The Gagauz SSR proclaimed independence on August 19, 1991; Transdniestria followed on September 2, 1991. Conflict began when both breakaway territories formed military units. Left-bank leaders, taking a pro-Soviet, "inter-nationalist" position to counter the Popular Front's Moldovan nationalism, viewed Popular Front initiatives as destructive to both socialism and the union. Chisinau attacked left-bank leaders for their opposition to Gorbachev's reforms and their adherence to antiquated political and economic policies. In response to Russian and Gagauz separatism, Chisinau reversed the Popular Front's initial nationalistic policies and championed minority rights and inter-national harmony. But the damage had already been done; left-bank Russians and Gagauz had developed their own minority nationalism in response to the majority's original exclusionary nationalistic agenda.

Before 1940 Transdniestria (the former Moldavian Autonomous Republic) was attached to Ukraine while most of the right bank was part of the Romanian state.[40] Both Moldovans and Ukrainians outnumber Russians on this strip of land east of the Dniester. Until the 1970s, Moldovans comprised an absolute majority on the left bank, even though the area never had been part of Romania. The 1989 census showed the Transdniestrian population of 546,400 to be 39.9 percent Moldovan, 28.3 percent Ukrainian, and 25.4 percent Russian. The rural areas remain predominantly Moldovan. Tiraspol', the administrative center of Transdniestria's five regions, has the appearance of a provincial Russian city. Its population of 195,500 is 41 percent Russian, 32 percent Ukrainian, and 18 percent Moldovan. Local leaders, however, claim a majority of "Russian-speakers," referring collectively to Russians, Ukrainians, Gagauz, and Bulgarians. Moldovans object to the "Russian-speaking" designation because they are themselves "Russian-speaking." The problem, in their view, is that the Russian-speakers are not "Moldovan-speaking."

The Russian population in Transdniestria consists primarily of migrants who arrived during postwar industrialization, drawn by all-union military enterprises and Red Army facilities. Igor Smirnov, the Transdniestrian leader, claims that 30 percent of Moldova's industry and 98.5 percent of its energy production is located on the left bank.[41]

In early 1992, Transdniestrian military personnel and communist leaders expanded control of left-bank Moldovan villages and made inroads to right-bank Russian-dominated cities. Described by Chisinau as a "creeping putsch," this expansion became progressively more violent. Transdniestrian secessionists, organized into paramilitary units by the Russian army and supported by local industrial enterprises, assumed administrative and security functions and replaced Moldovan personnel with Russians. On orders from Chisinau to avoid confrontation, local authorities offered little initial resistance. Finally, after numerous left-bank incidents and right-bank forays, Chisinau concluded that its appeasement had failed. On March 29, 1992, President Snegur declared a state of emergency, calling on Transdniestrian separatists to acknowledge Chisinau's authority.[42] Left-bank Russian leaders reacted with more extremist positions. Several Russian Federation deputies even noted that the Transdniestrian leaders had taken positions more extreme than the 1991 coup leaders.[43]

The Russian Fourteenth Army, the largest former Red Army unit in Moldova, headquartered in Tiraspol', furnished tacit support to the separatists in the beginning of the secession. By early 1992 its support became overt, with Russian troops taking an active role in the fighting. The conflict, responsible for 425 deaths between March and June, reached a crisis. In late June 1992, elements of the Fourteenth Army, reportedly numbering 5,000, crossed to the right bank to join the fighting around Bendery (Tighina), a city just ten miles from Tiraspol'. Moldovan troops were forced from the city. The Russian central command then named Major General Aleksandr Lebed', a Yeltsin supporter during the coup, as the new head of the Fourteenth Army. Lebed' called Transdniestria "part of Russia" and the right-bank city of Bendery "an inalienable part of the Dniester republic."[44] Moscow's interest in Transdniestria goes beyond national solidarity. With an army on the Dniester, Russia can maintain an important strategic position vis-à-vis Ukraine and the Balkans.[45]

In early July 1992, Snegur and Yeltsin agreed to divide the opposing forces. After attempts to use multilateral forces failed, Snegur and Yeltsin signed a bilateral agreement on Transdniestria, with Russian, Moldovan, and Transdniestrian troops serving as peacekeepers. Transdniestria formally received the right to decide its own fate if Moldova chose to unite with Romania in the future (an option offered to Transdniestrian leaders by Chisinau as early as January 1991). Chisinau offered the Transdniestrians positions in a coalition government in exchange for settling the dispute, demonstrating how far its positions had evolved from the original exclusionary nationalism of the Popular Front. The Transdniestrians rejected these initiatives, though Chisinau originally staffed these positions with temporary personnel to show its good faith. General Lebed', Russia's Fourteenth Army Commander, criticized both Yeltsin and Snegur for their agreement. Transdniestrian president Smirnov, although present at the signing ceremony with Yeltsin and Snegur, did not sign the document. Whether Smirnov disagreed with the accord or whether Snegur refused to sign with Smirnov as an equal participant remains unclear.[46]

The military conflict de-escalated in Fall 1992, with approximately two thousand troops separating the parties. The ten-battalion peacekeeping force consists not of outside guarantors but of the combatants themselves. As military analyst Neil Lamont notes, "the force was five Russian, three Moldovan and two Dniester battalions . . . [seven of which] were from the Russian side."[47] Despite their lack of neutrality (often shown by their support of Transdniestrian state-building efforts), the peacekeepers have contained the 1992 conflict, allowing political leaders to look for common ground. Trade and travel between left and right banks slowly resumed. Numerous daily trains run from Chisinau to Bendery to Tiraspol and back without interference.

Bendery, the disputed right-bank city, has remained under Transdniestrian control since 1992. Two-thirds the size of Tiraspol', Bendery has a population of 138,000 (30 percent Moldovan, 18 percent Ukrainian, and 42 percent Russian). Unlike the rest of Transdniestrian-controlled territory, Bendery was Romanian before 1940. Peacekeeping battalions have restored order in the city and most refugees who fled the fighting have returned. The civilian administration, put in place in June 1992, by Transdniestrians to replace fleeing Moldovan police and administrative officials, remains aligned with Tiraspol'.

Tiraspol's intervention in Bendery is often justified in reference to a 1990 referendum in which over 90 percent of the city's population voted to align with Transdniestria.[48] From Tiraspol's perspective, Bendery is under its "administrative-territorial" control and is part of the "Dniester Republic."[49] Transdniestrian political authorities continue to establish state structures throughout the left bank and in Bendery under protection of the peacekeeping forces.

With its strength estimated at 10,000, the Fourteenth Army remained the most formidable regional military force.[50] Furthermore, military leaders blurred the lines between the *Russian* Fourteenth Army and the *Transdniestrian* Guard by transferring soldiers back and forth and demobilizing army soldiers to the guard. The Transdniestrians thus claimed Russian forces as local rather than foreign. After the ceasefire in late Summer 1992, Russia and Moldova began talks on the Fourteenth Army's withdrawal. These negotiations constituted an implicit acknowledgement that Russia's troops were stationed on foreign territory. In articulating its "near abroad" policy, Russia demanded Transdniestrian bases for the Fourteenth Army and raised the possibility of leasing right-bank bases. Reminiscent of Baltic talks, Russia argued that it wanted to assure rights for Russians and pressed for a federal structure to protect Transdniestria in exchange for its troop withdrawal.

After two years of negotiations, a tentative agreement was reached during August 1994. Troop withdrawal would be "synchronized" with a grant of special status to Transdniestria and a settlement of the leftbank conflict. Military withdrawal would be completed within three years of the approval of the documents. With no consensus on the status of the left bank, this "agreement" effectively gives the Transdniestrians a veto while at the same time accepting the Russian demand to link troop withdrawal to a political settlement.[51] Nonetheless, it does concede that Russian troops are on foreign territory and will be withdrawn.

Gagauzia

The Transdniestrian position is strengthened by the Gagauz presence in the south. The Gagauz sided with the Transdniestrians in the conflict with Chisinau, both because of their russification during the Soviet period and their developing territorial nationalism. Under Soviet rule the Gagauz were thoroughly russified; few are proficient in Moldovan and many do not speak their own language.[52] The Gagauz opposed making Moldovan the state language, contending that the state language law discriminated against minority groups that already had learned Russian as a second language. Both Gagauz and Transdniestrian leaders advocate using Russian as the official language in their breakaway territories.

President Stepan Topal and other Gagauz leaders were members of the Communist Party hierarchy and originally supported continuation of Soviet rule. In the March 1991, referendum on union, the Gagauz voted almost unanimously to stay in the USSR; Moldovans living in the Gagauz area boycotted the election. Gagauz leaders then supported the 1991 coup, making rapprochement difficult. Like the left-bank Russians, the Gagauz especially fear unification of Moldova and Romania. While the Moldovan government has supported granting cultural autonomy to both the Gagauz and the Transdniestrians, until recently it has distinguished between cultural and territorial autonomy, viewing the latter as a threat to state aspirations.

However, in 1995 Chisinau granted territorial as well as cultural autonomy to Gagauzia, including the establishment of a "national-territorial autonomous unit" with elected executive and legislative officials and three official languages (Gagauz/Turkish, Russian, and Moldovan).[53] In reviewing the arrangements, the Council of Europe feared that Chisinau had gone too far in meeting ethnoterritorial demands for minority separatism and that its plan might set a bad precedent for other minority areas in Europe. The Council criticized the creation of an internal border which put most functions within it under local rather than central control. Likewise, the Council feared that the approach would put other groups living within the Gagauz-claimed territory at risk.[54] Having had little success with only cultural concessions, Chisinau appears to be testing whether territorial concessions will help it reestablish at least nominal control of its former borders. The March 5, 1995, elections "in 36 localities with a prevalent Gagauz population" to determine the territory to be under Gagauz rule is the first step in implementing this agreement on local autonomy.[55] The extent to which Chisinau will extend this same approach to Transdniestria remains to be seen, though by early 1995 both the Moldovan and the Transdniestrian authorities seemed to be moving in this direction.

External Perspectives

In Moldova's case, "external national homeland," to use Rogers Brubaker's terminology,[56] encompasses not only Russia but Romania, thus complicating both inter-national and inter-state politics. Moldova was the only Soviet republic where the titular nation had ethnic ties to the dominant nation in a country outside the former Soviet Union. However, Romania and Moldova view the relationship quite differently. Snegur and his government have stressed disinterest in unification with Romania, and the March 6, 1994, referendum showed overwhelming popular support "in favor of the development of Moldova as an independent state, whole and indivisible, within the borders valid on the date of the proclamation of sovereignty." To minority Russians and Gagauz, a "greater Romania" would reduce their status numerically, politically, and culturally; thus, "romanianization" is a threat that quickly incites the minorities and fuels left-bank and Gagauz separatism. Snegur has tried to finesse this issue by emphasizing "two Romanian states."

Despite Soviet efforts to differentiate Moldovans from Romanians, the cultures, languages, and much of the history are similar on both sides of the Prut. Nonetheless, Crowther's analysis of 1990–1992 surveys identifies attitudinal differences between Romanians and Moldovans, as well as between the residents in the region of the Romanian state known as Moldova and those in the Moldovan Republic to its east.[57] Yet these differences have not kept the two peoples from rediscovering a common heritage. Before the disintegration of the Soviet Union, Moldova had taken steps to emphasize its cultural unity with Romania. The Popular Front's nationalistic agenda called for political unity as well.

The Popular Front's nationalism provoked minority separatism. This separatism, in turn, resulted in the moderation of Moldovan policy and the development of Snegur's "two states" policy. The Romanian leadership originally articulated this "two-state" position, but soon most political forces in Romania advocated reunification. The Romanian public, however, remained indifferent.[58] A joint 1992 decree of the Romanian and Moldovan Parliaments recognized the important historical relationship between the two countries but affirmed the separate status of Romania and Moldova.[59] Some Romanian politicians still assume that Moldova's separate status is indeed temporary. Because Transdniestria was never under Romanian control, political forces in Bucharest are not opposed to a permanent division of a unified Moldovan-Romanian state at the Dniester, a position that makes reunification difficult for most Moldovans to contemplate.

The passage of the new Moldovan constitution in July 1994, establishing independence as part of the basic law, set off a new round of Romania-Moldovan recriminations. After several years of discussion, this document defined Moldova as an independent state with "Moldovan" (not Romanian) as its official language. The constitution also established the framework for autonomy for the Gagauz and left-bank regions. The Romanian government reacted with hostility to both of these provisions.[60]

Moldova has placed other legal obstacles in the way of unification with Romania. The Moldovan Parliament passed a law in 1992 requiring a referendum to approve any proposals for unification or separation. Likewise, in its attempts to bring Gagauzia and Transdniestria back under its control, Chisinau similarly promised these two regions the opportunity to separate if Moldova were to join Romania.

With the Agrarian Party's victory in the February 1994, elections and the clear mandate for independence in the March 1994, referendum, political ties with Romania are unlikely to become closer in the immediate future. The Popular Front, previously a major player in Moldovan politics, is now virtually powerless because of its insistence on reunification. The other pro-Romanian Party, the Congress of Intellectuals, has yielded to the popular mood and now advocates cultural rather than political linkages. Together, these two pro-Romanian parties won only 20 seats in the 104-seat parliament. The Russian minority's fear of Moldovan-Romanian unification should, for the present, be alleviated.

Russian-minority ties with Moscow, of course, remain. For two centuries migrating Russians travelled to the fringes of the Russian and Soviet empires, settled new lands and worked to develop the industrial infrastructure, never perceiving that they were going abroad. Soviet dissolution changed neither these Russians' psychological bonds to their homeland, nor Moscow's view that it had a responsibility for Russians' welfare beyond the Russian Federation. Russians in this "near abroad" remain both domestic and foreign policy issues for Moscow.

Moldova provides a particularly sensitive example of the interplay of Russia's domestic and foreign policies. Russian nationalists place Moldovan events in the context of the former Soviet Union or even the Russian empire. After the conservative strength shown in the 1993 Russian elections, the more moderate political leaders are careful not to alienate nationalist supporters. Events in Moldova (as well as in Latvia, Crimea, and Kazakhstan) provide opportunities for the conservatives to reapply their imperial worldview to Russian political and military relations with neighboring states. Although moderates express concern for fellow Russians, they have less confidence in Russia's ability to manage events in the successor states. Yet, because of demonstrated conservative electoral strength, the moderates outwardly take a harder line.

In spite of his recent hard-line statements supporting Russian minorities in the successor states, Russian Foreign Minister Kozyrev earlier took a more moderate position. On a tour of the successor states in April 1992, Kozyrev charged that those criticizing the Foreign Ministry for its neglect of Russians in other states were the same forces interested in continuing the old union. In addressing the Congress of People's Deputies, Kozyrev dealt with the Moldovan situation, but had little success in moderating the conservatives' intrusive stand:

> We cannot send a military helicopter for every Russian-speaking boy or girl in a school in Moldova. . . . We must not provoke Russophobic feelings in Moldova, because 75% of all the Russians and Russian speakers living in Moldova are beyond the Dniester, on the right bank of the Dniester.[61]

But that moderation changed with the internal Russian political situation. Moscow's rhetoric intensified during spring and summer 1992, reflecting the Transdniestrian escalation and the conservative challenge to Yeltsin.[62] Following the failure of various conflict resolution strategies, former vice president Rutskoi signaled a change in Russian policy when he announced that Russia would no longer tolerate ill treatment of Transdniestrian Russian-speakers.[63]

Both conservative successes in the 1993 Russian elections and weak Western reaction to Moscow's statements on the "near abroad" encouraged Russia's unyielding positions on Moldova and other former Soviet territories, again illuminating the connection between Russian domestic politics and foreign policy. Yeltsin's domestic opponents want continued influence in former Soviet space. Russian minorities provide justification for Moscow's exercising "special authority" in the "near abroad." Fearing that strong objection to this position would play into the hands of right-wing nationalists such as Zhirinovsky, the West has remained silent. A more interventionist Russian foreign policy has thus emerged, with leaders in Moldova, as in Ukraine and the Baltics, worrying that—by its silence—the West has consigned them once again to the Russian sphere.

Conflict Management

In pre-Gorbachev times, nationalism was limited by crosscutting identities and roles, heterogeneity within the nations, and pressure by Moscow.[64] Coercion and dependency provided effective mechanisms to manage conflict.[65] Without central control, nationalism has destabilized much of the former Soviet Union. The development of national feelings and symbols by indigenous populations has triggered minority Russian reaction. In Moldova, both cultural and territorial autonomy have been proposed to contain inter-national conflict.

In the years just before the Soviet collapse, Chisinau used cultural autonomy to validate minority rights. By supporting demands for linguistic, religious, and educational self-determination, cultural autonomy was intended to eliminate reasons for minority opposition. The Chisinau government hoped that the diverse populations would support the creation of a multinational polity that recognized diverse cultural claims. Yet the early nationalistic rhetoric of the Popular Front crowded out genuine efforts to provide for cultural autonomy.

Though non-Moldovans are not a majority in any geographic area of Moldova, concentrations of Russians and Ukrainians in Transdniestria and Chisinau, and of Gagauzi in the south, lend importance to addressing minority demands. After independence Chisinau took steps to accommodate minority cultural needs by developing schools, media, and cultural facilities. Nonetheless, the Transdniestrian Russians, a minority even where their population is most concentrated, were neither satisfied with "mere" cultural autonomy, nor willing to accommodate other nations inhabiting their claimed geographic regions. Left-bank Moldovans appealed to the inter-state community, pointing to "measures undertaken by the 'Dniester SSR,'" to restrict Latin script usage and Romanian speech in schools and to teach Soviet, rather than "Moldo-Romanian," history.[66]

In independent Moldova, citizenship was immediately granted to all; language policy was moderate; education was supported in several languages; and political representation was available to all groups. If the secessionist movements are construed as attempts by communists to hold power—with national issues serving as justification for insurgency rather than the cause—then the generally positive relationships between the nations on the right bank might be seen as constructive outcomes of cultural autonomy. The failure of right-bank Russians to support Transdniestrian separatism provides evidence for this interpretation. However, initial Popular Front rhetoric was provocative and anti-Russian; while accommodative policies toward minorities developed after independence, they could not undo Transdniestrian Russian fears of romanianization that resulted from the early positions of the Popular Front. These fears, combined with the communist leadership's desire to maintain its status, encouraged the secession.

A second strategy for conflict containment involves territorial autonomy, which grants a geographically concentrated population control over governmental functions such as education, media, local administration, and police. Territorial autonomy is attractive to minorities concentrated in defined areas within larger states. While benefitting from the larger political entity, they have greater influence over administrative policies directly affecting their group. But territorial autonomy can also have negative implications: Reinforcing national identification with territory can foster a desire for total independence. Education, culture, language, and media influence daily existence and accentuate national differences rather than political or economic similarities. By decentralizing control of some functions and services, territorial autonomy can potentially make state-building more difficult. In Moldova, the breakaway Russians and Gagauzi are themselves minorities in the territories that they claim. What becomes of the rights of other populations under such circumstances?

Nevertheless, as the stalemate in Transdniestria continues, a federative approach seems to be emerging. Chisinau demands control over all of former Soviet Moldova to preserve its prior borders and harness economic resources located in Transdniestria. The Transdniestrians demand autonomy, wishing to preserve Russian (and Soviet) culture. Both the Transdniestrians and Gagauzi now advocate a federation of three equal republics—Moldova, Transdniester, and Gagauz. Chisinau rejects "federation" but concedes "special status" and "autonomy" to

Transdniestria, thereby acknowledging significant local control. Likewise, President Snegur obtained Gagauz support for holding the February 1994, parliamentary elections on Gagauz territory by conceding that one of the first items that he would bring to the new parliament was autonomy for the area. The 1994 Constitution provides the framework for autonomy for both Gagauzia and Transdniestria. Recent elections in Gagauzia formalized local autonomy.[67] Negotiations with Tiraspol' appear to be headed in the same direction. Thus, a federal structure with significant territorial autonomy seems likely to emerge as the basis for a single state comprising the territory of the former Moldovan SSR.

Conclusion

Transdniestrian Russians and other minorities had legitimate fears about the nationalizing agenda originally championed by the Popular Front. Although a minority, Russians once had privileges of empire. Chisinau's current articulation of a policy of minority cultural autonomy in place of the original exclusionary nationalistic agenda of the Popular Front does not reduce the enormity of the change that Russians have undergone. Dismissing the Transdniestrian leaders as hard-line communists just interested in maintaining their former status masks the reality for Russians and other russified minorities experiencing this transition. Yet focusing solely on the left-bank secession obscures the generally positive situation among nations elsewhere in Moldova.

Chisinau's early policy of cultural autonomy, together with its renunciation of reunification, enabled many right-bank Russians, Ukrainians, and Bulgarians to support Moldovan independence.[68] A main goal of the Moldovan government has been to create conditions for inter-national cooperation. The accommodative policy can be credited with bringing right-bank Russians and Moldovans together in a multinational government, independent of both Moscow and Bucharest. But Moldovan state-building processes are being hampered by both inter-national and inter-state disputes. Mobilizing the indigenous population creates a reactive nationalism among Russians and other minorities that subsequently increases nationalist pressures for intervention by the Russian Federation. The challenge to Moldovan political leadership is to build a multinational coalition that can incorporate the minorities, and the territory with which they identify, into the developing political and economic infrastructure.

Notes

*On May 23, 1991, the Moldavian Soviet Socialist Republic renamed itself the Republic of Moldova, removing the "Soviet Socialist" designation. With the latinization of the alphabet, most western sources began using the Romanian forms Moldova and Chisinau (the capital) in place of Moldavia and Kishinev, forms that result from translation from the Russian or Cyrillic. (This change is more significant in appearance than in fact; Romanian speakers have always used Moldova and Chisinau, and Russian speakers continue to refer to Moldavia and Kishinev.) In this chapter we will use the Moldova and Chisinau except when the previous forms are found in direct quotations.

Designating the language and the majority population as "Moldovan" or "Romanian" is troublesome. All but the Transdniestrians have acknowledged that the same language is written and spoken in Romania and Moldova. Nonetheless, the language law designates the language as "Moldovan." In keeping with the legal designation, this chapter will use the term Moldovan to describe both the language and the Romanian-speaking majority.

The Moldovans may not constitute a nation in its strictest definition, but they have continued to look at themselves as different from their relatives in Romania, both in terms of history and future goals. In fact, since independence, they have rejected pan-Romanianism at every opportunity. While acknowledging that the question of Moldovan nationhood remains open, we have concluded that the term "Moldovan" is more appropriate for this discussion than either "Romanian" or "Romanian-speaker." Our choice of Moldovan is not intended to reflect any judgment on the question of a distinct Moldovan "nation."

1. Bessarabia declared itself an autonomous republic on December 2, 1917. The Bessarabian State Council then voted to reunite with Romania on March 27, 1918, ending four months of independence. See Nicolas Dima, *Bessarabia and Bukovina: The Soviet-Romanian Territorial Dispute* (New York: Columbia University Press, 1982).

2. Jonathan Eyal, "Moldavians," in Graham Smith, cd., *The Nationalities Question in the Soviet Union* (London: Longman, 1990), pp. 123–124.

3. The most complete discussion of this issue can be found in Charles King, "Moldovan Identity and the Politics of Pan-Romanianism," *Slavic Review*, Vol. 53, No. 2 (Summer 1994): 345–368.

4. *The Republic of Moldova* (Chisinau: Foreign Relations Committee of the Parliament of the Republic of Moldova, 1992), p. 16.

5. Eyal, "Moldavians," p. 124.

6. *Republic of Moldova*, p. 4.

7. Population data, unless otherwise noted, are from the 1989 census.

8. *Republic of Moldova*, p. 76.

9. Ibid.

10. Irina Livezeanu, "The Internationalization of Ethnic Politics in ex-Soviet Moldavia," (paper presented to the American Association of Slavic Studies Conference, Miami, November 1991), p. 9.

11. Ibid., p. 41.

12. William Crowther, "The Politics of Ethno-National Mobilization: Nationalism and Reform in Soviet Moldavia," *The Russian Review*, Vol. 50 (April 1991): 185–6.

13. Nicolae Tau, Moldovan Ambassador to the United States and former Foreign Minister (1990–1993), personal interview, Orlando, Florida, January 1994.

14. An earlier version of this section was published as "The Politics of Language in Moldova," *Demokratizatsiya*, Vol. 2, No. 2 (Spring 1994): 309–315.

15. *Actele legislative ale R.S.S. Moldovenesti cu privire la decretarea limbii moldovenesti limba de stat si revenirea ei la grafia latina / Zakonodatel'niye akti Moldovskoi SSR o pridanii moldavskomu yaziku statusa gosudarstvennogo i vozvrate emu latinskoi grafiku* (Chisinau: Cartea Moldoveneasca, 1990).

16. Crowther, "Politics of Ethno-National Mobilization," p. 189.

17. Irina Livezeanu, "Moldavia, 1917–1990: Nationalism and Internationalism Then and Now," *Armenian Review*, Vol. 43, No. 2–3/170–171 (Summer-Autumn 1990):157.

18. Ibid., p. 179.

19. "The Bessarabians," *The Economist*, April 6, 1991, p. 49.

20. Constantin Rusnac, Rector of the Academy of Music and former Deputy Minister of Culture, personal interview, Orlando, Florida, January 1994.

21. Crowther, "The Politics of Ethno-National Mobilization," p. 195.

22. Alexander Belopotapov, Director General of the Russian Cultural Center, personal interview, Chisinau, September 1993.

23. RFE/RL *Daily Report*, No. 26, February 8, 1994.

24. King, "Moldovan Identity," p. 355.

25. Mikhail Guboglo, "Demography and Language in the Capitals of the Union Republics," *Journal of Soviet Nationalities*, Vol. 1, No. 4 (Winter 1990–1991): 20, 40.

26. Dan Ionescu, "Soviet Moldavia: The State Language Issue," Radio Liberty, *Report on the USSR*, June 2, 1989, p. 20.

27. *Anuarul statistic al Republicii Moldova, 1992* (Chisinau: Universitas, 1994), p. 159. These data were provided by Charles King, New College, Oxford.

28. *Anuarul statistic al Republicii Moldova, 1991* (Chisinau: Departmentul de Stat pentru Statistica, 1992), p. 176; and *Anuarul statistic al Republicii Moldova, 1992* (Chisinau: Universitas, 1994), p. 170. These data were provided by Charles King, New College, Oxford.

29. Belopotapov, personal interview, Chisinau, September 1993.

30. Galina V. Galagan, Director of the Cultural Department of the Tiraspol Executive Committee, personal interview, Tiraspol', September 1993.

31. Konstantin Fedorovich Popovich, Director, Institute for the Study of National Minorities of the Moldovan Academy of Sciences, personal interview, Chisinau, September 1993.

32. Reuters/AP, April 1, 1994.

33. Chancy D. Harris, "Ethnic Tensions in the Successor Republics in 1993 and Early 1994," *Post-Soviet Geography*, Vol. 35, No. 4 (April 1994), p. 187.

34. Viktor Grebenshchikov, Counselor to President Snegur, personal interview, Chisinau, September 1993.

35. Vladimir Socor, "Opinion Polling in Moldova," RFE/RL *Research Report*, March 22, 1992, pp. 60–61.

36. Vladimir Socor, "Moldavia Defies Soviet Coup, Removes Vestiges of Communism," RFE/RL Research Institute, *Report on the USSR*, September 20, 1991, p. 21.

37. Ibid., p. 16, citing *Moldova Surverana*, September 11, 1991.

38. Valeriu Matei, Member of Parliament and Vice Chair of the Congress of Intellectuals, personal interview, Chisinau, September 1993.

39. RFE/RL *Research Report*, March 20, 1992, p. 69.

40. See Wilhelmus Petrus van Meurs, *The Bessarabian Question in Communist Historiography: Nationalist and Communist Politics and History-Writing* (Boulder: East European Monographs, 1994).

41. *The Economist*, April 6, 1991, p. 50.

42. RFE/RL *Research Report*, April 10, 1992, p. 63.

43. Vladimir Socor, "Creeping Putsch in Eastern Moldova," RFE/RL *Research Report*, January 17, 1992, p. 9.

44. RFE/RL *Research Report*, July 17, 1992, p. 73.

45. Ibid.

46. Neil V. Lamont, "Peacemaking or Warfighting? Ethnic Conflict in the Transdniester," Foreign Military Studies Office, Ft. Leavenworth, Kansas, unpublished paper, November 1993, p. 15.

47. Ibid., p. 14.

48. Valentin Ivanovich Yegoshin, Cultural Department of the Tiraspol' City Political Committee, personal interview, Tiraspol' September 1993.

49. Svetlana Gamova, "Question of the Status of Bendery—Test for the Politicians," *Izvestiya* (Moscow), September 3, 1992, p. 2, cited in *FBIS–USR–92–118*, September 16, 1992.

50. The Moldovan Ministry of Foreign Affairs (October 1994) estimated the size of the 14th Army at 10,000 in 1992 and 7,700 by 1994.

51. "Agreement on the Legal Status, Procedure and Timetable for the Withdrawal of Russian Military Forces Located Temporarily In Moldova," *Adevarul*, October 12, 1994; see also RFE/RL *Daily Report*, No. 152, August 11, 1994.

52. Stefan Bozbei, Director of the Moldovan Department of Nationalities, personal interview, Chisinau, September 1993.

53. RFE/RL *Daily Report*, No. 143, July 29, 1994.

54. RFE/RL *Daily Report*, No. 127, July 7, 1994.

55. *Adevarul*, March 6, 1995.

56. Rogers Brubaker, "National Minorities, Nationalizing States, and External National Homelands in the New Europe," *Daedalus*, Vol. 24, No. 2 (Spring 1995): 107–132.

57. William Crowther, "Exploring the Determination of Political Culture: a Comparative Analysis of Romania and Moldova," unpublished paper.

58. RFE/RL *Research Report*, October 16, 1992, p. 68.

59. *Monitorul Oficial al Romaniei*, No. 313, December 4, 1992.

60. RFE/RL *Daily Report*, Nos. 143 and 145, July 29, 1994, and August 2, 1994.

61. Bohdan Nahaylo, "Moldovan Conflict Creates New Dilemmas for Ukraine, RFE/RL *Research Report*, May 15, 1992, citing Radio Rossiya, April 18, 1992, p. 6.

62. Anatolie Gondiu, "Opreste, doamne, mina ucigasului," *Curierul National*, June 29, 1992, p. 1.

63. Serge Schmemann, "Yeltsin Plans Peacekeepers to End Fighting in Moldova," *New York Times*, July 7, 1992, p. A8.

64. Gail Lapidus, "Ethnonationalism and Political Stability: The Soviet Case," *World Politics*, Vol. 35 (1984): 375–380.

65. Paul Goble, "Ethnic Politics in the USSR," *Problems of Communism*, Vol. 38 (1989).

66. RFE/RL *Research Report*, January 10, 1992, p. 62.

67. Dimitry Solovyov, "Moldova's Gagauz Minority Backs Autonomy," Reuters, March 6, 1995; *Cronica Romana*, March 6, 1995; Infotag News Agency, March 2, 1995.

68. Vladimir Socor, "Why Moldova Does Not Seek Reunification with Romania," RFE/RL *Research Report*, January 31, 1992, p. 31.

Chapter 8

Kazakhstan

The "Russian question" is more complex and relatively more important for the future viability and democratization of Kazakhstan than for any of the other newly independent states with the possible exception of Ukraine. The 6.2 million Russians in Kazakhstan are second in number only to Ukraine, and account for nearly one quarter of all Russians living outside Russia.

Like Ukraine, Russians in Kazakhstan are geographically concentrated near the borderlands with Russia. However, unlike Ukraine, where Russians are a minority in every oblast except Crimea, Russians comprise a majority of the population in three of Kazakhstan's northern oblasts (East Kazakhstan, Karaganda, and North Kazakhstan) and a plurality in four others (Akmola, Kokchetav, Kustanay, and Pavlodar).[1] All of these oblasts either share a border with Russia (North Kazakhstan, Kustanay, Kokchetav, East Kazakhstan, Pavlodar) or are contiguous with one of the Russian-dominated border oblasts (Karaganda, Akmola). Moreover, this Russian-dominated northern region is the industrial and agricultural heartland of Kazakhstan and is tied more closely with Russia economically than with the southern part of the state. This geopolitical situation increases the likelihood of irredentism in Kazakhstan and makes the management of Russian-titular relations even more critical.

In this chapter we examine the development of Russian-Kazakh relations during the late 1980s and early 1990s. Kazakhstan has frequently been depicted both at home and in the West as a democratic state where inter-national harmony exists. In Kazakhstan, the "friendship of the peoples" myth did not die with the collapse of the USSR. On closer examination, however, relations between Russians and Kazakhs are anything but harmonious. Exclusionary ethnodemographic, sociocultural and political "kazakhization" policies and processes have the objective of redefining multinational Kazakhstan as a Kazakh nation-state. These policies and processes have resulted in rising Russian uneasiness within Kazakhstan and have also drawn Russia into the picture as the "defender of Russians in the near abroad." Kazakhstan, like Ukraine, is on the verge of an inter-national crisis between Russians and Kazakhs that has the potential to become an inter-state conflict between Russia and Kazakhstan.

Kazakhstan: Areas of Russian Concentration

Kazakhstan

Lake Balkhash

Almaty

Aral Sea

KAZAKHSTAN

Territorial Size (km²)	2,717,300	
Population Size (1/1/94)	16,942,400	
Titular (1/1/93)	7,296,942	43.2%
Percent Russian (1/1/93)	6,168,740	36.4%
Urban Population (1/1/93)	9,718,000	57.2%
Percent Titular (1989)	26.7	
Percent Russian (1989)	51.3	
Size of Capital City (1/1/93)	1,197,900	
Percent Titular (1/1/93)	25.1	
Percent Russian (1/1/93)	56.0	
Natural Increase (/1000, 1993)	9.4	
Titular NI (1989)	24.8	
Russian NI (1989)	7.3	
Life Expectancy (1989)	Men: 63.9	Women: 72.9
Titular e⁰ (1989)	Men: 63.7	Women: 72.6
Russian e⁰ (1989)	Men: 63.9	Women: 73.6
Net Migration To (−)/From (+) Russia (1989–1993)		
Total	−351,612	
Titular	26,140	
Russian	−274,465	
Employment[a] (1992)	78.9	
Trade (Export/Import Ratio, 1993)		
Intra-NIS Trade[b]	0.91	
Extra-NIS Trade[c]	3.15	

Notes: [a]Employment given as a percent of the working-age population. [b]Intra-NIS ratios calculated from trade among the republics of the former USSR and measured in the national currencies. [c]Extra-NIS ratios calculated from trade with countries outside the former USSR and measured in US dollars.

Sources: Goskomstat Respubliki Kazakhstan, *Demograficheskiy yezhegodnik Kazakhstana* (Almaty: Kazinformtsentr, 1993); Goskomstat Rossiyskoy Federatsii, *Chislennost' i sotsial'no-demograficheskiye kharakteristiki russkogo naseleniya v respublikakh byvshego SSSR* (Moskva: 1994); Statisticheskiy komitet SNG, *Statisticheskiy byulleten'* No. 20 (June 1994): 35–36; Statkom SNG, *Itogi vsesoyuznoy perepisi naseleniya 1989 goda* (Minneapolis, MN: East View, 1992), Vol. 7, Part 2; The World Bank, *Statistical Handbook 1994: States of the Former USSR* (Washington, DC: World Bank Studies of Economies in Transformation No. 14, 1994).

Demographic Trends

Russification

As noted in Chapter 2, in-migration of ethnic outsiders nearly always results in the nationalization of the indigenous population and in the activation of exclusionary nationalism. This process certainly occurred among the Kazakhs, who first became nationally conscious in reaction to the massive in-migration of Russian peasants and their appropriation of the best Kazakh grazing lands during the last three decades of tsarist Russia. A relatively pro-Russian attitude among Kazakhs "did not survive the advent of the Russian settlers, who descended on the Kazakhs at the turn of the century and robbed them of their lands."[2] The Kazakh national consciousness that arose in response to the flood of Russians was both anti-Russian and anti-tsarist.[3]

By 1917, 1.3 million Russians, comprising 20.5 percent of the population, lived in Kazakhstan. The number of Russians remained approximately the same between 1917 and 1926, but then nearly doubled to 2.5 million by 1939 as a result of collectivization and industrialization. During the same period Kazakhs suffered an absolute decline from 3.7 million to 2.3 million due to a combination of high mortality and emigration to western China.[4] By 1939, Russians had become a plurality in Kazakhstan with 40.3 percent of the total population, while Kazakhs had declined from a majority of 57.1 percent (1926) to only 38.2 percent.

This demographic russification continued after World War II, particularly as a result of Khrushchev's Virgin Lands Program that expanded the acreage under cultivation in the steppe region of northern Kazakhstan.[5] Russians increased from 2.5 million in 1939 to 4 million in 1959, reaching 42.7 percent of the population. In that year, Russians outnumbered Kazakhs in nine of fifteen oblasts and comprised 73 percent of the population in Almaty, the capital city.[6]

Each of the policy initiatives that resulted in massive in-migration of Russians and/or decimation of Kazakhs became a historic event which helped nationalize the Kazakhs and orient their mass-based nationalism against both Russian in-migrants and Moscow. These policies and their demographic consequences for Kazakhstan were utilized by Kazakh nationalists during the late 1980s to mobilize the Kazakh population behind a separatist political action program.[7]

Indigenization

Beginning in the 1960s, Kazakhstan experienced a demographic shift in favor of Kazakhs (Table 8.1). The Kazakh population nearly doubled between 1959 and 1979, increasing from 2.8 to 5.3 million. The Russian population increased from 4 to 6 million, but declined proportionately from 42.7 percent of Kazakhstan's population in 1959 to 40.8 percent in 1979. At the same time, Kazakhs increased their share of the total population from 30 percent to 36 percent.

Table 8.1
Russians and Kazakhs in Kazakhstan, 1959–1993
(Absolute number and percent of total population)

Nation	1959	1970	1979	1989	1993
Russians	3,974,229	5,521,917	5,991,205	6,227,549	6,168,740
Percent	42.7	42.4	40.8	37.8	36.5
Kazakhs	2,794,966	4,234,166	5,289,349	6,534,616	7,296,942
Percent	30.0	32.5	36.0	39.7	43.1

Sources: **1959:** TsSU SSSR, *Itogi vsesoyuznoy perepisi naseleniya 1959 goda* (Moskva: Gosstatizdat, 1962), Vol. *Kazakhskaya SSR*, p. 162; **1970:** TsSU SSSR, *Itogi vsesoyuznoy perepisi naseleniya 1970 goda* (Moskva: Statistika, 1973), Vol. 4, p. 223; **1979:** Goskomstat SSSR, *Itogi vsesoyuznoy perepisi naseleniya 1979 goda* (Moskva: Goskomstat SSSR, 1989), Vol 4, Part I, Book 2, p. 179; **1989:** Gosudarstvennyy komitet Kazakhskoy SSR po statistike i analizu (Goskomstat KSSR), *Itogi vsesoyuznoy perepisi naseleniya 1989 goda: Natsional'nyy sostav naseleniya Kazakhskoy SSR, oblastey i g. Alma-Ata* (Alma-Ata: Respublikanskiy informatsionno-izdatel'skiy tsentr, 1991), p. 23; **1993:** Goskomstat Respubliki Kazakhstan, *Demograficheskiy yezhegodnik Kazakhstana* (Almaty: Kazinformtsentr, 1993), p. 45.

This demographic indigenization occurred primarily because of a much higher birthrate among Kazakhs than among Russians in Kazakhstan.[8] In addition, the Russian net in-migration that had continued from the time of the original conquest of the Kazakh lands slowed considerably during the 1960s and was reversed during the 1970s, from which time there has been a net out-migration of Russians from the republic.[9]

Both the higher birthrate among Kazakhs and Russian net out-migration continued during the 1980s (Table 8.1). By 1989 Kazakhs outnumbered Russians in Kazakhstan for the first time since the 1920s. This demographic indigenization has increased since 1989, with relatively high Kazakh birthrates the most important causal factor. However, Russian out-migration has also increased dramatically, and the Russian population is declining absolutely for the first time since the conquest of Kazakhstan.

The reasons for this Russian out-migration have also changed since the late 1980s. During the 1970s and 1980s Russians were leaving primarily because greater economic opportunities existed in Russia than in Kazakhstan. In addition, Russians and other nonindigenes increasingly commented that ethnic favoritism toward Kazakhs put them at a comparative disadvantage, and that this change in the ethnic stratification system was also causing out-migration.[10] Kazakh over-representation in higher education and political representation, and the dramatic shift during the 1980s toward higher Kazakh participation in all sectors of the economy (even though proportional representation had not been achieved) provided an added incentive for Russian emigration.[11]

The new language law that proclaimed Kazakh the official state language, the new citizenship law that allowed citizenship for Kazakhs living outside Kazakhstan but did not allow dual citizenship for Russians, and the new constitution that proclaimed independence in the name of the Kazakh nation since 1989 contributed to the feeling among the Russians of relative deprivation and of favoritism toward the Kazakhs.[12]

The rising fear of worsening inter-national relations and the potential for inter-national conflict have accelerated the pace of Russian emigration in the 1990s. In 1991, only 10.9 percent of out-migrants from Kazakhstan named "worsening of inter-national relations" as the reason for their departure. This reason ranked behind "family circumstances" (33.6 percent), "changed work place" (14.1 percent) and "studies" (11.1 percent). Only Belarus, Russia and Ukraine had a lower percentage of out-migrants who claimed that the deterioration of inter-national relations was the cause of their migration decision.[13] A survey of potential emigrants from Kazakhstan taken in 1993 in Almaty shows a different picture. "Interethnic problems" were ranked as the principal factor in the decision to emigrate (29.2 percent), followed by "the economic situation" (25.6 percent), "the political situation" (24.0 percent), "personal reasons" (18.8 percent) and "the Law on Languages" (14.2 percent).[14]

Between 1989 and 1993, Russian net emigration from Kazakhstan totaled 267,000.[15] Russian net emigration to Russia more than tripled from 25,578 in 1991 to 82,371 in 1992, and increased to 104,400 in 1993.[16] This trend toward increasing Russian emigration is likely to continue: A 1994 public opinion poll found that approximately one-third of all Russians wished to leave Kazakhstan; this finding was true not only for Russians in southern oblasts where they were a demographic minority, but also in the Russian-dominated oblasts of northern Kazakhstan.[17]

Several analysts have recently concluded that Russians in Kazakhstan will emigrate rather than stay and fight kazakhization either through political opposition or by attempting to secede.[18] However, to date the number of Russians in Kazakhstan has not decreased significantly. Between January 1989 and January 1993, the Russian total had decreased by only 58,809 (Table 8.1). Even adding the 104,000 net emigrants for 1993 to this figure, and ignoring the natural increase among Russians in Kazakhstan for 1993, the total decrease in the number of Russians was less than 200,000 by January 1994, and the total number of Russians in Kazakhstan was still over six million.

In addition, public opinion polls about the desire to emigrate—on which several of the predictions of large-scale Russian emigration are based—are notoriously unreliable; a much higher percentage of Russians is likely to express dissatisfaction in a public opinion poll than actually emigrate from Kazakhstan. This disparity is especially true in northern Kazakhstan, where Russians have lived for generations, remain in the majority, and have developed a strong sense of homeland. According to the 1989 census, two-thirds of all Russians living in Kazakhstan were born there, the highest proportion in all of the non-Russian successor states, including Ukraine.[19] This relatively longer-term residence among Russians in Kazakhstan and the sense of homeland that has developed in the north suggest that irredentism is likely to become a viable alternative to emigration as Russians increasingly react to exclusionary Kazakh nationalism.

Demographic indigenization is also being enhanced by the return of Kazakhs from the former union republics and from foreign states. Of the 188,000 immigrants to Kazakhstan in 1992, 110,000 were Kazakhs. Most returned from Mongolia, where Kazakhs had fled from Stalinist persecution during the 1930s.[20] This repatriation has been fostered by the citizenship law (passed December 20, 1991), which grants automatic citizenship for Kazakhs from outside Kazakhstan. These Kazakhs are permitted to hold either dual citizenship (if their country of residence permits it), or they can obtain Kazakh citizenship upon their immigration to Kazakhstan. In addition to providing for the unobstructed return of all Kazakhs, the law provides funding for those Kazakhs previously forced to leave the republic due to persecution who now wish to return.[21] Most of these immigrants are being settled in northern Kazakhstan in what Russians perceive as a deliberate effort by the Kazakh government to "kazakhize" the population in the north.[22]

In addition to emigrating from Kazakhstan, Russians have increasingly become more concentrated in Kazakhstan's northern oblasts. This geographic segregation is occurring as a result of Russian migration from southern oblasts with Kazakh majorities to northern oblasts with Russian majorities or pluralities. In the south, Russians have become relatively more concentrated in Almaty, where they still comprised 56 percent of the population in 1993.[23]

The Russian concentration in the north is in part due to the geographic differentials in the phasing in of the law on languages, which has already been implemented in Kazakh-majority southern oblasts but which has been delayed in Kazakh-minority northern oblasts.[24] In addition, the implementation of the language law and similar pro-Kazakh legislation is actively resisted by the local Russian administrators in the north; this resistance has undoubtedly exerted a northward pull on Russians living in Kazakhstan's south.[25]

Despite the increasing Russian concentration in the northern oblasts, Kazakh population growth there has outpaced that of the Russians. The demographic indigenization has resulted from Russian emigration, from the immigration and the resettlement policies targeting Kazakhs returning from abroad, and from the higher birthrates among the Kazakhs (Table 8.2).

The geographic concentration of Russians in the north and the demographic kazakhization of that region is a potentially explosive combination. As Russians in the north begin to lose their majority or plurality status, they will be tempted to opt for secession while they still hold the majority rather than to wait for a time in which they will no longer be able to prevail in an independence referendum. As discussed later, other trends are also increasing the pressure on Kazakhstan's Russians to separate from Kazakhstan.

Table 8.2
Russian and Kazakh Population by Oblast, 1959–1993 (%)

Oblast	Russians					Kazakhs				
	1959	1970	1979	1989	1993	1959	1970	1979	1989	1993
South										
Aktubinsk	26.2	26.4	25.1	23.7	22.0	43.1	47.5	52.1	55.5	59.8
Almaty (Oblast)[a]	42.4	37.8	35.3	31.2	29.4	32.1	38.3	41.3	45.3	50.2
Gur'ev[b]	20.7	27.3	27.0	22.8	19.8	72.2	62.4	63.1	67.3	71.2
Zhambyl	31.4	32.4	30.4	26.5	24.1	39.1	40.7	44.0	48.8	56.7
Kzyl-Orda	15.3	18.6	15.3	13.3	11.6	72.2	69.9	76.2	79.4	83.9
Chimkent[c]	22.7	22.0	19.2	15.3	13.7	44.1	47.2	51.0	55.7	59.4
Almaty (capital)	73.0	70.3	66.0	59.1	56.0	8.6	12.1	16.4	22.5	25.1
North										
E. Kazakhstan	70.9	69.5	67.7	65.9	64.2	18.9	23.2	25.4	27.3	29.1
Kokshetau	41.7	40.4	40.4	42.1	39.5	18.5	22.8	26.3	28.9	31.6
Pavlodar	39.3	44.4	45.9	45.4	44.6	25.5	25.2	26.8	28.6	30.9
N. Kazakhstan	64.5	63.5	63.4	62.1	61.7	12.5	14.9	16.6	18.7	19.5
Semipalatinsk	45.2	40.9	39.1	36.0	34.5	35.8	43.7	48.0	51.9	55.6
Ural'sk[d]	41.5	38.4	37.2	34.4	33.3	45.9	49.3	51.5	55.8	57.6
Akmola+Karaganda+ Kustanay+Turgay+ Zhezkazgan[e]	44.2	47.3	47.5	45.7	45.7	18.8	18.7	21.1	23.7	26.0

Notes: [a]Figures for Almaty Oblast include Taldy-Kurgan Oblast, which was part of Almaty in 1959. [b]Figures for Gur'ev Oblast (renamed Atyrau in 1992) include Mangistau Oblast, which was part of Gur'ev in 1959, 1970 and 1989. [c]Chimkent Oblast was renamed South Kazakhstan in 1992. [d] Ural'sk Oblast was renamed West Kazakhstan in 1992. [e]In order to create a geographically comparable unit, it was necessary to combine figures for these oblasts. Zhezkazgan was part of Karaganda in 1959 and 1970; Turgay was part of Kustanay and Akmola (Tselinograd until 1992) in 1959 and 1989, and territory was reallocated from Akmola to Karaganda in 1993.

Sources: **1959:** TsSU SSSR, *Itogi vsesoyuznoy perepisi naseleniya 1959 goda* (Moskva: Gosstatizdat, 1962), Vol. *Kazakhskaya SSR*, pp. 168–172; **1970:** TsSU SSSR, *Itogi vsesoyuznoy perepisi naseleniya 1970 goda* (Moskva: Statistika, 1973), Vol. 4, pp. 232–252; **1979:** Goskomstat SSSR, *Itogi vsesoyuznoy perepisi naseleniya 1979 goda* (Moskva: Goskomstat SSSR, 1989), Vol 4, Part I, Book 2, pp. 188–277; **1989:** Gosudarstvennyy Komitet Kazakhskoy SSR po statistike i analizu (Goskomstat KSSR), *Itogi vsesoyuznoy perepisi naseleniya 1989 goda: Natsional'nyy sostav naseleniya Kazakhskoy SSR, oblastey i g. Alma-Ata* (Alma-Ata: Respublikanskiy informatsionno-izdatel'skiy tsentr, 1991), p. 22–116; **1993:** Goskomstat Respubliki Kazakhstan, *Demograficheskiy yezhegodnik Kazakhstana* (Almaty: Kazinformtsentr, 1993), p. 47–48.

Sociocultural Kazakhization

During the 1980s, Kazakh political and cultural elites began to reverse the sociocultural—and particularly linguistic—russification that had occurred during the Soviet era. Although nearly 99 percent of all Kazakhs in Kazakhstan proclaimed Kazakh to be their native language,[26] Kazakh cultural leaders such as Olzhas Suleymenov and even President Nursultan Nazarbayev complained throughout the 1980s that the Kazakh language was dying out.[27] Kazakh elites were particularly concerned about the status of Kazakh in the primary schools, which had increasingly been replaced by Russian during the previous two decades.

> During the 1960s and 1970s, the language of instruction in thousands of elementary schools throughout the republic had shifted from Kazakh to Russian. By the mid-1980's, as Suleymenov has repeatedly reminded audiences, approximately 40 percent of Kazakh youth were unable to read their native language.[28]

A concerted effort has been undertaken to convert the language of instruction from Russian to Kazakh. The number of hours of instruction in Kazakh was increased in 1987. The language law of 1989 made Kazakh a mandatory subject of study.[29] Partitions (called Berlin Walls) were installed in the Russian-language schools to divide classes into Kazakh and Russian-language instruction.[30] During the 1990s, the Russian-language schools were increasingly converted to Kazakh-language schools, particularly in the South.[31]

An increasing proportion of students are being educated in Kazakh-language schools (Table 8.3). This shift has brought the language of instruction closer to the Kazakh and Russian proportions of the student population, though even with these changes Kazakh continued to be under-represented at the beginning of the 1993–94 school year.

Table 8.3
Education by Language of Instruction, 1989–1994
(Percent of Schools and Students in Russian and Kazakh-Language Schools)

Year	Percent of Schools			Percent of Students in:	
	Kazakh	Russian	Mixed	Kazakh Schools	Russian Schools
1990/91	34.0	44.7	20.2	32.4	65.0
1991/92	35.3	41.7	21.9	34.3	63.1
1992/93	37.1	36.7	25.2	37.0	60.3
1993/94	38.3	33.9	26.8	40.1	57.2

Note: The figures above do not total to 100% because there are also Uzbek, Tajik, Uygur and German-language schools in Kazakhstan.

Source: Data provided by the Ministry of Education, Almaty, February 1994.

As noted in Chapter 4, a kazakhization of students, faculty and administrators in higher education was already taking place by the 1980s. The fact that Kazakh college students were at the forefront of the 1986 demonstrations in Almaty was not lost on the new regime that replaced Kunayev. Speeches and articles by political elites in 1987 decried both the favoritism shown Kazakhs in gaining admission to higher education, and the lack of "inter-nationalism" among college students and within the education system.[32] Clearly, higher educational attainment, even in an educational system dominated by the Russian language, had not resulted either in russification or sovietization.

In the wake of the 1986 demonstrations, one would have expected the new government to de-kazakhize higher education; however, this did not occur. Not only did Kazakhs continue to be over-represented among students in colleges, but Russians in faculty and administrative positions in the universities and within the Ministry of Education were increasingly replaced by Kazakhs. Between 1989 and 1992, the share of Russian executives in the Ministry of Education had declined from 43 percent to 14 percent, and Russian specialists in the Ministry had declined from 47 percent to 19 percent.[33] This kazakhization has continued in 1993 and 1994.[34]

Kazakhstan passed a "Law on Languages" in August 1989, which went into effect on July 1, 1990. Reflecting Nazarbayev's belief that the Kazakh language "should be preserved, enriched, and developed without encroaching on all the others which we have,"[35] the law proclaimed Kazakh to be the state language, but accorded Russian the status of language of inter-national communication. Under the provisions of the law, study of Kazakh is mandatory and competency in Kazakh is required for admission to higher education and for governmental employment. The implementation of these requirements varies by oblast, with the earliest dates in southern oblasts where Kazakhs hold the majority, and later implementation in northern areas with Russian majorities.

Nevertheless, Russians have for the most part resisted learning Kazakh. They contend that nearly all Kazakhs know Russian and almost no Russians know Kazakh; Russian is an inter-national language while the utility of Kazakh is limited outside Kazakhstan; and the need to know Kazakh is minimal for day-to-day life in the northern oblasts where Russians comprise the majority. The central government has delayed the original implementation deadlines to avert a confrontation with the Russians,[36] but this postponement will only delay a seemingly inevitable clash on the language issue.

Russian resistance to the perceived forced linguistic kazakhization is particularly intense in the northern oblasts, which Russian nationalists consider part of their homeland. Although one reaction to linguistic kazakhization has been Russian emigration, the dominant response has been Russian migration from southern to northern oblasts where both Russian authorities and the Russian population generally have thus far refused to learn Kazakh. The "forced acculturation" that Russians perceive in the law on languages is likely to serve as a catalyst for rising irredentism in the north. As an example of this, the law on languages was one of the factors cited by the "Organization for the Autonomy of Eastern Kazakhstan" in its decision to press for the conversion of East Kazakhstan Oblast into an autonomous republic.[37]

At the same time, Kazakh nationalists are pressuring the Nazarbayev government to proceed more rapidly with sociocultural kazakhization. Nazarbayev's attempts to protect the status of the Russian language and to emphasize the equality of languages have angered Kazakh nationalists. Organizations such as Alash—whose members favor an exclusionary "Kazakhstan for Kazakhs" political agenda and advocate the expulsion of Russians—staged demonstrations in 1992 calling for Nazarbayev's removal for being too inter-nationalist and for pandering to Russians. Nevertheless, Nazarbayev (like Ukraine's Kravchuk) has continued to speak in inter-nationalist terms. For example, in an interview given on February 6, 1993, Nazarbayev proclaimed that "only unity can ensure peace and prosperity for our land—the common motherland of all citizens of the republic regardless of ethnic origin."[38] In the same interview he argued against blaming Russians for Kazakhstan's problems:

> The Russian people have suffered most of all. During the Great Patriotic War who suffered the heaviest losses? The Russians. And in the thirties more Russians died from famine and repressions than any other nationality. That is why I say to my opponents: Do not identify the Russian people with the empire.[39]

In a speech in Almaty on May 11, 1993, Nazarbayev advocated the formation of a new civic nation—a multinational Kazakhstani people—which sounded strikingly similar to the "Soviet people" concept. Today this approach seems out of step with the rising inter-national tensions between Russians and Kazakhs in Kazakhstan, and reminds one of Gorbachev's mistaken belief that a Soviet people had emerged and that Soviet patriotism had successfully supplanted nationalism in the USSR.

Nazarbayev's attempts to find common ground between the Kazakh nationalist revival and Russian interests have assuaged neither Kazakhs intent on gaining national hegemony nor Russians worried about their loss of standing in the face of kazakhization. Nationalists want sociocultural kazakhization to proceed more rapidly to overcome past russification. Russians perceive kazakhization as forced acculturation and a means of replacing Russians with Kazakhs. Russians are thus increasingly concluding that they have no future in an independent and increasingly nationalistic and exclusionary Kazakhstan.

Political Kazakhization

The Alma-Ata Riots

One of the most important incidents in Russian-Kazakh relations took place on December 17–18, 1986, in Almaty, and was the first widely publicized international conflict after Gorbachev came to power. The Alma-Ata riots now seem minor in comparison to the events in other republics. Nonetheless, they mark the beginning of a political reorientation in Kazakhstan which culminated in its independence from Moscow and set the stage for the political kazakhization that followed.

The riots were triggered by the selection of Gennadii Kol'bin, a Russian who had served in Georgia under Shevardnadze, to the post of Communist Party First Secretary in Kazakhstan. Kol'bin replaced Kunayev, a Kazakh who had held the First Secretary position for the previous 25 years. The replacement of a Kazakh with a Russian followed a wave of political purges throughout Central Asia, in which titular elites were replaced by Slavs.

> The dismissal of Kunayev . . . spelled trouble. Having already seen the extent of the purge in Uzbekistan, and being aware of the Gorbachev leadership's tendency to appoint Slavs to positions that Central Asians had come to regard as their own and to abolish positive discrimination programmes, not to mention its tougher ideological policy towards the traditionally Moslem republics, it was hardly surprising that there were Kazakhs who feared the worst.[40]

A student demonstration over the appointment turned into a riot, resulting in three deaths and a large number of injuries. Subsequent investigations placed much of the blame on republican leadership for overreacting to a peaceful demonstration. These events reflected some Kazakhs' sensitivity to the national question, and in retrospect provide an indicator of the depth of anti-Russian feeling:

> The protests in Alma-Ata came across as the first real "Moslem" revolt. What was perhaps the most striking thing about them . . . was their anti-Russian nature. The idea of Soviet-educated youth from a traditionally Moslem background openly rebelling against the Russian "elder brother" while the Soviet Union was still embroiled in Afghanistan was enough to send shivers down many a spine in Moscow.[41]

Kazakhstan has undergone a series of political reorientations since these events. In their wake, "inter-nationalism" became the official policy in Kol'bin's Kazakhstan; overt nationalism was suppressed, though cultural kazakhization did continue during this period. Ironically, the 1986 events became a catalyst for further kazakhization, since it was effectively argued that Kazakh students reacted so strongly to the removal of Kunayev because of a history of linguistic russification, and also because there were "blank pages" in the history of their nation's relationship with Russians and Moscow.

Nazarbayev became Party First Secretary in 1989, but did not immediately adopt a nationalist political action program. As a Gorbachev supporter and apparently an inter-nationalist himself, Nazarbayev attempted to fulfill the Kazakh nationalist desire for greater sociocultural, economic and political kazakhization, while at the same time reassuring the Russians that their status would be protected. However, this formula proved unworkable, since increasing Kazakh privileges necessarily restructured the national stratification system to the detriment of Russians. Even inter-national equalization in a republic where Russian language and culture had been dominant would result in a loss of Russian status.

Kazakhstan's Declaration of Sovereignty

The Declaration of Sovereignty adopted October 25, 1990, shows the attempt to balance the Kazakh and Russian positions during the preindependence period, but nonetheless reflects the dominance of the nationalistic political action program. In the preamble, support for inter-national equality and "consolidating and strengthening the friendship of the peoples" is intermingled with the need to take "responsibility for the fate of the Kazakh nation."[42] In Article 2, sovereignty is declared for the "protection, defense and strengthening of *national* statehood," with "the revival and development of the distinctive culture, traditions and language, and the strengthening of the national dignity of the Kazakh nation" proclaimed as the primary tasks of the sovereign republic. Not until Article 12 is a guarantee of inter-national equality provided. Yet the labeling of non-Kazakhs as "outsiders," and the concern expressed for Kazakhs living outside Kazakhstan, provided strong indications that Kazakhs were "first among equals:"

> [Article 12] Representatives of nations and national groups living in the Kazakh SSR outside their national-state and autonomous formations or without such on the territory of the Union are guaranteed legal equality and equal opportunities in all spheres of life.
>
> The Kazakh SSR displays concern for satisfaction of the national-cultural, spiritual, and language requirements of Kazakhs living outside of the republic.[43]

This preferential treatment of Kazakhs was also found in the language law—passed at about the same time—which noted the equality of languages, but stressed the need to protect and promote the Kazakh language in education, business, and government.

During the preindependence period, political elites in the Russian Federation and Russian nationalists outside Kazakhstan played a small role in the development of Russian-Kazakh relations in Kazakhstan. Solzhenitsyn's 1990 article, which proclaimed northern Kazakhstan (due to its demographic composition) a part of Russia, struck a responsive chord with some Russians and Cossacks in the north, particularly in Eastern Kazakhstan Oblast, where Russian nationalists formed the "Organization for the Autonomy of Eastern Kazakhstan."[44] In addition, at the end of 1991 a close aide to Yeltsin declared that if Kazakhstan (and Ukraine) sought complete independence Russia would reserve the right to review the inter-state borders between them. However, Yeltsin immediately and publicly reiterated his support for the bilateral treaty signed with Kazakhstan that accepted the existing borders between the two republics. Kazakhstan's support for strong relations with a renewed "Union of Sovereign States" and later with Russia in the "Commonwealth of Independent States" kept inter-state tensions from rising, at least until 1992.

However, neither Kazakh nationalists nor Russians were satisfied with either the language law or the declaration of sovereignty.[45] Russians and Kazakhs were moving to more extreme positions between 1989 and 1991, but a survey at the end of the preindependence era indicated that inter-national attitudes between Russians and Kazakhs remained quite positive. Few anticipated that independence would result either in rising inter-national conflict or in a revision of borders with Russia.[46]

Kazakhization was apparent in the republic prior to independence and accelerated between 1989 and 1991. Nevertheless, this period marks an accommodative phase in Russian-Kazakh relations, with Kazakh political elites sensitive to Russian concerns about their loss of privileges, and with local Russians remaining moderately optimistic about their future in Kazakhstan. As an indication of this, Kazakhstan was the last republic to declare independence, and waited until Russia, Ukraine, and Belarus created the Commonwealth of Independent States. One reason for Kazakhstan's hesitance was concern that such a declaration would further alienate Russians in the north.[47]

Since the collapse of the USSR and Kazakhstan's independence in December 1991, Kazakh political elites have become less accommodative as they have become more intent on reconstructing their state to serve primarily if not exclusively the interests of the Kazakh nation. This more exclusionary political action program has further alienated Russians in Kazakhstan, who have responded in a variety of ways, including: emigration from Kazakhstan, internal migration to the more russified northern oblasts, political resistance to further kazakhization of the north, and increasing calls for territorial autonomy in Kazakhstan or secession from Kazakhstan and accession to Russia. Political elites in Russia have also responded with calls for dual citizenship for Russians in Kazakhstan. Both inter-national relations in Kazakhstan and inter-state relations between Kazakhstan and Russia have deteriorated since independence. This trend is certain to continue into the near future, despite Nazarbayev's call for a recentering of society around a multinational Kazakhstani identity.

The Kazakhization of Political Appointees

After independence and the dismantling of the Communist Party, Nazarbayev removed local political appointees throughout the country and installed his own personnel.[48] The reappointment process resulted in a kazakhization of political elites in the northern oblasts.[49] The Kazakhs appointed by the center often had no ties to local Russian communities, thus widening the rift between Russians and Kazakhs and between the northern periphery and central authorities in Almaty.

At the same time, political elites in Almaty began to treat nationalist organizations differently. In the past the Nazarbayev regime suppressed both Kazakh and Russian extremist groups equally. Beginning in 1992 the government increasingly tolerated Kazakh nationalist organizations, but Russian nationalist and Cossack organizations were denied registration or had their registrations revoked for engaging in anti-state or pro-separatist demonstrations.

Citizenship

The Law on Citizenship passed December 20, 1991, and effective March 1, 1992, provided a further cause for Russians to perceive discrimination in independent Kazakhstan.[50] The citizenship law adopted a "zero option" approach which automatically conferred citizenship on all permanent residents of Kazakhstan at the time the law went into effect. However, several clauses in the law were objectionable to Russians. First, the law rejected dual citizenship for Russians in Kazakhstan, but permitted Kazakhs living outside Kazakhstan and holding citizenship in another state to become citizens of Kazakhstan. Second, the law provided automatic citizenship to Kazakhs living outside the state upon their immigration to Kazakhstan, regardless of their place of birth.

> The Kazakhstan Republic creates the conditions for the return, to its territory, of persons who had been forced to leave the republic in periods of mass repressions, due to forced collectivization and as a result of other inhumane political acts, of their progeny, and of Kazakhs living in former Union republics.[51]

Coupled with the law on immigration which provided financial support for Kazakhs returning to Kazakhstan, the citizenship law resulted in an estimated 110,000 Kazakhs returning home in 1992 alone. Most of these returnees, as noted above, came from Mongolia and were resettled in northern Kazakhstan in an effort to dilute the Russian majority there.

Polls conducted in the first year of independence reflect a growing sense of Russian insecurity. A survey of inter-national attitudes conducted in August 1992, found that "a majority of Russian residents (57 percent) say they feel 'more insecure and fearful' as a result of the breakup of the Soviet Union and the shift of power to Kazakhstan," compared to only 13 percent who said they felt more secure and 20 percent who said they felt the same as before. In addition, a majority of Kazakhs and Russians felt that inter-national relations in Kazakhstan were bad, and only 36 percent of Kazakhs and 34 percent of Russians expressed the opinion that "relations among nationalities are essentially good."[52]

The New Constitution

Debates on the constitution of Kazakhstan were a further reason for growing insecurity within the Russian community. A Fall 1992 draft was much more nationalistic than the previous version, removing the article proclaiming Russian to be the language of inter-national communication, and requiring that the president of Kazakhstan must be a Kazakh.[53] The final version, adopted January 28, 1993, restored the more accommodative Russian-language article and stipulated only that the president must be fluent in Kazakh; nonetheless, the introduction of the draft itself caused growing concern about the status of Russians. In addition, the new constitution again rejected dual citizenship, though Russians had fought hard for it in debates leading up to final passage.

During 1993, inter-national relations between Russians and Kazakhs deteriorated further. Nazarbayev and other Kazakh political elites contended that there were no national problems in Kazakhstan. However, Russians increasingly felt that the government in Almaty was pursuing an evermore exclusionary nationalist political agenda. Adding to the growing tensions in the state, Russian Federation political elites and nationalists now openly sided with Russians in northern Kazakhstan. While nationalists such as Zhirinovsky talked of the reincorporation of lost territories, even more moderate politicians such as Foreign Minister Andrey Kozyrev promoted the dual citizenship agenda of the local Russians. Russia's defense of Russians in the "near abroad" provoked an angry response from Nazarbayev, who compared it with Hitler's defense of the Sudeten Germans which led to the conquest of Czechoslovakia in 1938.[54]

Dual Citizenship

Dual citizenship is presently the most explosive inter-national and inter-state issue facing Kazakhstan. Russians in Kazakhstan favor dual citizenship, arguing that it would provide security against what they view as a troubling Kazakh-centric government in Almaty. Kazakh political elites and nationalists believe that dual citizenship is an issue being fabricated in Moscow and that nearly all Russians would opt for Kazakhstan citizenship if forced to choose.[55] However, the Russians' growing sense that they are becoming an excluded minority in independent Kazakhstan indicates the reverse—if forced to choose, they will select Russian citizenship. Because of the geographic concentration of Russians in the North, this eventuality would present Almaty with de facto secession, since a majority of the population in the region would be citizens of another state.[56] Kazakh reaction to this de facto secession would certainly be severe. Thus, the citizenship issue could precipitate civil conflict between Russians and Kazakhs and ultimately inter-state conflict between Russia and Kazakhstan.

The March 1994 Parliamentary Elections

The parliamentary election of March 7, 1994, provides further evidence of political kazakhization in the state, and its detrimental effect on the development of democracy. Of the 177 parliamentary seats, 42 were filled by the president rather than by election. Over 700 candidates competed for the remaining 135 seats, giving the appearance of a democratic election. However, Kazakh electoral commissions struck 200 potential candidates from local ballots. These candidates tended to represent Russian nationalist positions. In addition, Cossack organizations were not allowed to field candidates on the grounds that Cossacks did not exist in Kazakhstan. As a result of such preelection maneuvering, only 128 Russian candidates appeared on the ballots, compared to 566 Kazakhs, even though voting-aged Russians outnumbered Kazakhs.[57] According to election results, 60 percent of the parliamentary seats were filled by Kazakhs, and 28 percent by Russians.[58]

The elections further exacerbated relations between Russians and Kazakhs and between Russia and Kazakhstan. Almaty's kazakhization of local political organizations in northern oblasts and rayons, coupled with the lack of Russian representation at the center, further encourages Russians to reorient themselves northward toward Russia. For some Russians this reorientation will mean emigration from Kazakhstan; for the majority it is more likely to trigger irredentist sentiments.

Conclusion

The interactive nationalism unfolding in Kazakhstan is less the result of ancient animosities than it is the consequence of events of the last several decades. The Kazakh nationalist political action program—itself a reactive project designed to replace Russian dominance with Kazakh hegemony—is precipitating the rise of counter-hegemonic nationalism among local Russians. As a result of this interactive process, a large portion of Kazakhstan's Russian population, geographically concentrated in northern Kazakhstan along Russia's border, is likely to opt for Russian citizenship and an irredentist geopolitical strategy. Partially as a reaction against this possibility and as an assertion of Kazakh claims to the northern region, but also as an effort to more fully integrate Kazakh South and Russian North, Kazakhstan's parliament voted in July 1994 to relocate the capital from Almaty to Akmola by 2000.[59]

The March 1994 elections provide the most recent example of Kazakh hegemony-seeking, and Russian counter-hegemonic nationalism as a response. The biased procedure in the selection and elimination of parliamentary candidates to guarantee Kazakh domination of the political process left Russians with little stake in the political system. Because this was the first true exercise in democracy in Kazakhstan, the Kazakh manipulation of candidate lists in order to ensure an outcome favorable to the Kazakh nationalist agenda is likely to convince an increasing number of Russians that inter-national relations will not be normalized with the democratization of Kazakhstan. This Kazakh approach seems even more damaging to inter-national relations than the Estonian case where those who could not trace their citizenship to the interwar republic were not able to vote in the first post-Soviet parliamentary election. At least in Estonia those wishing to participate in subsequent elections can control the factors necessary to qualify for future citizenship, and the election itself met democratic expectations. The uncertain political role that Russians will be allowed to play in independent Kazakhstan gives those excluded no reason to conclude that the future will be any more predictable or manageable than the past.

The center's appointment of local political elites in the North with no ties to the local Russian population is a second example of the exclusion of the Russian minority. While this step may in the short run give Nazarbayev greater power over local affairs in the North, it will ultimately fail because Russians will lose confidence that they will be included in the developing polity. Here the Moldovan situation provides an interesting contrast. While the initial agenda of the Moldovan Popular Front was nationalistic and provoked a minority reaction, it was reversed when it became clear that the consequences of such a course would drive the national groups further apart and destroy any hope for an independent state to survive. Exclusionary policies are unlikely to convince the Russian-dominated areas in northern Kazakhstan that their future lies with Almaty rather than with Moscow.

Especially now that the center has begun to replace local political elites in the North with Kazakhs loyal to Almaty, the sense among local Russians that they have no future in a centralized, unitary Kazakh nation-state is certain to fuel both emigration and separatist sentiments. Such sentiments cannot be dampened by greater centralism and authoritarianism, nor can they be eliminated by repression—the USSR's experience indicates that such efforts are counter-productive. Increased kazakhization is likely to result in conflict escalation in the north, and between the center and this new Russian periphery.

The increasing bifurcation of Kazakhstan into a Russian-oriented North and a more nationalistic Kazakh South does not leave one optimistic about the peaceful construction of either a unified Kazakh nation-state or a federated multinational state. In some ways the situation resembles Ukraine, with the historic left bank oriented toward Moscow, and the right bank more nationalistic. Likewise, economic ties pull Ukraine's East and Kazakhstan's North toward Russia.

Nonetheless, the Russian majority or plurality found in Kazakhstan's northern oblasts is an important distinction. None of Ukraine's eastern oblasts has a Russian majority; while the eastern Ukrainians may be russified, they at least identify nationally as Ukrainians and have important ties to the rest of Ukraine. Such is not the case in northern Kazakhstan. A federal approach providing a measure of local autonomy might alleviate some of the centrifugal forces in Ukraine; however, the same degree of autonomy granted the Russians in northern Kazakhstan would probably be insufficient to alleviate the inter-national and regional fragmentation in Kazakhstan.

While unlikely to cause Russians to reidentify with Almaty, territorial autonomy might be useful as a method of reducing the growing inter-national hostility, and of dampening the growing mood for secession in the North. However, such a decision would be difficult for the Kazakh government to take, particularly since Kazakh nationalists see northern Kazakhstan as part of their ancestral homeland taken from them by Russian imperialists. From a Kazakh nationalist perspective, a federal approach is a poor alternative to the ideal of a unitary, nationally homogeneous nation-state. However, territorial autonomy becomes relatively more attractive when compared to the alternatives of inter-national conflict or the partition of the state and the loss of the northern regions to Russia.

Notes

1. Gosudarstvennyy komitet Respubliki Kazakhstan po statistike i analizu (Goskomstat RK), *Demograficheskiy yezhegodnik Kazakhstana* (Almaty: Kazinformtsentr, 1993), pp. 47–48. The data are for January 1, 1993.

2. Shirin Akiner, *Islamic Peoples of the Soviet Union* (London: Kegan Paul International, 1983), p. 290.

3. Robert Kaiser, *The Geography of Nationalism in Russia and the USSR* (Princeton, NJ: Princeton University Press, 1994), pp. 57–58; Ralph Clem, "The Frontier and Colonialism

in Russian and Soviet Central Asia," in Robert Lewis, ed., *Geographic perspectives on Soviet Central Asia* (London: Routledge, 1992), pp. 19–36; and Martha Olcott, *The Kazakhs* (Stanford, CA: Hoover Institution Press, 1987), pp. 101–112.

4. Robert Lewis et al., *Nationality and Population Change in Russia and the USSR* (New York: Praeger, 1976), pp. 232–233; and Viktor Kozlov, *Natsional'nosti SSSR* (Moskva: Statistika, 1975), p. 111.

5. For a map of the "Virgin Lands" region, see Martin Gilbert, *Atlas of Russian History*, second edition (New York: Oxford University Press, 1993), p. 136.

6. The nine oblasts encompassed the entire northeastern half of the state, including Almata (which included Taldy-Kurgan in that year), East Kazakhstan, Karaganda (which included Dzhezkazgan in 1959), Kokchetav, Kustanay, Pavlodar, North Kazakhstan, Semipalatinsk, and Tselinograd. Tsentral'noye statisticheskoye upravleniye pri Sovete Ministrov SSSR (TsSU SSSR), *Itogi vsesoyuznoy perepisi naseleniya 1959 goda: Kazakhskaya SSR* (Moskva: Gosstatizdat, 1962), pp. 162–173.

7. Martha Olcott, "Perestroyka in Kazakhstan," *Problems of Communism* Vol. 39, No. 4 (July/August 1990):69.

8. Goskomstat SSSR, *Demograficheskiy yezhegodnik SSSR 1990* (Moskva: Finansy i Statistika, 1990), p. 184.

9. Yu. Arutyunyan and Yu. Bromley, *Sotsial'no-kul'turnyy oblik sovetskikh natsiy* (Moskva: Nauka, 1986), pp. 20–22; and Richard Rowland, "Demographic Trends in Soviet Central Asia and Southern Kazakhstan," in Robert Lewis, ed., *Geographic Perspectives on Soviet Central Asia*, pp. 228–229, 243.

10. Leonid Rybakovskiy and Nina Tarasova, "Migratsionnyye protsessy v SSSR: novyye yavleniya," *Sotsiologicheskiye issledovaniya* No. 7 (1990): 32–42.

11. See table 4.1 for the proportion of titular nations in higher education, among enterprise directors and among political representatives. On titular representation by economic sector, see Goskomstat SSSR, *Trud v SSSR* (Moskva: Finansy i statistika, 1988), pp. 20–25.

12. The national stratification in favor of Kazakhs apparent in these laws and documents is examined below.

13. Statkom SNG, "O prichinakh migratsii naseleniya," *Statisticheskiy byulleten'* No. 1 (April 1992).

14. Irina Malkova, "Kazakhstan Still Unshaken by the Exodus of Its People," *Caravan Business News*, Vol. 2, No. 8 (July 16–31, 1993):22.

15. Statisticheskiy komitet Sodruzhestva Nezavisimykh Gosudarstv, "O migratsii naseleniya v stranakh sodruzhestva," *Statisticheskiy byulleten'*, No. 40 (November 1994):72.

16. Federal'naya migratsionnaya sluzhba Rossii, *Vynuzhdennyye pereselentsy v Rossii: Statisticheskiy byulleten' no. 1* (Moskva: Goskomstat RF, 1993), p. 5. Figures for 1993 were provided by Lee Schwartz, "Emerging Regional, Political and Social Issues in Russia," (paper presented at the Association of American Geographers 91st Annual Meeting, Chicago, March 14–18, 1995).

17. John Dunlop, "Will the Russians Return from the Near Abroad," *Post-Soviet Geography*, Vol. 35, No. 4 (April 1994): 210; *The Current Digest of the Post-Soviet Press* Vol. 45, No. 48 (1993):20.

18. Schwartz, "Emerging Regional, Political and Social Issues;" Dunlop, "Will the Russians Return," *Post-Soviet Geography*, Vol. 35, No. 4 (April 1994): 210–211.

19. Statkom SNG, *Itogi vsesoyuznoy perepisi naseleniya 1989 goda* (Minneapolis: East View, 1992), Vol. 12, pp. 649–654.

20. *The Current Digest of the Post-Soviet Press*, Vol. 45, No. 20 (1993): 25.

21. Commission on Security and Cooperation in Europe (CSCE), *Human Rights and Democratization in the Newly Independent States of the Former Soviet Union* (Washington, DC: CSCE, 1993), pp. 195–196.

22. "Kazakhstan: The Question of Dual Citizenship is Entirely Appropriate," *The Current Digest of the Post-Soviet Press*, Vol. 45, No. 48 (1993): 20.

23. Goskomstat RK, *Demograficheskiy yezhegodnik Kazakhstana*, pp. 47–50.

24. Martha Olcott, "Kazakhstan: A Republic of Minorities," in Ian Bremmer and Ray Taras, eds., *Nations and Politics in the Soviet Successor States* (Cambridge: Cambridge University Press, 1993), p. 320.

25. Ian Bremmer, "Nazarbaev and the North: State-Building and Ethnic Relations in Kazakhstan," *Ethnic and Racial Studies*, Vol. 17, No. 4 (1994): 619–635.

26. Statkom SNG, *Itogi vsesoyuznoy perepisi naseleniya 1989 goda*, Vol. 7, Part II, p. 296.

27. Olcott, "Perestroyka in Kazakhstan," p. 68; "Nazarbayev Addresses Kazakh Supreme Soviet 15 October," *FBIS*-SOV No. 201 (17 October 1990): 73.

28. Olcott, "Perestroyka in Kazakhstan," p. 68.

29. Olcott, "Perestroyka in Kazakhstan," p. 68; "Law of the Kazakh Soviet Socialist Republic on Languages—22 August 1989," in Charles Furtado, Jr., and Andrea Chandler, eds., *Perestroika in the Soviet Republics: Documents on the National Question* (Boulder: Westview Press, 1992), pp. 479–481.

30. "Movement Opposes Ethnic Division in Kazakhstan," *FBIS*-SOV No. 201 (17 October 1990): 75.

31. Data provided by the Kazakhstan Ministry of Education, Almaty, February 1994.

32. "Kunayev Out; Riots in Alma-Ata," *The Current Digest of the Soviet Press* Vol. 38, No. 51 (21 January 1987):1–5; "Probing the Roots of Kazakhstan's Troubles," *The Current Digest of the Soviet Press* Vol. 39, No. 5 (1987): 13–15; "Faulty Education System Blamed for Riots," *JPRS-UPS* No. 29 (1987): 90–92.

33. "Discrimination Against Russian Speakers Reviewed," *FBIS*-USR No. 146 (14 November 1992): 92–93.

34. Interviews with Ninel Fokina, director of the Almaty Helsinki Committee on Human Rights, and Sergey Skorokhodov, Russian correspondent in Almaty for *Rossiskaya Gazeta* , 17 February 1994.

35. "Nazarbayev Addresses Kazakh Supreme Soviet 15 October," *FBIS*-SOV No. 201 (17 October 1990):73.

36. Olcott, "Kazakhstan: A Republic of Minorities," p. 320.

37. Olcott, "Kazakhstan: A Republic of Minorities," pp. 322–323.

38. "Nazarbayev Interviewed on Future of CIS," *FBIS*-SOV No. 29 (16 February 1993): 54.

39. "Nazarbayev Interviewed on Future of CIS," p. 55.

40. Bogdan Nahaylo and Victor Swoboda, *Soviet Disunion* (New York: Free Press, 1991), p. 254.

41. Nahaylo and Swoboda, *Soviet Disunion* (New York: Free Press, 1991), p. 256.

42. "Kazakh Declaration on State Sovereignty," *FBIS*-SOV No. 245 (20 December 1990):70.

43. "Kazakh Declaration on State Sovereignty," pp. 71–72.

44. Aleksandr Solzhenitsyn, "Kak nam obustroit' Rossiyu," *Komsomol'skaya pravda* (spetsial'nyy vypusk) (18 September 1990):2; Olcott, "Perestroyka in Kazakhstan, p. 76.

45. Bess Brown, "Kazakhstan: Interethnic Tensions, Unsolved Economic Problems," Radio Liberty, *Report on the USSR* , January 4, 1991, pp. 29–30.

46. James Critchlow, "Kazakhstan: The Outlook for Ethnic Relations," RFE/RL *Research Report* Vol 1, No. 5 (January 31, 1992):34–39.

47. Olcott, "Kazakhstan: A Republic of Minorities," p. 326.

48. Olcott, "Kazakhstan: A Republic of Minorities," p. 326.

49. Bremmer, "Nazarbaev and the North."

50. "Law on Citizenship," *FBIS*-USR No. 54 (5 May 1992):66–72.

51. "Law on Citizenship," p. 67.

52. U.S. Information Agency, "Kazakhs and Russians Close on Nationality Issues in Kazakhstan," *Opinion Research Memorandum* (Washington, DC: USIA, March 19, 1993).

53. CSCE, *Human Rights and Democratization*, pp. 192–193; "Nazarbayev, Kazakh Parliament Fight for Power," *The Current Digest of the Post-Soviet Press* Vol. 45, No. 5 (1993):9.

54. Bess Brown, "Central Asia: The Economic Crisis Deepens," RFE/RL *Research Report* Vol 3, No. 1 (January 7, 1994):62.

55. Mikhail Ivanovich Issinaliyev, Chairman of Azat Civil Democratic Movement, personal interview, Almaty, February 18, 1994.

56. Nurbulat Masanov, Professor of History and ethnographer, personal interview, Kazakhstan State University, Almaty, February 18, 1994. See also Nurbulat Masanov and Nurlan Amrekulov, "O dikom natsionalizme i podlinnom patriotizme," *Karavan* (January 14, 1994):10–11; and Nurbulat Masanov and Nurlan Amrekulov, "Budushchyeye Kazakhstana bez Rossii nevozmozhno," *Karavan* (February 4, 1994):10–11.

57. Figures supplied by Nurbulat Masanov, February 18, 1994, personal interview, and confirmed in RFE/RL *Daily Report*, No. 45 (7 March 1994).

58. Figures include the 42 parliamentary members selected by Nazarbayev. No breakdown of the two sets of figures was given. RFE/RL *Daily Report*, No. 54 (March 18, 1994).

59. "New Kazakhstan Capital," *New York Times* (7 July 1994):A6; "Will Kazakhstan Have a New Capital?" *The Current Digest of the Post-Soviet Press*, Vol. 45, No. 40 (1993):32.

Chapter 9

Central Asia

The relationship between Russians and Central Asians has been shaped principally by the imperialistic nature of the relationship between Moscow and Central Asia. From Russia's conquest of Turkestan during the "age of imperialism" to the "welfare colonialism" of the Brezhnev era, Russians established and maintained a dominant position in Central Asia and the region itself became an economic dependency of Russia. This imperialistic relationship started to unravel during the 1970s, and decolonization accelerated during the 1980s. Local Russians, reacting to decreasing economic opportunities in the region and increasing competition from upwardly mobile Central Asians, began to leave in increasing numbers during the last two decades of the Soviet era. Russian emigration has increased dramatically since 1989.

Nevertheless, in the 1990s with their nominal independence, the Central Asian states remain economic dependencies of Russia, and are dependent on the skills of Russians living in the region. Indigenous political elites in Central Asia have been relatively accommodative of Russians in an effort to reduce the Russian "brain drain" from the region. However, this official accommodation is opposed by indigenous nationalists, who favor a more rapid derussification and indigenization of their homelands.

For their part, Russians have refused to adapt to the new Central Asia. Having retained an imperialistic mentality toward Central Asia and never having developed a sense of homeland toward it, few Russians are willing to live and work as equals in Central Asian society and even fewer are willing to acculturate to it. While some Russians will stay and fight for cultural autonomy, most will emigrate from the region as decolonization continues.

In this chapter, we briefly trace the changing nature of Russian-titular relations through the three main stages of imperial conquest and colonization, welfare colonialism, and decolonization. This review is followed by a more detailed analysis of the divergence in indigenous treatment of local Russians (i.e., official accommodation versus mass-based anti-Russian sentiments) that has developed since the late 1980s, and the varying Russian responses to such treatment. We conclude by considering the complex interconnection between democratization,

Central Asia: Areas of Russian Concentration

CENTRAL ASIA

	Uzbekistan	Kyrgyzstan	Tajikistan	Turkmenistan
Territorial Size (km²)	447,400	198,500	143,100	488,100
Population Size (1/1/94)	22,192,500	4,462,600	5,703,700	4,361,300
Percent Titular (1989)	71.4	56.5[a]	62.3	72.0
Percent Russian (1989)	8.3	18.8[a]	7.6	9.5
Urban Population (1993)	8,489,000	1,678,700[a]	1,689,000[b]	1,718,000[b]
Percent Titular (1989)	53.7	29.9	50.5	53.8
Percent Russian (1989)	19.5	39.5	22.0	20.3
Size of Capital City (1/1/91)	2,113,300	624,200[a]	582,400	412,200
Percent Titular (1989)	44.2	28.1[a]	38.3	50.8
Percent Russian (1989)	34.0	52.2[a]	32.8	32.4
Natural Increase (/1000, 1993)	24.9	18.2	24.2	25.2
Titular NI (1989)	31.5	29.8[a]	36.8	31.0
Russian NI (1989)	4.1	0.7[a]	5.3	4.0
Life Expectancy (1989)	Men: 65.8 Women: 71.6	Men: 64.2 Women: 71.8	Men: 66.2 Women: 70.8	Men: 61.8 Women: 68.2
Titular e⁰ (1989)	Men: 66.9 Women: 71.8	Men: 64.7 Women: 71.6	Men: 67.6 Women: 71.5	Men: 62.0 Women: 67.6
Russian e⁰ (1989)	Men: 63.1 Women: 72.9	Men: 64.1 Women: 73.1	Men: 63.0 Women: 73.1	Men: 61.6 Women: 71.9
Net Migration To (−)/From (+) Russia (1989–1993)				
Total	−300,313	−180,360	−194,074	−33,053
Titular	8,652	6,487	−2,272	4,796
Russian	−201,491	−143,245	−139,380	−29,628

(continues)

CENTRAL ASIA (continued)

	Uzbekistan	Kyrgyzstan	Tajikistan	Turkmenistan
Employment[c] (1993)	77.6	82.0[d]	73.1[d]	83.2[d]
Trade (Export/Import Ratio, 1993)				
Intra-NIS Trade[e]	0.76[f]	0.75	0.60	1.50[f]
Extra-NIS Trade[g]	1.15	1.00	0.70	1.54

Notes: [a]Percents for Kyrgyzstan are for 1/1/93; and were provided by Nurbek Omuraliev, Center of Social Research, National Academy of Sciences of Kyrgyzstan, Bishkek, in February 1994, or in Gosudarstvennoye Statisticheskoye Agentstvo Kyrgyzskoy Respubliki, *Demograficheskiy Yezhegodnik Kyrgyzskoy Respubliki 1992* (Bishkek: 1993). [b]Urban population for Tajikistan and Turkmenistan given for 1992. [c]Employment given as a percent of working-age population. [d]Employment figures for Kyrgyzstan, Tajikistan and Turkmenistan are for 1992. [e]Intra-NIS ratios calculated from trade among the republics of the former USSR and measured in the national currencies. [f]Intra-NIS ratios for Uzbekistan and Turkmenistan are for 1992. [g]Extra-NIS ratios calculated from trade with countries outside the former USSR and measured in US dollars.

Sources: Goskomstat SSSR, *Chislennost' naseleniya soyuznykh respublik po gorodskim poseleniyam i rayonam na 1 yanvarya 1991 goda* (Moskva: 1991); Goskomstat Rossiyskoy Federatsii, *Chislennost' i sotsial'no-demograficheskiye kharakteristiki russkogo naseleniya v respublikakh byvshego SSSR* (Moskva: 1994); Statistichesky komitet SNG, *Statisticheskiy byulleten'* No. 20 (June 1994): 35–36; Statkom SNG, *Itogi vsesoyuznoy perepisi naseleniya 1989 goda* (Minneapolis, MN: East View, 1992), Vol. 7, Part 2; Mikhael Guboglo, "Demography and Language in the Capitals of the Union Republics," *Journal of Soviet Nationalities* Vol. 1, No. 4 (Winter 1990–1991): 9–13; The World Bank, *Statistical Handbook 1994: States of the Former USSR* (Washington, DC: World Bank Studies of Economies in Transformation No. 14, 1994).

political stability, and inter-national conflict emerging in Central Asia since 1990, and place this unfolding relationship in the theoretical framework of interactive nationalism.

Two cautionary comments about the analysis of Russian-titular relations in Central Asia are necessary. First, due both to the lack of democratization in Turkmenistan and Uzbekistan and to the political instability in Tajikistan, primary sources of data are quite limited for this region. Kyrgyzstan is the only republic where vital statistics, socioeconomic data, and surveys of public opinion are being published regularly. For this reason, our analysis relies on primary sources from Russia and on secondary sources for Tajikistan, Turkmenistan, and Uzbekistan.

Second, the analysis of Russian-titular relations in Central Asia is complicated by the limited degree to which national consciousness exists among indigenes in the region. As noted in Chapter 3, the process of nationalization was only beginning in Turkestan prior to 1917. The formation of nations around Uzbek, Tajik, Turkmen, and Kyrgyz identities was facilitated during the Soviet era, but the limited migration and social mobilization of rural indigenes prior to the 1960s resulted in the retention of relatively strong ties to locality and clan. The continuing relevance of *intra*-national ethnic identities has become increasingly apparent in the Tajik civil war, as well as in the localism and nepotism of political elites in Turkmenistan, Uzbekistan, and Kyrgyzstan. What appears to the outside observer as indigenous nationalism may on closer inspection turn out to be a more localized ethnic favoritism. The limited extent of national consciousness in the region helps to explain the failure of titular nationalists to mobilize their 'nations' in support of independence, as well as the failure of nationalists to attain power in Central Asia following independence.

An investigation of the importance of subnational identities in Central Asia is complicated by the limited number of studies that have been conducted and data that have been collected on this subject. While Soviet ethnographers studied national communities as integrated wholes, western analysts frequently focused on the supranational scale (a pan-Islamic or a pan-Turkic identity).[1] Nevertheless, events in the region since 1990 have made the continuing relevance of subnational identities increasingly apparent. It is not possible to gauge precisely the relative strengths of a national as compared to a subnational consciousness; likewise, the relevance of each level of identity changes with political, socioeconomic, and cultural circumstances. Nonetheless, we will highlight the times and places in which the subnational identities of Central Asia have impinged on the unfolding Russian-titular relationship through the periods of colonialism and decolonization.

Russian Colonization of Central Asia

Russia conquered and incorporated Turkestan at the end of the nineteenth century in much the same way that other European powers expanded into Asia and Africa during the age of imperialism. Russians entered the region as an imperial elite and settled primarily in the region's cities. This pattern was unlike the Russian peasant migration to Kazakhstan, Siberia, and the Kuban region of northern Caucasia which occurred at approximately the same time. Russia and Russians viewed Siberia and Kazakhstan as frontier zones into which large numbers of Russian peasants resettled, often demographically overwhelming the indigenous peoples. Turkestan, on the other hand, was treated as an imperial holding where a thin layer of Russian political and military administrators was placed atop the indigenous peoples and their society which, for the most part, remained intact. While Russia's relationship to Kazakhstan and Siberia thus can be compared to the European conquest and resettlement of the Americas and Australia, the Russian conquest of Central Asia was more comparable to the European expansion into South Asia and Africa.[2]

By 1911, over 1.5 million Russians had migrated to the Asiatic steppe oblasts of present-day Kazakhstan. Of these, 1.3 million settled in the most fertile rural regions of northern Kazakhstan, displacing Kazakh nomads. Only 18 percent of the Russian immigrants settled in urban areas.[3] As we noted in Chapter 8, this flood of Russians to the rural areas and the disruption it caused in the Kazakhs' way of life resulted in the emergence of a Kazakh national identity.

Central Asia offers a striking contrast to the frontier settlement and indigenous nationalism that occurred in Kazakhstan. First, by 1911 only 407,000 Russians had moved to Turkestan, constituting just 6 percent of its population. The majority of Russians were rural peasants, and over half of them settled in Semirich'e Oblast (Krgyzstan). Thus, the history of Russian-Kyrgyz interaction is in many ways more comparable to Kazakhstan than to the rest of Central Asia. Approximately 202,000 Russians moved to the remaining oblasts of Turkestan by 1911, and the overwhelming majority of them settled in cities.[4]

One reason for the difference in settlement patterns was climatic. The desert environment afforded fewer opportunities for sedentary agriculture, and the limited arable lands were already densely settled by indigenes. This situation was unlike the Asiatic steppe, which had fertile soils but was sparsely settled.

The Russian conquest of Turkestan thus followed the European imperialistic pattern. A thin layer of Russian military and administrative personnel controlled the region from urban centers where they mostly segregated themselves from the indigenous population.[5] The Russian rulers sought neither to russify the indigenous peoples of Turkestan nor to dispossess them of their land; rather, they wanted military, political, and economic dominion over the region.

Russia had several motives for expanding into Turkestan. Concern with stability along its southern border continued to serve as justification for southward expansion. The conquest of Turkestan also established Russia more firmly as a European imperial power, while denying the region to the British Empire which was making inroads from the south through India. More specifically, Russia viewed Central Asia as a "cotton colony" needed to satisfy the demand of Russia's growing textile industry, particularly after the American Civil War convinced Russia's rulers that its overseas supply of cotton was unreliable.[6]

The indigenous reaction to Russia's conquest and imperial domination of Turkestan was mixed. The local population was extremely fragmented along ethnic lines and unable to unite to offer serious resistance to the Russian invasion. Indigenous uprisings against local rulers were more frequent than were attempts by Central Asians to resist the Russians. The intraregional interethnic conflicts during the latter half of the nineteenth century weakened the region internally, and facilitated the Russian conquest of Turkestan.[7]

Russia's conquest and incorporation of Central Asia into the empire had only a limited effect on the making of nations in the region. At the time of its conquest, the indigenous population was divided into scores of ethnolinguistic communities. The members of each community lived highly localized lives in which loyalties revolved around family, clan, and tribe. By the turn of the twentieth century, communities of belonging and interest as broad as nations had not yet been imagined by the vast majority of indigenes in Turkestan.

Additional factors limited the degree to which Russia's conquest and incorporation of Turkestan served as a catalyst for rising nationalism. Unlike the situation in Kazakhstan, Russian in-migration to Central Asia was not an agent for nationalization. This was due both to the limited number of Russians entering the region and to the geographic and class segregation of most Russians in urban areas. In addition, in true imperial fashion, Russians did not attempt to russify the Central Asians, treating them instead as an unassimilable inferior population. Ironically, since tsarist russification policies in the European parts of the empire were often a catalyst for rising indigenous nationalism, the lack of a forcible russification program in Central Asia may be seen as one factor delaying the onset of nationalization in the region. Finally, nationalization was also delayed by the traditional Islamic elites, who viewed the rise of nations both as a threat to the unity of the Islamic world and also as a competitor with Islam for the loyalty of members.[8]

Specific policies such as the decision in 1916 to draft Central Asians for service at the front during World War I caused a strong reaction within the region; nonetheless, such reactions against the tsarist regime cannot be labeled nationalism. In general, the handful of nationalized elites that had emerged by the end of the tsarist era had little success in mobilizing the indigenous masses behind the goals of national self-determination.

Welfare Colonialism During the Soviet Era

The imperialistic relationship established between Russians and Central Asians during the tsarist period continued during the Soviet era, albeit in modified form. Russians migrated to Central Asian cities with industrialization between 1926 and 1970, becoming an economic rather than an imperial elite. These urbanized Russians never perceived Central Asia as their homeland.[9] They were tied more closely to Russia and especially Moscow than to the Central Asian countryside which surrounded them. Demographically, culturally, and economically, the cities in which they lived became Russian enclaves divorced from and alien to Central Asia.

The Russian population in Central Asia nearly doubled between 1917 and 1926, increasing from 289,000 to 437,000.[10] It then more than tripled between 1926 and 1937, increasing to 1.3 million.[11] This rapid increase resulted primarily from the in-migration of skilled Russians that accompanied industrialization in the region.[12] The outcome was the demographic russification of Central Asia; Russians increased their share of the total population from 6 percent in 1926 to 13 percent in 1937.[13]

Between 1937 and 1959, the demographic russification of Central Asia continued, but at a slower pace. The Russian population grew from 1.3 million to 2.3 million during the twenty-year period, increasing from 13 percent to 17 percent of the total population in Central Asia.[14] The russification was greatest in Kyrgyzstan, where Russians comprised 30 percent of the population by 1959, with the Kyrgyz constituting only 41 percent. In Uzbekistan and Tajikistan, Russians made more modest gains, while in Turkmenistan there was a demographic indigenization, as Turkmen increased their share of the total from 59 percent to 61 percent.[15]

Unlike northern Kazakhstan, where the entire region was inundated by Russians, large geographic regions in Central Asia were not russified. Instead, Russians migrating to Central Asia overwhelmingly settled in cities. Indigenes remained primarily in rural areas. By 1959, 78 percent of all Russians living in Central Asia lived in cities. Kyrgyzstan was the only exception to this rule, but even there 58 percent of Russians lived in cities by 1959 (Table 9.1).

The migration of skilled Russians and other Europeans to the developing urban/industrial centers of Central Asia had a number of important consequences. First, this class-specific immigration created a national stratification system that favored Russians and the Russian language throughout the urban/industrial sector, with indigenes employed primarily in agriculture, small-scale enterprises, and handicraft production.[16] This "cultural division of labor" is a classic case of "internal colonialism."[17]

However, the national stratification did not initially foster a nationalization of rural Central Asians in opposition to Russian hegemony, as we might have predicted from our model of interactive nationalism. Because no indigenous industrial work force had developed prior to Russian immigration, russification did not displace indigenes. The limited degree to which Russians and indigenes competed in the work place limited the indigenous reaction against the Russian presence. The russification of the urban industrial work force might be an inhibitor of the nationalization of indigenous Central Asians, since it impeded the urbanization and social mobilization of rural indigenes and helped to preserve local, sub-national clan ties and a localist mentality.

The imperialistic relationship between Russians and Central Asians during the tsarist era changed after 1917 into what some analysts have described as "welfare colonialism," which Rywkin defined as:

> a politically opportunistic attempt to combine three diverse elements: a genuine interethnic economic equalitarianism of Leninist inspiration, a social welfarism

Table 9.1

Russians in Central Asia, 1959–1989

(Total Number of Russians, Percent of Russians in Urban Areas, and Russian Percent of Urban Population)

Republic	Russians (000s)				Russian % of Total				Russian % of Urban				% of Russians in Urban			
	1959	1970	1979	1989	1959	1970	1979	1989	1959	1970	1979	1989	1959	1970	1979	1989
Total USSR	114,114	129,015	137,397	145,155	54.6	53.4	52.4	50.8	65.8	64.5	62.9	60.4	57.7	68.0	74.4	78.2
Uzbekistan	1,091	1,473	1,666	1,653	13.5	12.5	10.8	8.3	33.4	30.4	24.8	19.5	83.7	89.1	93.4	94.8
Kyrgyzstan	624	856	912	917	30.2	29.2	25.9	21.3	51.8	51.4	46.4	39.5	57.8	65.9	68.6	69.9
Tajikistan	263	344	395	388	13.3	11.9	10.4	7.6	35.3	30.0	28.3	22.0	86.9	93.8	94.1	93.9
Turkmenistan	263	313	349	334	17.3	14.5	12.6	9.5	35.4	31.2	25.7	20.3	94.5	95.7	96.5	96.9
Central Asia	2,240	2,987	3,322	3,292	16.4	15.1	13.0	10.1	36.7	33.2	28.2	22.4	78.1	83.7	87.0	88.0

Source: **1959:** TsSU SSSR, *Itogi vsesoyuznoy perepisi naseleniya 1959 goda* (Moskva: Gosstatizdat, 1962), Central Asian volumes; **1970:** TsSU SSSR, *Itogi vsesoyuznoy perepisi naseleniya 1970 goda* (Moskva: Statistika, 1973), Vol. 4; **1979:** Goskomstat SSSR, *Itogi vsesoyuznoy perepisi naseleniya 1979 goda* (Moskva: Goskomstat SSSR, 1989), Vol 4, Part I; **1989:** Statkom SNG, *Itogi vsesoyuznoy perepisi naseleniya 1989 goda* (Minneapolis: East View Press, 1992), Vol. 7.

reminiscent of the American attitudes toward its minorities, and a good deal of prudent tolerance for the increasingly numerous Muslim inhabitants in this politically sensitive geopolitical arena.[18]

Economically, Central Asia remained primarily a producer of raw materials (fossil fuels and industrial crops such as cotton) which were processed predominantly outside the region.[19] This economic dependency resulted from investment decisions made in Moscow that kept the imperialistic relationship intact. Those industries with all-union significance were tied directly to Moscow and were staffed primarily by Russians and other Europeans. Central Asians lived primarily in rural areas where they were employed in agriculture and in the "nonproductive" sectors of the economy (e.g. education and health).

On the other hand, the federalization of the state structure and *korenizatsiya* policies during the 1920s and 1930s encouraged indigenes to think in national terms and to see their homelands as more geographically expansive than the local village. In addition, *korenizatsiya* facilitated both the development of standardized written languages using the Latin script, literacy and education in these languages, and the more rapid upward mobility of indigenes by targeting them for preferential treatment in hiring. Russians and other non-Central Asians were told not only to hire indigenes over nonindigenes, but to study the indigenous languages or face unemployment.[20] Not surprisingly, the indigenous elites created under these conditions tended to be more nationalistic and exclusionary than in the past.

With their hegemony challenged by indigenization in the 1920s, Russians resisted learning the indigenous languages and hiring unqualified Central Asians. This placed local Russian elites in conflict with Moscow; however, they did not have to resist these central edicts for long. By the mid-1930s, Moscow shifted emphasis away from indigenization and toward russification. The developing Central Asian languages were russified through the use of Russian loan words and the replacement of the Latin script with Cyrillic. In 1938, study of Russian was made mandatory.[21] As the pressure from Moscow for preferential treatment of Central Asians in education and hiring diminished, local nonindigenous elites carried out their own de-indigenization campaign.[22] During the last two decades of the Stalin era Russians were able to reestablish their dominance in urban Central Asia; and indigenes wishing to advance economically were hindered by the Russian presence.

The post-Stalin period presents a mixed picture. First, the demographic russification of Central Asia reached its peak in 1959. Then, demographic indigenization began. This shift occurred primarily because of a high indigenous natural increase, which outpaced the Russian demographic growth that resulted from natural increase and in-migration. By the 1970s, the pace of demographic indigenization increased, primarily because more Russians were leaving. This out-migration increased substantially during the 1980s. The Russian population declined in Tajikistan, Uzbekistan, and Turkmenistan between 1979 and 1989, and increased only slightly in Kyrgyzstan (Table 9.2).

Table 9.2

Demographic Indigenization of Rural and Urban Populations, 1959–1989

(Titular Nation as a Percent of the Rural, Urban and Capital City Populations, by Republic)

Republic	Rural Population				Urban Population				Capital Cities			
	1959	1970	1979	1989	1959	1970	1979	1989	1959	1970	1979	1989
Uzbekistan	74.8	79.5	82.8	83.5	37.2[a]	41.1	48.1	53.7	33.8	37.1	40.9[a]	44.2
Kyrgyzstan	54.4	59.9	63.4	66.2	13.2	16.9	22.9	29.9	9.4	12.3	17.0	22.7
Tajikistan	63.4	66.6	67.2	68.0	31.8	38.6[a]	42.8	50.5	18.5	26.2	30.7	38.3[a]
Turkmenistan	83.5	86.1	87.2	87.0	34.7	43.4[a]	47.6	53.8	29.8	38.2	40.4	50.8[a]

Notes: [a]Signifies the date in which the titular nation exceeded the Russians in urban areas and in the capital cities.

Source: Rural and Urban Population: Robert Kaiser, "Ethnic Demography and Interstate Relations in Central Asia," in *National Identity and Ethnicity in Russia and the New States of Eurasia,* The International Politics of Eurasia, ed. Roman Szporluk, vol. 2 (Armonk, NY: M.E. Sharpe, 1994), 240. Capital Cities: Mikhail Guboglo, "Demography and Language in the Capitals of the Union Republics," *Journal of Soviet Nationalities* Vol. 1, No. 4 (Winter 1990–1991): 27–33.

Demographic indigenization occurred not only in rural areas where indigenes were already dominant, but also in the previously russified cities. It occurred even in the republics' capital cities, which had served as strong magnets attracting Russians in the past (Table 9.2). Nonetheless, indigenes remained overwhelmingly rural between 1959 and 1989, just as Russians remained highly concentrated in the cities (Table 9.1).

Russians continued to be over-represented in the urban/industrial sectors of Central Asia's economy and indigenes continued to be concentrated in agriculture.[23] However, indigenes were increasingly "being drawn into modern sectors of the labor force."[24] The indigenization of the urban/industrial sectors of Central Asia increased the inter-national competition between Russians and upwardly mobile members of the titular groups, tending to heighten national consciousness among indigenous elites and to increase inter-national tension between them and Russians.

The Russian language became even more dominant during the post-Stalin era. In principle, Central Asians could still receive a college education in their native languages, but in reality fewer schools offered instruction in these languages—particularly in the capital cities. For example, in Bishkek 42 percent of Kyrgyz children did not receive an education in the Kyrgyz language in 1988.[25] In part, this situation was due to pressure from the center to accelerate the pace of sovietization by more rapid linguistic russification of non-Russians. Central Asian political elites also pressed for greater linguistic russification of indigenes.[26] Indigenous parents who viewed Russian as the language of upward mobility also wanted their children to enroll in Russian-language schools, although this varied according to class status of the parents. Skilled blue-collar and midlevel white-collar workers favored Russian-language schooling for their children more strongly than either unskilled blue-collar or high-level directors.[27] This indicates that as indigenes became more upwardly mobile, they favored Russian for their children in order to make upward mobility easier for the next generation. In contrast, indigenes who had already achieved elite status more often viewed the indigenous language as an instrument to give their children an edge over others, most likely Russians, competing for elite positions in Central Asia.

Yet for all the support that the Russian language had throughout Central Asia, especially in the cities, little linguistic russification occurred, at least as measured by the postwar censuses (Table 9.3). In urban areas, where Russians and their language were dominant, a linguistic derussification occurred between 1959 and 1989 in all Central Asian republics except Turkmenistan. In rural areas, linguistic russification made no gains during the same three decades, except in Turkmenistan, where a very limited linguistic russification of Turkmen occurred.

An increasing proportion of Central Asians claimed fluency in Russian between 1970 and 1989, but Russian was named as a second language, while their indigenous languages retained the status of first languages (Table 9.4).

For all republics but Kyrgyzstan, the rate of increase in Russian bilingualism was slower during the 1980s than during the 1970s. Two factors contributed to

Table 9.3
Linguistic Russification of Indigenes in Central Asia, 1959–1989
(Percent of indigenes claiming Russian as the first language, and percentage point change)

	Homeland Urban					*Homeland Rural*				
Nation	*1959*	*1970*	*1979*	*1989*	*% point chg*	*1959*	*1970*	*1979*	*1989*	*% point chg*
Uzbek	1.4	1.3	1.3	1.2	−0.2	0.1	0.1	0.1	0.1	0.0
Kyrgyz	1.2	1.3	1.3	1.0	−0.2	0.1	0.1	0.1	0.1	0.0
Tajik	1.7	1.5	1.9	1.6	−0.1	0.1	0.1	0.1	0.1	0.0
Turkmen	1.9	2.0	2.1	2.0	0.1	0.0	0.0	0.1	0.1	0.1

Source: Robert Kaiser, *The Geography of Nationalism in Russia and the USSR*, p. 276.

Table 9.4
Indigenous Mastery of Russian in Central Asia, 1970–1989
(Percent of Indigenes in Urban and Rural Areas Claiming Fluency in Russian as a
Second Language)

	Homeland Urban					*Homeland Rural*				
				% point change					*% point change*	
Nation	*1970*	*1979*	*1989*	*1970–79*	*1979–89*	*1970*	*1979*	*1989*	*1970–79*	*1979–89*
Uzbek	32.6	63.6	42.0	31.0	−21.6	7.2	48.6	13.6	41.4	−35.0
Kyrgyz	53.0	59.3	66.1	6.3	6.8	14.1	21.6	28.8	7.5	7.2
Tajik	33.8	46.0	47.4	12.2	1.4	10.7	21.7	23.6	11.0	1.9
Turkmen	30.8	41.0	47.6	10.2	6.6	7.4	15.9	17.4	8.5	1.5

Source: <u>1970:</u> TsSU SSSR, *Itogi vsesoyuznoy perepisi naseleniya 1970 goda* (Moskva: Statistika, 1973), Vol. 4; <u>1979:</u> Goskomstat SSSR, *Itogi vsesoyuznoy perepisi naseleniya 1979 goda* (Moskva: Goskomstat SSSR, 1989), Vol. 4, Part I, Books 2 and 3; <u>1989:</u> Statkom SNG, *Itogi vsesoyuznoy perepisi naseleniya 1989 goda* (Minneapolis: East View, 1992), Vol. 7, Part 2.

this deceleration. First, the changing political climate during the 1980s led both to increasingly vocal complaints about the inferior status of the titular languages, and to calls for their official protection and promotion. This promotion of indigenous languages during the latter half of the 1980s undoubtedly reduced the spread of Russian. In 1989, as in the other union republics, language laws were passed that declared the titular languages to be the official languages of the republics.

Second, the 1979 figures overstate the level of Russian fluency among Central Asians in both urban and rural areas (particularly in Uzbekistan, but also apparently in Tajikistan and Turkmenistan). Dissatisfied with the levels of Russian fluency indicated in the 1970 census, political elites in Uzbekistan put pressure on census takers to encourage Central Asians to declare themselves fluent in Russian in the 1979 census. This pressure resulted in wildly inflated figures, which were brought back into line in the 1989 census. This incident provides a good example of the pro-russification orientation of the political leaders in Central Asia during the 1970s. Ironically, the extremely rapid rise in Russian fluency indicated by the falsified 1979 figures was used by Central Asian nationalists as a catalyst to mobilize support for the preservation and enhanced status of the Uzbek language and culture.

Though the Russian language was becoming dominant throughout urban Central Asia during the 1960s and 1970s, certain aspects of indigenization were also promoted. However, titular elites in the republics, not political elites in Moscow, were responsible for the reemergence of *korenizatsiya* during the post-Stalin period. Titular students were given preferential treatment in access to higher education, resulting in an indigenization of universities between 1959 and 1989 in all four Central Asian republics. This trend was due not only to the demographic indigenization of the population overall, but to a concerted effort on the part of titular elites in the republics to increase the proportion of titular students attending college.[28] By 1989, titular students were over-represented in universities in Kyrgyzstan, Tajikistan, and Turkmenistan, and had achieved parity in Uzbekistan (Table 9.5).

An indigenization of elite positions in the economy was also occurring. Russians remained over-represented in heavy industry and in highly skilled positions such as engineering, but indigenes were increasingly appointed to enterprise directorships. By 1989, indigenes were over-represented in this elite economic

Table 9.5

Indigenous Proportions of Students Entering Higher Education,
by Republic (Percent)

Republic	Indigenous Percent of Students			Indexed Values[a]		
	1960/61	1970/71	1989/90	1959	1970	1989
Uzbekistan	47	57	71	77	88	100
Kyrgyzstan	47	47	65	115	107	125
Tajikistan	47	50	63	89	89	102
Turkmenistan	55	65	78	90	98	108

Notes: [a]Indigenous percent of students indexed to the indigenous percent of the total population (% of students/% of total population), and presented as a percent. Values under 100 indicate relative under-representation, 100 equals parity, and values over 100 indicate relative over-representation.

Source: 1960/61 and 1970/71: Rasma Karklins, "Ethnic Politics and Access to Higher Education: The Soviet Case," *Comparative Politics* (April 1984): 284; 1989/90: Robert Kaiser, *The Geography of Nationalism in Russia and the USSR*, p. 233.

category in Kyrgyzstan and Tajikistan, were at parity in Turkmenistan, and were slightly under-represented in Uzbekistan (Table 4.1).

Finally, an indigenization of local and republican political elites was occurring at the same time that decision-making authority devolved to the republics during the Brezhnev era. Even Party first secretaries who promoted linguistic russification in their republics, such as Kyrgyzstan's Usubaliyev, also pressured Moscow for greater control over the selection of personnel at the local and republic levels, and tended overwhelmingly to appoint members of the titular group to those positions when personnel was decentralized.[29] This indigenization was reversed to some extent under Gorbachev, when a massive political purge occurred in Central Asia. However, in 1989, indigenes in all four Central Asian republics were still over-represented in the republican Supreme Soviets and were even more dominant in the local soviets (Table 4.1).

The indigenization occurring between 1970 and 1989 may be seen as the onset of decolonization. As indigenes became more socially mobilized, they increasingly competed with Russians for dominance in Central Asia. Indigenes were successful in gaining greater control over the local power structures, although the region as a whole remained economically dependent on Moscow and linguistic russification continued to be promoted by the center. From their elite positions at the local and republican scales, titular elites used *korenizatsiya* to gain a competitive advantage over outsiders, including Russians.

However, this indigenization does not provide convincing evidence of decolonization nationalism. Titular elites frequently promoted fellow indigenes, not because they were members of the same nation, but because they were from the same locality, clan, or extended family.[30] Such a distinction hardly mattered to the Russians who lost out in this process. However, it was significant for the Central Asian "nations," since it prolonged and even widened *intra*-national cleavages and limited the degree to which indigenization coincided with nationalization. The consequences of this failure to successfully nationalize the titular populations have already been felt in Tajikistan, which has been torn apart by intra-national interethnic civil war. Similar intra-national conflicts are possible in the other three Central Asian republics.

Decolonization

The process of de-colonization that began with indigenization during the 1970s accelerated during the late 1980s. In addition to the indigenes' increasing success in out-competing Russians for elite positions, a related set of circumstances developed which increased the level of tension between upwardly mobile Central Asians and Russians. Rapid indigenous social mobilization–particularly the rapid rise in educational attainment–fueled an equally rapid rise in Central Asians' expectations for a better life. However, as indigenous expectations were increasing most rapidly, economic growth in Central Asia stagnated and then declined. This combination of rising expectations and economic decline created the conditions for a rapid rise in feelings of relative deprivation among indigenes, particularly because they occurred when nonindigenes, especially Russians, occupied privileged positions.[31] The tension resulting from this explosive increase in relative deprivation among indigenes was directed against nonindigenes in a series of violent nativistic confrontations at the end of the 1980s.[32]

Moscow must take some responsibility for the economic decline which precipitated the rise in nativism in Central Asia.[33] Beginning in 1972, central authorities began to reduce their commitment to the economic equalization of Central Asia with the rest of the USSR. On the fiftieth anniversary of the founding of the USSR, Brezhnev declared that the goal of inter-regional equalization had been achieved; thereafter, equalization was no longer mentioned as an economic objective in five-year plans.[34] The relative economic neglect of Central Asia during the Brezhnev era continued under Gorbachev, as investments were redirected toward the economic revitalization of the European industrial core. Later, Yeltsin announced that Russia would no longer support the Central Asian periphery economically and would make investments in the region only on the basis of economic merit.

During the 1970s and early 1980s, Russians in Central Asia reacted to economic stagnation and rising competition with indigenes by leaving the region in increasing numbers, reversing a century-long trend of immigration. Other regions had become relatively more attractive as areas of economic opportunity, and fewer Russians migrated to Central Asia. However, changing economic conditions alone cannot explain the accelerating rate of Russian emigration, since Russians were leaving relatively secure high-status positions in Central Asia, often for an uncertain future in Russia. Surveys taken during the 1980s began to show that Russians and other nonindigenes were leaving Central Asia because of the perception of favoritism that was being given to indigenes over nonindigenes.[35] Russians increasingly felt that their futures, and those of their children, were not secure in Central Asia.

As the tendency toward indigenous favoritism in Central Asia became better known throughout the former USSR, it served as a disincentive for those Russians still considering migration to Central Asia as well as an incentive for those who were already in Central Asia to leave. Russians were losing their previous competitive edge as indigenous status became a more important factor in admission to universities and advancement in the workplace. This change in the national stratification system resulted in rising Russian and nonindigenous emigration from the region, thus accelerating the pace of demographic indigenization.

Between 1971 and 1975, all of Central Asia had a net in-migration of 137,000, though a net out-migration had already begun in Kyrgyzstan. Between 1976 and 1980, the region as a whole experienced a net out-migration of 47,000, and emigration was greater than immigration in all four republics.[36] Between 1979 and 1988, an estimated 1,008,616 left Central Asia, with Russians accounting for 216,883 (21.5 percent) of the total.

Between 1989 and 1991, another 595,000 emigrated from the region, including 201,000 (33.8 percent) Russians.[37] Between 1989 and 1993, 705,500 emigrated from Central Asia to Russia, of which 511,700 (72.5 percent) were Russians. Not only was the rate of emigration increasing dramatically during this period but the proportion of emigrants who were Russians was also rising.[38] By January 1, 1994, approximately 16 percent of all Russians living in Central Asia in 1989 had left for Russia.

Two factors contributed to the relatively rapid increase in emigration beginning in 1989. First, the more informal favoritism shown indigenes during the previous two decades became formalized in language laws and other legislation, as was also the case in the other republics of the non-Russian periphery. In 1990, along with the other union republics, the Central Asian republics declared their sovereignty. These declarations were then followed by declarations of independence in 1991 following the failed August coup attempt. In 1992, new constitutions and citizenship laws were passed in Turkmenistan, Uzbekistan, and Kyrgyzstan, while civil war erupted in Tajikistan.

Although these laws were more inclusive than those passed in many of the other newly independent states, they radically altered the status of Russians from a position of dominance to at best a position of equals with the titular nations, and at worst as their inferiors in the new national stratification system being constructed. Russians in Central Asia were less willing to accept their new subordinate situation than they were in other parts of the former USSR, and responded by emigrating to Russia and abroad.

Second, at the end of the 1980s indigenous nativism turned violent. As economic conditions worsened and indigenous unemployment rose, resentment against "foreigners" increased, particularly among young Central Asians who had experienced the greatest rise in expectations due to increased educational attainment. Faced with diminishing prospects as the economy collapsed around them, young unemployed indigenes reacted violently against nonindigenes who were seen as economically privileged. Though Russians were rarely targeted directly, these violent incidents heightened the sense among Russians that they were not welcome in Central Asia and that they had no future in the region.

Formal Indigenization

Language Laws. Language laws passed in Central Asia during 1989 and 1990 varied by republic in their treatment of the Russian language and also in the degree to which they promoted the indigenous languages. All four language laws, in addition to declaring the titular language to be the "state language," preserved Russian as the "language of inter-national communication."[39] However, the Kyrgyz and Turkmen language laws emphasize the link among language, national identity, and cultural preservation, and the need to protect, preserve, and develop the use of these titular languages is more forcefully articulated than is the case with the Uzbek and Tajik language laws.

One reason for this emphasis is the more limited historical development of Turkmen and Kyrgyz as literary languages, together with the greater linguistic russification that occurred in these two republics. In addition, Kyrgyzstan had experienced a greater degree of democratization by 1989, and this gave the nationalist opposition a greater voice in the writing of this legislation. In Turkmenistan, President Niyazov favored the equal status of Russian and Turkmen, but allowed the more nationalistic version of the language law to pass "when his already suspect nationalist credentials came under fire from Turkmen intellectuals."[40]

In contrast, the Uzbek language law treats Russian and Uzbek almost equally. The limited Uzbek nationalism apparent in this law is reflective of the harsh treatment that the Uzbek nationalist opposition—and particularly the nationalist group *Birlik*—has received from the government in Uzbekistan. While the Uzbek language law stresses in its opening paragraphs the "equal status of the languages of the peoples of the Uzbek SSR," the Kyrgyz law emphasizes that "the legal establishment of the status of the Kyrgyz language as a state language creates the basis for the protection and development of the Kyrgyz language and the national culture of the Kyrgyz people."[41]

The original draft of the Tajik language law, which opened with a statement about the need to provide the Tajik language "state protection," is closer to the Kyrgyz variant.[42] However, the law as passed on July 22, 1989, stresses the equality of languages and peoples in Tajikistan and is thus more comparable to the Uzbek law.[43]

Since 1989, the status of Russian has become even more precarious in Kyrgyzstan, where an increasingly nationalistic parliament is pushing a "Kyrgyz first" political agenda, often over the objection of the more inter-nationally oriented president, Askar Akayev. The president had lobbied for the retention of a clause in the new constitution preserving Russian as the language of international communication. However, the May 5, 1993, Constitution eliminates any special status for Russian, aside from the statement that the "Kyrgyz Republic guarantees the preservation, equality and free development and functioning of Russian and other languages which are used by the population of the republic."[44] Akayev opened a Slavonic University in Bishkek in 1992, and has viewed this university as a way to reduce the flight of Russians from Kyrgyzstan. However, migration data do not indicate any slowing in the emigration of Russians.

The fortunes of the Russian language have also changed dramatically in Tajikistan. The coalition of democrats, nationalists, and Islamic revivalists who came to power briefly in 1992 attempted to enforce the language law and accelerate the shift from Russian to Tajik, now to be written in the Arabic script rather than Cyrillic. The victory of this nationalistic coalition, much more pro-Tajik and anti-Russian than its predecessor, caused a dramatic increase in Russian emigration. However, in December 1992, the conservative forces were restored to power. The more conservative government has talked about redrafting the law on languages to place Russian on a par with Tajik as a second state language, hoping to slow the pace of Russian emigration.[45] To date, little evidence suggests that the relatively pro-Russian stance of this government has had the desired effect.

Declarations of Sovereignty. The Central Asian republics declared their sovereignty during the fall of 1990 along with the other union republics in the USSR.

All four declarations contained articles supportive of inter-national equality; however, differences regarding the special status of the titular nation appeared among the republics. The alignment of republics on sovereignty was somewhat different than that found in the language laws.

All four declarations proceeded from the right of nations to self-determination, and this was not surprising since it was a right enshrined in the Soviet constitution. However, Tajikistan declared sovereignty in the name of "its historical responsibility for the fate of the Tajik people and their national statehood." Turkmenistan cited "its responsibility for the fate of the Turkmen nation" as the reason for declaring sovereignty.[46] In contrast, in Uzbekistan and Kyrgyzstan the declarations were made in the name of "the historical responsibility for the fate of the people of Uzbekistan," and "the historical responsibility for the fate of the people of Kirgizia."[47] In addition, article one of Turkmenistan's declaration described the republic as a "sovereign national state;" Kyrgyzstan and Tajikistan both defined themselves as sovereign *multi-national* states. Uzbekistan's declaration does not contain a comparable clause.

Judging by these statements, Turkmenistan took the most nationalistic position, followed by Tajikistan. Kyrgyzstan is the most surprising, since its declaration was the least nationalistic, even though its language law appeared most nationalistic. The reason for the change in position can be explained by the timing of Kyrgyzstan's declaration of sovereignty. It came just after the violent confrontation between Kyrgyz and Uzbeks in Osh Oblast, and its more inter-nationalist orientation undoubtedly reflects the concern about inter-national relations in the state following the ethnoterritorial conflict in Osh. As indicated by Kyrgyzstan's more nationalistic constitution, this brief rise in inter-nationalism did not last long (discussed later).

New Constitutions.   After independence, Turkmenistan was the first Central Asian republic to pass a post-Soviet constitution. This is ironic, because Turkmenistan is the least democratic of the Central Asian republics. Turkmenistan's authoritarian nature is reflected in its redefinition from a "national state" in its declaration of sovereignty to a "presidential state" in the constitution.[48] President Niyazov's political dominance and his suppression of *Agzybirlik* (Turkmenistan's national front organization) indicate that the early signs of Turkmen nationalism have not developed since independence, and that Niyazov has consolidated power. Niyazov, by most accounts relatively pro-Russian, has provided a stable environment for Russians in the republic; this stability helps explain the relatively limited emigration from Turkmenistan through 1993.

On December 8, 1992, Uzbekistan became the second Central Asian state to pass a new constitution. This follows the inverse correlation with democratization noted in Turkmenistan, since Uzbekistan is, after Turkmenistan, the least democratic state in the region. Like its declaration of sovereignty, Uzbekistan's constitution is relatively neutral regarding the status of Uzbeks and non-Uzbeks. Uzbek national opposition groups such as *Birlik* and *Erk*, which would have created a more nationalistic document if given the chance, have been harassed since their founding in the late 1980s. Both faced even harsher treatment in 1992, when the success of the democratic-nationalist opposition in Tajikistan was used by Karimov to repress opposition in Uzbekistan.[49] This repression of the nationalistic opposition continues.[50] As in Turkmenistan, Russians view Karimov as the only individual capable of maintaining Uzbekistan's political stability.

The Kyrgyzstan constitution, passed May 5, 1993, provides convincing evidence that Krygyzstan has become more nationalistic as a result of increasing democratization since independence. Kyrgyzstan's constitution opens by proclaiming that the state's primary mission is "to provide for the national rebirth of the Kyrgyz." This statement is followed by the goal of protecting and developing "the interests of representatives of all nationalities." The constitution also proclaims Kyrgyzstan's "devotion to the rights and freedoms of humankind and the idea of national statehood."[51] The combination of nationalism and inter-nationalism in these statements reflects the struggle between a more inter-nationalistic president and a nationalistic parliament.

Kyrgyzstan was renamed the Kyrgyz Republic, which was thought to be a name more in concert with the "idea of national statehood" enunciated in the preamble.[52] Aside from the more nationalistic preamble and the name change, Kyrgyz nationalism is indicated more by what is missing from the document than by what is included. Russian as "the language of inter-national communication" was rejected by Parliament, as was dual citizenship, an objective of Russians throughout Central Asia. Although much of the Kyrgyz constitution conforms to worldwide norms regarding human rights and the treatment of national minorities, it represents a decisive defeat for Russians in the republic, who wanted their special historic status enshrined in this document.

Tajikistan has not passed a new constitution. The democratic-nationalist-Islamic alliance that gained power in February 1992, was more anti-Russian and anti-Uzbek than either the government that came before it or the one that ousted it in December 1992.[53] If it had retained power and drafted a constitution, it would certainly have been more nationalistic and more anti-Russian than the documents cited above. On the other hand, the conservative political elites who came to power at the end of 1992 are more pro-Russian than even the pre-1992 Tajik government, since they owe their success to military intervention by Russia and Uzbekistan. They are also desperate to stem the tide of Russian emigration, which has created a "brain drain" that has devastated the Tajik economy. As noted above, Tajik political elites have promised to make the Russian language equal in status to Tajik, and have also spoken favorably about dual citizenship, although neither step has yet been taken.

Citizenship Laws and Dual Citizenship. A primary political objective of Russians throughout Central Asia, as well as political elites in Russia, is the passage of dual citizenship laws that would permit Russians to hold citizenship in both the Central Asian state in which they currently reside and in the Russian Federation. The alignment of republics on this issue is similar, but not identical, to that of the new constitutions.

Turkmenistan and Uzbekistan have passed citizenship laws incorporating the "zero option" principle. Uzbekistan was the first to pass a citizenship law in July 1992.[54] In addition to the zero option, it has no language requirement for "foreigners" who wish to become citizens of Uzbekistan. Individuals need only renounce their foreign citizenship and be permanent residents in Uzbekistan for five years (article 17). However, Uzbekistan does not allow for dual citizenship, except that "compatriots who are citizens of a foreign state . . . may also be accepted as citizens of the Republic of Uzbekistan, if they or their parents, their grandfather, or grandmother were at one time forced to leave their homeland because of the regime in existence at the time" (article 10). This exception aids in the repatriation of Uzbeks from other successor states and Afghanistan. It has also become a source of resentment among Russians who are themselves denied the right to hold citizenship in Russia and Uzbekistan. Former Russian Foreign Minister Andrey Kozyrev pressed Karimov for dual citizenship for Russians, and 74 percent of Russians in Tashkent in a recent poll favored dual citizenship over citizenship in either Uzbekistan or Russia.[55] However, to date Russian demands have drawn only an angry response from Uzbek political elites, who argue that there are no violations of Russian rights.[56]

Turkmenistan passed its citizenship law in September 1992. In addition to the zero option, foreign citizens can be naturalized if they show competency in the Turkmen language and provide proof of permanent residence for seven years. This law stands out as the only one thus far passed in Central Asia to allow dual citizenship.[57] This provision reinforces the view that Turkmenistan, under the authoritarian leadership of Niyazov, is the most pro-Russian of the Central Asian states. During 1994, approximately 20,000 Russians registered for dual citizenship. According to Russia's ambassador to Turkmenistan, "over 95 percent of those who have registered have decided to go to Russia."[58]

The Kyrgyz parliament discussed the possibility of dual citizenship during constitutional debates and rejected it. However, support for dual citizenship remains strong among Russians in Kyrgyzstan: 58 percent of Russians surveyed favor dual citizenship over citizenship in either Kyrgyzstan or Russia.[59] The issue apparently has not been decided definitively. Kozyrev pressed for dual citizenship on his January 1994 visit to Bishkek, and Akayev responded that passing such a law to allay the fears of Russians in the republic may still be possible. However, Kyrgyz nationalist parties strongly oppose such a law.[60]

Tajikistan has not passed a citizenship law to date, again due to the political turmoil in the republic. The leaders of the conservative government that took power in December 1992, favor dual citizenship as a means of convincing Russians to remain in Tajikistan. Given the political and military dependency of the Tajik conservatives on Russia, the passage of a dual citizenship law in the near future is likely. However, prospects that such a law will stem the outflow of Russians remain doubtful.

A recent survey asked Russians in Tashkent and the cities of Kyrgyzstan what form of citizenship they favored: dual, in the republic of residence, or in Russia.[61] The majority of Russians favored dual citizenship in both Tashkent

(74 percent) and Kyrgyzstan (58 percent). Only 10 percent of Russians in Tashkent and 15 percent of Russians in Kyrgyzstan favored citizenship in Russia alone. This low proportion is not surprising, because this choice would force Russians to close the door on their lives in Central Asia, a prospect that most Russians had only begun to consider by 1992. Only 5 percent of Russians in Tashkent and 15 percent of Russians in Kyrgyzstan favored citizenship in Uzbekistan or Kyrgyzstan respectively. This response also is not surprising since Russians had not developed a sense of homeland in Central Asia and were feeling increasingly alienated from these Central Asian republics.

The Tashkent survey also asked Russians which citizenship they would prefer if dual citizenship were not an option. The responses were divided, with 42 percent opting for Russian citizenship and 47 percent favoring citizenship in Uzbekistan.[62] No follow-up questions were asked, so explaining the relatively high proportion saying Uzbekistan is difficult. These figures indicate indecision among Russians who had previously viewed themselves as citizens of the USSR, and who have thus far failed to develop a sense of attachment to either the state in which they reside or to Russia.

Additional Factors.   Specific cultural, political, and economic events in the Central Asian republics have become additional factors weighed by Russians deciding whether to stay or leave. For example, all three Turkic republics agreed in September 1993, to change their alphabets to the Latin script, and the Tajik democratic-nationalist opposition parties, while in power in Tajikistan, accelerated the conversion of Tajik to the Arabic script.[63] All four republics have also accelerated the pace of indigenization of political personnel since independence.[64] Except for Tajikistan, all have also introduced their own currencies. Each of these moves has further alienated Russians culturally, politically, and economically from Central Asia.

In Kyrgyzstan, the parliament attempted to pass a land law which stated that only members of the Kyrgyz nation had the right to own land. Only with great effort was president Akayev successful in removing this article from the privatization bill that ultimately passed.[65] Nevertheless, such debates provide a clear signal to Russians that their future in the republic would be tenuous at best if Kyrgyz nationalists take control. On the other side of the ledger, a Slavonic University was opened in Bishkek as part of an effort by Akayev to hold Russians in Kyrgyzstan. However, the shift to Kyrgyz-language schools has been rapid, and Russians doubt that they will be able to educate their children in the Russian language.[66]

Overall, the political elites in Turkmenistan have been the most pro-Russian, and Turkmenistan is the republic with the fewest Russian emigrants. However, this pro-Russian attitude is likely to last only as long as President Niyazov retains power.

In Uzbekistan, laws have been relatively accommodative of Russians, but the acceleration of indigenization has alienated an increasing number of Russian residents. Again, the relatively pro-Russian policies of the state are likely to continue only so long as Karimov retains power. Democratization in either Turkmenistan or Uzbekistan will provide a greater political voice to indigenous nationalists, who will increase pressure on Russians to accept a subordinate position or leave. In Kyrgyzstan, democratization has occurred to some extent, resulting in a more assertive nationalist opposition with greater political power. Thus far, that nationalistic voice has been balanced by a more inter-nationalist president. In Tajikistan, the relatively pro-Russian former communists were ousted by the more anti-Russian and anti-Uzbek coalition of democrats, nationalists, and Islamic revivalists. The more conservative force that took power in 1993 is more pro-Russian, but the chaos of this struggle for power has convinced most Russians that they have no future in Tajikistan.

Indigenous Nativism

At the end of the 1980s and the beginning of the 1990s, a third factor influenced Russians who were increasingly deciding to leave Central Asia. Beyond economic decline and growing difficulties in competing with indigenes, acts of violence carried out against foreigners served as a powerful catalyst for Russian emigration. Most of these violent displays of nativism—the Uzbek riots against Meskhetian Turks in 1989 or the anti-Armenian violence in several cities throughout Central Asia between 1989 and 1990—were led by young unemployed indigenes who viewed outsiders as receiving preferential treatment in jobs, wages, and access to housing.

This rising nativism was not only directed against non-Central Asians. In Osh Oblast, the conflict pitted local Kyrgyz, who held most of the political power in the region, against Uzbeks, who were an economically privileged group locally. A growing wave of young unemployed Kyrgyz migrated to Osh in search of work and adequate housing, both of which had become increasingly scarce. The fact that Uzbeks occupied prestigious economic positions in Osh "generated a feeling among part of the Kirghiz population, especially young people, of wounded pride and deprivation in their own land."[67] Kyrgyz political elites reallocated land from a predominantly Uzbek collective farm to provide housing exclusively for Kyrgyz. This set in motion conflict escalation that left over 200 people dead, and triggered a rapid rise in Uzbek refugee migration from Osh Oblast to Uzbekistan.[68]

Even though Russians were rarely targets of rising nativism in Central Asia, these incidents served as a wake-up call to Russians throughout the region, telling them that they were no longer welcome. A survey of people who wished to leave Dushanbe in the aftermath of the February 1990 riots gave the following reasons:[69]

	percent
"fear of the recurrence of the events of February"	20.2
"change in the linguistic situation"	11.6
"deterioration in the material conditions of life"	10.5
"unsuitable climate"	8.4
"change in family's position"	4.5

Table 9.6
Reasons for Out-Migration (Percent)

Reasons	Uzbekistan	Kyrgyzstan	Tajikistan	Turkmenistan
School	8	8	5	13
Change in Place of Work	10	13	9	14
Worsening Inter-National Relations	27	33	41	15
Worsening Crime	3	4	6	1
Family Circumstances	26	22	23	30
Unsettled Living Conditions	10	6	4	6
Other	20	14	12	21

Source: Statkom SNG, "Napravleniya i prichiny migratsii naseleniya," *Statisticheskiy byulleten'* No. 14 (October 1992): 129.

A survey conducted in 1992 throughout the CIS indicated that "worsening inter-national relations" was given as the principal reason for emigration in all of the Central Asian states except Turkmenistan (Table 9.6).

A more recent survey of Russians in Kyrgyzstan indicated that "worsening inter-national relations" has become an even more important factor, with 60 percent stating that it was the most important reason for their decision to leave. The second and third reasons listed were also associated with the changing relationship between Kyrgyz and Russians: "adoption of laws which infringe upon the rights of Russians" (29.4 percent), such as language laws, and "infringement of the national dignity of Russians" (19.8 percent).[70] Another recent survey found that 83 percent of Russians in Tajikistan assessed the inter-national situation negatively, as did 69 percent in Uzbekistan.[71]

Responding to a combination of factors, including economic decline, rising competition as indigenes restructure the stratification systems to favor the titular group, the rise of anti-Russian nationalist forces, and rising nativism among the increasingly relatively deprived young indigenes, Russians have left Central Asia in increasing numbers since 1989. We examine this Russian emigration and possible alternatives to emigration in the next section.

The Russian Refugees

Russian emigration since 1989 has increasingly taken on the appearance of a refugee migration as tens of thousands have left Central Asia for an uncertain future in Russia (Table 9.7). The Russian emigration between 1989 and 1993

Table 9.7

Total and Russian Net Migration from Central Asia to Russia, 1989–1993

Republic	Total (000s)					Russians (000s)					Russian % of Total Emigration					Emigrants as a % of Russians in 1989
	1989	1990	1991	1992	1993	1989	1990	1991	1992	1993	1989	1990	1991	1992	1993	
Uzbekistan	41.6	65.9	35.8	84.3	70.7	17.7	40.2	27.8	64.2	50.7	42.5	61.0	77.7	76.2	71.7	12.1
Kyrgyzstan	4.9	21.2	17.7	49.8	86.2	3.8	16.1	15.4	41.5	66.5	77.6	75.9	87.0	83.3	77.1	15.6
Tajikistan	5.7	40.3	17.6	66.7	62.9	5.4	31.7	14.4	45.9	40.9	94.7	78.7	81.8	68.8	65.0	35.6
Turkmenistan	4.6	6.1	4.5	12.2	6.8	2.9	4.4	4.7	10.8	6.7	63.0	72.1	104.4	88.5	98.5	8.8
Central Asia	56.8	133.5	75.6	213.0	226.6	29.8	92.4	62.3	162.4	164.8	52.5	69.2	82.4	76.2	72.7	15.5

Source: Lee Schwartz, paper presented in the roundtable discussion "Emerging Regional, Political, and Social Issues in Russia," at the 91st Annual Meeting of the Association of American Geographers, Chicago, 14–18 March 1995.

exceeded the rate for the previous decade in Tajikistan, Kyrgyzstan, and Uzbekistan; only in Turkmenistan was the 1989–1993 Russian emigration less than it was in 1979–1988.[72]

Emigration increased dramatically between 1989 and 1990, in conjunction with the rising inter-national discomfort felt by Russians as the Central Asians passed language laws, declarations of sovereignty, and other legislation designed to enhance the status of the indigenous nation. This discomfort also increased in response to inter-national violence in Dushanbe, Tashkent, Fergana valley, and Osh Oblast in Kyrgyzstan, though Russians were not the targets of this violence.[73] In 1991 the level of Russian and total emigration declined as republic elites attempted to reassure local Russians that their status was secure. The agreement reached in April with Gorbachev to form a new Union of Sovereign States was undoubtedly also a factor in the declining level of emigration in 1991.

Since independence at the end of 1991, Russian emigration has once again increased dramatically. The number leaving Central Asia for Russia nearly tripled, increasing from 62,300 in 1991 to 162,400 in 1992. Increases were particularly dramatic in Tajikistan, where intra-national civil war erupted almost immediately after independence was declared. Russian emigration increased substantially in all republics, including Turkmenistan. In 1993 the number of Russians leaving Central Asia remained at approximately the 1992 level. Russian emigration decreased somewhat in Tajikistan with the ouster of the nationalist coalition and the return of relatively more pro-Russian forces to power. The number leaving Uzbekistan and Turkmenistan also decreased in 1993, and this was undoubtedly correlated with the antinationalist dictatorships that had established firm control in these republics by 1993. By way of contrast, democratization in Kyrgyzstan that resulted in a relatively more nationalistic parliament encouraged an increasing number of Russians to leave in 1993.

An increasing number of Russians in 1991 and 1992 made firm decisions to leave Central Asia (Table 9.8). The shift toward emigration was particularly dramatic in Tajikistan and Kyrgyzstan; by 1992, in each of these two states the proportion that had decided to leave exceeded the proportion that had made a firm decision to remain. In Tajikistan, in addition to the 66 percent who had decided to leave by 1992, another 15 percent were leaning toward emigration, making a total of 81 percent who said they favored emigration. In Uzbekistan, an additional 16 percent of Russians were inclined toward emigration, bringing the total favoring emigration in that state to 59 percent.[74] In Kyrgyzstan, over two-thirds of Russians surveyed between 1991—1992 were "thinking about leaving."[75] Unfortunately, no 1992 data were available for Turkmenistan. However, given that the 1991 figure of those who had decided to leave was higher than those in Uzbekistan and Kyrgyzstan, and given the increase in actual emigration between 1991 and 1992, it is likely that Russians in Turkmenistan have undergone a similar rise in discomfort, with an increasing number of them making firm decisions to emigrate.

Table 9.8
Migration Intentions of Russians in Central Asia (Percent of Respondents)

State	Firm Decision to Leave			Firm Decision to Stay			No Firm Decision		
	1991	1992ª	1992ᵇ	1991	1992ª	1992ʰ	1991	1992ª	1992ᵇ
Uzbekistan	25	31	43	35	33	18	40	36	39
Kyrgyzstan	24	36	na	33	25	na	43	38	na
Tajikistan	36	52	66	23	17	6	41	31	28
Turkmenistan	28	na	na	32	na	na	40	na	na

Notes: ªData of the Russian Center for the Study of Public Opinion. ᵇData of the Laboratory of Population Migration.

Source: Data provided by Zhanna Zayonchkovskaya and Galina Vitkovskaya, Laboratoriya migratsii naseleniya, Institut narodnokhozyaystvennogo prognozirovaniya, Rossiyskaya akademiya nauk, March 1994.

Migration trends and survey data suggest that the majority of Russians in Central Asia will leave for Russia in the near future. Russians leaving between 1991 and 1993 increasingly viewed themselves—and were increasingly viewed by Russia—as refugees forced to leave the region in the face of mounting anti-Russian discrimination and anti-outsider violence.

Alternatives to Emigration

With the majority of Russians opting for emigration from Central Asia, what alternatives exist for those who wish to remain, and why are they less attractive? In this section we examine two variants of the "stay and fight" option, as well as the "stay and adapt" option for Russians who wish to remain in Central Asia.

Stay and Fight

For Russians who wish to stay in Central Asia and continue living as Russians, two options are possible: territorial and cultural autonomy. However, the Russians of Central Asia appear to consider only the latter worth pursuing. Few Russians have expressed a desire for territorial autonomy in the region, and this reticence appears related to the limited degree to which urbanized Russians have developed a localized sense of homeland in Central Asia. Unlike areas of Kazakhstan, Estonia, Moldova, or Ukraine, Russians in Central Asia have developed no particular attachment to the locality in which they live.

Surveys have consistently shown that the majority of Russians living in Central Asia consider the USSR or Russia to be their homeland (all figures are in percent):

Country of Residence	Late 1970s –early 1980s.[76]	1991[77]	After USSR Breakup[78]
	Russians who viewed the USSR to be their homeland		Viewed Russia as homeland
Kyrgyzstan		78	52	12
Tajikistan		87		
Uzbekistan (Tashkent)	70	88	50	15
	Russians who considered the republic of residence to be their homeland		
Kyrgyzstan		7	28	
Tajikistan		18		
Uzbekistan (Tashkent)		11	20	

A somewhat more significant proportion of Russians is willing to stay and fight for cultural autonomy. As discussed above, local Russians—frequently assisted by political elites from Russia—have put pressure on the Central Asian regimes to enhance the status of the Russian language and to reduce favoritism toward indigenes. Russians have been relatively successful in this effort, primarily because the Central Asian states continue to be dependent both on the local skilled Russian labor force and on trade with Russia.

A survey of Russians in Kyrgyzstan found that while 40 percent felt that the majority of Russians would emigrate, 25 percent believed that the majority would stay and "actively fight for their rights."[79] The latter figure matched fairly closely the proportion of Russians who considered Kyrgyzstan to be their homeland. Although survey data on this question for the other republics are not available, it is likely that fewer Russians in Tajikistan, Uzbekistan, and Turkmenistan would favor a "stand and fight" alternative, because more Russians have a sense of homeland in Kyrgyzstan, a higher proportion of Russians were born in Kyrgyzstan,[80] and a higher proportion of Russians live in rural areas in Kyrgyzstan than in any other Central Asian republic.

Stay and Adapt
Even fewer Russians will opt to stay and adapt. One indication of this is the extremely small number of Russians who learned the Central Asian languages, even as second languages. Only 3 percent of Russians in Central Asia claimed to have mastered the Central Asian languages in 1989.[81] This figure can be interpreted as a measure of Russians who had accommodated themselves to Central Asian society by the end of the Soviet era. A larger number of Russians may now be willing to learn the indigenous languages under the new political and cultural circumstances; nonetheless, the extremely low starting point indicates that those likely to stay and adapt is quite small.

The survey of Russians in Kyrgyzstan noted above found that 13 percent believed that "the majority of Russians would stay and adapt to the situation that is taking shape." The Russians' response to the questions were greatly influenced by age. Those under 25 were most oriented toward emigration, those over 50 were more willing to stay and fight, and those aged 30–50 were more willing to stay and adapt.[82] These age correlations make sense: Retirees living in the region want to return to the status quo ante, those who have established careers in Kyrgyzstan are more willing to adapt in order to preserve the time and energy that they have already invested, and those who are just beginning their lives as adults see little future for Russians in the region and are most able to make a clean break.

There is undoubtedly a small segment who will not only adapt, but will acculturate. However, judging by the number of Russians who claimed a Central Asian language as their native or first language, this segment of Russians is exceedingly small. In the 1989 census in all four republics, only 1,351 (0.04 percent) of Russians claimed to have adopted the language of the titular group as their first language.[83] Even in the new environment, this number is unlikely to increase substantially, both because of the ethnocultural distance between Russians and Central Asians, and also because of the imperialistic mentality of the Russians in Central Asia.

Conclusion

Continued Emigration of Russians

The data presented above indicate that the dominant response of Russians to their new status in Central Asia will be emigration, though the actual number of emigrants cannot be accurately predicted. A very small number of Russians will stay in Central Asia and adapt to a new way of life, and a somewhat more sizable number will stay and fight for greater cultural autonomy.

The decision to stay or leave is being made on the basis of a complex set of factors including regional economic conditions (compared to those in Russia), the degree to which the state is promoting indigenization, the level of anti-Russian sentiments and nativism, the degree of political stability in the republic, and the degree to which each individual Russian has come to view the Central Asian republic as home. Many of these factors are themselves affected by Russian emigration. For example, the rising emigration of skilled Russians has caused a "brain drain" which has forced numerous Central Asian enterprises to close their doors. These economic consequences further disrupt the local economies, causing greater anti-Russian sentiments and nativism among a larger number of young unemployed indigenes, which in turn provides the impetus for greater Russian emigration. This downward spiral has been apparent in the region since 1990.

Russian political elites in Moscow have taken on the role as defenders of Russians in Central Asia. Moscow has pressured the Central Asian regimes to alleviate the fears of the Russian population by improving the status of the Russian language and accepting dual citizenship. Two reasons are apparent in Russia's attempts to improve conditions for Russians in Central Asia. First,

Russia is having difficulty coping with refugee migration from the region. The cost to Russia is political as well as financial, since Russians forced to leave Central Asia tend to be nationalistic and to join right-wing political organizations such as those that support politicians like Zhirinovsky.

Second, Russian elites in the Yeltsin government continue to view Central Asia as an imperial appendage of Russia. Andrey Kozyrev, the most outspoken advocate for Russians in Central Asia, made statements in October 1993, indicating that he continued to view Central Asia as a Russian possession, or at least an exclusive Russian sphere of influence.[84] Similarly Pavel Grachev, Russia's Defense Minister, defended the use of Russian troops on the border between Tajikistan and Afghanistan on the basis of the strategic importance of the region to Moscow,[85] and declared that "the Russian side regards the attack on the 12th border post on the Tajik-Afghan border as a tragedy for *Russia*. This is a direct threat of interference in *Russia's domestic affairs* and an undeclared war waged by some militant groups against *Russia* (emphasis added)."[86] Such statements coming from Moscow are likely to reinforce the existing imperialistic mentality among Russians in Central Asia, further reducing the number of Russians in Central Asia likely to stay and adapt.

Impact on Democratization

Democratization has made limited inroads into Central Asia, and is really in evidence only in Kyrgyzstan. Yet Russians are leaving Kyrgyzstan at a faster rate than any other Central Asian republic except Tajikistan, where civil war and political chaos have dominated. An inverse relationship appears to exist between democratization and the comfort level of Russians in the region. The main reason for this negative correlation appears to be that many Russians oppose democratization if it means accepting a subordinate or even an equal position with the titular nations in Central Asia.

Democratization is also perceived as linked to political instability. Russians have strongly supported dictatorial rulers such as Karimov and Niyazov because they have provided political stability in Uzbekistan and Turkmenistan. In these two cases, "political stability" appears to be equated with harsh repression of indigenous national front organizations such as *Birlik* and *Agzybirlik*.

The evidence from Central Asia strongly suggests that democratization results in a stronger political voice for titular nationalists, who in turn press more forcefully for a new national stratification system that favors indigenes over Russians and all other outsiders. Both Kyrgyzstan and Tajikistan allowed the development of multiple political parties, and parties in both tend to be nationally specific. The nationalist parties in parliament have obtained a powerful political voice in Kyrgyzstan, which is balanced only by the more inter-nationally oriented president.

In Tajikistan, the nationalist opposition gained power in February 1992, and adopted a more pro-Tajik and anti-Russian (and anti-Uzbek) political agenda. However, *Rastokhez*, the Tajik nationalist movement, could not rally the support of all Tajiks, but only those who were politically disenfranchised by the old order. A second nationalist party, *Lali Badakhshan*, promoted an anti-Tajikistan separatist agenda and drew support from the Pamiris who do not perceive themselves to be part of the Tajik nation. This fragmented "national" opposition was not successful in holding power, and indicates that the consolidation of all Tajiks into a unified national identity overriding all other levels of identity has not taken place. This intra-national splintering of the Tajik opposition forces has worked to the benefit of Russians and other non-indigenes in Tajikistan.

Likewise, the limited degree to which national consciousness has assumed primacy among all indigenes in Kyrgyzstan, Turkmenistan, and Uzbekistan has also limited the degree to which a nationalist opposition has been successful in attaining political hegemony in the independent states. However, independence will no doubt accelerate the nation-making process in the states of Central Asia, and as nationalization proceeds, the position of Russians in the region will become even more precarious.

Imperialism and Interactive Nationalism in Central Asia

Central Asia conforms to the 'internal colonialism' model more closely than any other region of the former USSR. However, the behavior of Central Asians toward the dominant group has not conformed to the predictions of internal colonialism. According to theory, Central Asians should have been the most nationalistic groups in the USSR (i.e., the most separatist). However, Central Asia was the least separatist region in the USSR. In addition, the nationalist political organizations formed in these republics (e.g., *Birlik, Erk, Agzybirlik*) have had the most difficult time mobilizing the titular masses in this region behind a national self-determination agenda.

Part of the reason for this relates to the limited degree of nationalization, which in turn is largely the result of the imperialistic nature of Russia's relations with the region. Indigenous migration, urbanization, and social mobilization—all processes that facilitated the formation of nations in other regions of the Russian Empire and the USSR—were stifled in Central Asia until the post-Stalin period. The limited amount of industrialization that occurred in Central Asia was accompanied by Russian in-migration, not indigenous mobilization and nationalization. This was changing during the 1970s and 1980s. Central Asians experienced dramatic increases in the level of educational attainment, and those with a higher education and positions in the intelligentsia were more nationalistic. However, when expectations among young educated Central Asians were increasing most rapidly, socioeconomic development in the region stalled as Moscow reduced the level of investment in Central Asia. This created conditions of increasing relative deprivation among the young, educated, and unemployed Central Asians. Because the level of national consciousness remained limited, this relative deprivation resulted not in massive pro-independence demonstrations, but rather in sporadic, spontaneous displays of nativism which tended to be much more localized.

Nevertheless, even though indigenous nationalization in Central Asia has been limited, an interactive process comparable to interactive nationalism is in evidence. First, titular nativism has targeted members of nontitular groups because they are outsiders and because members of the titular groups perceive them as privileged. Nontitular groups have responded to the threat posed by rising nativism, primarily by emigrating from Central Asia.

To the extent that titular elites have sought to establish their group's hegemony in the state through language laws and "constitutional nationalism," Russians have sought to counter these policies, primarily through the preservation of cultural autonomy, the promotion of equal rights, and through attempts to obtain dual citizenship with Russia. However, few Russians have developed a sense of homeland in Central Asia, and so few are willing to stay and fight. As titular nationalists gain greater political control in Central Asia, and pass laws that enhance the hegemony of their groups in their homelands, Russians will continue to respond by emigrating from the region.

Notes

1. For an example of the Soviet ethnographic view, see Yu. Bromley, "Etnograficheskoye izucheniye sovremennykh natsional'nykh protsessov v SSSR," *Sovetskaya etnografiya* No. 2 (1983): 4–14. For an example of the western pan-Islamic view, see Alexandre Bennigsen, "Several Nations or One People? Ethnic Consciousness Among Soviet Central Asian Muslims,"*Survey* Vol. 24, No. 3 (Summer 1979): 51–64. Studies at the subnational level were conducted during the Soviet era. For example, see R. Dzharylgasinova and L. Tolstova, eds., *Etnicheskiye protsessy u natsional'nykh grupp Sredney Azii i Kazakhstana* (Moskva: Nauka, 1980). For a current assessment of identity in Central Asia, see Jo-Ann Gross, ed., *Muslims in Central Asia: Expressions of Identity and Change* (Durham: Duke University Press, 1992). The Central Asian chapters in Ian Bremmer and Ray Taras, eds., *Nations and Politics in the Soviet Successor States* (Cambridge: Cambridge University Press, 1993) also highlight the importance of subnational identities in the region.

2. Ralph Clem, "The Frontier and Colonialism in Russian and Soviet Central Asia," in Robert Lewis, ed., *Geographic Perspectives on Soviet Central Asia* (London: Routledge, 1992), pp. 19–36. Russians in northern Kyrgyzstan are more comparable to Russians in northern Kazakhstan than they are to Russians in the rest of Central Asia because they entered the Semirech'e region as peasants in search of land, and their descendants have remained in the region for generations.

3. Richard Pierce, *Russian Central Asia 1867–1917. A Study in Colonial Rule* (Berkeley: University of California Press, 1960), p. 137.

4. Pierce, *Russian Central Asia*, p. 137.

5. Elizabeth Bacon, *Central Asians Under Russian Rule* (Ithaca: Cornell University Press, 1980), p. 106.

6. Bacon, *Central Asians Under Russian Rule*, pp. 107–109.

7. Beatrice Manz, "Central Asian Uprisings in the Nineteenth Century: Ferghana Under the Russians," *The Russian Review*, Vol. 46 (1987): 267–281.

8. See Chapter 3.

9. To some extent, the Russians who migrated to rural Kyrgyzstan during the tsarist era, and whose descendants remained there during the Soviet period, are an exception to this general rule.

10. The fact that the 1917 figure for Russians in Central Asia is smaller than the 1911 figure given for Russians in Turkestan does not necessarily mean that Russians were leav-

ing the region, though Russians did go to the front in sizable numbers during World War I. However, the 1911 figure for Russians includes Ukrainians and Belarusians, who were treated as parts of the Russian "tribe" at that time. The Russian figure in 1917 included only ethnic Russians. In addition, the borders of Central Asia are not comparable to the borders of the Turkestani oblasts.

11. S. Bruk and V. Kabuzan, "Dinamika chislennosti i rasseleniya russkikh posle velikoy oktyabr'skoy sotsialisticheskoy revolyutsii," *Sovetskaya etnografiya* No. 5 (1982): 7. For 1937 figures, see "Vsesoyuznaya perepis' naseleniya 1937 g.," *Vestnik statistiki* No. 7 (1990):65–79.

12. Robert Lewis, et al., *Nationality and Population Change in Russia and the USSR* (New York: Praeger, 1976), pp. 144–151.

13. Bruk and Kabuzan, "Dinamika chislennosti," p. 7; For 1937 figures, see "Vsesoyuznaya perepis' naseleniya 1937 g."

14. Bruk and Kabuzan, "Dinamika chislennosti," p. 7; For 1937 figures, see "Vsesoyuznaya perepis' naseleniya 1937 g."

15. Viktor Kozlov, *Natsional'nosti SSSR* (Moskva: Statistika, 1975), pp. 111–112.

16. Michael Sacks, "Roots of Diversity and Conflict: Ethnic and Gender Differences in the Work Force of the Former Republics of Soviet Central Asia," (revised paper originally presented at the Conference on Central Asia and the Middle East, Tel Aviv University, Israel, October 12–14, 1993 [November 1993]).

17. Michael Hechter, *Internal Colonialism* (Berkeley: University of California Press, 1975). See also Ronald Liebowitz, "Soviet Geographical Imbalances and Soviet Central Asia," in Robert Lewis, ed., *Geographic Perspectives on Soviet Central Asia*, pp. 119–120.

18. Michael Rywkin, *Moscow's Muslim Challenge* (Armonk, NY: M. E. Sharpe, 1982), p. 57.

19. Alastair McAuley, "The Central Asian Economy in Comparative Perspective," in Michael Ellman and Vladimir Kontorovich, eds., *The Disintegration of the Soviet Economic System* (London and New York: Routledge, 1992).

20. William Fierman, "Language Development in Soviet Uzbekistan," in Isabelle Kreindler, ed., *Sociolinguistic Perspectives on Soviet National Languages* (Berlin: Mouton de Gruyter, 1985), pp. 207–208.

21. Mikhael Guboglo, "Razvitiye obshchestvennykh funktsiy yazykov narodov SSSR v sfere shkol'nogo obrazovaniya," in Yu. Bromley et al., eds, *Sovremennyye etnicheskiye protsessy v SSSR* (Moskva: Nauka, 1977), p. 267.

22. Fierman, "Language Development in Soviet Uzbekistan," pp. 213–220.

23. Yu. Arutyunyan, et al., *Russkiye: Etnosotsiologicheskiye ocherki* (Moskva: Nauka, 1992), pp. 95, 100; Sacks, "Roots of Diversity and Conflict," pp. 3–4.

24. Sacks, "Roots of Diversity and Conflict," p. 4.

25. G. Yagodin, "Sovershenstvovaniye mezhnatsional'nykh otnosheniy i shkola," *Sovetskaya pedogagika*, No. 8 (1989): 5.

26. Eugene Huskey, "The Politics of Language in Kyrgyzstan," *Nationalities Papers*, Vol. 23, No. 3 (September 1995): 552; Fierman, "Language Development in Soviet Uzbekistan," pp. 220–221.

27. Yu. Arutyunyan and Yu. Bromley, *Sotsial'no-kul'turnyy oblik sovetskikh natsiy* (Moskva: Nauka, 1986), pp. 306–309.

28. Rasma Karklins, "Ethnic Politics and Access to Higher Education: The Soviet Case," *Comparative Politics* (April 1984):288–290.

29. Huskey, "Politics and Elections in Kyrgyzstan, 1989–1990," unpublished paper, pp. 5–7.

30. *Srednyaya Aziya: Spravochnyye materialy* (Moskva: institut gumanitarno-politicheskikh issledovaniy, 1992), pp. 9–10, 44–45, 65, 88–89.

31. Socioeconomic developments in Central Asia during the 1970s and 1980s are a classic example of "aspirational deprivation." See Ted Gurr, *Why Men Rebel* (Princeton, NJ: Princeton University Press, 1970).

32. The same set of circumstances also gave rise to nativism in India. See Myron Weiner, *Sons of the Soil* (Princeton, NJ: Princeton University Press, 1978), pp. 274–294.

33. Other factors include rapid population growth and the rapid rise in the number of highly educated Central Asians, both of which would have been difficult to absorb even under favorable economic conditions.

34. Gertrude Schroeder, "Nationalities and the Soviet Economy," in Lubomyr Hajda and Mark Beissinger, eds., *The Nationalities Factor in Soviet Politics and Society* (Boulder: Westview Press, 1990), pp. 43–44; Ronald Liebowitz, "Spatial Inequality Under Gorbachev," in Michael Bradshaw, ed., *The Soviet Union: A New Regional Geography?* (London: Belhaven, 1991), p. 17.

35. Leonid Rybakovskiy and Nina Tarasova, "Migratsionnyye protsessy v SSSR: novyye yavleniya," *Sotsiologicheskiye issledovaniya* No. 7 (1990): 39–40.

36. Arutyunyan and Bromley, *Sotsial'no-kul'turnyy oblik sovetskikh natsiy*, p. 20.

37. Robert Kaiser, "Ethnic Demography and Interstate Relations in Central Asia," in *National Identity and Ethnicity in Russia and the New States of Eurasia*, The International Politics of Eurasia, ed. Roman Szporluk, vol. 2 (Armonk, NY: M. E. Sharpe, 1994), p. 251.

38. Lee Schwartz, "Emerging Regional, Political, and Social Issues in Russia," (paper presented at the 91st Annual Meeting of the Association of American Geographers, Chicago, March 14–18, 1995). Comparable data are also found in "O migratsii naseleniya v stranakh Sodruzhestva," *Statisticheskiy Byulleten'* (Statisticheskiy Komitet SNG), No. 40 (November 1994): 69–85.

39. Charles Furtado and Andrea Chandler, eds., *Perestroika in the Soviet Republics: Documents on the National Question* (Boulder: Westview Press, 1992), pp. 509–513, 530–533, 546–551, 567–571.

40. Christopher Panico, "Turkmenistan Unaffected by Winds of Democratic Change," RFE/RL *Research Report* Vol 2., No. 4 (22 January 1993):10.

41. Furtado and Chandler, eds., *Perestroika in the Soviet Republics*, pp. 509, 530.

42. Furtado and Chandler, eds., *Perestroika in the Soviet Republics*, pp. 546–551.

43. "Tajik SSR Law on Languages," *JPRS-UPA* No. 63 (December 5, 1989):37–40.

44. *Konstitutsiya Kyrgyzskoy Respubliki*, Bishkek, May 5,1993, article 5, section 2.

45. "Prime Minister Pledges Equal Status for Russian Citizens," *FBIS*-SOV No. 68 (12 April 1993):63.

46. Furtado and Chandler, eds., *Perestroika in the Soviet Republics*, pp. 553, 572.

47. Furtado and Chandler, eds., *Perestroika in the Soviet Republics*, pp. 523, 536.

48. Commission on Security and Cooperation in Europe, *Human Rights and Democratization in the Newly Independent States of the Former Soviet Union* (Washington, DC: CSCE, 1993), p. 180.

49. Bess Brown, "Tajik Civil War Prompts Crackdown in Uzbekistan," RFE/RL *Research Report* Vol. 2, No. 11 (March 12, 1993): 1–6.

50. Yalcin Tokgozoglu, "Uzbek Government Continues to Stifle Dissent," RFE/RL *Research Report* Vol. 2, No. 39 (October 1, 1993): 10–15.

51. *Konstitutsiya Kyrgyskoy Respubliki*, preamble.

52. Bess Brown, "Central Asia: The Economic Crisis Deepens," RFE/RL *Research Report* Vol. 3, No. 1 (January 7, 1994): 63–64.

53. Bess Brown, "Tajikistan: The Conservatives Triumph, RFE/RL *Research Report* Vol. 2, No. 7 (February 12, 1993): 10.

54. Uzbekistan, "Republic Law on Citizenship," *FBIS*-USR No. 121 (September 24, 1992): 178–184.

55. A. Ginsberg et al., *Russkiye v novom zarubezh'e: Srednyaya Aziya*, p. 87; "Kozyrev in Uzbekistan," *RFE/RL Daily Report* No. 27 (February 9, 1994).

56. "Karimov: No Violation of Russian Rights," *FBIS-SOV* No. 219 (November 16, 1993): 96.

57. CSCE, *Human Rights and Democratization*, p. 183.

58. Commission on Security and Cooperation in Europe, *Report on the Parliamentary Election in Turkmenistan December 11, 1994* (Washington, DC: CSCE, 1995), p. 10. The CSCE report states that dual citizenship for Russians was only allowed after the December 1993 electoral success of Zhirinovsky in Russia. However, the dual citizenship provision was part of the 1992 citizenship law. The CSCE report appears to be in error, although it is possible that the provision was not implemented until January 1994.

59. Ginsberg et al., *Russkiye v novom zarubezh'e*, p. 88.

60. "Dispute Over Dual Citizenship Continues in Kyrgyzstan," RFE/RL *Daily Report*, No. 12 (19 January 1994).

61. Ginsberg et al., *Russkiye v novom zarubezh'e*, p. 87–89.

62. Ginsberg et al., *Russkiye v novom zarubezh'e*, p. 88.

63. Brown, "Central Asia: The Economic Crisis Deepens," p. 68; Bess Brown, "Tajik Opposition to be Banned," RFE/RL *Reseach Report* Vol. 2, No. 14 (April 2, 1993): 10.

64. John Dunlop, "Will the Russians Return from the Near Abroad?" *Post-Soviet Geography* Vol. 35, No. 4 (April 1994): 207–209.

65. Gregory Gleason, "Central Asia: Land Reform and the Ethnic Factor," RFE/RL *Research Report* Vol. 2, No. 3 (January 15, 1993):30.

66. John Dunlop, "Will the Russians Return from the Near Abroad?" p. 208; personal interview with Yuri Razgulyayev, chairman of the "inter-national" movement *Narodnoye yedinstvo*, Bishkek, February 24, 1994.

67. Aynur Elebayeva, "The Osh Incident: Problems for Research," *Post-Soviet Geography*, Vol. 33, No. 2 (February 1992): 79. See also A. Elebayeva, A. Dzhusupbekov, and N. Omuraliyev, *Oshskiy mezhnatsional'nyy konflikt: Sotsiologicheskiy analiz* (Bishkek: Otdel problem natsional'nykh otnosheniy, Institut filosofii i prava, Akademiya nauk Respubliki Kyrgyzstan, 1991).

68. Elebayeva, "The Osh Incident: Problems for Research;" Elebayeva, et al., *Oshskiy mezhnatsional'nyy konflikt: Sotsiologicheskiy analiz*; Gosudarstvennoye statisticheskoye agentstvo Kyrgyzsoy Respubliki, *Demograficheskii ezhegodnik Kyrgyzskoy Respubliki 1992* (Bishkek: Gosudarstvennoye statisticheskoye agentstvo Kyrgyzsoy Respubliki, 1993), pp. 193–195.

69. "Tajikistan's Tension Shows No Sign of Abating," *FBIS*-SOV No. 181 (September 18, 1990): 73–74.

70. Ginsberg et al., *Russkiye v novom zarubezh'e*, p. 94.

71. Galina Vitkovskaya, "Russians in the Non-Russian Former Republics," (paper presented at the workshop: *Geodemography of the Former Soviet Union*, Radford University, August 7, 1994). See also, Galina Vitkovskaya, *Vynuzhdennaya migratsiya: Problemy i perspektivy* (Moskva: Programma po Issledovaniyu Migratsii, Institut Narodnokhozyaystvennogo Prognozirovaniya, Rossiyskaya Akademiya Nauk, 1993), Vypusk III.

72. Kaiser, "Ethnic Demography and Interstate Relations," p. 251.

73. Vitkovskaya, *Vynuzhdennaya migratsiya*, pp. 17–18.

74. Vitkovskaya, *Vynuzhdennaya migratsiya*, p. 95.

75. Ginsberg et al., *Russkiye v novom zarubezh'e*, p. 90.

76. Leokadiya Drobizheva, "Etnicheskoye samosoznaniye russkikh v sovremennykh usloviyakh: ideologiya i praktika," *Sovetskaya etnografiya* no. 1 (1991): 5. In contrast to the Russian response, 80% of Uzbeks in Tashkent felt that Uzbekistan was their homeland.

77. Results are from a survey conducted by the All-Union Center of Public Opinion Research, as reprinted in Donald Carlisle, "Uzbekistan and the Uzbeks," *Problems of Communism* Vol. 40, No. 5 (September–October 1991):40.

78. Ginsberg, et al., *Russkiye v novom zarubezh'e*, p. 89.

79. Ginsberg, et al., *Russkiye v novom zarubezh'e*, p. 90.

80. Statkom SNG, *Itogi vsesoyuznoy perepisi naseleniya 1989 goda* (Minneapolis: East View, 1992), Vol. 12, pp. 649–654.

81. Statkom SNG, *Itogi vsesoyuznoy perepisi naseleniya 1989 goda*, Vol. 7, Part 2.

82. Ginsberg, et al., *Russkiye v novom zarubezh'e*, p. 90.

83. Statkom SNG, *Itogi vsesoyuznoy perepisi naseleniya 1989 goda*, Vol. 7, Part 2.

84. Suzanne Crow, "Kozyrev on Maintaining Conquests," RFE/RL *Research Report Supplement* Vol. 2, No. 41 (October 8, 1993):7.

85. Stephen Foye, "Russian Forces to Defend Against Fundamentalism," RFE/RL *News Briefs* (February 8–12, 1993):8.

86. "Grachev Arrives in Dushanbe, Discusses Border Situation," *FBIS*-SOV No. 136 (July 19, 1993):63.

Chapter 10

Transcaucasia

The Russian/titular relationships in Transcaucasia are similar, but not identical, to those in Central Asia. Russia's incorporation of Transcaucasia can be compared to the colonial conquest and control of Turkestan. A small number of Russians entered both regions as a ruling layer placed atop the indigenous societies. However, Central Asia became a magnet for skilled and urbanized Russians migrating from the European part of the country, and Russians established themselves as the hegemonic group in Central Asia's urban/industrial centers. With the exception of Baku, Russians never established the same local economic hegemony in Transcaucasia, and the region never served as a magnet for large-scale Russian in-migration.

Nationalization and sociocultural, economic, and political indigenization proceeded much further in Transcaucasia than in Central Asia. With little competitive advantage, fewer Russians migrated to Transcaucasia, and a net out-migration of Russians began relatively early in the 1960s. Since the late 1980s Russian emigration from Transcaucasia has been relatively greater than even the Central Asian rate. Although several thousand Russians—many of whose ancestors came to the region in the early nineteenth century—will undoubtedly remain in Transcaucasia, the overwhelming majority of Russians has left or is in the process of leaving.

Russian emigration from Transcaucasia is motivated by two fears similar to those expressed by the Russians of Central Asia: worsening inter-national relations and possible involvement in the violent inter-national conflict that has engulfed the region. The emigration is greater in Transcaucasia than in Central Asia both because inter-national conditions are worse and because the governments themselves are much more nationalistic. Nativism is not only a mass-based phenomenon among indigenes who feel relatively deprived but is also fostered by the ruling nationalist elites in each republic. While most of this state-sponsored nativism has been directed against non-Russians, Russians have also felt alienated because of the general rise in anti-outsider sentiments. In response, even greater proportions of Russians have left Transcaucasia than have left Central Asia.

Transcaucasia: Areas of Russian Concentration

TRANSCAUCASIA

	Georgia	Azerbaijan	Armenia
Territorial Size (km²)	69,700	86,600	29,800
Population Size (1/1/94)	5,425,700	7,430,700	3,741,600
Percent Titular (1989)	70.1	82.7	93.3
Percent Russian (1989)	6.3	5.6	1.6
Urban Population (1993)	3,004,000ᵃ	3,893,000ᵃ	2,533,000
Percent Titular (1989)	67.6	76.7	96.1
Percent Russian (1989)	9.8	9.8	2.0
Size of Capitol City (1/1/91)	1,279.000	1,080,500	1,125,458ᵇ
Percent of Titular (1989)	66.0	61.8	96.5
Percent Russian (1989)	10.0	18.0	1.9
Natural Increase (/1000, 1993)	7.9ᶜ	16.2	8.5
Titular NI (1989)	7.6	23.1	16.9
Russian NI (1989)	−2.0	−5.3	5.9
Life Expectancy (1989)	Men: 68.0 Women: 75.4	Men: 66.4 Women: 73.5	Men: 64.6 Women 67.4
Titular e⁰ (1989)	Men: 68.8 Women: 76.0	Men: 66.4 Women: 74.1	Men: 64.5 Women: 67.1
Russian e⁰ (1989)	Men: 63.3 Women:72.5	Men: 63.5 Women: 72.6	Men: 62.9 Women: 67.2
Net Migration To (−) From (+) Russia (1989–1993)			
Total	−165,291	−204,365	−53,885
Titular	332	22,751	−22,110
Russian	−95,636	−129,558	−21,337
Employment ᵈ (1993)	66.0ᵉ	74.4ᵉ	74.5
Trade (Export Import Ratio, 1993)			
Intra-NIS Tradeᶠ	0.48ᵍ	1.21	0.78
Extra-NIS Tradeʰ	1.43ᵍ	1.46	0.15

Notes. ᵃUrban population totals for Georgia and Azerbaijan are for 1992. ᵇFigure for Yerevan is from the 1989 census. ᶜFigure for NI in Georgia is for 1991. ᵈEmployment given as a percent of the working-age population. ᵉEmployment percents in Georgia and Azerbaijan are for 1992. ᶠIntra-NIS ratios calculated from trade among the republics of the former USSR and measured in the national currencies. ᵍTrade ratios for Georgia are for 1992. ʰExtra-NIS ratios calculated from trade with countries outside the former USSR and measured in US dollars.

Sources: Goskomstat SSSR, *Chislennost' naseleniya soyuznykh respublik po gorodskim poseleniyam i rayonam ma l yanvarya 1991 g.* (Moskva: 1991); Goskomstat Rossiyskoy Federatsii, *Chislennost' sotsial' no-demograficheskiye kharakteristiki russkogo naseleniya v respublikakh byvshego SSSR* (Moskva: 1994); Statisticheskiy komitet SNG, *Statisticheskiy byulleten'* No. 20 (June 1994): 35–36; Statkom SNG, *Itogi vsesoyuznoy perepisi naseleniya 1989 g.* (Minneapolis, MN: East View, 1992), Vol. 7, Part 2; Mikhael Guboglo, "Demography and Language in the Capitals of the Union Republics," *Journal of Soviet Nationalities* Vol. 1, No. 4 (Winter 1990–1991): 9–13; The World Bank, *Statistical Handbook 1994: States of the Former USSR* (Washington, DC: World Bank Studies of Economies in Transformation No. 14, 1994).

Nevertheless, the absence of a sizable Russian community in Transcaucasia does not mean that the region is unimportant to Russia. Transcaucasia retains geopolitical significance for Russia today for much the same reason as in the eighteenth and nineteenth centuries. Positioned between Russia, Turkey, and Iran, and with the homelands of Armenians and Azeris dissected by inter-state borders, Transcaucasia was a shatterbelt over which the Persian, Ottoman, and Russian Empires competed for control. Russia prevailed in this competition and turned Transcaucasia into a Russian colonial holding during the first three decades of the nineteenth century. Transcaucasia remained a Russian and Soviet possession, with the exception of a brief period of independence during the civil war (1918–1921). Since the late 1980s, the nations of Transcaucasia have reasserted their independence. However, surrounded by much more powerful neighbors, the region is likely again to become a shatterbelt over which Iran, Turkey, and Russia will compete for influence.[1]

Russians in Transcaucasia: 1800–1917

Georgia's annexation began as a voluntary accession to Russia as a protectorate to thwart incursions from Persia and Turkey, and was followed by formal annexation of eastern Georgia in 1801. The western Georgian provinces became Russian protectorates between 1803 and 1810, and were formally annexed between 1810 and 1867. In two successful wars with Persia, Russia gained control of northern Azerbaijan (1804–1813), and eastern Armenia (1826–1828). Russia was also successful in war against the Ottoman Turks, gaining the port cities of Poti and Sukhumi in the Treaty of Adrianople (1829) and the Kars region in 1878.[2] With the exception of the loss of Kars to Turkey at the end of World War I and the brief independence which Georgia, Azerbaijan, and Armenia experienced between 1918 and 1921, Transcaucasia remained a Russian and then Soviet possession until 1991.

Russian colonization of the Caucasus region was similar to the pattern followed in Kazakhstan and Central Asia. The northern Caucasus steppe zone (i.e., Kuban, Stavropol', and Tersk guberniyas), like northern Kazakhstan, became a frontier into which an estimated 1.4 million Russian and Ukrainian peasants migrated between 1871 and 1916, overwhelming the indigenous peoples.[3] By 1897, most of the people were "Russian."[4]

Population	Stavropol' %	Kuban %	Tersk %
Great Russian	55	43	29
Ukrainian	37	48	5
"Russian"	92	91	34

In contrast to the Russian frontier settlement of the northern Caucasus steppe, Russia viewed "Transcaucasia as a supplier of raw materials rather than an area to be developed economically."[5] In this respect the imperialistic relationship between Russia and Transcaucasia was similar to that between Russia and Turkestan. Russian in-migration during the tsarist era was limited by the lack of economic development and by the prior development of an Armenian-dominated merchant class. Russians entering Transcaucasia were primarily military and administrative personnel who settled overwhelmingly in cities, particularly in Tiflis (Tbilisi) and Baku. Even with the economic development that took place during the last third of the nineteenth century, this ethnically differentiated structure did not change, although it was made more complex by the increasing in-migration of unskilled indigenes to the cities in search of work.[6]

The number of Russians in Transcaucasia increased eight-fold from 32,000 in 1858 to 261,000 by 1897. Even by the latter date Russians represented only 5 percent of the region's total population, and only 0.5 percent of all Russians in the empire.[7] Russians and Ukrainians together comprised no more than 10 percent of any one guberniya or oblast in Transcaucasia in 1897.[8] However, they made up over one-third of the population and were the largest ethnic component of Baku, an oil boom town that attracted thousands of Russians after 1870.[9] The number of Russians in Transcaucasia increased to 474,000 by 1917, but still constituted only 6 percent of the total population in Transcaucasia and less than 1 percent of all Russians in the empire.[10]

Nationalization had advanced further in Transcaucasia than in Central Asia by the turn of the twentieth century. Azeri, Armenian, and Georgian nationalized intelligentsias were discernible by the last quarter of the nineteenth century, and mass-based nationalization was occurring by the end of the tsarist era. Indigenous rural to urban migration was much greater in Transcaucasia than in Turkestan. As indigenes entered their homelands' cities, they increasingly came into contact and competition with socially mobilized nonindigenes. Georgians entering Tiflis and Azeris entering Baku faced an ethnic stratification system in which they found themselves at a competitive disadvantage with economically dominant Armenians and politically dominant Russians. The nationalization process of Georgians and Azeris was thus both anti-Armenian and anti-Russian and reflected a rising sense of national exclusiveness among the indigenous urban/industrial work force.[11] The anti-Armenian reaction by Azeris migrating to Baku and finding the local economy dominated by Armenians was a critical catalyst in the Armenian-Azerbaijani War of 1905. The war in turn became a potent agent facilitating further Azeri nationalization.[12]

For Armenians in Yerevan guberniya, social mobilization was restricted by the lack of economic development rather than by the existence of an ethnic stratification system dominated by nonindigenes. The capital city of Yerevan remained "a sleepy oriental town of 30,000 in 1914."[13] Russians and Ukrainians made up only 2 percent of Yerevan's total population in 1897; Azeris were 38 percent of the population, but they did not represent an economic or a political elite.[14] For the most part, socially mobilized Armenians lived and worked in the cities outside Yerevan guberniya, and this geographic separation of elites and masses impeded the nationalization process. Armenian nationalism rose during the first two decades of the twentieth century, but this was primarily a reaction against threats to the Armenian people and homeland posed by both the Ottoman and Azeri Turks.

Local Russians served as only a minor catalyst for the rising nationalism found in Azerbaijan and Georgia during the last four decades of the tsarist era, and did not play this role in Armenia. Indigenous nationalism coincided with a rising sense of exclusiveness against outsiders, but the foreigners against whom the indigenes rallied were primarily Armenians in Georgia and Azerbaijan, and Turks in Armenia.

Between 1918 and 1921, Georgia, Armenia, and Azerbaijan all gained independence from Russia. However, this independence was born of necessity rather than as an affirmation of national self-determination. The collapse of tsarist authority and the flood of Russian soldiers into the region as they left the front with Turkey necessitated greater political, military, and economic autonomy. Similarly, outright independence, declared by the Transcaucasian Federative Republic on April 9, 1918, was forced on Transcaucasia by Turkey, which set this independence as a precondition for peace negotiations.[15] The following month Georgia declared its independence from the federation. However, this move was taken out of concern about a possible Azerbaijani-Turkish alliance and taken at the suggestion of Germany, rather than as an assertion of Georgian national self-determination. Likewise, Armenia and Azerbaijan declared their independence because of Georgia's declaration.[16]

During the two years of independence, Georgia, Azerbaijan, and Armenia had little real autonomy. They again constituted a geopolitical shatterbelt over which Germany, Turkey, Britain, France, and the emergent Soviet Union competed for control. Nevertheless, Georgian, Azeri, and Armenian nationalists today remember this short period as a golden age in their nations' histories. The symbols of statehood adopted prior to the Soviet takeover reappeared at the end of the 1980s as the titular nationalists again declared their sovereignty. An April 9, 1989, demonstration in Tbilisi commemorating Georgia's original day of independence from the Russian Empire became the scene of violent conflict between Georgian nationalists and Soviet troops, imbuing this date with even greater meaning. In addition, both Georgia and Armenia based the legitimacy of their declarations of independence in 1990 on their independence between 1918 and 1921. Thus, the period of nominal independence during which all three states were dominated by outside powers has nonetheless become a historic event of transcendent importance for nationalists today.

Russians in Transcaucasia: The Soviet Era

The Russian population declined dramatically in Georgia and slightly in Azerbaijan between 1917 and 1926 (Table 10.1). A combination of factors contributed to this decrease, including domination by foreign powers hostile to

Russia (and presumably to Russians), excess mortality caused by war, return migration of many Russians attracted by the promise of a share of land in Russia (and afraid that they would miss out if they remained in independent Transcaucasia), and a rise in indigenization and nativism among indigenes during the short period of independence.[17]

Armenia, Azerbaijan, and Georgia were conquered and reincorporated into the USSR as the Transcaucasian Soviet Federated Socialist Republic. The decision to amalgamate the three republics was in part a reflection of the weak position of local Russians in Georgia, particularly compared to Baku, the capital from which the TCSFSR was run. In addition, combining the three republics into one federated republic reduced the risk of secession from the USSR; under the Soviet system, self-determination, up to and including secession, was a right applied to the constituent republics, not to their territorial subdivisions or titular nations. In 1936 the TCSFSR was dissolved and replaced by the Georgian, Armenian, and Azerbaijan Soviet Socialist Republics; by then Moscow had reestablished firm control in the region.[18]

As noted previously, local Russians lost status during the brief period of Transcaucasian independence. Reincorporation into the USSR did not immediately alter their standing vis-à-vis members of the titular nations. As in the USSR's other national homelands in the 1920s, Moscow promoted the indigenization of political and economic elites, the education system, and other sociocultural institutions in Transcaucasia. Though each national homeland had not been given union republic status, indigenization was promoted in all three homelands.

Indigenization was particularly extensive in Armenia and Georgia. In Azerbaijan, indigenization was tempered by the center's interest in maintaining control over Baku's oil, the center's fears of pan-Turkic and pan-Islamic sentiments among indigenous elites, and the area's potential for irredentism.[19] With relatively high levels of literacy and education, both Armenians and Georgians were able to take advantage of opportunities afforded by *korenizatsiya*. By 1939 all three republics had literacy rates over eighty percent. Georgians and Armenians exceeded their republics' averages for educational attainment in both urban and rural areas, and had higher urban rates than Russians. Azeris continued to lag behind both the republic averages and the Russian rates in both urban and rural locations.[20]

Politically, Georgians came to dominate local party and governmental structures by the end of the 1920s, largely at the expense of Russians and Armenians.[21] Armenians also dominated the local bases of political power in Armenia. However, Azeris lost ground between 1923 and 1925 to both Russians and Armenians. In 1925, 76 percent of Russian Communists in Transcaucasia were in Azerbaijan, where they comprised 38 percent of the Azerbaijan Communist party. Azeris accounted for only 43 percent of the Azerbaijan Communist party, compared to a Georgian rate of 93 percent in Georgia and an Armenian rate of 71 percent in Armenia.[22]

This dichotomy in Transcaucasia was also apparent in the occupation structure. Georgians were relatively under-represented in high status occupations in

Table 10.1

Russians in Transcaucasia, 1917–1989 (Absolute and Percent)

Republic	Total Number of Russians (000s)							Russians as a Percent of Total Population						
	1917	1926	1939	1959	1970	1979	1989	1917	1926	1939	1959	1970	1979	1989
Georgia	190	96	309	408	397	372	341	6.7	3.6	8.7	10.1	8.5	7.4	6.3
Azerbaijan	224	221	528	501	510	475	392	8.7	9.6	16.5	13.6	10.0	7.9	5.6
Armenia	13	20	51	56	66	70	52	1.2	2.3	4.0	3.2	2.7	2.3	1.6

Source: 1917–79: S. Bruk and V. Kabuzan, "Dinamika chislennosti i rasseleniya Russkikh posle Velikoy Oktyabr'skoy Sotsialisticheskoy Revolyutsii," *Sovetskaya etnografiya* No. 5 (1982): 7.

Georgia in 1926, but had become over-represented by 1939. Armenians were relatively over-represented in high status occupations in Armenia in both years. Indigenization of high status occupations reflects the greater competitive advantages enjoyed by Armenians and Georgians in their homelands, and helps explain why Russian in-migration to these two republics was relatively limited.[23] In contrast to the indigenization in Armenia and Georgia, Azeris were relatively underrepresented in high status occupations in Azerbaijan in both 1926 and 1939, although they had come closer to parity by 1939.[24] Azerbaijan and the status of Azeris in their homeland were more comparable to Central Asia than to the other Transcaucasian republics.

Georgians and Armenians lost some of their competitive advantage during the 1930s, when *korenizatsiya* was replaced by russification throughout the USSR. This shift from an indigenes-first to a Russians-first policy encouraged Russian in-migration to the cities of all three republics between the 1930s and the 1950s. However, even while the Russian language and culture attained the status of "first among equals," Georgians and Armenians retained dominance in their respective homelands, and the cities of Azerbaijan actually experienced a demographic indigenization. Only in Georgia did Russian population growth (total and urban) exceed the indigenous rate between 1926 and 1959 (Table 10.2). The limited demographic russification of cities is also distinct from Central Asia, where cities became Russian demographic and cultural enclaves during this period.

Between 1959 and 1989, even the limited demographic russification of the previous two decades was reversed. First, as in Central Asia, indigenous natural increase was relatively high during this period, particularly among Azeris. Second, Armenians living outside Armenia migrated to their homeland in increasing numbers over these thirty years. The Armenian in-migrants came primarily from the other republics of Transcaucasia, and therefore also increased the demographic indigenization of Azerbaijan and Georgia. Third, beginning as early

Table 10.2
Indigenous and Russian Percent of the Total and Urban Population,
by Republic 1926–1959

	Total				Urban			
	Indigenes		Russians		Indigenes		Russians	
Republic	1926	1959	1926	1959	1926	1959	1926	1959
Georgia	67.0	64.3	3.6	10.1	48.2	52.9	11.8	18.8
Azerbaijan	62.1	67.4	9.6	13.6	37.6	51.3	27.0	24.8
Armenia	84.4	88.0	2.3	3.2	89.3	91.9	3.2	4.5

Source: V. Kozlov, *Natsional'nosti SSSR* (Moskva: Statistika, 1975), pp. 86–88.

Table 10.3

Titular Nation as a Percent of Total Population,
and Percent of Titular Nation Living in the Home Republic, 1959–1989

Republic	Indigenous % of Total Population				% of Indigenes in Republic			
	1959	1970	1979	1989	1959	1970	1979	1989
Georgia	64.3	66.8	68.8	70.1	96.6	96.5	96.1	95.1
Azerbaijan	67.5	73.8	78.1	82.7	84.9	86.2	86.0	85.7
Armenia	88.0	88.6	89.7	93.3	55.7	62.0	65.6	66.7

Source: Robert Kaiser, "Nationalism: The Challenge to Soviet Federalism," in Michael Bradshaw, ed., *The Soviet Union: A New Regional Geography?* (London: Belhaven, 1991), p. 50.

as 1960, a net out-migration of Russians from Transcaucasia began, preceding the onset of out-migration of Russians from Central Asia by more than a decade (Table 10.3).

Demographic indigenization in Transcaucasia occurred in cities as well as in the countryside (Table 10.4). Russians had never demographically, culturally or economically dominated the urban/industrial sector of this region as they had in Central Asia. The only Transcaucasian capital that came close to the russification found in Central Asian was Baku, but even here Russian domination was more limited.

The social, political, and economic indigenization in Transcaucasia coincided with demographic indigenization. Russians and members of other non-titular nations faced increased competition from upwardly mobile indigenes, who were increasingly favored in their own homelands. This favoritism was especially true of Georgians in Georgia and Armenians in Armenia, but also applied to Azeris in Azerbaijan.

Indigenes were particularly favored in access to higher education (Table 10.5). Georgians were the most over-represented group, but both Armenians and Azeris were also over-represented. In contrast to the situation in Central Asia, these three groups had attained dominance by 1959, and indigenous domination of higher education in both Georgia and Azerbaijan increased during the next thirty years. Armenians, whose degree of over-representation fell between 1970 and 1989, provide the only exception to this pattern, but Armenians constituted nearly 100 percent of both the general and student population and thus could hardly increase their numbers.

Russians were under-represented in higher education in Georgia. The Russian proportion of students was approximately equal to the Russian proportion of the total population in Armenia, and Russians were slightly over-represented in Azerbaijan. In addition, Russians were concentrated in the technical higher educational institutions (*VUZy*) such as the Oil and Gas Institute, while Azeris were over-represented in Azerbaijan State University.[25] Overall,

Table 10.4

The Derussification of Cities in Transcaucasia, 1959–1989

(Russian percent of urban and capital city population, and Russian concentration in urban areas)

Republic	Russian % of Urban				Russian % of Capitals				% of Russians in Urban			
	1959	1970	1979	1989	1959	1970	1979	1989	1959	1970	1979	1989
Georgia	18.8	14.7	12.4	9.8	18.1	14.0	12.3	10.0	79.1	82.8	84.9	86.3
Azerbaijan	24.9	18.3	14.1	9.8	34.7	27.7	22.7	18.0	87.6	92.2	94.1	95.0
Armenia	4.5	3.5	2.9	2.0	4.4	2.9	2.6	1.9	71.0	79.4	82.5	85.2

Source: 1959: Tsentral'noye statisticheskoye upravleniye pri Sovete Ministrov SSSR (Ts SU SSSR), *Itegi vsesoyuznoy perepisi naseleniya 1959 goda* (Moskva: Gosstatizdat, 1963), Gruzinskaya SSR, Azerbaydzhanskaya SSR, Armyanskaya SSR volumes, table 53; 1970: Ts SU SSSR, *Itogi vsesoyuznoy perepisi naseleniya 1970 goda* (Moskva: Statistika, 1973), Vol. 4; 1979: Goskomstat SSSR, *Itogi vsesoyuznoy perepisi naseleniya 1979 goda* (Moskva: Goskomstat SSSR, 1989), Vol. 4, Part 1, Book 3; 1989: Statkom SNG, *Itogi vsesoyuznoy perepisi naseleniya 1989 goda* (Minneapolis: East View, 1992), Vol. 7, Part 2; Capitals: Mikhael Guboglo, "Demography and Language in the Capitals of the Union Republics," *Journal of Soviet Nationalities* Vol. 1, No. 4 (Winter 1990–1991): 22–26.

Table 10.5
Indigenous Proportions of Students Entering Higher Education, 1959–1989
(Percent of Students, and Indexed Values[a])

Republic	Indigenous % of Students			Indexed Values		
	1960/61	1970/71	1989/90	1959	1970	1989
Georgia	77	83	89	120.3	123.9	127.1
Azerbaijan	71	78	91	104.4	105.4	109.6
Armenia	94	96	99	106.8	107.9	106.5

Notes: [a]Indexed Values = Indigenous % of Students/Indigenous % of Total Population. A value over 100.0 indicates indigenous over-representation, a value of 100.0 indicates parity, and a value of less than 100.0 indicates under-representation.

Source: 1959–1970: Rasma Karklins, "Ethnic Politics and Access to Higher Education: The Soviet Case," *Comparative Politics* (April 1984): 284; 1989–90: see Table 4.1.

Russians were in a less competitive position regarding their access to higher education only in Estonia.[26]

The indigenous domination of higher education went beyond the number of students admitted. In Armenia and Georgia, indigenous languages were the primary languages of instruction, and the linguistic russification of schools was much less apparent than in Central Asia. Azeri was not as dominant in Azerbaijan as Armenian and Georgian were in their respective homelands, but it too was in a relatively better position than the indigenous languages of Central Asia.[27] Azeris had resisted enhancing the status of the Russian language in schools during the late 1950s, while at the same time the Azeri language became a required subject of study in Russian-language schools.[28] The indigenous languages in all three Transcaucasian union republics had become official state languages long before the late 1980s; attempts by Moscow to eliminate this clause from the 1978 Georgian Constitution resulted in demonstrations in Tbilisi and the restoration of the language clause.

The growing strength of the indigenous languages is reflected in the linguistic derussification that indigenes experienced between 1959 and 1989 (Table 10.6). This linguistic indigenization was particularly intense in urban areas, and was indicative of the declining dominance of Russians in the urban/industrial sectors of Transcaucasia. The decreasing proportion of indigenes claiming Russian as their native language was especially dramatic between 1959 and 1970 in Armenia and Azerbaijan. In 1970 a "second-language" question was added to the census; a number of indigenes who had claimed Russian as their native language in 1959 apparently demoted Russian to a second language, claiming their indigenous language as their language of first choice. Another substantial decrease occurred between the 1979 and 1989 censuses, reflecting the region's rising nationalism.

Table 10.6
Percent of Indigenes Claiming Russian as Their First Language,
1959–1989 (Urban and Rural)

Republic	Urban					Rural				
	1959	1970	1979	1989	% point change	1959	1970	1979	1989	% point change
Georgia	1.1	0.9	0.9	0.4	−0.7	0.1	0.1	0.1	0.0	−0.1
Azerbaijan	2.1	1.8	2.2	0.7	−1.4	0.1	0.0	0.1	0.1	0.0
Armenia	1.3	0.3	0.7	0.3	−1.0	0.1	0.0	0.2	0.3	0.2

Source: Robert Kaiser, *The Geography of Nationalism in Russia and the USSR*, p. 276.

Fluency in the Russian language was nonetheless increasing among indigenes in both urban and rural areas throughout this period (Table 10.7). However, almost all of the increase in Georgia and Azerbaijan occurred during the 1970s; very little change was registered during the 1980s, with the exception of rural Georgians. In Armenia, the increasing proportion of Armenians claiming Russian fluency during both the 1970s and 1980s was caused mostly by the in-migration of Armenians who had lived outside Armenia for a substantial period of time, and who thus tended to be fluent in Russian.

In Transcaucasia, the linguistic assimilation of Russians to the titular languages was higher than the linguistic russification of indigenes in Georgia and Armenia. This linguistic indigenization of Russians was also higher in the capital than in the republic as a whole in Georgia and Armenia, providing further evidence that the titular nations rather than Russians had established dominance in these two republics. A substantial proportion of Russians also claimed fluency in

Table 10.7
Percent of Indigenes Claiming Russian as a Second Language,
1959–1989 (Urban and Rural)

Republic	Urban				Rural			
	1970	1979	1989	% pt change	1970	1979	1989	% pt change
Georgia	35.8	38.7	39.7	3.9	8.3	13.4	22.7	14.4
Azerbaijan	29.7	41.7	45.1	15.4	4.6	16.1	18.8	14.2
Armenia	31.6	41.7	51.5	19.9	9.5	17.7	28.3	18.8

Source: 1970: Ts SU SSSR, *Itogi vsesoyuznoy perepisi naseleniya 1970 goda* (Moskva: Statistika, 1973), Vol. 4; *1979:* Goskomstat SSSR, *Itogi vsesoyuznoy perepisi naseleniya 1979 goda* (Moskva: Goskomstat SSSR, 1989), Vol. 4, Part 1, Book 3; *1989:* Statkom SNG, *Itogi vsesoyuznoy perepisi naseleniya 1989 goda* (Minneapolis: East View, 1992), Vol. 7, Part 2.

Table 10.8

Russians Claiming the Indigenous Language as a First or Second Language, 1989
(Percent in Republic and in Capital Cities)

Republic	% Claiming Indigenous Language as First Language		% Claiming Indigenous Language as Second Language	
	Total	Capital	Total	Capital
Georgia	1.2	1.9	22.5	42.6
Azerbaijan	0.2	0.1	14.3	11.6
Armenia	1.4	1.6	32.2	34.5

Source: Statkom SNG, *Itogi vsesoyuznoy perepisi naseleniya 1989 goda* (Minneapolis: East View, 1992), Vol. 7, Part 2.

Georgian and Armenian as second languages (Table 10.8). In Azerbaijan, the linguistic indigenization of Russians was more limited, and was lower in Baku than in the republic as a whole. This also held true for Russians who claimed fluency in Azeri as a second language, making the Russian-titular relationship in Azerbaijan closer to the situation found in Central Asia than in Georgia and Armenia.

The titular nations of Transcaucasia were also among the most dominant in high-status employment. Only the Baltic nations were at a comparable rate of over-representation in the high-end economic category "directors of enterprises" (Table 4.1). Data for local and republic-level political representation are not available, but indigenous political dominance—particularly in Georgia and Armenia—was clearly well-established by the late 1950s.[29]

The sociocultural, economic, and political indigenization occurring in Transcaucasia between 1959 and 1989 placed greater competitive pressures on local Russians than existed in Central Asia, and the indigenous push for dominance occurred much earlier. As a result of the increasing subordination of Russians to members of the titular nations (particularly in Armenia and Georgia), Russians began to emigrate from Transcaucasia as early as 1960.[30] An estimated 359,000 Russians left Azerbaijan and Georgia between 1959 and 1989, with the number increasing over time.[31] The same indigenization process was reducing the competitive advantages historically enjoyed by Armenians in Baku and Tbilisi, leading an increasing number of them to migrate to Armenia. This process furthered the national homogenization of all three Transcaucasian homelands.

Russification processes in Transcaucasia were mostly limited to the urban/industrial centers. However, because the titular nations of Transcaucasia—and particularly the Armenians and Georgians—were much more urbanized and socially mobilized than the Central Asians, Russians had greater difficulty establishing hegemony in Transcaucasia. Indigenes were relatively more successful in gaining a privileged sociocultural, economic, and political status in their own homelands, and Armenians and Georgians attained a dominant position during the last three decades of the Soviet era. If the Russian-titular relationship is characterized as "internal colonialism," then the process of decolonization was well underway in Armenia and Georgia as early as the mid–1950s.

Azeris were improving their position vis-à-vis Russians and Armenians in Baku and elsewhere in Azerbaijan, but continued to lag behind these two socially mobilized groups. For Azeris, rapidly rising educational attainment and socioeconomic expectations were comparable to the experience of the titular groups in the Central Asian republics. Although Azeris were relatively more successful than Central Asians in becoming upwardly mobile and attaining elite positions, a sense of relative deprivation among those who perceived their pathways to be blocked by Russians and Armenians developed, as did a rising anti-outsider nativism. In this way, Russian-titular relations in Azerbaijan are again more comparable to developments in Central Asia than to those in Georgia and Armenia.

Independence Movements, Inter-National Conflict, and Russian Emigration

Russian emigration from Transcaucasia has increased dramatically since 1989. As in Central Asia, the reasons for the increasing emigration are related to precipitous economic decline in the region, an increase in indigenization pressures on Russians, and an increase in anti-outsider nativism resulting in violent inter-national conflict. Russians have not often been the direct targets of such nativism, but they clearly feel persecuted in all three states.[32] The degree of political instability, the intensity of inter-national conflict, and the level of state-sponsored national exclusivity are much greater in Transcaucasia than in Central Asia. This more hostile, nativistic environment, coupled with the relatively more hegemonic position of the titular nations in their homelands, has increased the pressure on Russians and members of other nontitular groups to leave.

A dramatic national homogenization process has occurred in each of the three states. The processes in Armenia and Azerbaijan have approximated the "ethnic cleansing" found in Bosnia, as Armenians have been forced to flee Azerbaijan for Armenia and Azeris have been forced out of Armenia. At a more local geographic scale, Azeris have been cleared from Nagorno-Karabakh and the borderlands between Armenia and Nagorno-Karabakh, Georgians have fled the ethnoterritorial conflict in Abkhazia, and Ossetian refugees have left Georgia for North Ossetia.

Inter-national conflict over the territorial extent of each national homeland has engulfed the entire region, delaying the passage of new constitutions and citizenship laws in all three states. It has also undermined the process of democratization and the establishment of law-governed societies.[33] As in Central Asia, this lack of democracy is not necessarily viewed unfavorably by the Russian minority. However, both the success of nationalistic forces and political instability are perceived as threats by the dwindling Russian minorities.

The overwhelming Russian response to these perceived threats has been emigration, and one would predict from the model of interactive nationalism that this response should be greatest in the state with the most nationalistic and hegemony-seeking titular group. However, the scale of emigration does not correspond to the degree of national exclusivity displayed by the titular elites (Table 10.9).

Georgia has been the most nationalistic republic in the region. Unlike most of the other successor states, Georgia's language law contains no reference to the equality of languages or to Russian as the language of inter-national communication.[34] Official publications are published only in Georgian, and by 1992 one had a difficult time conversing in Russian in hotels and shops.[35] Georgia was also the only Transcaucasian republic that refused to participate in discussions on the renewal and redefinition of the union, and instead focused on restoring its independence lost in 1921. The 1921 constitution was readopted after independence, as were the 1918–1921 symbols of statehood. Former President Zviad Gamsakhurdia proposed that citizenship be based on the population of independent Georgia, and stated that he was not certain whether 1921 or 1801 would be the date adopted.[36] As in the Baltics, such an approach would make all Soviet-era immigrants ineligible for citizenship. Gamsakhurdia also declared that all autonomous lands in Georgia belong exclusively to Georgia, and accused first the USSR and then Russia of fomenting inter-national conflict in Georgia in order to reconquer the republic.[37]

Despite such anti-Russian laws and sentiments, Russian emigration was proportionately lower from Georgia than from Azerbaijan or Armenia. It is interesting, however, that the lull in emigration found elsewhere in 1991 did not occur in Georgia, supporting the conclusion that the lower level of emigration from other republics was tied to the improved political climate brought on by the new confederal arrangements negotiated in April of that year. Georgian nationalist political elites refused to participate in this process, and pushed instead for complete independence from the USSR, which encouraged an increasing number of Russians to leave.

Azerbaijan until 1992 was the least nationalistic of the three states. Its language law was the most inter-nationalist, emphasizing the importance of Russian and the equality of all languages in the republic.[38] It was the only Transcaucasian republic to declare its sovereignty as a union republic within the USSR, rather than its independence from the Soviet Union. Azerbaijan also based its sovereignty declaration on "the inalienable right of the people of the Azerbaijani SSR to determine . . . their destiny," and on "the Treaty on the Formation of the USSR and the provisions of the current USSR Constitution."[39] The "Act of Independence" of October 18, 1991, also emphasized inter-national equality in the republic, not Azeri dominance.[40] The relatively pro-Russian Communist party retained power in Azerbaijan until 1992, and this too should have been seen as a stabilizing factor by Russians. However, Russian emigration was greatest from Azerbaijan in numerical terms and second in proportional terms of the Transcaucasian republics.

Table 10.9

Total and Russian Net Migration from Transcaucasia to Russia, 1989–1993

Republic	Total (000s)					Russians (000s)					Russian % of Total Emigration					Emigrants as a % of Russians in 1989
	1989	1990	1991	1992	1993	1989	1990	1991	1992	1993	1989	1990	1991	1992	1993	
Armenia	8.6	1.4	4.1	12.0	27.8	3.4	3.6	3.3	5.5	6.4	39.5	257.1	80.5	45.8	23.0	43.0
Azerbaijan	37.7	52.0	20.8	50.7	43.2	11.0	42.9	17.6	35.1	22.9	29.2	82.5	84.6	69.2	53.0	33.0
Georgia	10.9	14.5	28.8	46.2	65.1	4.6	9.5	18.1	29.7	33.8	42.2	65.5	62.8	64.3	51.9	28.0
Transcaucasia	57.2	67.9	53.7	108.9	136.1	19.0	56.0	39.0	70.3	63.1	33.2	82.5	72.6	65.6	46.4	31.5

Source: Lee Schwartz, paper presented in the roundtable discussion "Emerging Regional, Political, and Social Issues in Russia," at the 91st Annual Meetings of the Association of American Geographers, Chicago, 14–18 March, 1995.

Armenia's state-sponsored nationalism occupied a middle position between Georgia and Azerbaijan during this period. The language law emphasized the importance of strengthening the position of Armenian, but acknowledged Russian as the language of inter-national communication.[41] Armenia declared its intention to secede from the USSR in 1990, basing this decision on its independence in 1918, on the right of nations to self-determination, and on its right to take responsibility for the fate of the Armenian people.[42] However, Armenia also declared its intention to follow the law on secession passed by the USSR earlier that year.[43] This declaration also included a "zero option" citizenship clause and a statement that "diaspora Armenians have the right to citizenship in the Armenian Republic," without specifying the conditions that they would have to fulfill in order to become citizens.[44] Armenia also maintained observer status during the negotiations for a new union treaty, and joined the CIS. Yet in proportional terms, Russian emigration was greatest from Armenia; nearly one-half of all Russians living in Armenia in 1989 had left by 1993.

Beyond state-sponsored nationalism, Russian emigration throughout Transcaucasia has been in response to the rapidity of economic decline (which posed a threat to their material well-being), as well as to the degree of political instability and inter-national violence found in each republic. Russian emigration from Armenia has been driven mostly by the precipitous decline in living standards since the initiation of the war with Azerbaijan over the status of Nagorno-Karabakh.

The severe economic hardships caused by this inter-national and inter-state conflict have convinced an increasing number of Armenians as well as Russians that their future lies elsewhere. According to the Russian embassy in Yerevan, approximately 10,000 Armenians wish to adopt Russian citizenship and emigrate to the Russian Federation.[45] A poll taken in November, 1993, also indicated that 70 percent of the population wants to emigrate because of the economic situation and the war.[46]

Economic hardship—even economic hardship borne of inter-national conflict—does not qualify those seeking to leave Armenia for refugee status. This inability to attain refugee status holds whether they attempt to emigrate to Europe, the United States, or Russia, the latter of which has adopted a law on refugees similar to international law.[47] Relatively few people who migrated to Russia from Armenia sought refugee status between July 1, 1992, and September 1, 1993 (2,023), and only 816 (40.3 percent) were approved. This approval rate was the lowest in Transcaucasia.[48]

The refugee status of Armenians and Russians seeking to leave Armenia highlights the artificiality of the division between economically-motivated and politically-motivated emigration. Surveys indicated that the principal reason people wished to leave Armenia in 1990 and 1991 was "worsening inter-national relations," not economic collapse.[49] Economic conditions subsequently deteriorated due to the "worsening inter-national relations," yet today few who wish to leave the republic (except Azeris) are treated as refugees. Nevertheless, until the conflict over Nagorno-Karabakh is resolved and inter-state relations are normalized, the economic crisis in Armenia will continue and the pressure on Russians to leave will likely increase.

The primacy of economic problems in explaining why Russians in Armenia wish to emigrate does not imply that political conditions are positive. Democratization has been derailed by the conflict with Azerbaijan; no constitution or citizenship law has yet been passed. The relatively moderate President Levon Ter-Petrosyan has also increasingly accumulated power in his own hands.[50] He is opposed by more nationalistic Armenians (the National Pact) who have demanded his resignation because of the poor economy and the failure to provide sufficient support for Nagorno-Karabakh.[51] Should Ter-Petrosyan lose power, which may well occur in a more democratic Armenia, Russians will face even more pressure to leave. In Armenia as in most other successor states, majoritarian democracy implies greater titular domination of the political, social, and economic environment.

Russian emigration from Azerbaijan resembles the pattern found in Tajikistan, though the flight from Azerbaijan is not as intense. First, Russians in Azerbaijan were highly concentrated in Baku; 75 percent of all Russians living in the republic lived in the capital, compared to only 37 percent in Tbilisi and 43 percent in Yerevan.[52] Russians in Azerbaijan have therefore been especially effected by changes in the capital's political climate. Unlike Yerevan or Tbilisi, Baku and its suburbs have been rocked by violent inter-national conflict since 1987. In January 1990, Baku was the scene of anti-Armenian pogroms, which led to the intervention of Soviet troops and their over-reaction against the Azeri population. These events sparked increased anti-Soviet and anti-Russian sentiments in the capital, and consequently an escalation of Russian emigration during that year.[53] During 1991, the Communist party retained power through what most analysts consider to have been fraudulent elections held in September 1990. This kept the more nationalistic and anti-Russian Popular Front from political power. Russians in Baku perceived the retention of power by the Communist party as a stabilizing factor, and this plus Azerbaijan's participation in the new union treaty discussions helps to explain the sharp decline in Russian emigration in 1991.

The next year was marked by political turmoil in the capital and renewed conflict over Nagorno-Karabakh, which in turn provoked increased Russian emigration. Between March 6 and June 7, 1992, the political leadership changed three times, twice by force. Elchibey, the Popular Front leader elected on June 7, was perceived as pro-Turkey and anti-Russian, though once in office the Popular Front moderated its anti-Russian rhetoric. Nevertheless, a survey on reasons for emigration taken at that time found that Azerbaijan had a higher proportion of emigres (47.9 percent) who cited "worsening inter-national relations" than any other republic in the former USSR.[54]

Russians in Baku complained to representatives of the Helsinki Commission in 1992 about antiforeigner discrimination, restrictions on the use of the Russian language, and the seizure of apartments by Azeri refugees from the war with

Armenia.[55] The Azerbaijani government and the Popular Front attempted to reassure the Russians, and issued a decree on September 16, 1992, to protect national minority rights.[56] Nonetheless, Russian fear of Azeri persecution caused a sharp escalation in emigration to Russia. Most of these emigres were treated as refugees: of the 71,109 emigres from Azerbaijan who applied for refugee status in Russia, 61,924 (87.1 percent) received it.[57]

When the war over Nagorno-Karabakh escalated in 1993, Azerbaijan lost control over much of its western territory, and political instability increased once again. Elchibey was forced to resign over war losses, and Geidar Aliyev was elected in October.[58] An estimated 1.1 million refugees—most of them internally displaced Azeris—were living in Azerbaijan by June 1994.[59] This placed additional pressure on Russians and other non-Azeris to leave.

Until the conflict over Nagorno-Karabakh is resolved, Azerbaijan, like Armenia, will remain politically unstable and Russians and other non-Azeris will continue to emigrate. While a cease-fire was signed in May 1994, it did not resolve the basic conflict between Azeris, who view the territorial integrity of Azerbaijan as an issue beyond compromise, and Armenians, who view their right to national self-determination (in Nagorno-Karabakh) in a similarly uncompromising way.[60]

Unlike the pattern in Armenia and Azerbaijan, Russian emigration from Georgia increased every year between 1989 and 1993 (Table 10.9). The relatively low level of emigration in 1989 and 1990 probably resulted from the limited degree to which Russian-Georgian relations changed during this period. As noted above, the Georgian law on language and declaration of independence were more exclusionary than those of Armenia and Azerbaijan. However, Georgians had become dominant in their homeland by the late Soviet era, and the Russians who chose to live in Georgia had undoubtedly already accommodated themselves to this reality. The April 9, 1989, demonstration in Tbilisi and the Soviet overreaction heightened anti-Soviet and pro-independence sentiments among Georgians. These sentiments were in part also anti-Russian, but aside from a generally more hostile atmosphere, no violence against Russians occurred. Georgia's high standard of living was apparently enough to offset the growing anti-Russian climate and the increasing political instability during 1989 and 1990.

The election of Gamsakhurdia as president in October 1990 changed this situation. Both exclusionary nationalism and pressure for secession increased dramatically from that point forward. Georgia refused to participate in negotiations for a new union treaty, and in place of the March 1991, all-union referendum on the future of the USSR, Georgia held its own referendum on independence, which was supported by an overwhelming majority of the electorate. The readoption of the 1921 Constitution, together with Gamsakhurdia's discussion of tying citizenship to the resident population of 1921 or even 1801, threatened to isolate and subordinate Russians further in an independent Georgia. In response to this rising Georgian nationalism, both Abkhazia and South Ossetia declared their independence from Georgia.[61] Georgia responded by abolishing South

Ossetia as an autonomous oblast,[62] which triggered a civil war that continued from late 1990 to 1992. The situation in South Ossetia has still not returned to normal.

As noted above, Russian emigration from Georgia did not decrease in 1991, as it did in the other Transcaucasian (and Central Asian) republics. A survey taken on the reasons for migration in early 1992 found that "worsening inter-national relations" was cited most frequently (42.1 percent), and that only Azerbaijan had a higher proportion that responded in this way.[63]

The violent overthrow of Gamsakhurdia and his replacement by Eduard Shevardnadze in early 1992, and the cease-fire agreement reached in South Ossetia, appear to have dampened the rising tide of Russian emigration. However, beginning in 1992 the civil war between Gamsakhurdia supporters and the government, and inter-national conflict in Abkhazia have increased the polit-ical instability and economic decline in Georgia. These conflicts have resulted in a rising tide of Georgian refugees internally and Russian and other non-Georgian refugees fleeing to Russia.

Nearly 75,000 Russians lived in Abkhazia in 1989;[64] it is likely that the fighting there has driven a substantial number of them to Russia. Of the 77,994 emigres from Georgia to Russia who sought refugee status between July 1, 1992, and September 1, 1993, 77,884 (99.9 percent) were approved.[65] Nevertheless, overall Russian emigra-tion for 1993 was not much higher than for 1992; the conclusion of the civil war in Abkhazia's favor, and the agreement by Shevardnadze to accept Russian military assistance and CIS membership, have reduced the impetus for Russian emigration.

Georgian nationalists have blamed Moscow for all their troubles in Abkhazia and South Ossetia, undoubtedly increasing local anti-Russian sentiments. However, so long as conflict in Georgia is limited to its autonomous republics and a more nationalistic and exclusionary government does not gain power in Tbilisi, a large-scale Russian emigration from Georgia is doubtful.

Conclusion

Russian-titular relations in Transcaucasia began in much the same way as they did in Central Asia. Marked as they were by Russian dominance, they too may be viewed as an imperialistic colonial relationship, or as a form of internal colonial-ism. Nevertheless, the Transcaucasian relationships had a number of differences from Central Asia that became more apparent as the Soviet era unfolded. Russian hegemony was never as firmly established in Transcaucasia, and the titular groups were gradually able to gain significant control over their own lives in their home-lands. This titular local control was particularly true for Armenians and Georgians, who had attained a dominant position in their republics by the 1960s.

In response to growing titular dominance, Russians began to emigrate from Transcaucasia beginning in the 1960s, and the rate of emigration accelerated dur-ing the 1970s and 1980s as indigenization pressures increased. Independence movements at the end of the 1980s—particularly in Armenia and Georgia—were a logical next step for Transcaucasia, with the impetus for independence coming from within the nations themselves. This situation was quite unlike that found in Central Asia, with the exception of Azerbaijan.

Nationalist elites in Transcaucasia have been more exclusionary and more successful in gaining political power. These titular nationalist attempts to establish hegemony for their nation throughout the territory of their former union republic (or throughout the territory that they perceive as their nation's ancestral homeland) have in turn initiated a wave of counter-hegemonic nationalism among the indigenous minorities in each republic. This downward-spiraling interactive nationalism has escalated out of control, causing inter-national conflicts that have destabilized the political and economic systems of each of the republics.

The local Russian minorities have been peripheral to the interactive nationalism process between Armenians and Azeris, Georgians and Ossetians, and Georgians and Abkhazians, though Georgian, Armenian, and Azeri nationalists view Russians (or at least Moscow) as directly involved.[66] The economic and political instability caused by these inter-national conflicts—even if the conflicts are with indigenous minorities—have convinced an increasing number of Russians to leave Transcaucasia for Russia. This trend of Russian emigration is likely to continue as long as these conflicts go unresolved, and the emigration will cause the smaller number of remaining Russians to perceive themselves as an even more vulnerable minority.

The inter-national conflicts in Transcaucasia have thwarted democratization, but the changing nature of the Russian-titular relationship is not central to the failure of the democratization process. From the limited evidence available, the conclusions drawn regarding democratization and the status of Russians in Central Asia also apply in Transcaucasia.

To the extent that it has occurred, democratization in Transcaucasia has tended to favor the election of titular nationalists, who have used political power to reorient their states toward a more exclusionary nationalist political action program. This was the case with Gamsakhurdia in Georgia and Elchibey in Azerbaijan; in Armenia at the time he was elected Ter-Petrosyan was a relatively moderate nationalist, who has had to become less democratic and more nationalistic in order to retain power. Russians and indigenous minorities in Transcaucasia see this relationship between democratization and titular nationalism as a threat to their status; while indigenous minorities have mobilized behind counter-hegemonic separatist and irredentist agendas, the Russians have overwhelmingly opted for emigration from the region. These trends are certain to continue in the foreseeable future.

Notes

1. This subject in its entirety is beyond the scope of this study. The discussion of these inter-state geopolitical issues is limited to their potential effects on Russians in the region.

2. Allen Chew, *An Atlas of Russian History: Eleven Centuries of Changing Borders*, rev. ed. (New Haven and London: Yale University Press, 1970), pp. 72–75.

3. S. Bruk and V. Kabuzan, "Dinamika chislennosti i rasseleniya russkogo etnosa (1678–1917)," *Sovetskaya Etnografiya* No. 4 (1982):23.

4. N. Troynitsky, ed., *Obshchiy svod" po imperii rezul'tatov" razrabotki dannykh" pervoy vseobshchey perepisi naseleniya, proizvedennoy 28 yanvarya 1897 goda* (St. Petersburg": Tsentral'nyy statisticheskiy komitet, 1905), Vol. 2, pp. vii–viii. At the time of the 1897 census, 'Russian' included Great Russians, "Little Russians" (Ukrainians), and Belarusians as three branches of the same ethnic or ethnolinguistic community. When this broader meaning of Russian is used, the term will appear as "Russian" in the text.

5. Ronald Suny, *The Making of the Georgian Nation* (Bloomington, IN: Indiana University Press, 1988), p. 91.

6. Suny, *Making of the Georgian Nation*, pp. 115–116; Audrey Altstadt-Mirhadi, "Baku: Transformation of a Muslim Town," in Michael Hamm, ed., *The City in Late Imperial Russia* (Bloomington, IN: Indiana University Press, 1986), pp. 289–293.

7. Bruk and Kabuzan, "Dinamika chislennosti i rasseleniya russkogo etnosa," pp. 17–24.

8. Troynitsky, *Obshchiy svod" po imperii rezul'tatov" razrabotki dannykh" pervoy vseobshchey perepisi naseleniya*, Vol. 2, p. viii.

9. Altstadt-Mirhadi, "Baku: The Transformation of a Muslim Town," p. 289.

10. Bruk and Kabuzan, "Dinamika chislennosti i rasseleniya russkogo etnosa," pp. 17–18.

11. Robert Kaiser, *The Geography of Nationalism in Russia and the USSR* (Princeton, NJ: Princeton University Press, 1994), pp. 39–42; 65–82; Suny, *Making of the Georgian Nation*, pp. 139–156.

12. Kaiser, *The Geography of Nationalism*, p. 82; Tadeusz Swietochowski, "National Consciousness and Political Orientations in Azerbaijan, 1905–1920," in Ronald Suny, ed., *Transcaucasia: Nationalism and Social Change* (Ann Arbor, MI: University of Michigan Slavic Publications, 1983), p. 212.

13. Richard Hovannisian, "Caucasian Armenia Between Imperial and Soviet Rule: The Interlude of National Independence," in Suny, ed., *Transcaucasia: Nationalism and Social Change*, p. 260.

14. Troynitsky, *Obshchiy svod" po imperii rezul'tatov" razrabotki dannykh" pervoy vseobshchey perepisi naseleniya*, Vol. 2, pp. viii, xxv.

15. Richard Pipes, *The Formation of the Soviet Union*, rev. ed. (New York: Atheneum, 1974), pp. 103–107.

16. Pipes, *Formation of the Soviet Union*, pp. 194–195.

17. Frank Lorimer, *The Population of the Soviet Union* (Geneva: League of Nations, 1946), pp. 36–43.

18. Kaiser, *Geography of Nationalism*, pp. 109, 134.

19. Audrey Altstadt, *The Azerbaijani Turks* (Stanford, CA: Hoover Institution Press, 1992), pp. 113–125.

20. Kaiser, *Geography of Nationalism*, pp. 130–131.

21. Suny, *The Making of the Georgian Nation*, p. 235.

22. Altstadt, *Azerbaijani Turks*, pp. 122–123.

23. Robert Lewis et al., *Nationality and Population Change in Russia and the USSR* (New York: Praeger, 1976), pp. 158, 254.

24. Kaiser, *Geography of Nationalism* p. 133.

25. Altstadt, *Azerbaijani Turks*, p. 186.

26. Rasma Karklins, "Ethnic Politics and Access to Higher Education: The Soviet Case," *Comparative Politics* (April 1984): 284.

27. Karklins, "Ethnic Politics and Access to Higher Education," pp. 285–286.

28. Altstadt, *The Azerbaijani Turks*, p. 175. Altstadt notes that Azeri resistance to the USSR's 1958 language law brought the removal of Azerbaijan's Communist party first secretary Mustafayev in 1959. After Mustafayev's removal, the 1958 language law favoring Russian while making the study of other languages voluntary was adopted in Azerbaijan.

29. Suny, *Making of the Georgian Nation*, pp. 298–304.

30. Yu. Arutyunyan and Yu. Bromley, *Sotsial'no-kul'turnyy oblik sovetskikh natsiy* (Moskva:Nauka, 1986), p. 20; A. Vishnevskiy and Zh. Zayonchkovskaya, *Migratsiya iz SSSR: Chetvertaya volna* (Moskva:SP "Evik" and Tsentr demografii i ekologii cheloveka, 1991), p. 9.

31. A. Topilin, "Vliyaniye migratsii na etnonatsional'nuyu strukturu," *Sotsiologicheskiye issledovaniya* No. 7 (1992):36.

32. Elizabeth Fuller, "The Transcaucasus," RFE/RL *Research Report* Vol. 3, No. 16 (April 22, 1994):40; CSCE, *Human Rights and Democratization in the Newly Independent States of the Former Soviet Union* (Washington, DC: CSCE, 1993), pp. 118–119.

33. CSCE, *Human Rights and Democratization*, pp. 96–160.

34. "State Program for the Georgian Language," *JPRS-UPA* No. 63 (December 5, 1989): 6–10.

35. Observations made during a June 1992 visit to Tbilisi.

36. "Gamsakhurdia on South Ossetia, Citizenship," FBIS-SOV No. 246 (December 21, 1990):59–60.

37. "Zviad Gamsakhurdia: We Have Tolerated Separatists Too Long," *Moscow News* No. 48 (1990):7.

38. "Resolution on Measures for Ensuring More Active Functioning of the Azeri Language as the State Language in the Azerbaijan SSR," *JPRS-UPA* No. 63 (December 5, 1989):4–6.

39. "Constitutional Law of the Azerbaijani Soviet Socialist Republic: 'On the Sovereignty of the Azerbaijani SSR'–23 September 1989," in Charles Furtado Jr., and Andrea Chandler, eds., *Perestroika in the Soviet Republics: Documents on the National Question* (Boulder:Westview Press, 1992), p. 449.

40. CSCE, *Presidential Elections and Independence Referendums in the Baltic States, the Soviet Union and Successor States* (Washington, DC: CSCE, 1992), p. 112.

41. "Draft Resolution on Measures to Further Improve the Use and Comprehensive Employment of the Armenian Language," *JPRS-UPA* No. 63 (December 5, 1989): 1–4.

42. "Declaration of the Armenian SSR Supreme Soviet on the Independence of Armenia–23 August 1990," in Furtado and Chandler, eds., *Perestroika in the Soviet Republics*, p. 441–443.

43. CSCE, *Presidential Elections and Independence Referendums*, p. 67.

44. "Declaration of the Armenian SSR Supreme Soviet," p. 442.

45. RFE/RL *Daily Report* No. 120 (June 27, 1994).

46. Elizabeth Fuller, "The Transcaucasus: War, Turmoil, Economic Collapse," RFE/RL *Research Report* Vol. 3, No. 1 (January 7, 1994):51–52.

47. "Zakon RF 'O bezhentsakh'," *Etnopolis* No. 2 (1993): 25–30. See also Sheila Marnie and Wendy Slater, "Russia's Refugees," RFE/RL *Research Report* Vol. 2, No. 37 (September 17, 1993):46–53; Lee Schwartz, "Refugee Flows in the Former Soviet Union: Policies and Prospects," (paper presented at the annual meeting of the Association of American Geographers, Atlanta, April 9, 1993); A. Zdravomyslov, ed., *Bezhentsy* (Moskva: Rossiyskiy nezavisimyy institut sotsial'nykh i natsional'nykh problem, 1993).

48. *Vynuzhdennyye pereselentsy v Rossii: Statisticheskiy byulleten' no. 1* (Moskva: Federal'naya migratsionnaya sluzhba rossii, 1993), p. 3.

49. Statkom SNG, "O prichinakh migratsii naseleniya," *Statisticheskiy byulleten'* No. 1 (April 1992); V. Chervyakov, V. Shapiro, and F. Sheregi, *Mezhnatsional'nyye konflikty i problemy bezhentsev* (Moskva: Institut sotsiologii, Akademiya Nauk SSSR, 1991), Part 2, pp. 9–10.

50. Fuller, "The Transcaucasus: War, Turmoil, Economic Collapse," pp. 51–52.

51. CSCE, *Human Rights and Democratization*, pp. 99–102.

52. Statkom SNG, *Itogi vsesoyuznoy perepisi naseleniya 1989 goda* (Minneapolis: East View, 1992), Vol. 7, Part 2.

53. Elizabeth Fuller, "Azerbaijan's Relations with Russia and the CIS," RFE/RL *Research Report* Vol. 1, No. 43 (October 30, 1992):52; see also Table 10.9.

54. Statkom SNG, "O prichinakh migratsii naseleniya."

55. CSCE, *Human Rights and Democratization,* pp. 118–119.

56. CSCE, *Human Rights and Democratization,* pp. 119–121.

57. *Vynuzhdennyye pereselentsy v Rossii,* p. 3.

58. Fuller, "The Transcaucasus: War, Turmoil, Economic Collapse," pp. 53–55.

59. Michael Specter, "Azerbaijan, Potentially Rich, Is Impoverished by Warfare," *New York Times* (June 2, 1994): A1.

60. Elizabeth Fuller, "Karabakh Cease-Fire Agreement," RFE/RL *Daily Report,* No. 91 (May 13, 1994).

61. "South Ossetia Proclaims Democratic Republic," *FBIS-SOV* No. 217 (November 8, 1990):89–90; Elizabeth Fuller, "Democratization Threatened by Interethnic Violence," RL *Report on the USSR* Vol. 3, No. 1 (January 4, 1991): 43.

62. Andrew Bond, "Georgian Supreme Soviet Votes to Abolish South Ossetian Autonomous Oblast," *Soviet Geography* Vol. 32, No. 1 (January 1991):68–71.

63. Statkom SNG, "O prichinakh migratsii naseleniya."

64. Statkom SNG, *Itogi vsesoyuznoy perepisi naseleniya 1989 goda,* Vol. 7, Part 2.

65. Federal'naya migratsionnaya sluzhba Rossii, *Vynuzhdennyye pereselentsy v Rossii: Statisticheskiy byulleten' No. 1,* (Moskva: Goskomstat RF, 1993), p. 3.

66. Local Russians have been more involved in Abkhazia, where a large number of them reside along the border adjacent to Russia.

Part III

Conclusions

Chapter 11

Conclusions and Implications

The unfolding relationships between the titular nations in the newly independent non-Russian states and the local Russians living in them vary from state to state, but generally conform to the model of interactive nationalism developed in Chapter 2. The titular nationalist elites have attempted to restructure the national stratification systems in their homelands to secure the hegemony of the titular nation, which they view as its "rightful" position in its homeland. Russians—the formerly hegemonic group in the USSR as a whole—have sought to reduce their loss of status by developing counter-hegemonic strategies or by emigrating to Russia or abroad. Such counter-hegemonic strategies have been championed by Russian Federation political elites, thus adding an inter-state dimension to this interactive inter-national process.

In this chapter we assess the degree to which the actual development of titular-Russian relations conforms to our theoretical expectations. First, the range of titular attempts to establish hegemony in their homelands, and the Russian reactions to the changing titular-Russian relations, is summarized and compared to theoretically predicted outcomes. The chapter concludes with an examination of the theoretical implications that these findings have for studies of international conflict and the potential for conflict management.

Titular Nationalism

Titular nationalists were most successful in gaining political power early and implementing a hegemonic political action program in the Baltic states, Georgia, and Moldova. Hegemony-seeking nationalists have had to share power in Ukraine, Azerbaijan, Kazakhstan, and Kyrgyzstan; in Azerbaijan and Tajikistan, nationalist elites held power briefly, but were not able to dominate long enough to implement an exclusionary nationalistic program. In Armenia, more moderate nationalists have held power. In Turkmenistan and Uzbekistan, political elites from the old Soviet system have succeeded in keeping the nationalistic opposition from developing into a viable political force.

Changes in the degree of exclusion have occurred since the late 1980s. The most exclusionary states at the outset have moderated their positions since independence. This moderation is particularly apparent in Lithuania and Moldova. Latvia, Estonia, and Georgia have remained more highly exclusionary, although they too have become more inclusive since independence. At the other end of the spectrum, Kazakhstan and Kyrgyzstan—states that were much more inclusionary during the late 1980s and early 1990s—have become more exclusionary as titular nationalists have gained greater influence over the decision-making process.

This ranking of states according to the successful implementation of an exclusionary nationalist political action program does not match the expectations of the internal colonialism/uneven development model, one of the main theories discussed in Chapter 2. This theory would predict that the most underdeveloped republics and most subordinate nations should have been most nationalistic and exclusionary, while the most developed republics and most dominant titular nations prior to independence should have been least nationalistic and exclusionary. The reverse has been true: The most developed republics and most dominant titular nations have proven to be most nationalistic and exclusionary.

Estonians, Latvians, Georgians, and Armenians were the most advanced nations in the USSR, with a level of dominance in their homelands unmatched by the other nations in the Soviet Union. Yet these were the first nations to implement exclusionary political action programs. In both Transcaucasia and the Baltics, the titular nations had gained significant local control prior to the late 1980s; nonetheless, they were not satisfied with their relatively more dominant status, and pursued hegemony-seeking agendas as soon as opportunities arose to do so.

In contrast, the least developed Central Asian republics and nations, whose relationship with Moscow most closely approximated internal colonialism, have been the least nationalistic and exclusionary. In addition, Belarusians faced the greatest cultural russification pressure (*i.e.,* internal colonialism in the ethnocultural sphere), but they have proven to be the least nationalistic of all the groups with homelands designated as union republics in the former USSR. Only Moldova appears to conform to the least developed/most nationalistic predictions of internal colonialism. However, the early nationalism in Moldova denied the existence of a Moldovan nation, contending that Moldovans and Moldova were part of the Romanian nation and homeland, and that reunification with Romania was the ultimate objective. This irredentist nationalism, rather than economic underdevelopment, was the principal cause of the early titular nationalism in Moldova.

Factors beyond level of dependency and level of development were critical in explaining the variation in the successful implementation of an exclusionary nationalist agenda by titular nationalists. We will now provide a brief review of the most salient of these factors.

Mass-Based National Consciousness

The degree to which "national consciousness" had become mass-based well before Soviet dissolution is critically important. All of the indigenous groups studied in this volume have nationalist elites, but not all of these elites have been equally able to mobilize their masses behind an exclusionary nationalist political action program. Their success in the Baltic republics, Georgia, and Armenia was directly related to the existence of mass-based national consciousness within these national communities. As discussed in Chapter 3, these were the regions where sociocultural, economic, and political conditions during the Russian Empire facilitated early nationalization.

In contrast, nationalist oppositions have had little success in mobilizing indigenous mass support in Central Asia because of the limited mass-based national consciousness found there. Within Central Asia, nationalists have been relatively more successful in Kyrgyzstan and Kazakhstan than in Turkmenistan and Uzbekistan. Belarusians are the least nationally conscious group, thus explaining their lack of hegemony-seeking nationalism. These were the regions in the Russian Empire where indigenes were least nationalized. Although nationalization processes took place during the Soviet era in Central Asia and Belarus, they were inhibited by Russian dominance, and titular nations as mass-based communities of interest and belonging were much less firmly established in these two regions.

In Azerbaijan and Tajikistan, democratization brought nationalists to power, but democratization itself has been curtailed. Azeri national consciousness has become mass-based—primarily as a result of rallying against Armenians (both historically and at present). On the other hand, the Tajik civil war showed the limited degree to which the Tajik nation has emerged as an overriding identity unifying the ethnic communities indigenous to Tajikistan.

Ukrainian national consciousness is strongly felt and mass-based in the West, but is less developed in the East. This geographic division has limited the degree to which Ukrainian nationalists have been successful in dominating the political institutions of the state, and consequently has hampered their ability to implement an exclusionary nationalist political action program.

Moldova and Moldovans again provide an exception. The early national self-determination movement was promoted by Romanian nationalists seeking reunification of Moldova with Romania. For these nationalist elites in Moldova, a Romanian rather than a Moldovan national consciousness existed. However, these Romanian nationalists were unable to mobilize the titular community behind their reunification agenda, indicating the lack of a mass-based Romanian national consciousness. The absence of popular support has caused a moderation of the nationalist objectives within Moldova, while raising questions about the degree to which a mass-based "Moldovan" national consciousness has emerged.

A History of Independence

In the late 1980s, nationalist elites used a variety of historical justifications to mobilize support for their separatist movements. The Baltic nations were independent during the interwar period. The recency of this experience, coupled with the nature of their incorporation into the USSR, were important factors in understanding the early rise of national independence movements in these republics. Nationalists in Armenia and Georgia also used the period of nominal independence between 1918 and 1921 as historical justification both for independence from the USSR in the late 1980s and for titular dominance in the newly independent states. Like the Baltics, the notion of the illegality of Soviet incorporation helps to explain the early nationalism in Moldova, which was also annexed to the USSR as a result of the Molotov-Ribbentrop Pact.[1] When nationalists in the Baltics successfully challenged the legality of this document, the legitimacy of Moldova's incorporation into the Soviet Union was similarly undermined, opening the way for Romanian nationalists seeking reunification.

Western Ukraine—while never an independent state—was not part of the Russian Empire or the USSR prior to 1945; not surprisingly, this region served as the core nationalist region in Ukraine. Western Belarus was also separated from the USSR during the interwar period. However, the indigenous population in western Belarus was subjected to polonization pressures during that time, so this period of independence from Russian hegemony did not result in the emergence of a Belarusian national consciousness. The absence of recent independence in Central Asia and Kazakhstan both limited the development of a national consciousness and deprived the nationalists of a historical justification for national independence during the late 1980s.

The timing of previous independence is thus critically important; if it coincided with the rise of a mass-based national consciousness, a historical period of independence becomes a crucial event through which present-day nationalists can rally the national membership behind the goals of national self-determination and exclusionary nationalism. However, if the most recent independence period preceded the onset of nationalization, nationalist elites are relatively unsuccessful in using it to mobilize the indigenous masses.

Demographic Trends

The importance of demographic factors appeared throughout this volume. In explaining the difference in levels of exclusionary nationalism between Estonia and Latvia on the one hand and Lithuania on the other, the demographic russification of the former two republics is critical. The in-migration of Russians raised serious concerns about the future viability of the Estonian and Latvian nations; their nationalist elites thus pursued exclusionary policies to help restore the titular nations to political, sociocultural, and economic, if not demographic, dominance. Lithuanians never faced the same demographic threat, and thus felt less pressure to exclude Russians from political, economic, and sociocultural life.

Demographic trends are also important in today's titular-Russian relations. In this regard Kyrgyzstan and Latvia make an interesting comparison. The proportion of the total population comprised of the titular nation is approximately the same in each (52 percent), but Latvians have been much more exclusionary in their policies than have the Kyrgyz toward the Russians. Between 1959 and 1989, Kyrgyzstan experienced a demographic indigenization, as Kyrgyz natural increase outpaced the growth of the Russian population; while Latvia experienced a demographic russification, as Russian in-migration exceeded Latvian natural increase. Our research suggests that indigenous demographic dominance, or a trend in that direction, reduces the degree to which members of the titular nation perceive the nontitular population as a threat, and makes inter-national accommodation more likely.

The demographic concentration of the Russian population within several of the newly independent states is also an important factor in inter-national conflict. Certain regions of the newly independent states—northeastern Estonia, Crimea and left-bank Ukraine, northern Kazakhstan, and Transdniestria—have been dominated by Russians (or russophones) demographically as well as politically, culturally, and economically. Titular attempts to assert their dominance over these areas, especially in regard to language, encounter greater resistance than in those locations where the Russians are less concentrated. Because these regions also pose the greatest threat for irredentism, titular policies have oscillated between attempts to dominate and attempts to accommodate in an effort to find a formula to maintain at least nominal titular control of these demographically Russian areas.

A Sense of Relative Deprivation

The titular nation's perception of its status—in comparison with the national membership's expectations—is more important than its actual economic, political, and sociocultural status. As noted throughout this study, indigenes were improving their position vis-à-vis the formerly dominant Russians throughout the postwar period; nonetheless, titular nationalists continued to feel relatively deprived. In the more developed republics such as Estonia and Latvia, nationalists felt that their nations and homelands would have developed further had they retained their interwar independence. They compared their level of socioeconomic development not with Russia and the USSR average (against which they would have looked relatively advantaged), but with Finland, against which they felt their homelands to be relatively deprived.[2] In the less developed republics, the relatively greater prosperity of the Russian core was seen as the baseline against which local nationalists judged their own situations. At each end of the developmental spectrum, the titular nations' status fell short of their expectations.

Indigenous expectations rose along with development and equalization. As young indigenes became more educated, urbanized, and upwardly mobilized, they expected greater status and societal rewards, particularly in their own homelands. The gap between expectations and actual capabilities was growing in Central Asia and Kazakhstan, as educational attainment (and socioeconomic expectations along with them) rose at the same time as the local economies first stagnated and declined. However, this "aspirational deprivation" did not fuel separatist movements, but rather served as a catalyst for rising anti-outsider nativism, as young educated unemployed indigenes struck out at nonindigenes perceived as receiving preferential treatment. Because a mass-based nationalization had made limited inroads in Central Asia, titular nationalist elites were not able to capitalize on this explosive rise in relative deprivation and antiforeigner nativism and convert it into national self-determination movements.

The relatively more advantaged indigenes in the developed republics also felt a sense of relative deprivation, since they had only limited control over their own lives in their own homelands. Their relative deprivation resulted not from economic inequality, but from a lack of sociocultural, economic, and political dominance. Here, titular nationalists were able to utilize these feelings of relative deprivation to rally members of the titular nations in support of first economic, and then political independence movements.

Relative deprivation theory, because it has explanatory utility in both less-developed and more-developed contexts, is more useful than internal colonialism in explaining and predicting where and when indigenous nationalism will emerge and become independence-oriented or hegemony-seeking. Inter-national equalization—the solution to inter-national conflict according to the internal colonialism model—remains a goal of titular elites whose groups hold a subordinate position in their own homelands. However, inter-national equalization has not proven to be a solution to the "national problem." Titular nationalists feel that their nation should be dominant—not equal—in its ancestral homeland, and anything less results in feelings of relative deprivation.

This finding suggests that inter-national tension and conflict rise with inter-national equalization, as members of the titular nation come into more intensive contact and competition with nontitular members, and especially with Russians. Projecting forward, it also implies that once the titular nation attains a dominant or hegemonic position in its homeland, inter-national competition and with it inter-national tension and conflict should decrease, increasing the possibility for the accommodation and inclusion of national minorities.

Russian Reactions

Just as titular behavior toward nontitular groups in this study ranged from accommodation and inclusion to denial and exclusion, local Russian responses ranged from acceptance and adaptation to rejection and opposition. Because the theory of interactive nationalism views minority nationalism as a reaction to and counter-hegemonic strategy against majority nationalism, one would predict that the more exclusionary toward Russians the titular nation becomes the more likely Russians are to reject and oppose the new relationship. However, our study does not fully support this hypothesis. Latvians and Estonians have been the most exclusionary in their political treatment of the Russians in their states. Yet few Russians have emigrated, and political opposition to the new order appears to be relatively more muted in these states. Russians seem more willing to tolerate the new reality in Latvia and Estonia than in many of the other successor states that have been more accommodative of the local Russians living there.

The Russian response in Estonia and Latvia stands in stark contrast to Russian behavior in Central Asia. We have found little evidence of an exclusionary, anti-Russian agenda within the independent Central Asian polities; the political elites in each republic, recognizing that their new states need the skills that the

Russians offer, have attempted to retain Russians by crafting more inclusionary policies. Nevertheless, Russians have responded to Central Asian independence by emigrating. The Russians who remain are more likely to oppose even the limited nationalization underway in Central Asia, i.e., to "stay and fight" rather than to "stay and adapt."

Two factors help explain this seeming anomaly. First, economic conditions in Central Asia have deteriorated rapidly, while the standard of living in the Baltics has stabilized at a relatively high level (especially when compared with conditions in Russia). However, this explanation is problematic, because many Russians in Central Asia are choosing to leave even though they hold high-status, well-paying jobs. Nevertheless, with the regional economic collapse, Russian fears about their future economic well-being have substance.

Second, although governmental policies in Central Asia are more inclusive than those in the Baltics, they cannot overcome the Russian perception of a greater indigenous threat. This fear of worsening inter-national relations in Central Asia derives in part from the violent anti-outsider nativism that has emerged in the region since the late 1980s, as well as from the civil war in Tajikistan. Though this violence has not been directed at Russians, it has heightened their feelings of insecurity.

This perception of greater risk in Central Asia also derives from a Russian imperialistic mentality toward the region. Many Russians view themselves as superior to Central Asians; thus, they would rather emigrate than accept a subordinate or even equal status to the titular groups. This mentality is not present in the Baltics, where many of the local Russians view the titular nations as more European, and hence superior to the Russian nation. Russian willingness to adapt to Baltic dominance is thus greater than their willingness to do so in Central Asia.

In the remaining successor states, the relationship between the degree of titular-nation exclusion/inclusion and the extent of Russian rejection/acceptance conforms more closely to the expectations of the interactive nationalism model. In Transcaucasia, titular dominance and Russian subordination/exclusion predated the Soviet dissolution of the late 1980s, and has subsequently increased greatly. Russians have been emigrating from Transcaucasia since the 1960s, with the outflow continuing to the present time. Local Russians in Abkhazia have reportedly been assisting Abkhazian separatists break free from Georgian hegemony, thus demonstrating another form of rejection/opposition. Emigration has been relatively greater from Armenia and Azerbaijan than from Georgia, even though Georgian nationalism has been more exclusionary and anti-Russian. This apparent divergence from the interactive nationalism model is, like the case of Central Asia, explained by the greater level of physical risk and economic collapse present in Azerbaijan and Armenia.

In Kazakhstan, as titular political elites have shifted from accommodative and inclusive toward more exclusionary anti-Russian policies, Russians have also shifted toward the rejection/opposition end of the spectrum. Russian emigration has increased since independence, and internal migration has led to a greater

Russian demographic concentration in the northern oblasts of the state. Irredentism has not yet become a predominant counter-hegemonic strategy; however, a majority of Russians in the north may opt for Russian Federation citizenship, which amounts to de facto irredentism. Such an outcome would likely result in the escalation of inter-national conflict, which in turn may expand to inter-state conflict with the Russian Federation defending Russians who have chosen Russian citizenship.

In Ukraine, nationalists have thus far been unable to obtain enough political power in Kiev to enact an exclusionary agenda. Their failure reflects the limited geographic support of Ukrainian nationalism—a more nationalistic West and center confronting a more russocentric East. The more limited Ukrainian nationalist agenda has brought about a relatively moderate Russian reaction. The Russian reaction to Ukrainian nationalism holds the potential for irredentism, particularly in Crimea; however, Russians and russophone Ukrainians in eastern Ukraine are at present pushing for closer ties between Ukraine and Russia and for greater territorial autonomy in a federal Ukraine.

In Moldova and Lithuania, early exclusionary nationalist rhetoric quickly gave way to more inclusive policies with independence. However, the Russian reaction was quite different in the two cases. In Lithuania, Russians responded with acceptance and adaptation, though cultural adaptation toward greater fluency in the Lithuanian language has been slow. In Moldova, the early reunification effort of the Romanian nationalists caused a strong reaction among the Russians (and Ukrainians) in the Transdniestrian region, an area which had not historically been part of Romania. Later Moldovan moderation and more inclusive policies have helped win greater acceptance among the Russians living on the right bank, but Russians in Transdniestria still seek independence. As Moldovans more clearly assert that they represent a distinct nation with a separate national consciousness, left-bank Russians are beginning to give up their quest for independence from Moldova and to indicate their willingness to accept territorial autonomy within Moldovan borders.

Finally, in Belarus, almost no exclusionary nationalism among Belarusians has developed. Indeed, by late 1995 Belarus appeared to be moving closer to the Russian Federation in many of its policies. Not surprisingly, the Russian response has been acceptance, since little if any adaptation has been required of the Russians' living in Belarus.

Overall, the development of inter-national relations between members of the titular nations and local Russians conforms to the expectations of the interactive nationalism model. Titular nationalists, pursuing exclusionary policies within what they consider to be their ancestral homelands, adopt positions threatening to the Russians and other minorities, which in turn lead to minority mobilization. At least in the context of this specific set of inter-national relationships, this pattern suggests that conflict escalation results not from ancient, primordial animosities, but rather from recent interactions and political agendas. This conclusion also suggests that (with the possible exception of Central Asia) titular nationalist elites have some ability to reduce inter-national tensions between their nations and local Russians. To the extent that the hegemonic politics of the titular nations provoke minority reaction, then accommodative policies in turn should ameliorate inter-national conflict.

Russia's Role

The unfolding interaction between Russians and titular nations in the newly independent states is complicated by the presence of the Russian Federation; its political elites have increasingly become involved as defenders of Russians in the "near abroad." Russia has repeatedly relied on former Soviet military assets to exert its influence in the newly independent states. Troop withdrawal has been used as a bargaining chip in Estonia, Latvia, and Moldova to force indigenous political elites to take a more inclusive approach toward the local Russians. Negotiations over the Black Sea fleet are connected specifically with the status of Crimea and more generally with that of Russians in Ukraine. The Russian military has also played a role in Abkhazia, where a large number of Russians are concentrated along the Georgian-Russian border, and in Tajikistan, where at least one of Russia's justifications for using its army was to defend local Russians.

Russia has also used economic leverage to influence conditions for Russians in the "near abroad." Withholding energy resources and refusing to fulfill previously concluded trade arrangements with the successor states are typically justified on financial grounds (i.e., nonpayment for previous shipments). However, the treatment of Russians is also a factor in the development and normalization of economic relations between Russia and the non-Russian states. According to Tatyana Regent, head of Russia's Federal Migratory Service, a closer connection between economic relations and treatment of Russians will be made by Russia in the future:

> I am firmly convinced that in addition to negotiating . . . we must make full use of economic levers. Russia must more effectively use economic levers to protect its compatriots living outside its borders. I am not talking about gross interference, but economic levers and a system of preventive measures can well be put into place, and we are planning to go ahead with this in the immediate future.[3]

Beyond military and economic leverage, Russia's Foreign Ministry has become increasingly involved in the successor states to preserve as many Russian privileges as possible. Andrey Kozyrev took the lead as Russia's spokesperson for Russians in the near abroad by lobbying for equality between the titular and Russian languages and more recently for dual citizenship for Russians living outside Russia.

Russia has three important reasons for its interest in the fate of Russians in the non-Russian successor states. First, Russia wishes to stem the rising tide of Russian immigration, seen as a current economic and political burden rather than a future benefit. In addition to the costs of resettlement and higher unemployment, Russian immigrants—particularly forced migrants and refugees from the near abroad—have tended to throw their political support behind the most nationalistic politicians and parties. Yeltsin's political interests thus involve keeping these Russians in place since their presence in Russia accelerates the rise of nationalism within Russia itself. Second, Russia views the over 20 million Russians outside Russia as a potential asset through which it may exert its influence in the "near abroad." Third, Yeltsin is attempting to steal the thunder of the more extreme Russian nationalists such as Zhirinovsky by defending Russians outside Russia.

Russia's effect on the developing Russian-titular relations in the successor states is difficult to assess, because it is only one aspect of a much more complicated interactive process, and also because Russia's role has varied over space and time. Nonetheless, a few generalizations may be offered.

First, Russia's attempts to preserve Russian privileges in the successor states is resented by titular political elites. For example, Kazakh political elites in Almaty argue that no national problem exists in Kazakhstan between Russians and Kazakhs, and that Moscow is behind all local Russian opposition. The belief that Moscow is behind all the inter-national tensions faced by the successor states is widely held by titular nationalists and has made them more intransigent in dealings with local Russians. Because this view often misrepresents the cause of local Russian discontent, the tendency to blame Moscow and ignore real inter-national problems has exacerbated tensions between local Russians and titular nations.

Second, Russia's attempts to preserve Russian privileges in the newly independent states has also tended to make local Russians more intransigent. For the most part, Russia's actions have encouraged local Russians to refuse to accept or adapt to their new subordinate status; they continue to hold out hope that the recent reversals in their fortunes may only be temporary. Beyond passive resistance, Russia's involvement has also encouraged some of the more extreme Russian nationalists living in the successor states to oppose the changing nature of inter-national relations. Transdniestrian and Crimean Russians serve as two examples. In general, Russia's role as defender of Russians in the "near abroad" makes more extreme counter-hegemonic strategies by the local Russians more likely, and thereby enhances the likelihood of conflict escalation.

Inter-National Conflict Management

The interactive Russian-titular relationships in the newly independent states continue to be dominated by exclusionary, hegemony-seeking titular nationalists on the one hand and Russians who are resisting (either overtly or passively) their new, more subordinate status, on the other. This conflictual starting point, with only limited exceptions, has not yet resulted in violent confrontation, and such conflict can still be avoided. However, the necessary perceptual adjustments required on the part of titular nationalists, Russians, and Russia are not yet apparent in most of the successor states. Unless all participants in this interactive process arrive at workable solutions, inter-national and inter-state conflict escalation remain possible.

Rising inter-national tension between Russians and members of the titular nations in the successor states is not the result of ancient animosities. Rather, it is a consequence of recent Russian dominance and current steps by titular nationalists to reconstruct the national stratification system to ensure their political, economic, and sociocultural hegemony. In other words, inter-national conflict and conflict escalation are interactive processes with contemporary causes. This interpretation implies that the dominant nations have some control over the situation and thus have the potential to moderate potential conflict by accommodating minority interests. We do not suggest that all conflict can be avoided; a regime ruling in the interest of the titular nation will almost certainly provoke a reaction from national minorities. Nonetheless, those holding the levers of power retain some control over the extent to which the interests of the titular nation must be promoted at the expense of the national minorities, and thus have the ability to ameliorate or exacerbate potential conflict.

What Titular Nationalists Can Do

To reduce inter-national tension, titular nationalists can take steps to develop a greater sense of membership in the political community among Russians and other national minorities. Balanced treatment of both the titular nation and national minorities in the new constitutions, together with more inclusive laws, particularly regarding citizenship, language, and property rights, serve as examples. However, titular political elites—even those with an inclusive orientation—have difficulty balancing the demands of the titular nationalists seeking hegemony in their homelands and the demands of national minorities seeking equal treatment. Titular accommodation and inclusion of Russians and other national minorities is unlikely until such time as titular nationalists can proclaim their nation to be dominant in the newly independent states.

Nevertheless, once the titular nations' dominant position is established, indigenous political elites should find it easier to accommodate national minorities. Hegemony, once established, need not be overtly expressed politically. Hennayake takes this one step further, arguing that "the hegemony of the nation-state and thus the majority nation is maintained through the consent of the minorities. The nation-state practices its hegemony because it tends to operate in such a way that it projects itself as a non-ethnic, non-partisan institution."[4]

A shift from highly exclusionary policies toward a more inclusive stance is occurring in Lithuania, Moldova, and to some extent in Estonia. In Lithuania and Estonia, this shift toward minority inclusion appears to result from the establishment of titular dominance or hegemony, which has tended to reduce the perceived threat posed by the Russian minority presence. In Moldova, the shift from exclusion to inclusion occurred not because Moldovans attained hegemony in their homeland, but because the original political action program itself (i.e., reunification with Romania) changed.

In contrast to those states that have become more inclusive with the attainment of titular hegemony, there has been a tendency in some republics to move toward more exclusionary policies, even where inter-nationally oriented leaders remain in power (e.g., Kazakhstan and Kyrgyzstan). In these states, the original, more inclusive policies did not reflect successful titular hegemony, but the failure of titular nationalists to attain power early on. Over time, with democratization, titular nationalists have gained greater political power and have reoriented these states toward indigenization. Once titular hegemony is secured in these states, and in the remaining states where exclusionary policies are still in the ascendance, minority accommodation will become more acceptable to the titular nationalists.

Beyond more inclusive, ethnically neutral laws, titular political elites can also reduce inter-national tensions by assuring local Russians that they will be able to maintain their cultural autonomy. The cultural dominance of Russians within the USSR was a source of great resentment in the non-Russian republics, and titular nationalists have reacted against the privileged status of the Russian language and culture since independence. For example, in 1992 Georgia refused to publish official materials in Russian, and Kiev sent all official documents to the russophone areas of eastern Ukraine written only in Ukrainian. The concerted effort to establish titular linguistic and cultural hegemony has caused growing concern among Russians, who fear that neither they nor their children can compete in a language other than Russian. Once the indigenous national languages and cultures have achieved dominance, titular nationalists should have less reason to be threatened by Russian culture, and are likely to become more open to Russian demands for cultural autonomy.

Finally, in northern Kazakhstan, eastern Ukraine and Crimea, northeastern Estonia, and left-bank Moldova, titular nationalists will need to consider forms of territorial autonomy to avoid growing Russian irredentism. Support for minority territorial autonomy might also serve the interests of the larger state in maintaining sovereignty:

> A new principle of international law can be discerned in the interstices of contemporary definitions of sovereignty, self-determination, and the human rights of individuals and groups, which will support creative attempts to deal with conflicts over minority and majority rights before they escalate into civil war and demands for secession. This right to autonomy recognizes the right of minority and indigenous communities to exercise meaningful internal self-determination and control over their own affairs in a manner that is not inconsistent with the ultimate sovereignty—as that term is properly understood—of the state.[5]

Our interest is not whether a legal basis for autonomy can be found in international law. Nonetheless, we arrive at a similar conclusion: That minorities' "meaningful internal self-determination and control over their own affairs" serve the political good of the state. Such an approach is not only "not inconsistent" with sovereignty, but perhaps protective of the state's ultimate sovereignty by providing the conditions necessary for the minority to affirm its own way-of-life at the local or regional level while accepting the legitimacy of the overarching state. As another analyst noted:

> Probably the only means of preserving cultural and consensus values, and the only means of integration in the long term, is through local autonomy in the short term. Separation promotes a sense of security from which there can be

cooperative transactions between communities, leading finally to a higher degree of functional cooperation, if not integration.[6]

Most titular nationalists are pursuing the objective of unitary nation-states, even though the territories that they claim contain multi-national populations. Such nationalists view territorial autonomy for minorities—or federalization of their national homelands—as problems to be rectified. However, if conflict is to be avoided or curtailed, titular nationalists must in some situations utilize federalism and territorial autonomy as instruments of inter-national conflict management to maintain the territorial integrity of their states in the face of minority irredentism.

Territorial autonomy was held by Lenin to be a **solution** to the national problem, and it certainly was not. Indeed, in reinforcing exclusionary claims made by titular groups toward their ancestral homelands, the federal structure of the USSR made the national problem more intractable. On the other hand, titular nationalists hold that providing territorial autonomy for minorities in the newly independent states is **the national problem,** and this is certainly not the case either. Indigenous minorities, including Russians who have lived in the same place for generations and have developed a sense of homeland there, feel that their futures will only be secured once they have a degree of local control over their own lives. Seen from this perspective, territorial autonomy for national minorities is neither the national problem itself nor the solution to the national problem, but rather is a potentially useful instrument in inter-national conflict management.

What Russians Can Do

Since conflict escalation is an interactive process, local Russians must also reorient their thinking. At a minimum, Russians must give up the dream that their past privileges will somehow be restored. The Russian imperialistic mentality—that all the territory of the former Soviet Union is the Russian homeland and Russians deserve to be dominant everywhere—must be eroded if inter-national conflict is to be successfully managed. This reorientation requires neither Russian acculturation nor assimilation to the titular nations; nor does it require that Russians accept the exclusionary, hegemony-seeking policies of the titular nationalists. It does, however, require Russian commitment to learn the titular languages, to become citizens of the states in which they live, and to develop a sense of citizenship (if not a sense of homeland) in the newly independent states. As part of this perceptual adjustment, Russians must be satisfied with limited cultural and local territorial autonomy in the successor states. Obviously, such a perceptual shift can more easily be made if the titular nationalists treat the Russians more inclusively.

What Russia Can Do

Russia has exacerbated tensions between local Russians and titular nations by playing the role of defender of Russians in the newly independent states. Russia has considered this role to be the essential equivalent of defending the privileges that Russians enjoyed in the non-Russian republics. To date, the involvement of the Russian Federation in the defense of the Russian minorities has fanned titular nationalism and encouraged local Russians to remain apart from the developing political institutions. Consequently, Russia's foreign policy goals, which encourage such involvement in the so-called near abroad, have worked against state-building and inter-national accommodation in the successor states.

For Russia to play a positive role in inter-national conflict management, Russia's political elites must also adjust to the reality of titular-nation dominance in the newly independent states. This shift requires a perceptual adjustment away from an imperialistic mentality within Russia itself where many still view the "near abroad" as Russian land. This perceptual adjustment does not imply that Russia must consign Russians living outside the Russian Federation to a hostile fate. It does require that Russia—to play a constructive role—must redefine its mission from defender of Russian privileges to defender of the universal human rights of Russians in the successor states.

The titular nations face the arduous task of building successful political and economic entities from the rubble of Soviet disintegration. This task is complicated by the presence of Russian minorities with questionable loyalties. How can the new states gain at least the passive acquiescence of their Russian populations, if not their outright support?

The evidence from this study suggests that policies of exclusion are more likely to provoke rather than contain conflict. Providing means for minorities to participate in the new states—that is, giving them a political voice—seems a necessary precondition to gaining minorities' loyalty.

Nonetheless, the most likely outcome for the political systems of the successor states is ethnic democracy[7] or constitutional nationalism[8]—granting political rights and civil liberties to all—while institutionalizing the dominance of the titular nation. Such an approach has an internal contradiction: Minorities, not fully equal, will always have reason to question the legitimacy of the political system and to cast themselves in opposition. By placing the nation above the state, the titular nation acknowledges this situation and seems willing to live with its consequences.

Notes

1. Robert King, *Minorities under Communism* (Cambridge: Harvard University Press, 1973), p. 32.

2. As indicated in this case, the titular sense of relative deprivation can be contingent on other factors, such as a history of independence. Latvians and Estonians compared their standards of living with Finland because it also gained its independence from Russia during World War I, but retained it after 1940.

3. Lexis-Nexis, "Press Conference by the Russian Federal Migratory Service Tatyana Regent on Problems of Migration in Russia," *Official Kremlin International News Broadcast* (June 29, 1992): 6.

4. Shantha Hennayake, "Interactive Ethnonationalism," *Political Geography* Vol. 11, No. 6 (November 1992):527–528.

5. Hurst Hannum, *Autonomy, Sovereignty, and Self-Determination: The Accommodation of Conflicting Rights*, (Philadelphia, University of Pennsylvania Press, 1990), pp. 475–476.

6. John Burton, *Conflict: Resolution and Prevention* (New York: St. Martin's Press, 1990), p. 140.

7. Sammy Smooha and Theodor Hanf, "The Diverse Modes of Conflict-Regulation in Deeply Divided Societies," in Anthony D. Smith, ed., *Ethnicity and Nationalism* (Leiden: E.J. Brill, 1992), pp. 31–32.

8. Robert M. Hayden, "Constitutional Nationalism in the Formerly Yugoslav Republics," *Slavic Review* Vol 51, No 4 (Winter 1992):655–656.

Suggested Reading

Books

Altstadt, Audrey. *The Azerbaijani Turks*. Stanford: Hoover Institution Press, 1992.

Anderson, Benedict. *Imagined Communities*. London: Verso, 1983.

Bremmer, Ian, and Ray Taras, eds. *Nations and Politics in the Soviet Successor States*. Cambridge: Cambridge University Press, 1993.

Breuilly, John. *Nationalism and the State*. 2nd ed. Chicago: University of Chicago Press, 1994.

Burton, John. *Conflict: Resolution and Prevention*. New York: St. Martin's Press, 1990.

Commission on Security and Cooperation in Europe (CSCE). *Human Rights and Democratization in the Newly Independent States of the Former Soviet Union*. Washington, DC: CSCE, 1993.

———. *Presidential Elections and Independence Referendums in the Baltic States, the Soviet Union and Successor States*. Washington, DC: CSCE, 1992.

Connor, Walker. *Ethnonationalism: The Quest for Understanding*. Princeton, NJ: Princeton University Press, 1994.

———. *The National Question in Marxist-Leninist Theory and Strategy*. Princeton, NJ: Princeton University Press, 1984.

Critchlow, James. *Nationalism in Uzbekistan*. Boulder: Westview Press, 1991.

Denber, Rachel, ed. *The Soviet Nationality Reader: The Disintegration in Context*. Boulder, CO: Westview Press, 1992.

Dunlop, John. *The Faces of Contemporary Russian Nationalism*. Princeton, NJ: Princeton University Press, 1983.

Fierman, William. *Soviet Central Asia: The Failed Transformation*. Boulder: Westview Press, 1991.

Gellner, Ernest. *Nations and Nationalism*. Ithaca, NY: Cornell University Press, 1983.

Gleason, Gregory. *Federalism and Nationalism*. Boulder: Westview Press, 1990.

Hajda, Lubomyr, and Beissinger, Mark, eds. *The Nationalities Factor in Soviet Politics and Society*. Boulder: Westview Press, 1990.

Hannum, Hurst. *Autonomy, Sovereignty, and Self-Determination: The Accommodation of Conflicting Rights*. Philadelphia: University of Pennsylvania Press, 1990.

Hobsbawm, Eric. *Nations and Nationalism since 1780*. Cambridge: Cambridge University Press, 1990.

Hroch, Miroslav. *The Social Preconditions for National Revival in Europe*. Cambridge: Cambridge University Press, 1985.

Kaiser, Robert. *The Geography of Nationalism in Russia and the USSR*. Princeton, NJ: Princeton University Press, 1994.

Karklins, Rasma. *Ethnopolitics and Transition to Democracy: The Collapse of the USSR and Latvia*. Washington, DC: Woodrow Wilson Center Press, 1994.

Lapidus, Gail, and Zaslavsky, Victor, with Goldman, Philip, eds. *From Union to Commonwealth: Nationalism and Separatism in the Soviet Republics*. Cambridge: Cambridge University Press, 1992.

Lewis, Robert, ed. *Geographic Perspectives on Soviet Central Asia*. London: Routledge, 1992.

Lewis, Robert; Richard Rowland; and Ralph Clem. *Nationality and Population Change in Russia and the USSR*. New York: Praeger, 1976.

Motyl, Alexander, ed. *The Post-Soviet Nations*. New York: Columbia University Press, 1992.

Olcott, Martha. *The Kazakhs*. Stanford: Hoover Institution Press, 1987.

Raun, Toivo. *Estonia and the Estonians*. 2nd ed. Stanford: Hoover Institution Press, 1991.

Shlapentokh, Vladimir; Munir Sendich; and Emil Payin, eds. *The New Russian Diaspora: Russian Minorities in the Former Soviet Republics*. Armonk, NY: M. E. Sharpe, 1994.

Smith, Anthony. *The Ethnic Origins of Nations*. Oxford: Basil Blackwell, 1986.

Smith, Graham, ed. *The Baltic States: The National Self-Determination of Estonia, Latvia, and Lithuania*. New York: St. Martin's Press, 1994.

——. *The Nationalities Question in the Soviet Union*. London: Longman, 1990.

Stalin, Joseph. *Marxism and the National and Colonial Questions*. New York: International Publishers, 1934.

Suny, Ronald. *The Making of the Georgian Nation*. 2nd ed. Bloomington, IN: Indiana University Press, 1994.

——. *The Revenge of the Past: Nationalism, Revolution, and the Collapse of the Soviet Union*. Stanford: Stanford University Press, 1993.

Suny, Ronald, ed. *Transcaucasia: Nationalism and Social Change*. Ann Arbor, MI: University of Michigan Slavic Publications, 1983.

Szporluk, Roman, ed. *National Identity and Ethnicity in Russia and the New States of Eurasia*. Armonk, NY: M. E. Sharpe, 1994.

Tiryakian, Edward, and Ronald Rogowski, eds. *New Nationalisms of the Developed West*. Boston: Allen & Unwin, 1985.

Tucker, Robert, ed. *The Lenin Anthology*. New York: W. W. Norton, 1975.

Vakar, Nicolas. *Belorussia: The Making of a Nation*. Cambridge: Harvard University Press, 1956.

Weber, Eugen. *Peasants into Frenchmen*. Stanford: Stanford University Press, 1976.

Zaprudnik, Jan. *Belarus: At a Crossroads in History*. Boulder: Westview Press, 1993.

Articles

Bremmer, Ian. "Nazarbaev and the North: State-Building and Ethnic Relations in Kazakhstan." *Ethnic and Racial Studies* 17, no. 4 (October 1994):619–635.

——. "The Politics of Ethnicity: Russians in the New Ukraine." *Europe-Asia Studies* 46 (1994):261–283.

Carlisle, Donald. "Uzbekistan and the Uzbeks." *Problems of Communism* 40, no. 5 (September-October 1991):23–44.

Clem, Ralph. "The Frontier and Colonialism in Russian and Soviet Central Asia." In *Geographic Perspectives on Soviet Central Asia*, edited by Robert Lewis. London: Routledge, 1992, pp. 19–36.

Crowther, William. "The Politics of Ethno-National Mobilization: Nationalism and Reform in Soviet Moldavia." *The Russian Review* 50 (April, 1991):183–203.

Dreifelds, Juris. "Immigration and Ethnicity in Latvia." *Journal of Soviet Nationalities* 1, no. 4 (Winter 1990–1991):43–81.

Dunlop, John. "Will the Russians Return from the Near Abroad?" *Post-Soviet Geography* 35, no. 4 (April 1994):204–215.

Guboglo, Mikhail. "Demography and Language in the Capitals of the Union Republics." *Journal of Soviet Nationalities* 1, no. 4 (Winter, 1990–1991):1–42.

Guthier, Steven. "The Belorussians: National Identification and Assimilation, 1897–1970, Parts 1 and 2." *Soviet Studies* 29, nos. 1 and 2 (1977).

Harris, Chancy. "Ethnic Tensions in Areas of the Russian Diaspora." *Post-Soviet Geography* 34, no. 4 (April 1993):233–239.

———. "Ethnic Tensions in the Successor Republics in 1993 and Early 1994." *Post-Soviet Geography* 35, no. 4 (April 1994):185–203.

———. "The New Russian Minorities: A Statistical Overview." *Post-Soviet Geography* 34, no. 1 (January 1993):1–27.

Hayden, Robert. "Constitutional Nationalism in the Formerly Yugoslav Republics." *Slavic Review* 51, no. 4 (Winter 1992):654–673.

Hennayake, Shantha. "Interactive Ethnonationalism: An Alternative Explanation of Minority Ethnonationalism." *Political Geography* 11, no. 6 (November 1992):526–549.

Kaiser, Robert. "Nationalism: The Challenge to Soviet Federalism." In *The Soviet Union: A New Regional Geography?*, edited by Michael Bradshaw. London: Belhaven Press, 1991, pp. 39–66.

King, Charles. "Moldovan Identity and the Politics of Pan-Romanianism." *Slavic Review* 53, no. 2 (Summer 1994):345–368.

Kirch, Aksel. "Russians as a Minority in Contemporary Baltic States." *Bulletin of Peace Proposals* 23, no. 2 (1992):205–206.

Kirch, Aksel, Marika Kirch; and Tarmo Tuisk. "Russians in the Baltic States: To Be or Not To Be." *Journal of Baltic Studies* 24, no. 2 (1993):173–188

Marples, David. "Belarus': The Illusion of Stability." *Post-Soviet Affairs* 9, no. 3 (July-September 1993):253–277.

Motyl, Alexander. "From Imperial Decay to Imperial Collapse: The Fall of the Soviet Empire in Comparative Perspective." In *Nationalism and Empire: The Habsburg Empire and the Soviet Union*, edited by Richard Rudolph and David Good. New York: St. Martin's Press, 1992, 15–43.

Nielsen, Francois. "Toward a Theory of Ethnic Solidarity in Modern Societies." *American Sociological Review* 50 (1985):133–149.

Pettai, Vello. "Estonia: Old Maps and New Roads." *Journal of Democracy* 4, no. 1 (January, 1993):117–125.

Pigolkin, Albert, and Marina Studenikina. "Republican Language Laws in the USSR: A Comparative Analysis." *Journal of Soviet Nationalities* 2, no. 1 (1991):38–76.

Robinson, John, et al. "Ethnonationalist and Political Attitudes Among Post-Soviet Youth: The Case of Russia and Ukraine." *PS: Political Science and Politics* 26, no. 3 (September 1993):516–521.

Smooha, Sammy, and Theodor Hanf. "The Diverse Modes of Conflict-Regulation in Deeply Divided Societies." In *Ethnicity and Nationalism*, edited by Anthony Smith. Leiden: E. J. Brill, 1992, 26–47.

Solchanyk, Roman. "Ukraine, the (Former) Center, Russia, and 'Russia'." *Studies in Comparative Communism* 25, no. 1 (March 1992):31–45.

Williams, Colin. "The Question of National Congruence." In *A World in Crisis? Geographical Perspectives*, 2nd ed., edited by R. J. Johnston and P. J. Taylor. Oxford: Basil Blackwell, 1989, 229–265.

About the Book and Authors

Twenty-five million Russians live in the newly independent states carved from the territory of the former Soviet Union. When they or their ancestors emigrated to these non-Russian areas, they seldom saw themselves as having moved "abroad." Now, with the dissolution of the USSR, these Russians find themselves to be minorities—often unwelcome—in new states created to fulfill the aspirations of indigenous populations.

Will the governments of these newly independent states be able to accept the fact that their populations are multi-national? Will the formerly dominant and privileged Russians be able to live with their new status as equals or, more often, subordinates? To what extent do the new regimes' policies of accommodation or exclusion establish lasting patterns for relations between the titular majorities and the minority Russians?

Developing the concept of interactive nationalism, this timely book explores the movement of Russians to the borderlands during the Russian Empire and Soviet times, the evolution of nationality policies during the Soviet era, and the processes of indigenization during the late Soviet period and under the newfound independence of the republics. The authors examine questions of citizenship, language policy, and political representation in each of the successor states, emphasizing the interaction between the indigenous population and the Russians. Through the use of case studies, the authors explore the tragic ethnic violence that has erupted since the demise of the Soviet Union, and weigh strategies for managing national conflict and developing stable democratic institutions that will respect the rights of all ethnic groups.

Jeff Chinn is associate professor of political science at the University of Missouri–Columbia. **Robert Kaiser** is assistant professor of geography at the University of Missouri–Columbia.

Index